[illegible] QUEST 2

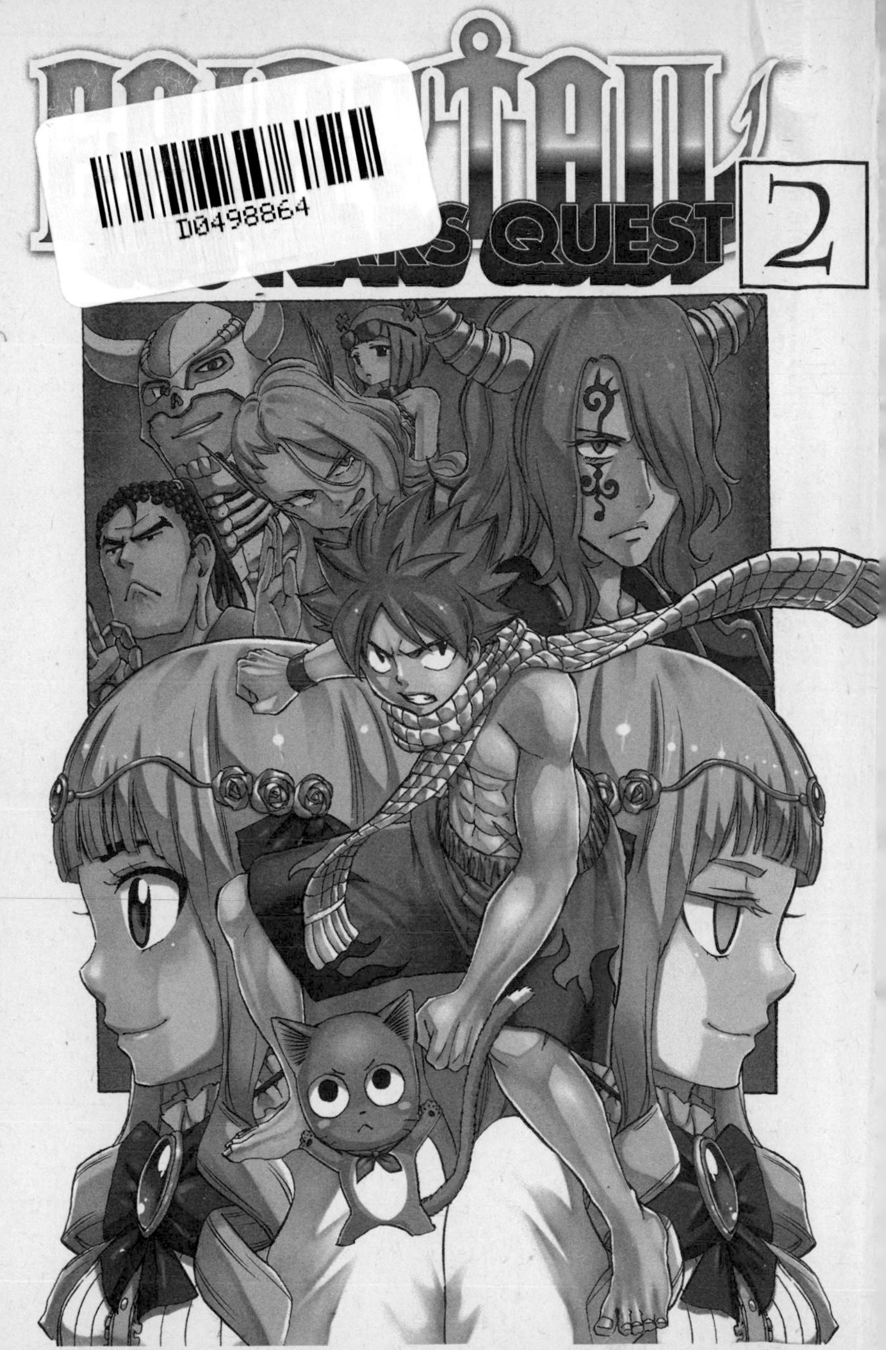

HIRO MASHIMA ATSUO UEDA

FAIRY TAIL 100 YEARS QUEST 2

CONTENTS

FAIRY TAIL
100 YEARS QUEST

Chapter 10: Diabolos of the Cutting Heart

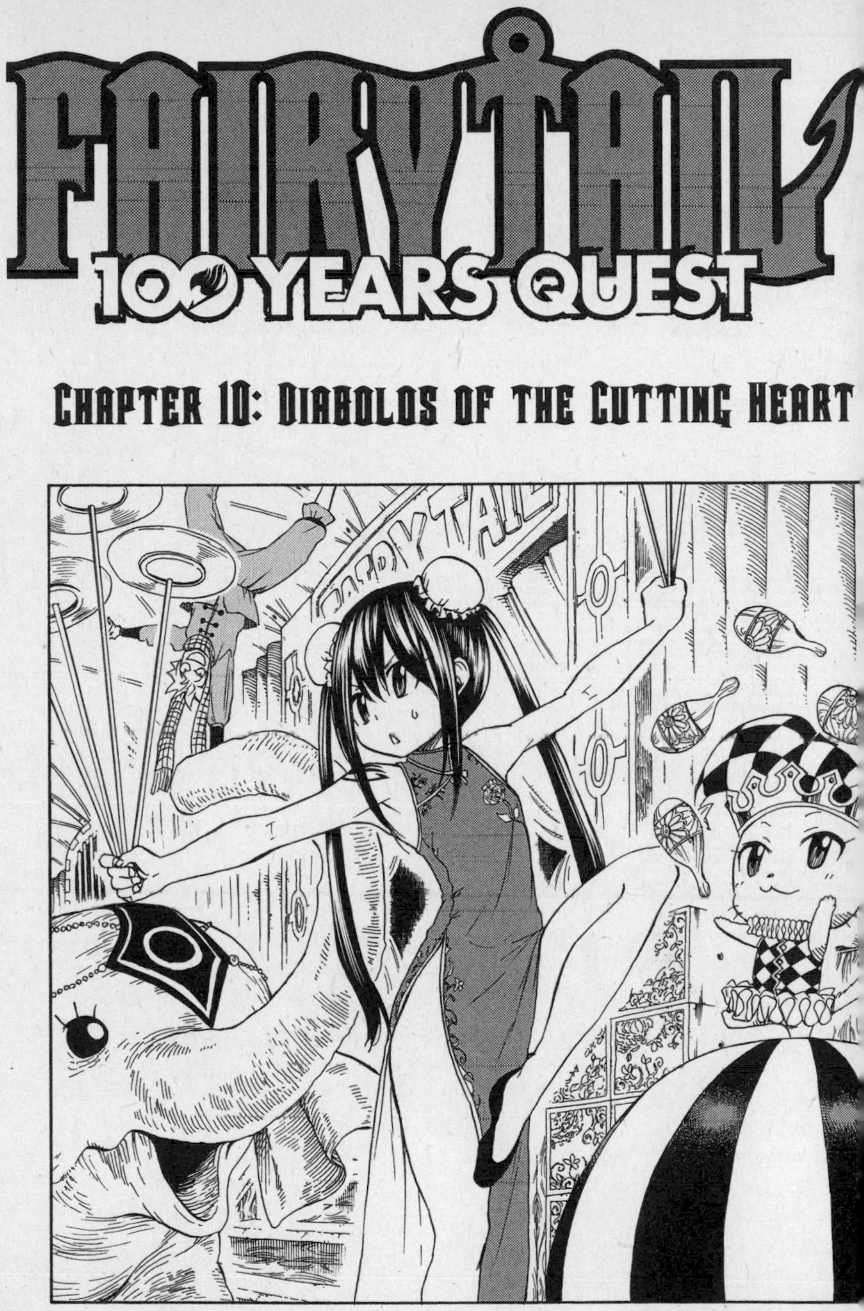

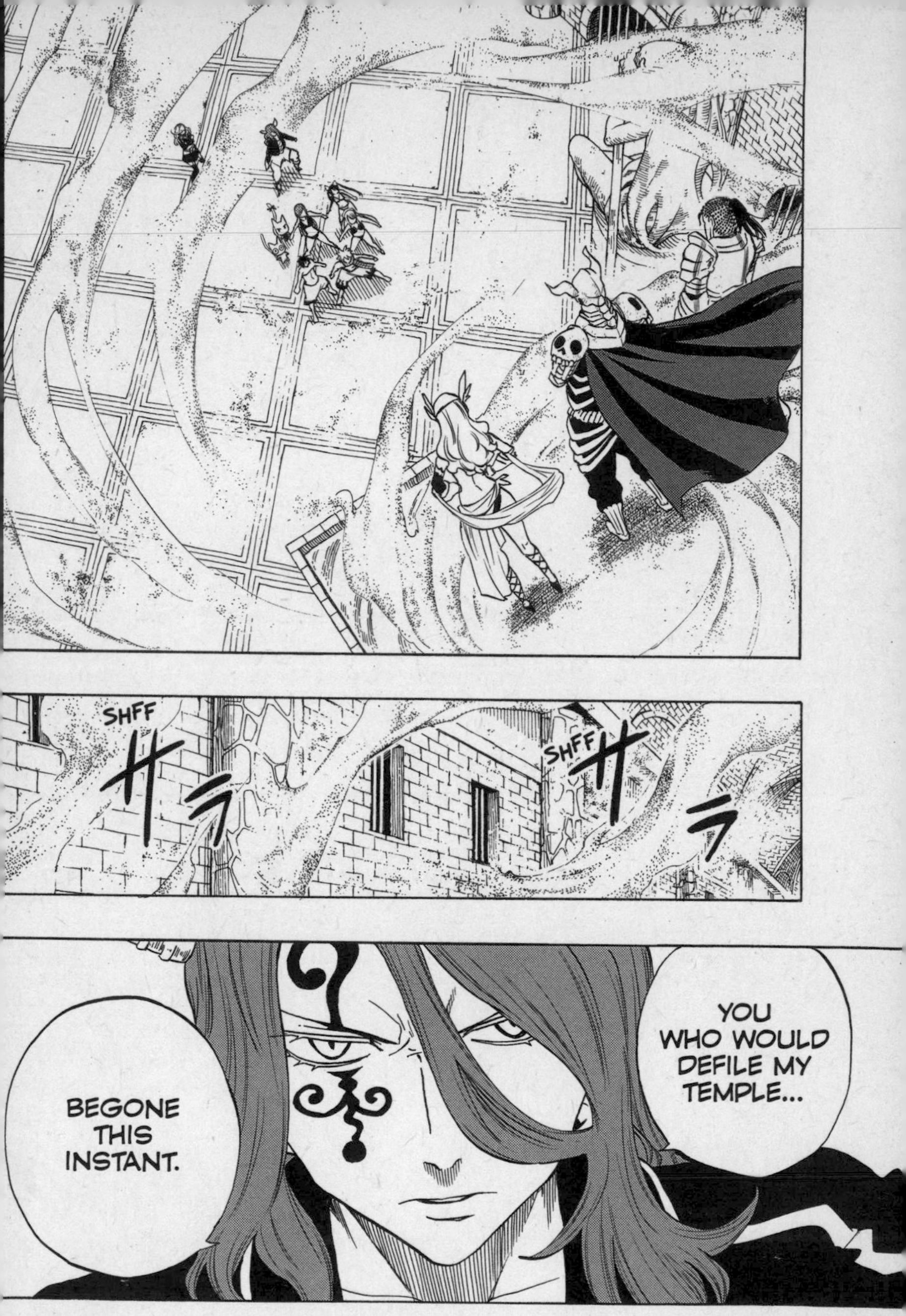
SHFF
サラ
SHFF
サラ
YOU WHO WOULD DEFILE MY TEMPLE...
BEGONE THIS INSTANT.

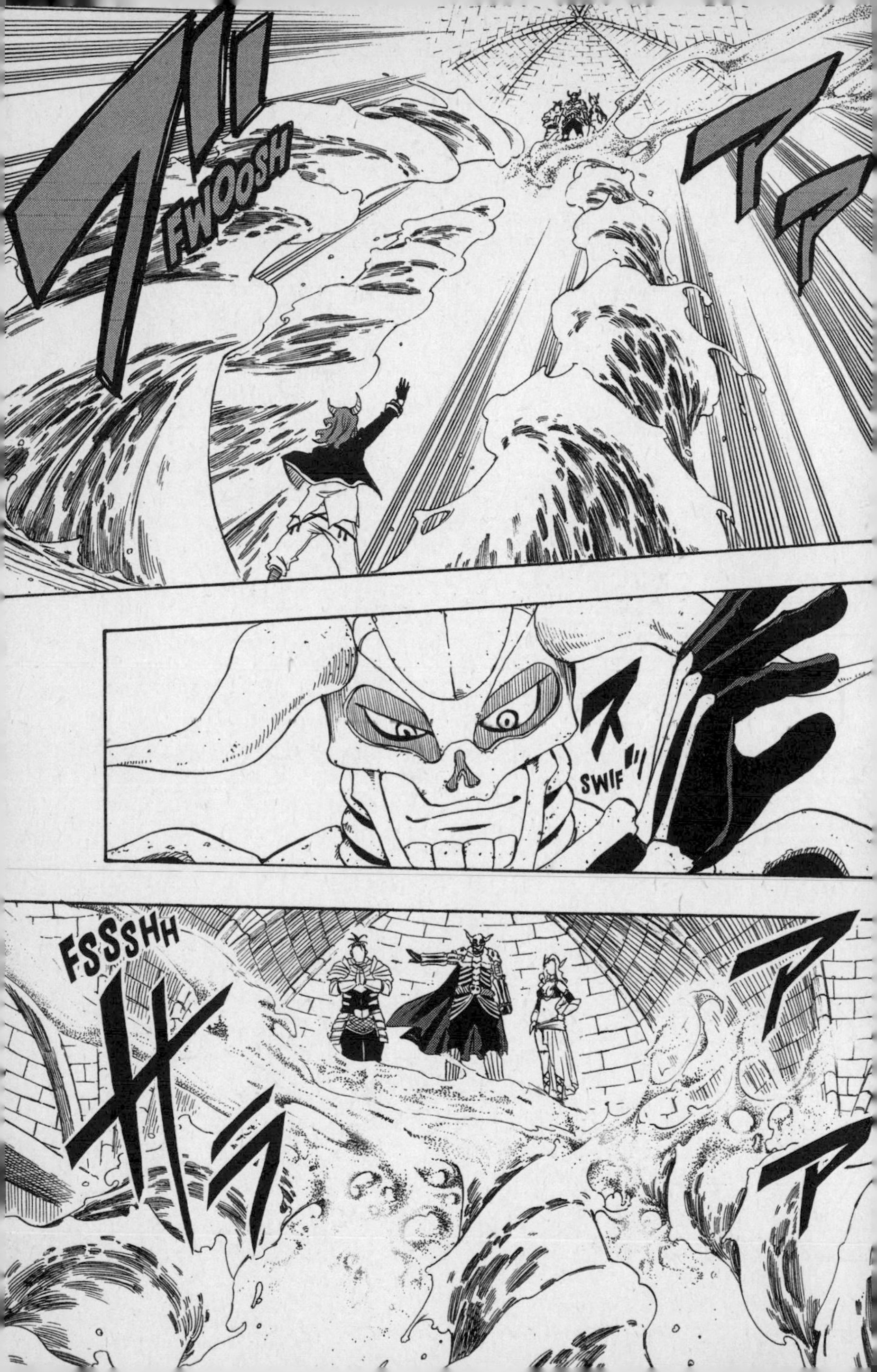
FWOOSH
SWIF
FSSSHH

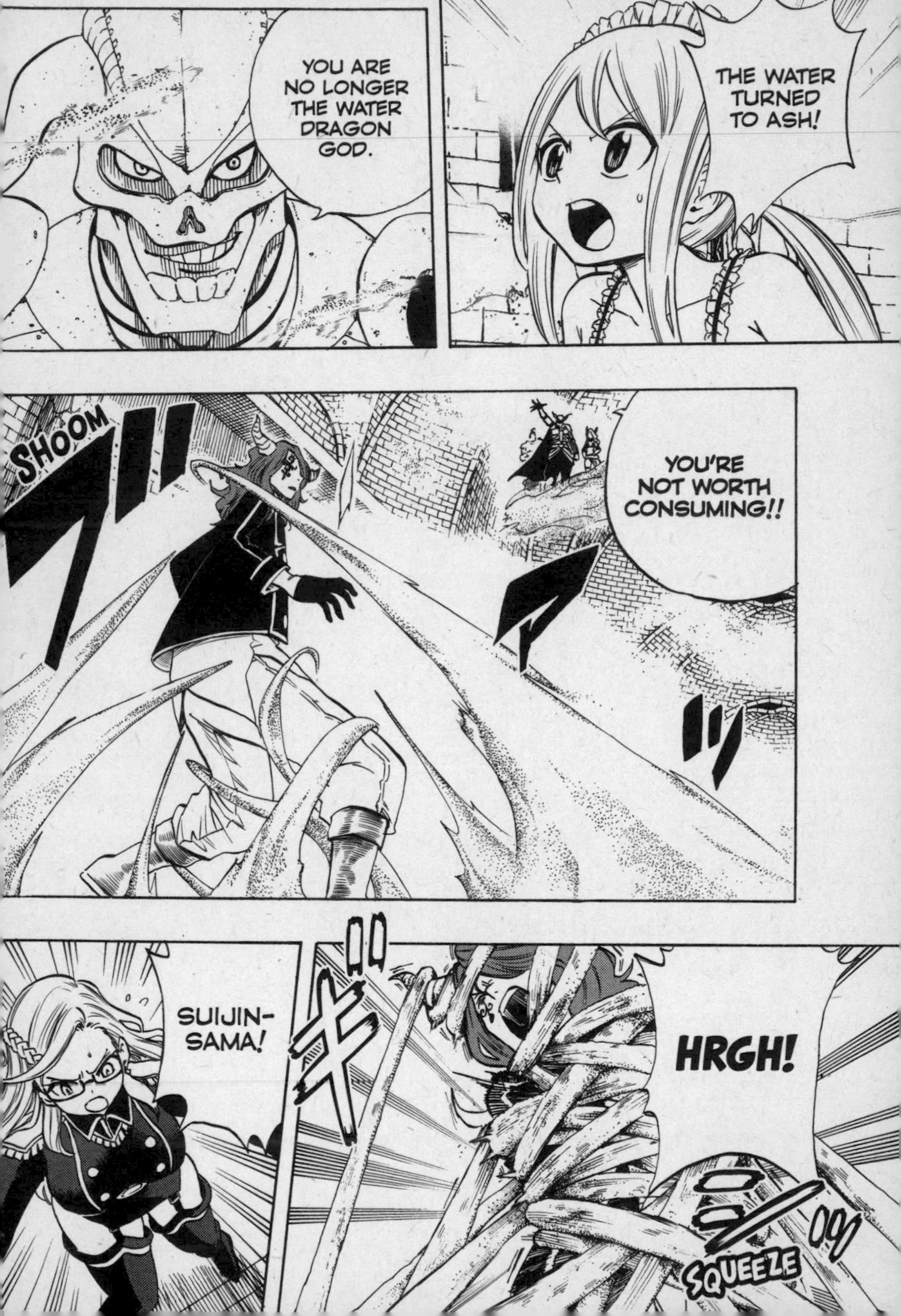
THE WATER TURNED TO ASH!
YOU ARE NO LONGER THE WATER DRAGON GOD.
YOU'RE NOT WORTH CONSUMING!!
SHOOM
HRGH!
SQUEEZE
SUIJIN-SAMA!

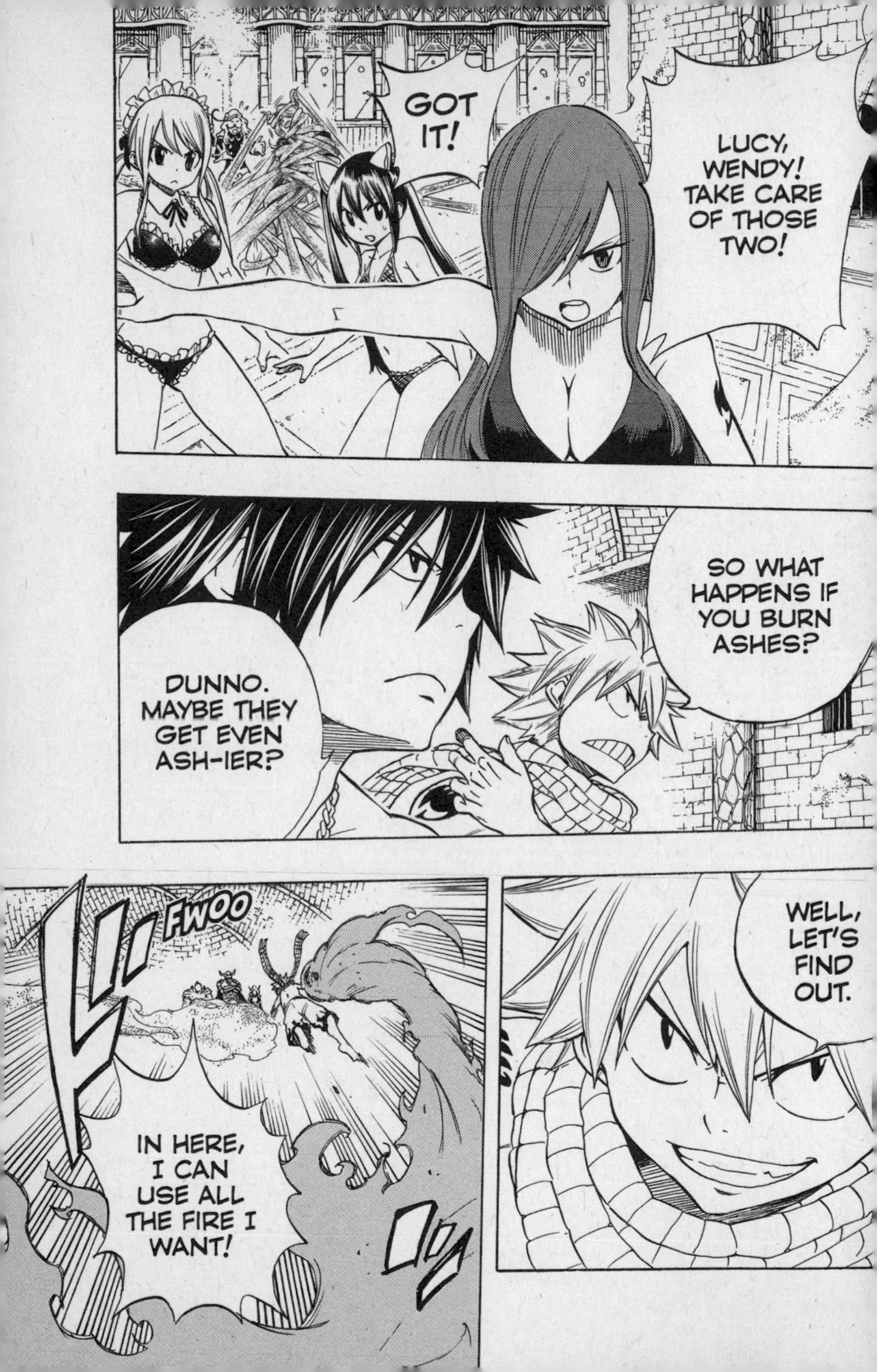
LUCY, WENDY! TAKE CARE OF THOSE TWO!
GOT IT!
SO WHAT HAPPENS IF YOU BURN ASHES?
DUNNO. MAYBE THEY GET EVEN ASH-IER?
WELL, LET'S FIND OUT.
FWOO
IN HERE, I CAN USE ALL THE FIRE I WANT!

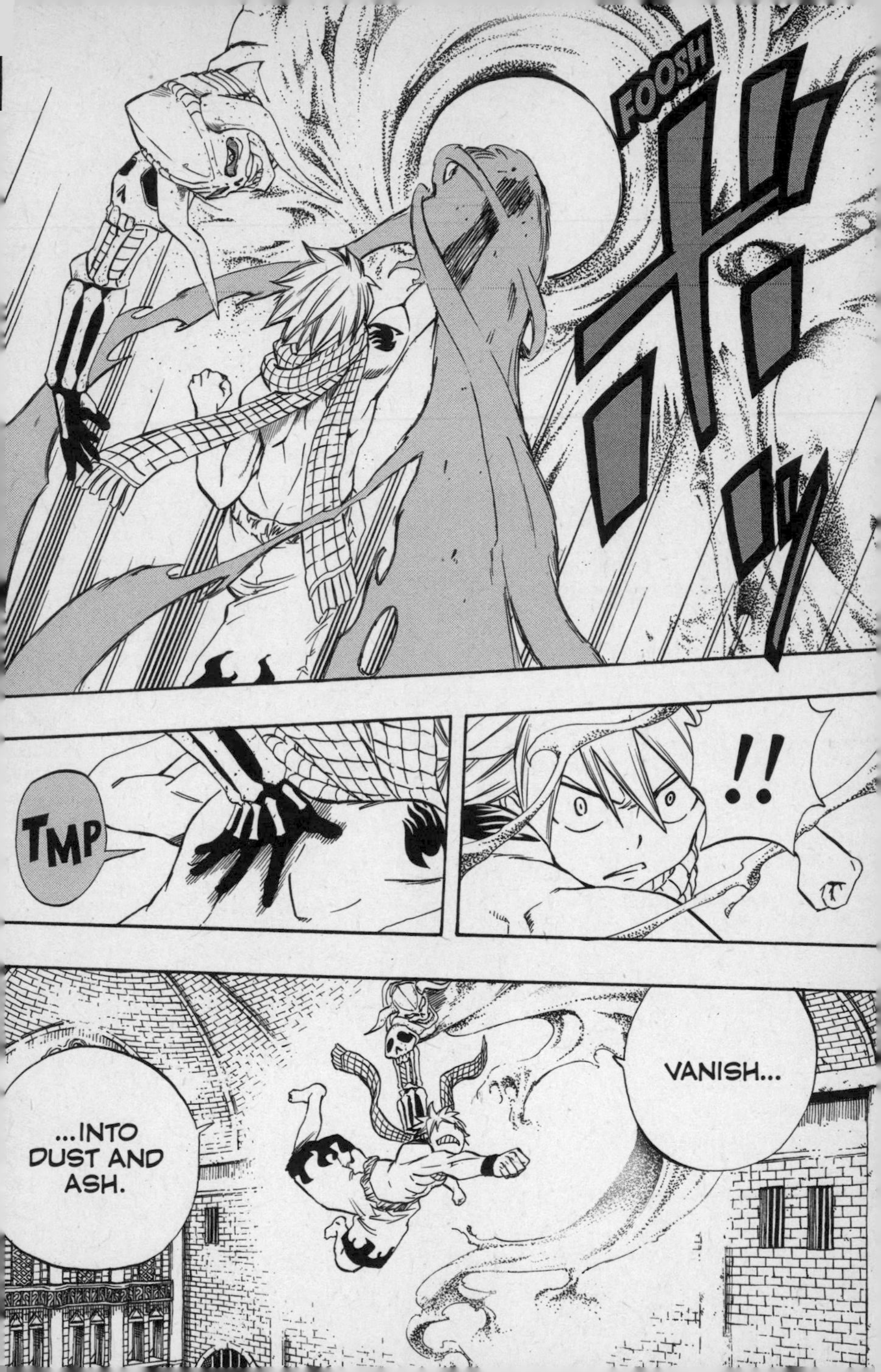
FOOSH
!!
TMP
VANISH...
...INTO DUST AND ASH.

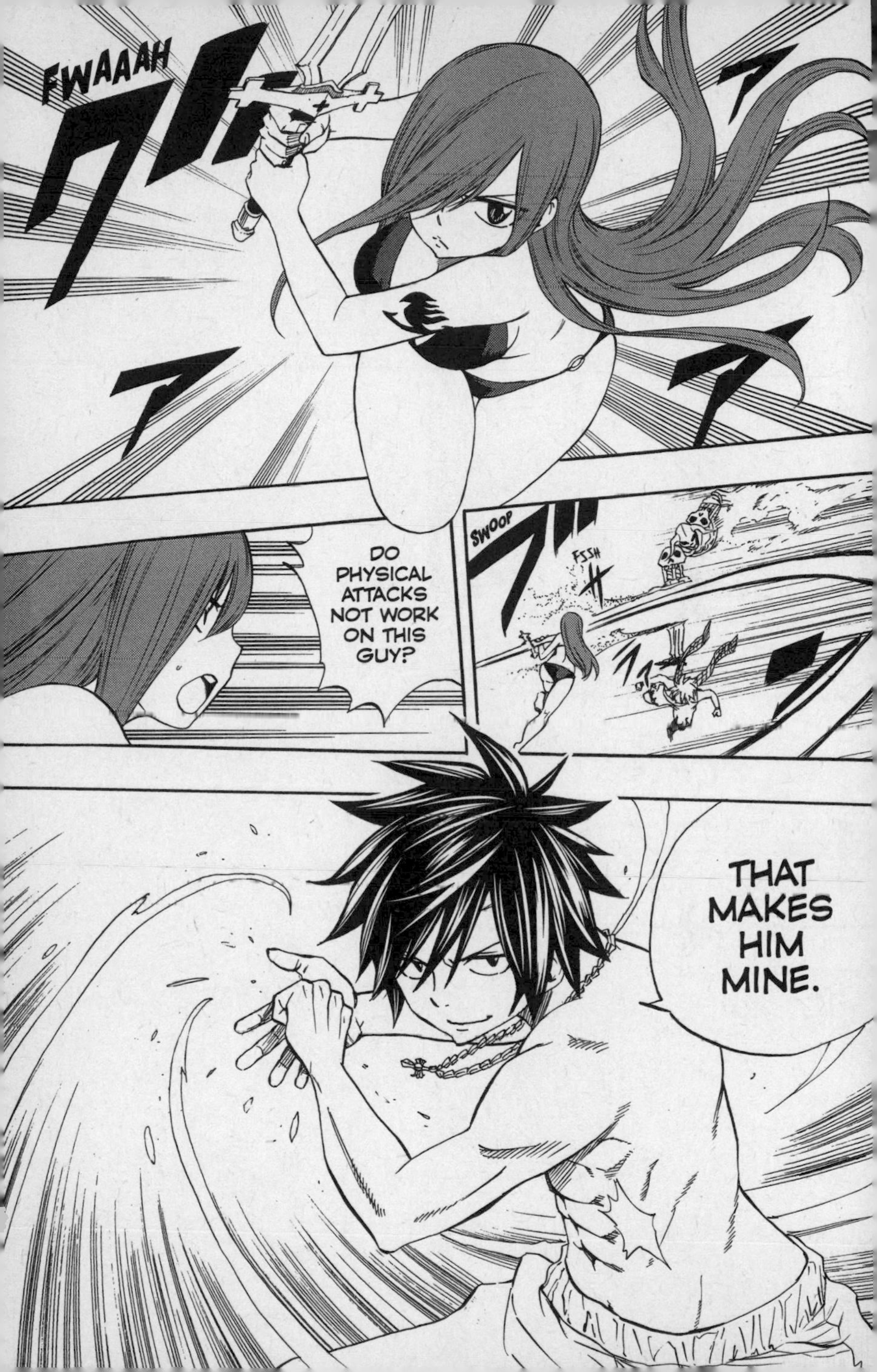
FWAAAH
SWOOP
FSSH
DO PHYSICAL ATTACKS NOT WORK ON THIS GUY?
THAT MAKES HIM MINE.

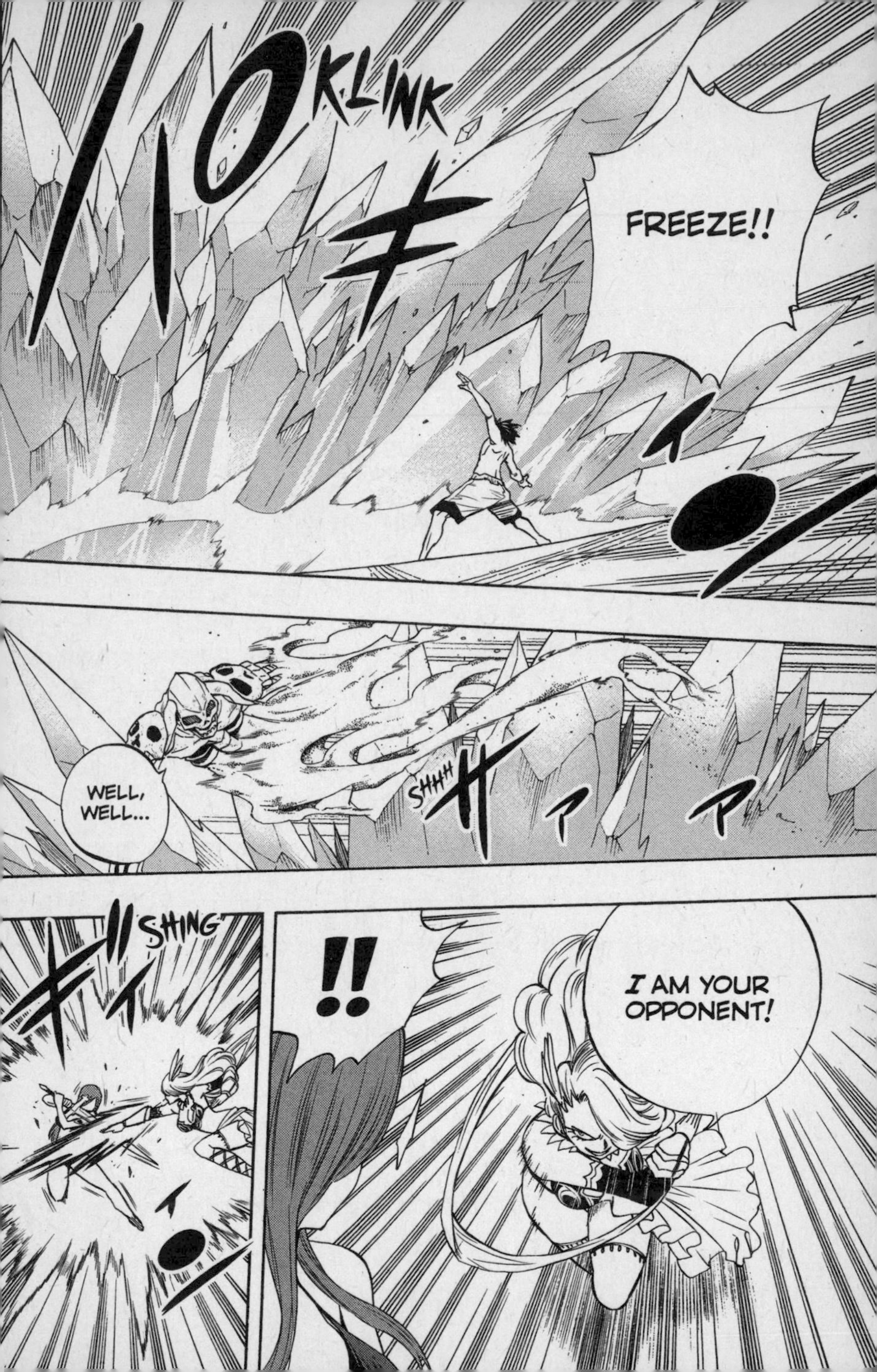
FREEZE!!
KLINK
SHHH
WELL, WELL...
I AM YOUR OPPONENT!
!!
SHING

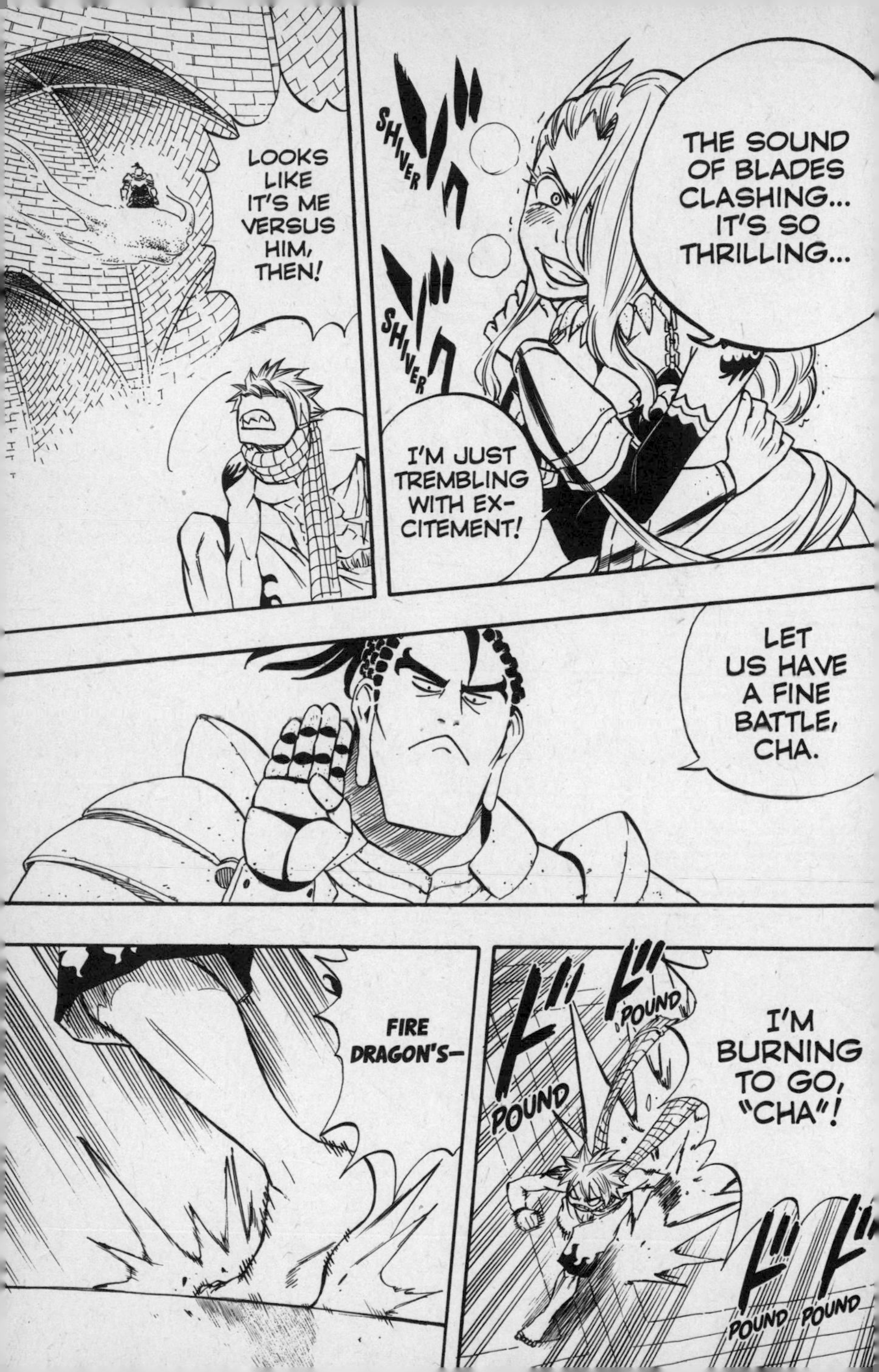
THE SOUND OF BLADES CLASHING... IT'S SO THRILLING...
SHIVER
SHIVER
I'M JUST TREMBLING WITH EX- CITEMENT!
LOOKS LIKE IT'S ME VERSUS HIM, THEN!
LET US HAVE A FINE BATTLE, CHA.
I'M BURNING TO GO, "CHA"!
POUND
POUND
POUND POUND
FIRE DRAGON'S—

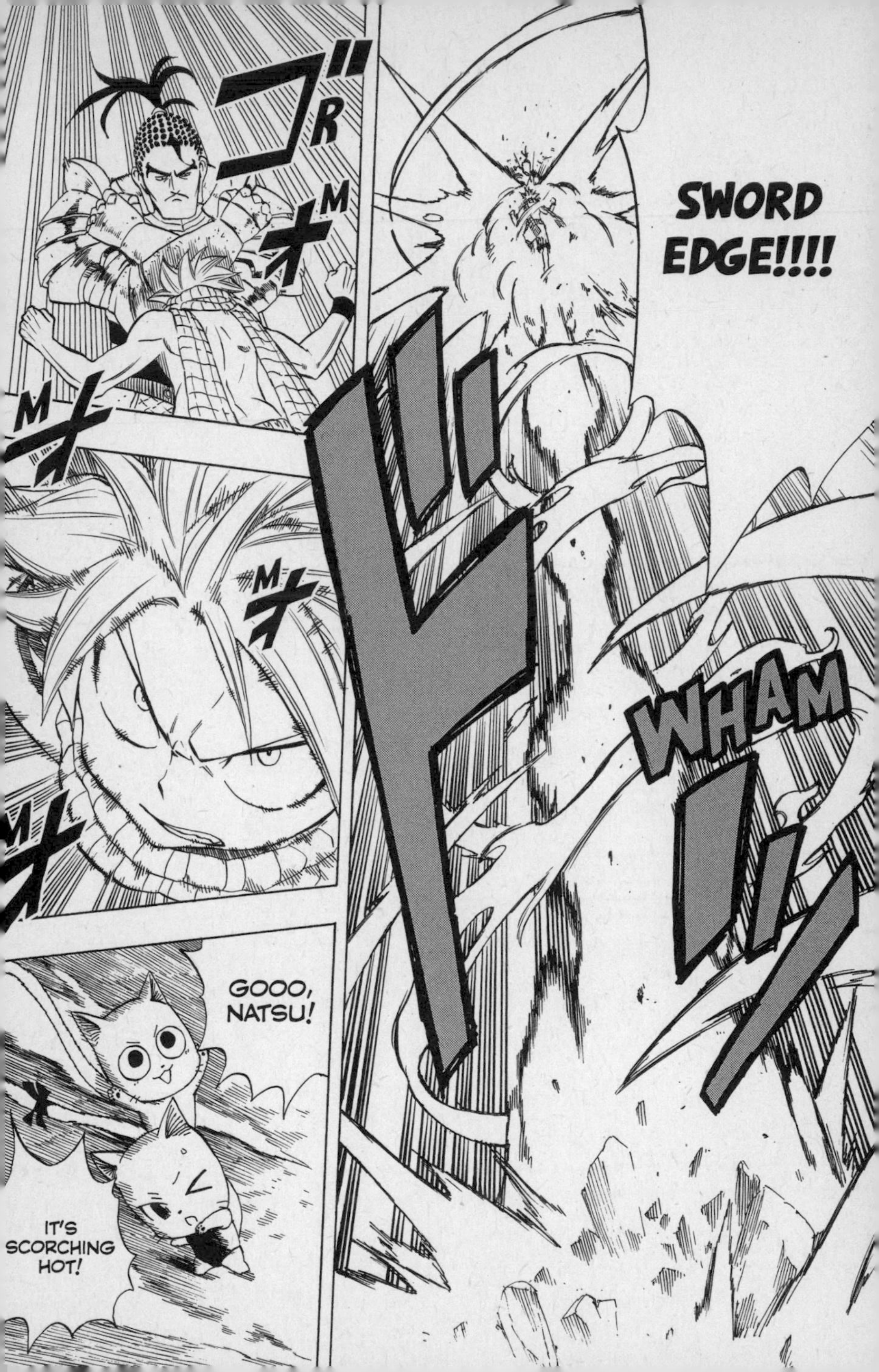
SWORD EDGE!!!!
WHAM
GOOO, NATSU!
IT'S SCORCHING HOT!

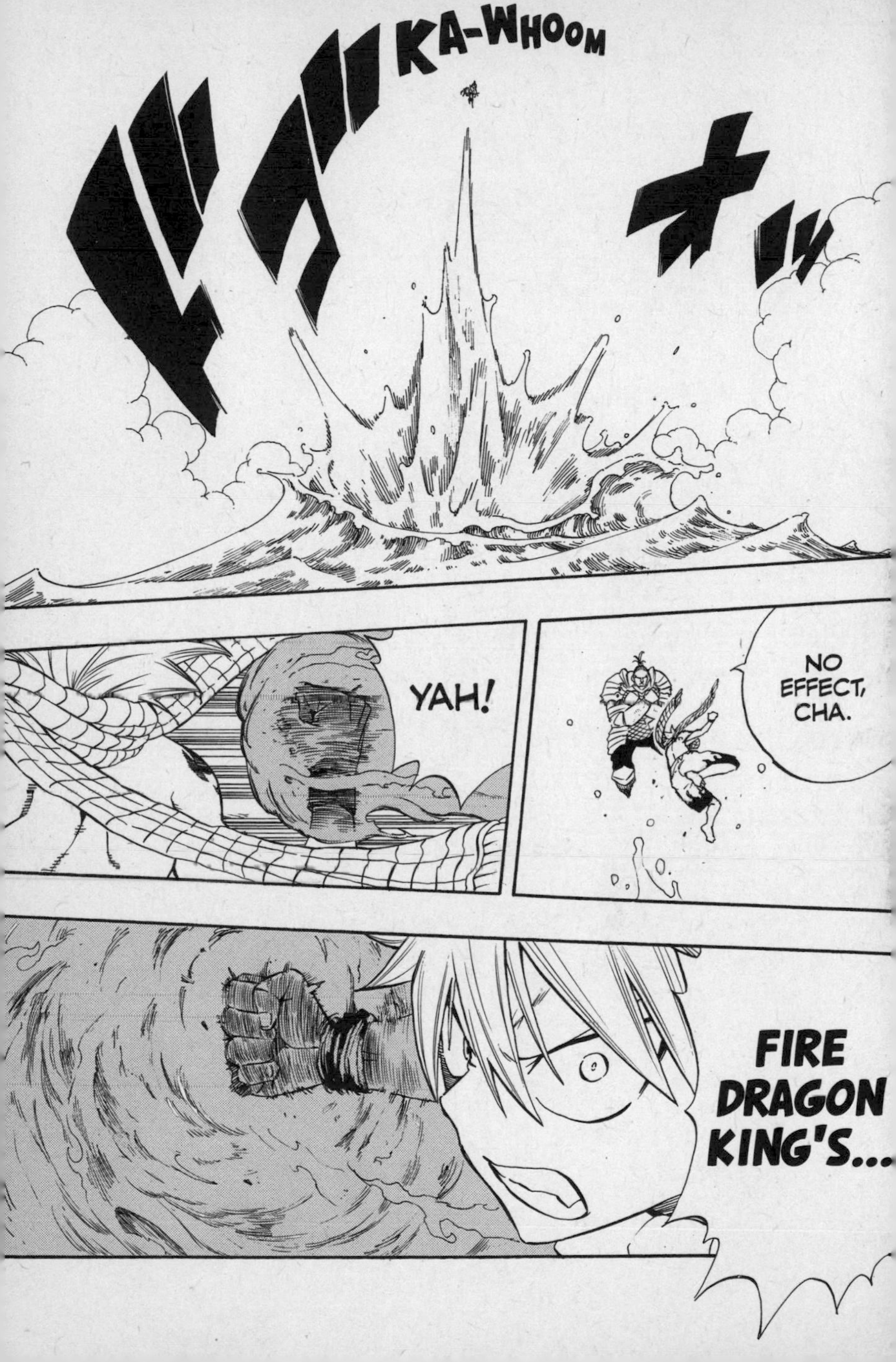
KA-WHOOM
NO EFFECT, CHA.
YAH!
FIRE DRAGON KING'S...

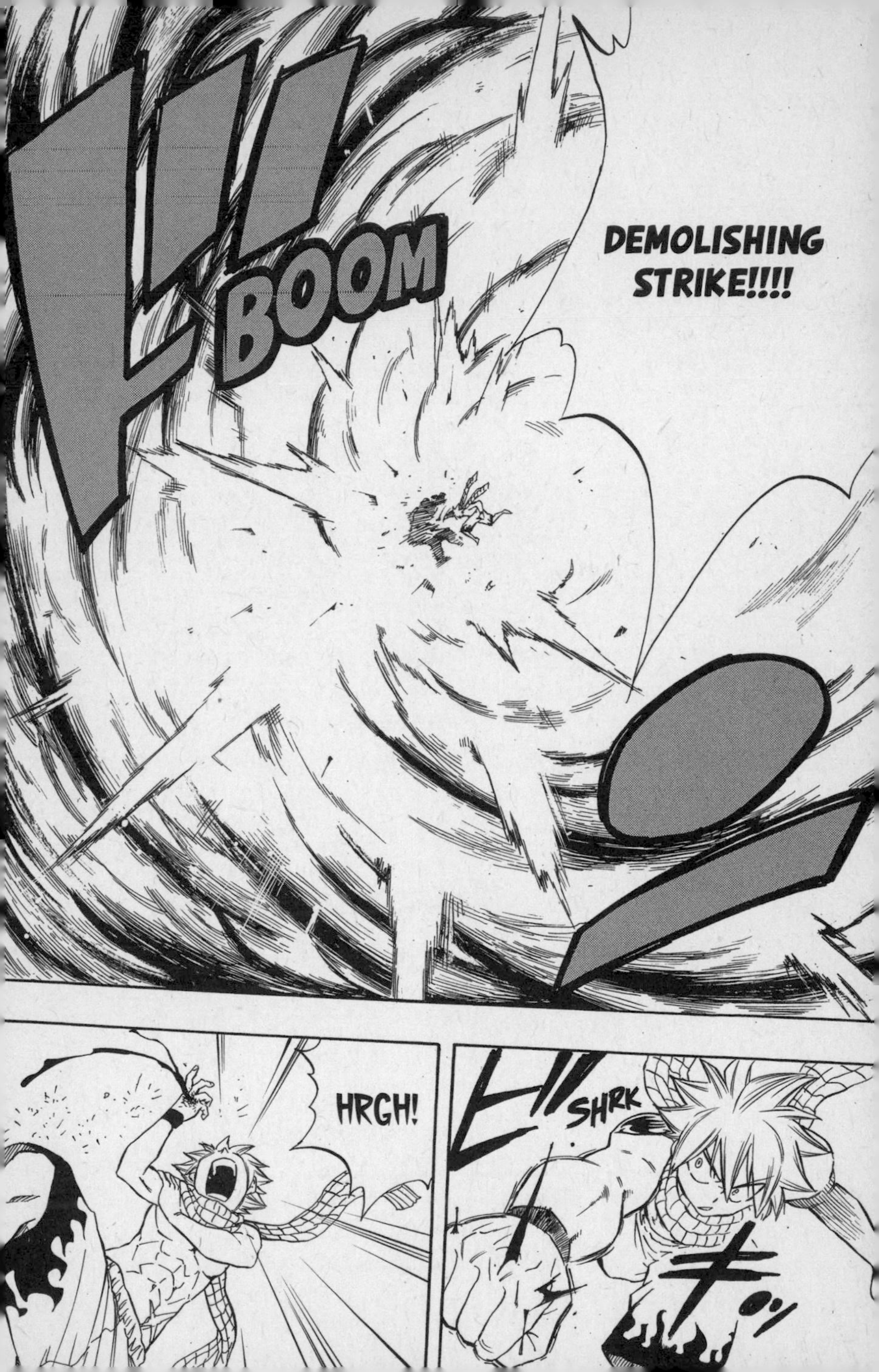
DEMOLISHING STRIKE!!!!
BOOM
SHRK
HRGH!

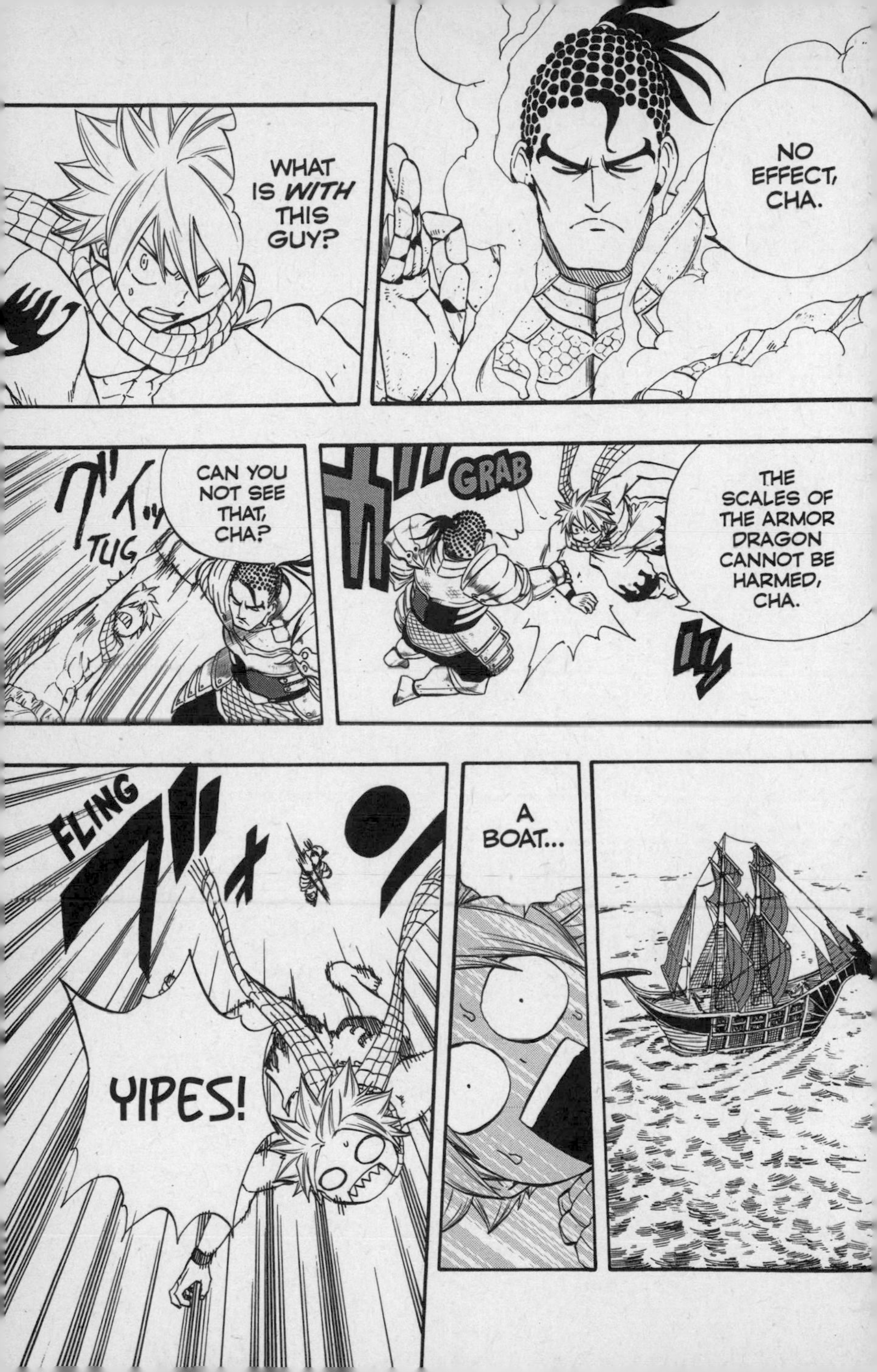
NO EFFECT, CHA.
WHAT IS WITH THIS GUY?
GRAB
THE SCALES OF THE ARMOR DRAGON CANNOT BE HARMED, CHA.
TUG
CAN YOU NOT SEE THAT, CHA?
A BOAT...
FLING
YIPES!

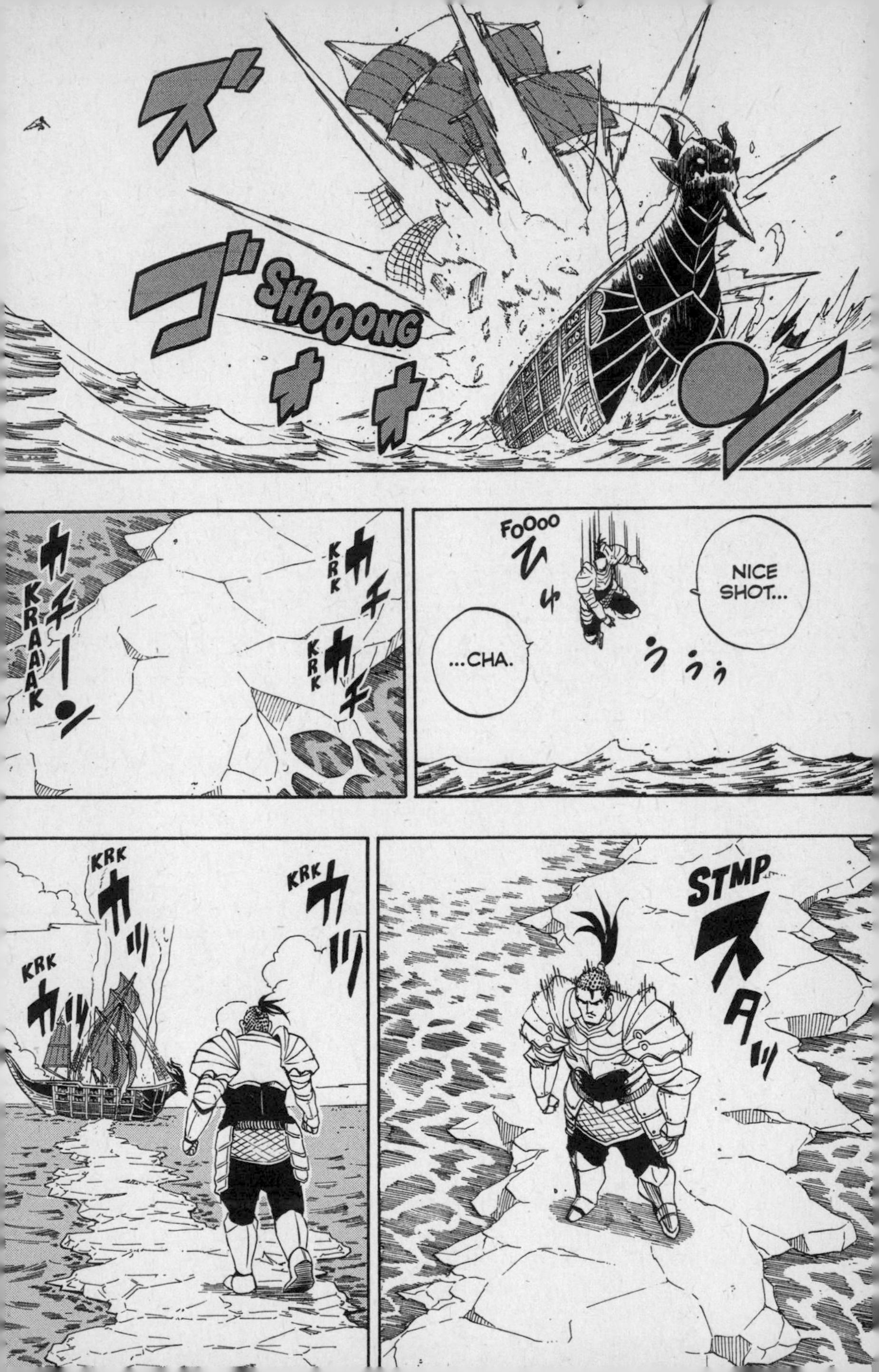
ズゴオオン
SHOOONG
FOOOO
ひゅ
NICE SHOT...
...CHA.
ううぅ
KRK
カチ
KRK
カチ
KRAAAK
カチーン
STMP
スタッ
KRK
カッ
KRK
カッ
KRK
カッ

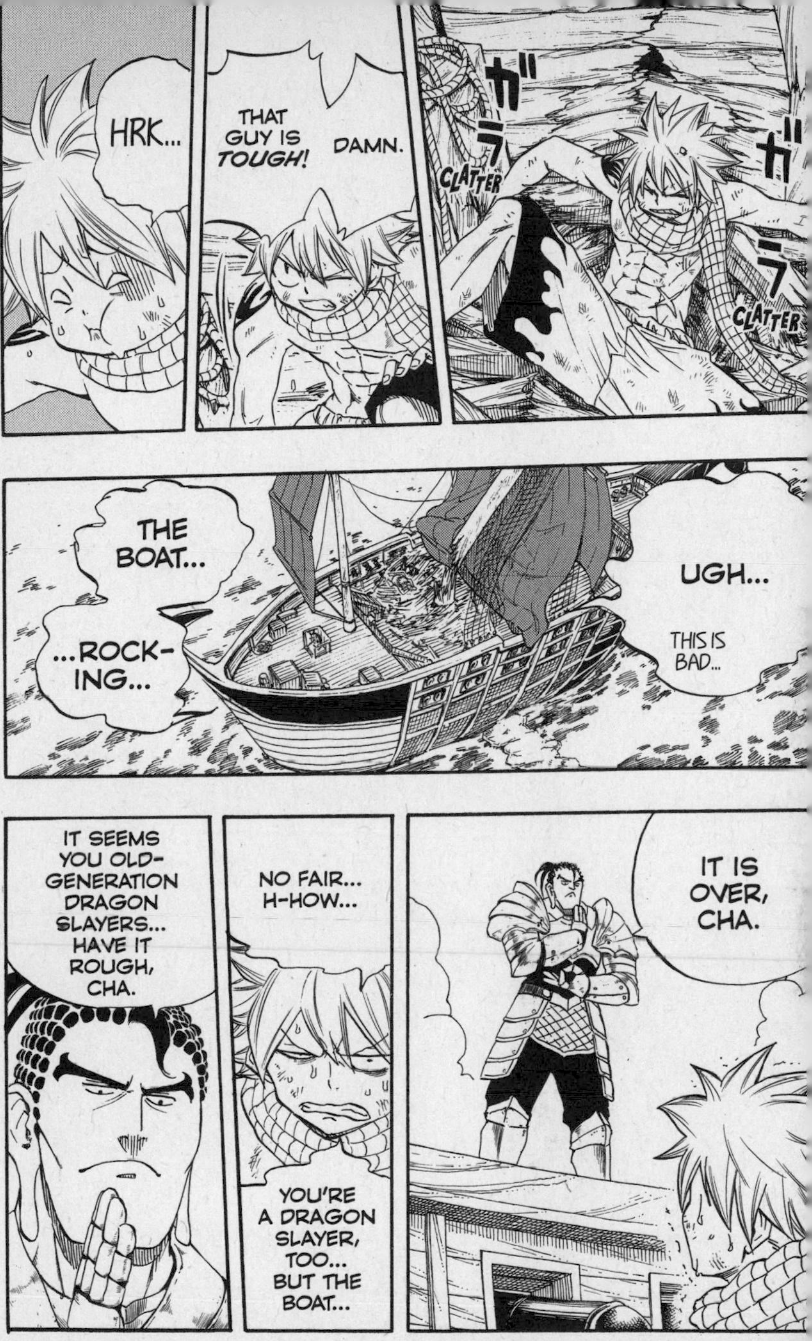
ガラ
CLATTER
ガラ
CLATTER
DAMN.
THAT GUY IS *TOUGH!*
HRK...
UGH...
THIS IS BAD...
THE BOAT...
...ROCKING...
IT IS OVER, CHA.
NO FAIR... H-HOW...
YOU'RE A DRAGON SLAYER, TOO... BUT THE BOAT...
IT SEEMS YOU OLD-GENERATION DRAGON SLAYERS... HAVE IT ROUGH, CHA.

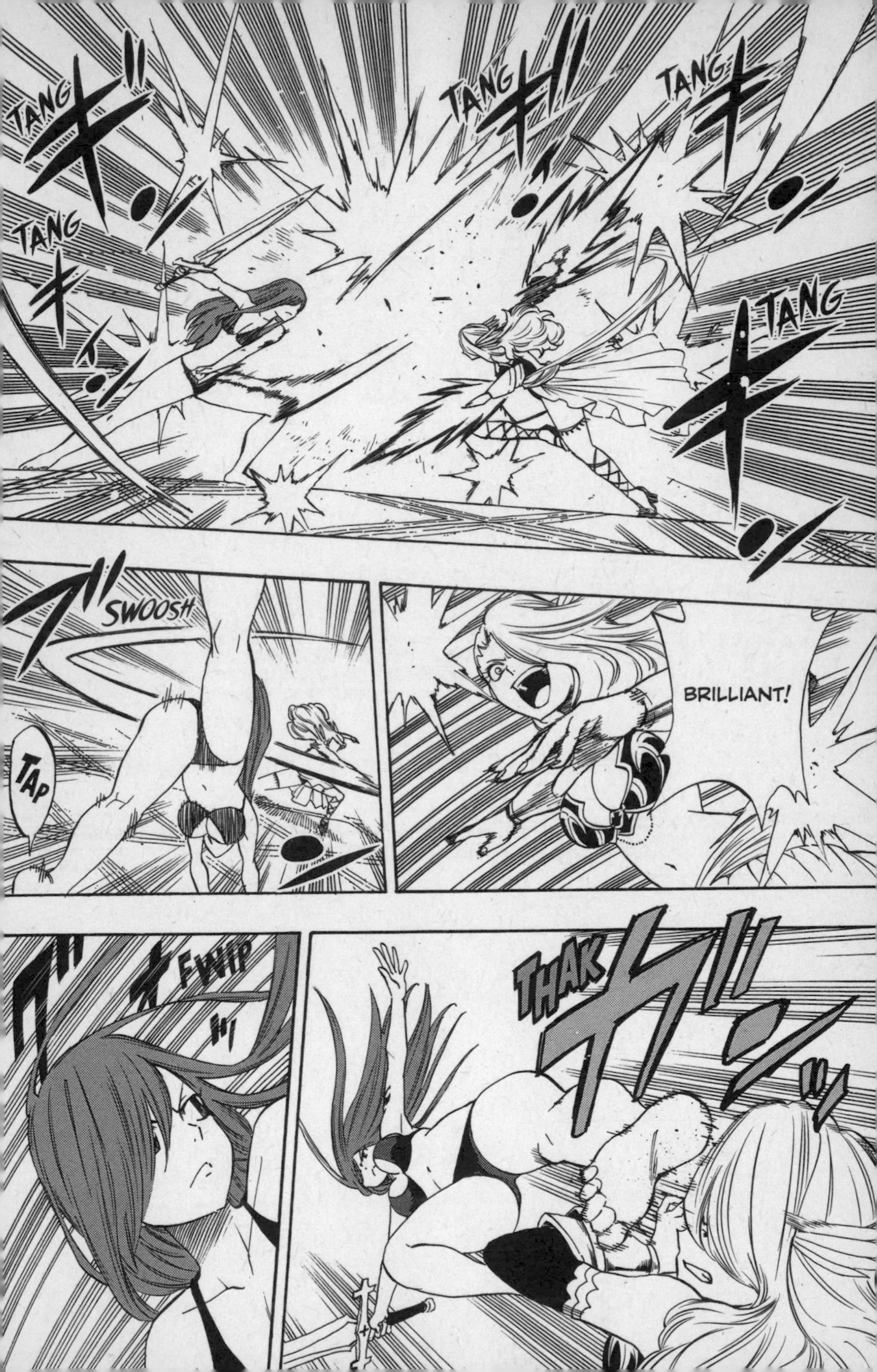
TANG
TANG
TANG
TANG
TANG
BRILLIANT!
SWOOSH
TAP
THAK
FWIP

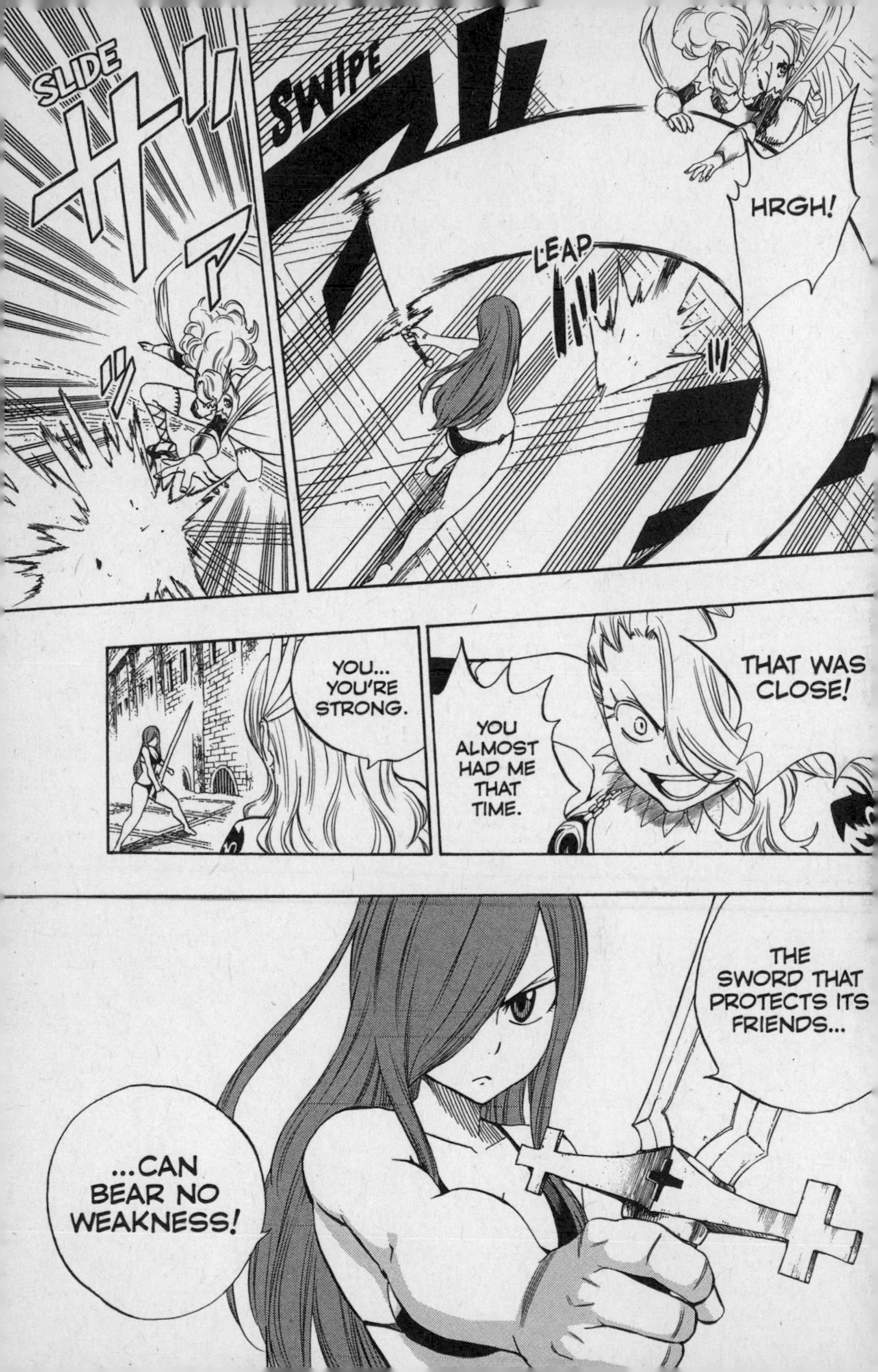
HRGH!
SWIPE
LEAP
SLIDE
THAT WAS CLOSE!
YOU ALMOST HAD ME THAT TIME.
YOU... YOU'RE STRONG.
THE SWORD THAT PROTECTS ITS FRIENDS...
...CAN BEAR NO WEAKNESS!

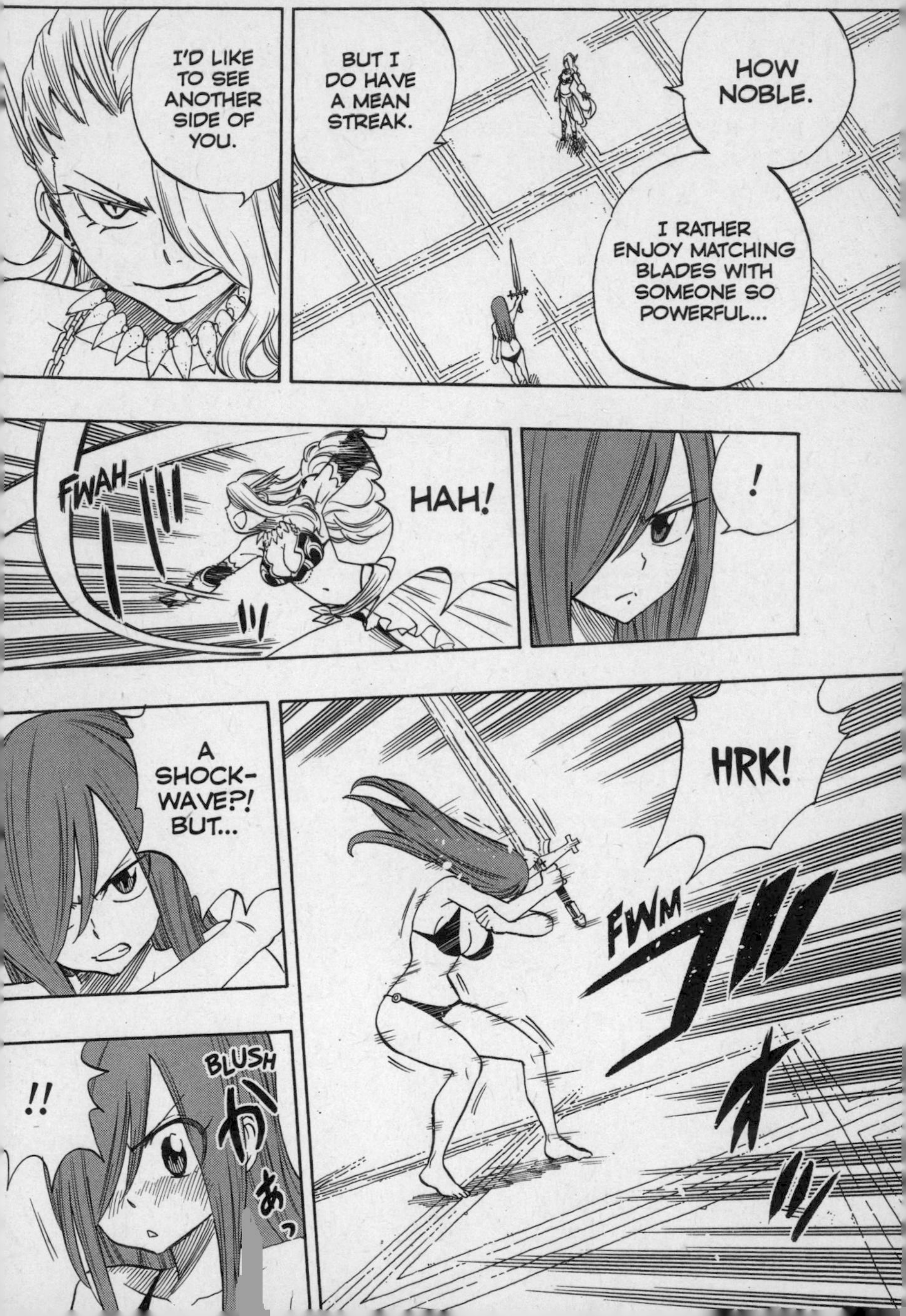
HOW NOBLE.
I RATHER ENJOY MATCHING BLADES WITH SOMEONE SO POWERFUL...
BUT I DO HAVE A MEAN STREAK.
I'D LIKE TO SEE ANOTHER SIDE OF YOU.
!
HAH!
FWAH
HRK!
FWM
A SHOCK-WAVE?! BUT...
BLUSH
かあっ
!!

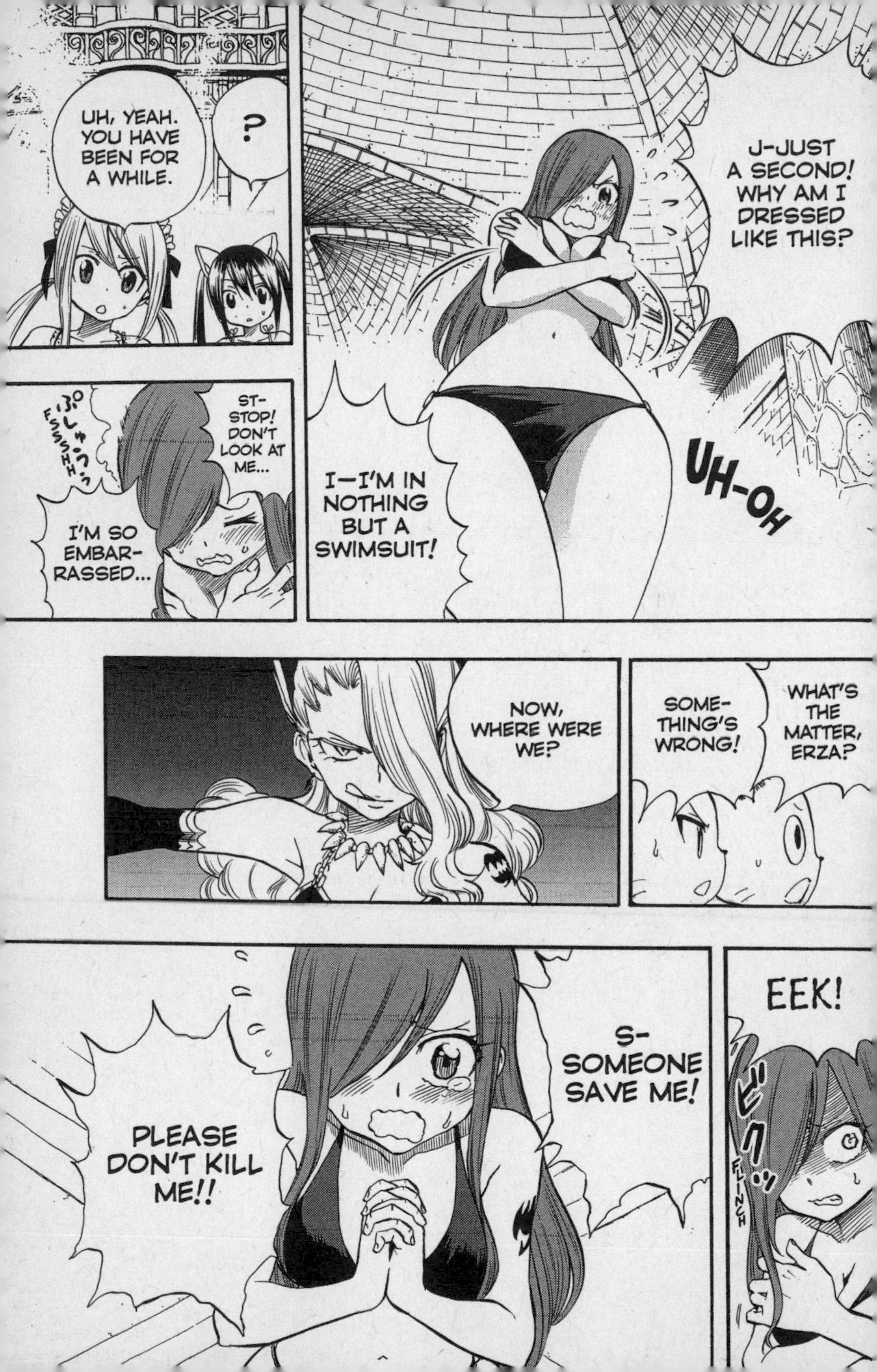
J-JUST A SECOND! WHY AM I DRESSED LIKE THIS?
UH-OH
I—I'M IN NOTHING BUT A SWIMSUIT!
?
UH, YEAH. YOU HAVE BEEN FOR A WHILE.
ST-STOP! DON'T LOOK AT ME...
FSSSHH
I'M SO EMBAR-RASSED...
WHAT'S THE MATTER, ERZA?
SOME-THING'S WRONG!
NOW, WHERE WERE WE?
EEK!
FLINCH
S-SOMEONE SAVE ME!
PLEASE DON'T KILL ME!!

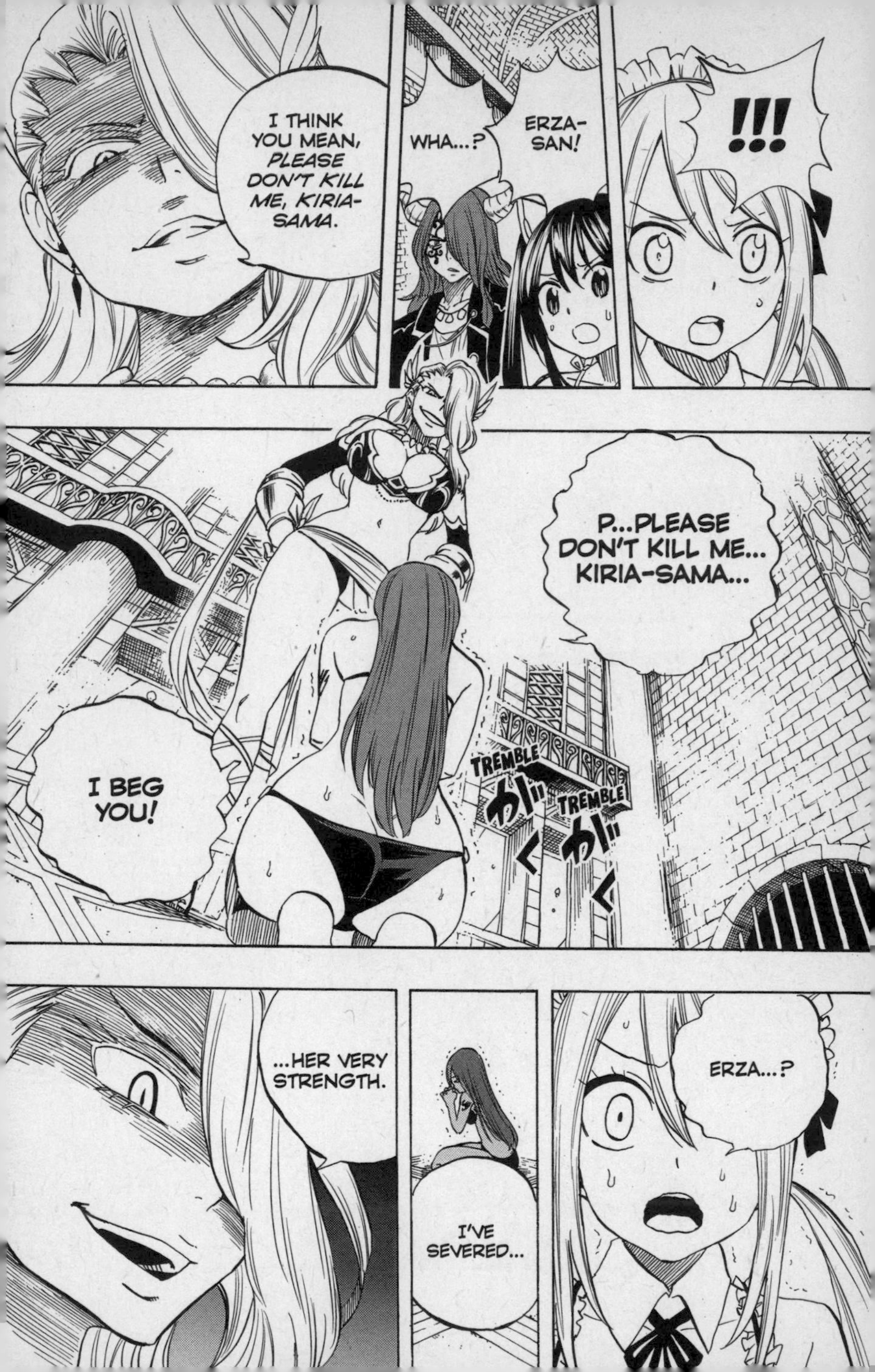
!!!
ERZA-SAN!
WHA...?
I THINK YOU MEAN, PLEASE DON'T KILL ME, KIRIA-SAMA.
P...PLEASE DON'T KILL ME... KIRIA-SAMA...
TREMBLE
TREMBLE
I BEG YOU!
ERZA...?
I'VE SEVERED...
...HER VERY STRENGTH.

FAIRY TAIL 100 YEARS QUEST

Chapter 11: Blade, Armor, Ash

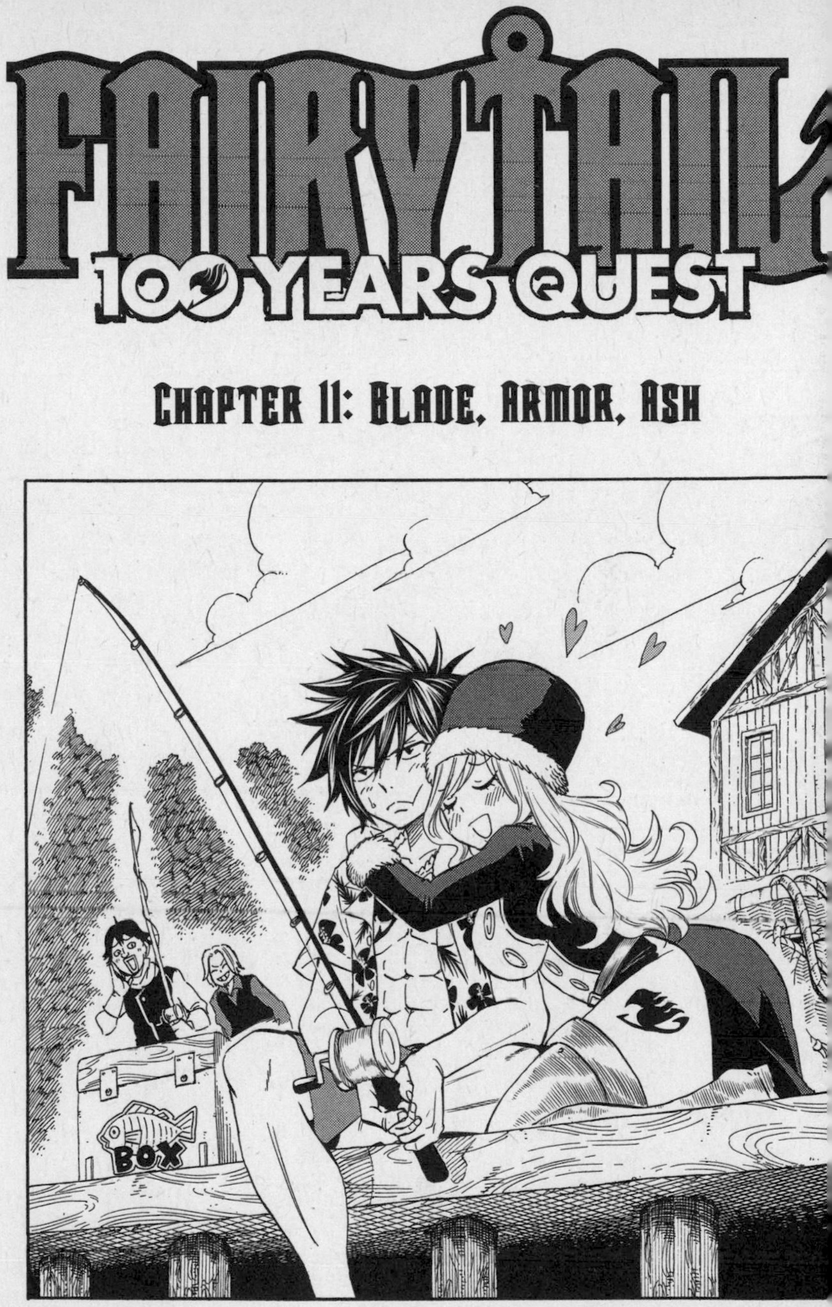
BOX

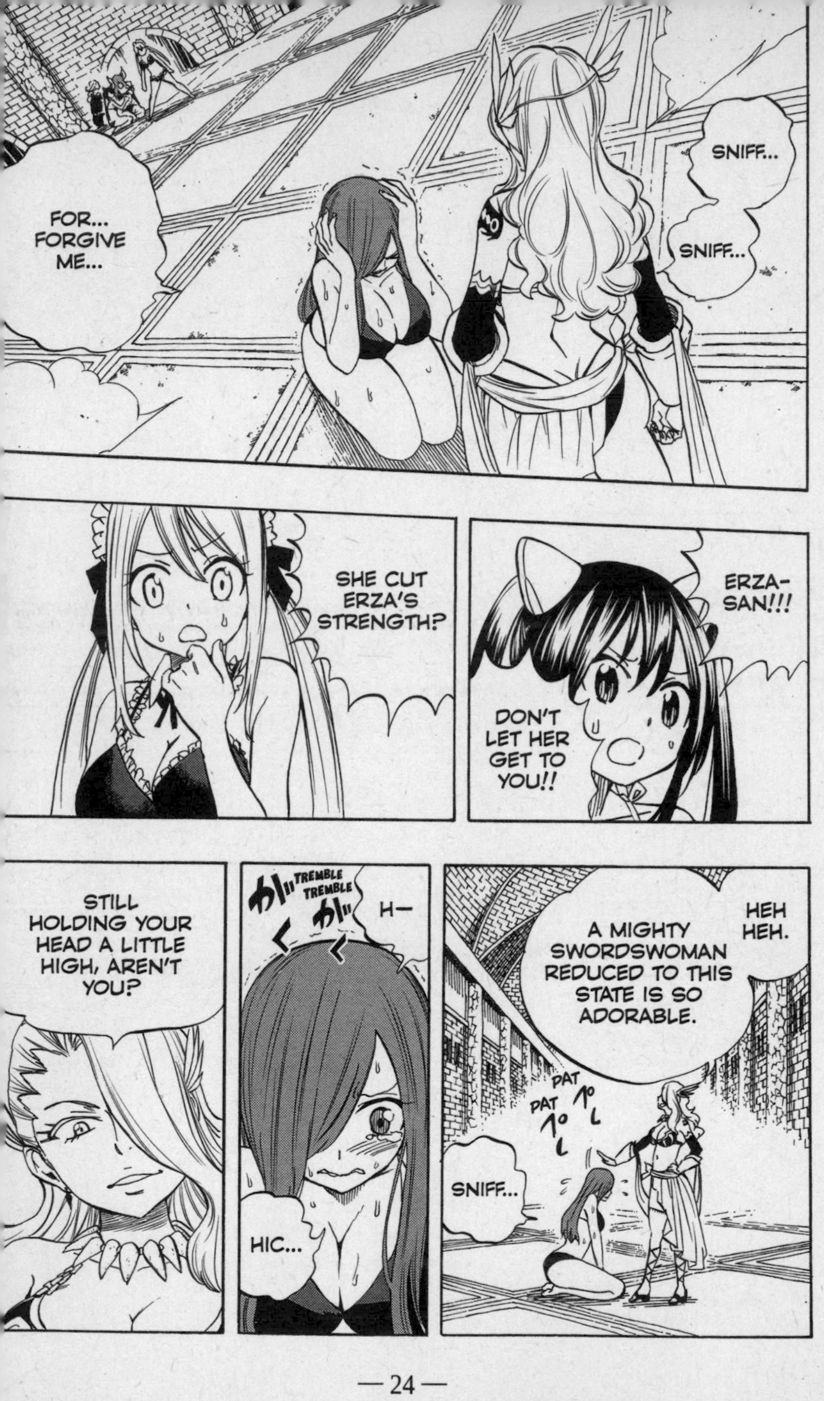
SNIFF...
SNIFF...
FOR... FORGIVE ME...
ERZA-SAN!!!
DON'T LET HER GET TO YOU!!
SHE CUT ERZA'S STRENGTH?
HEH HEH.
A MIGHTY SWORDSWOMAN REDUCED TO THIS STATE IS SO ADORABLE.
PAT PAT
SNIFF...
TREMBLE TREMBLE
H—
HIC...
STILL HOLDING YOUR HEAD A LITTLE HIGH, AREN'T YOU?

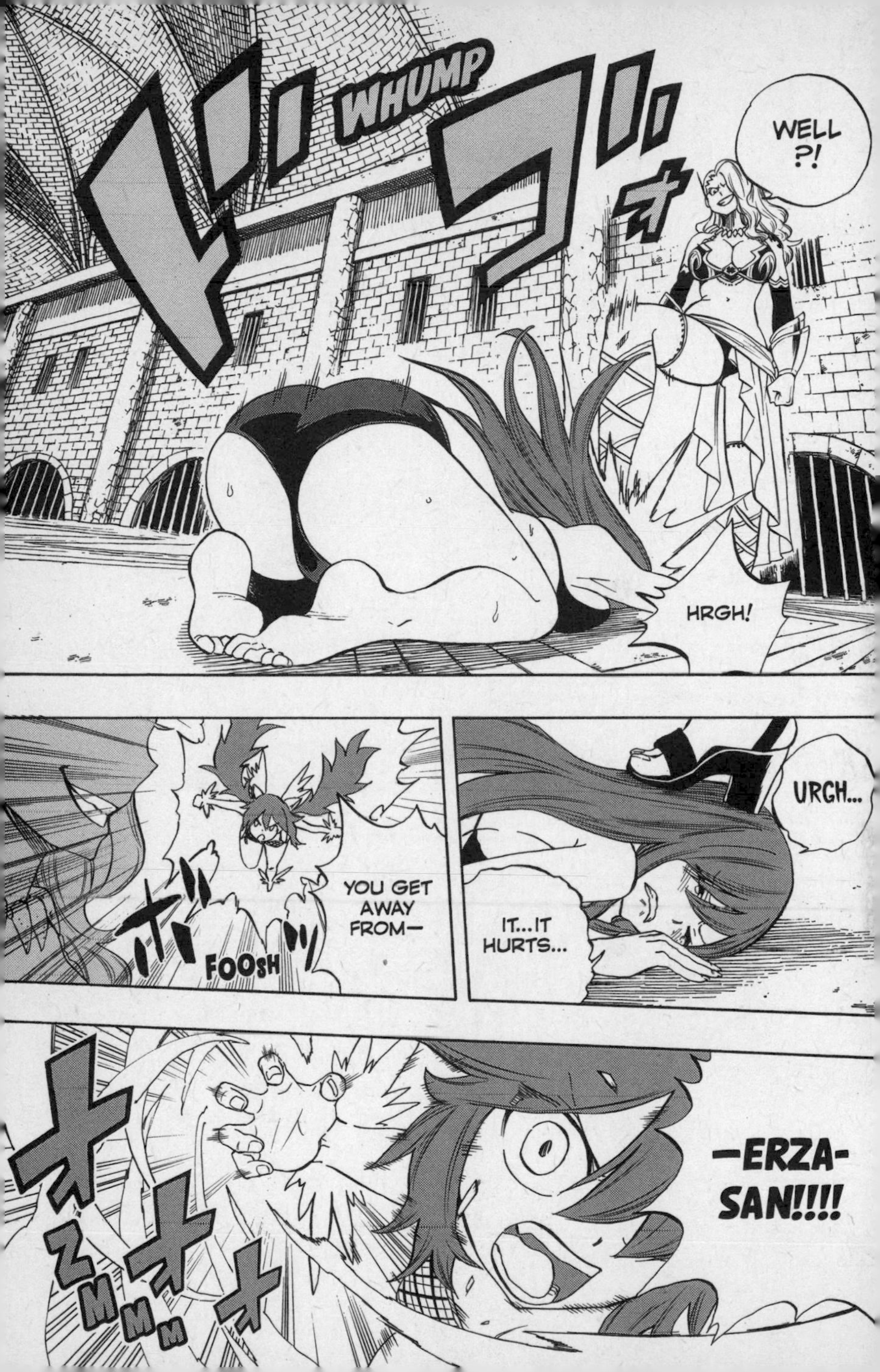
WELL ?!
WHUMP
HRGH!
URGH...
IT...IT HURTS...
YOU GET AWAY FROM—
FOOSH
—ERZA-SAN!!!!
ZMMM

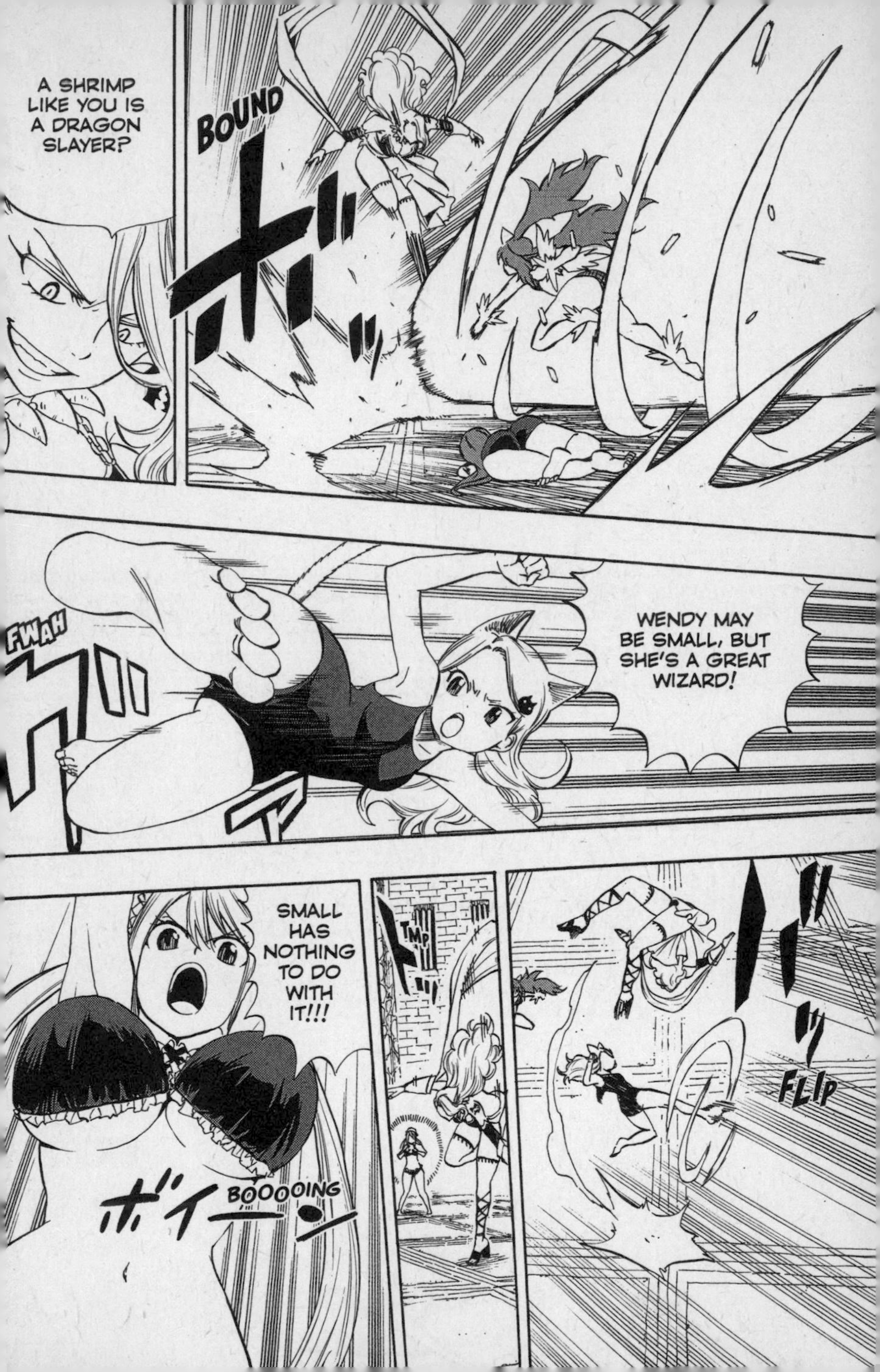
BOUND
A SHRIMP LIKE YOU IS A DRAGON SLAYER?
WENDY MAY BE SMALL, BUT SHE'S A GREAT WIZARD!
FWAH
FLIP
TMP
SMALL HAS NOTHING TO DO WITH IT!!!
BOOOOING

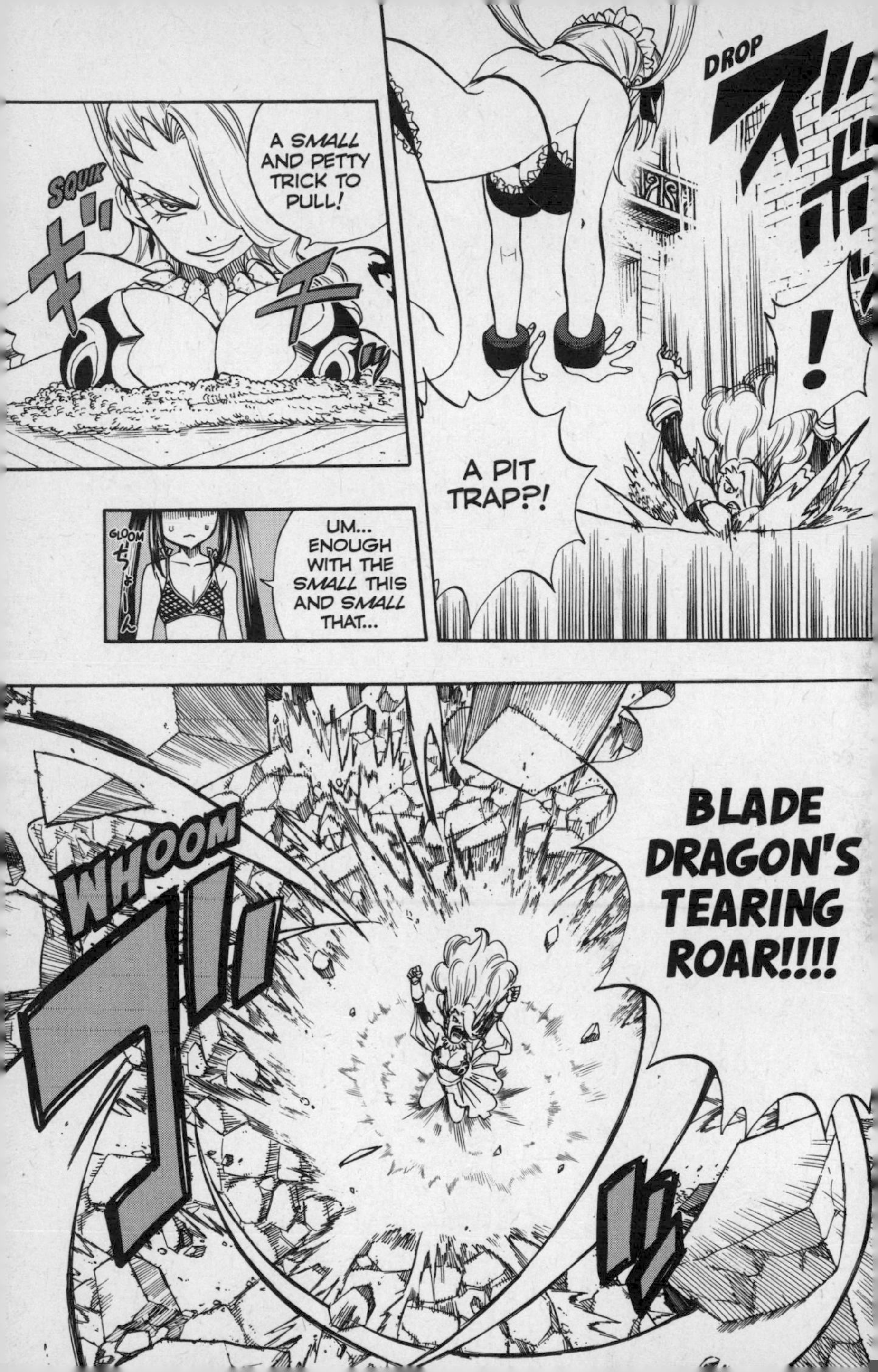
DROP
A PIT TRAP?!
SQUIK
A SMALL AND PETTY TRICK TO PULL!
GLOOM
UM... ENOUGH WITH THE SMALL THIS AND SMALL THAT...
BLADE DRAGON'S TEARING ROAR!!!!
WHOOM

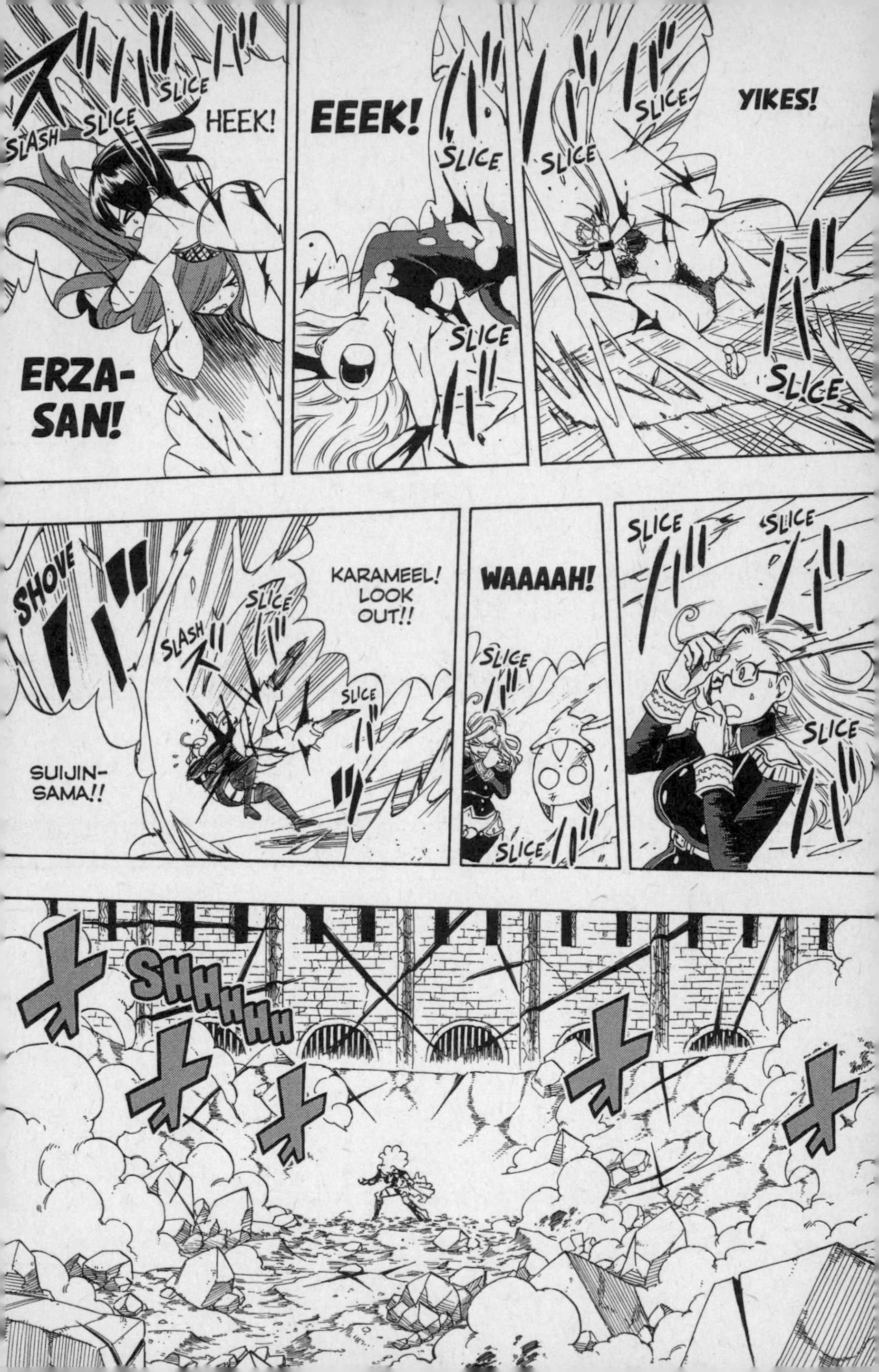
SLICE
YIKES!
SLICE
SLICE
EEEK!
SLICE
SLICE
HEEK!
SLICE
SLICE
SLASH
ERZA-SAN!
SLICE
SLICE
SLICE
WAAAAH!
SLICE
SLICE
KARAMEEL! LOOK OUT!!
SHOVE
SLICE
SLASH
SLICE
SUIJIN-SAMA!!
SHHHHHH

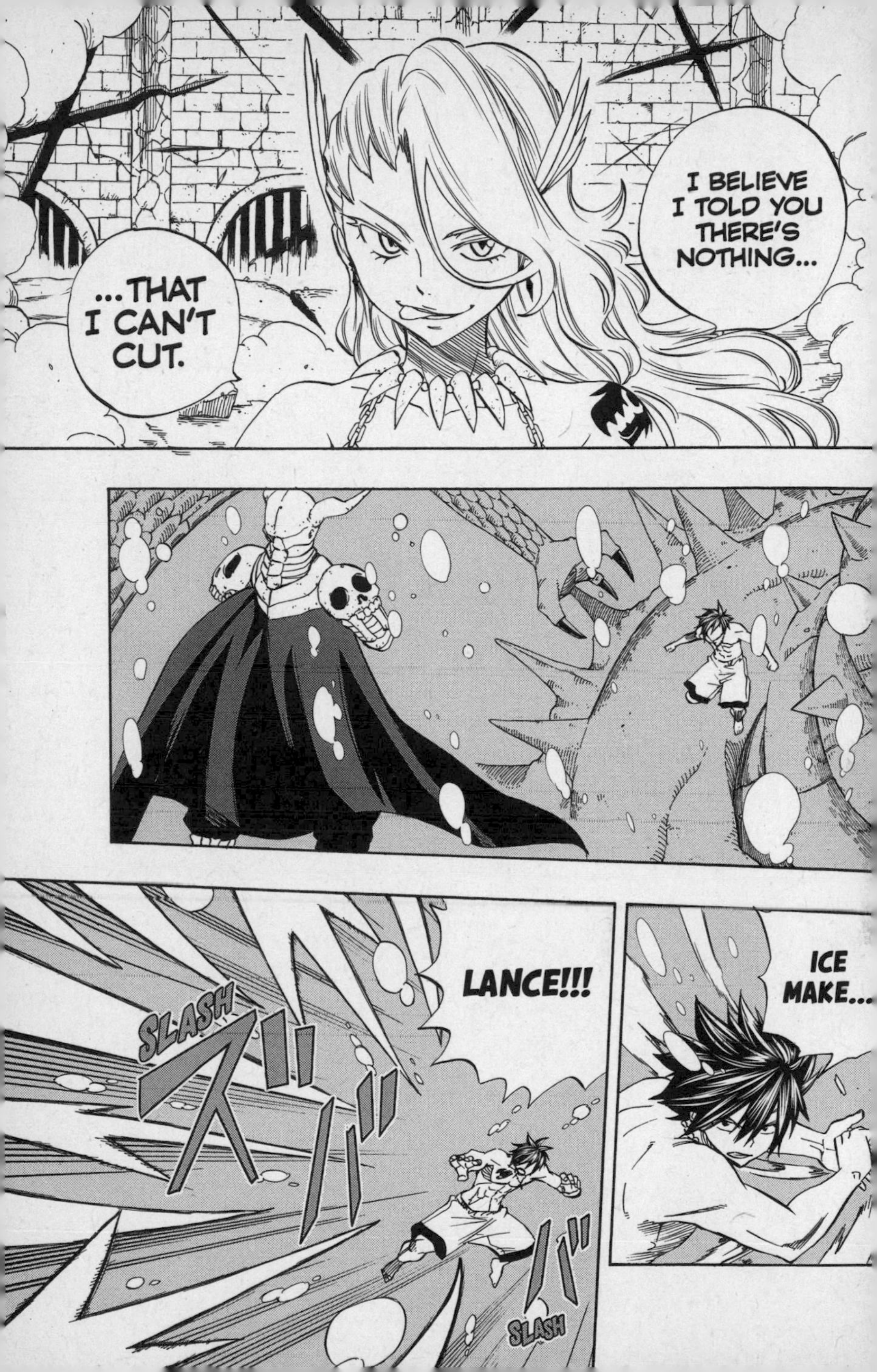
I BELIEVE I TOLD YOU THERE'S NOTHING...
...THAT I CAN'T CUT.
ICE MAKE...
LANCE!!!
SLASH
SLASH

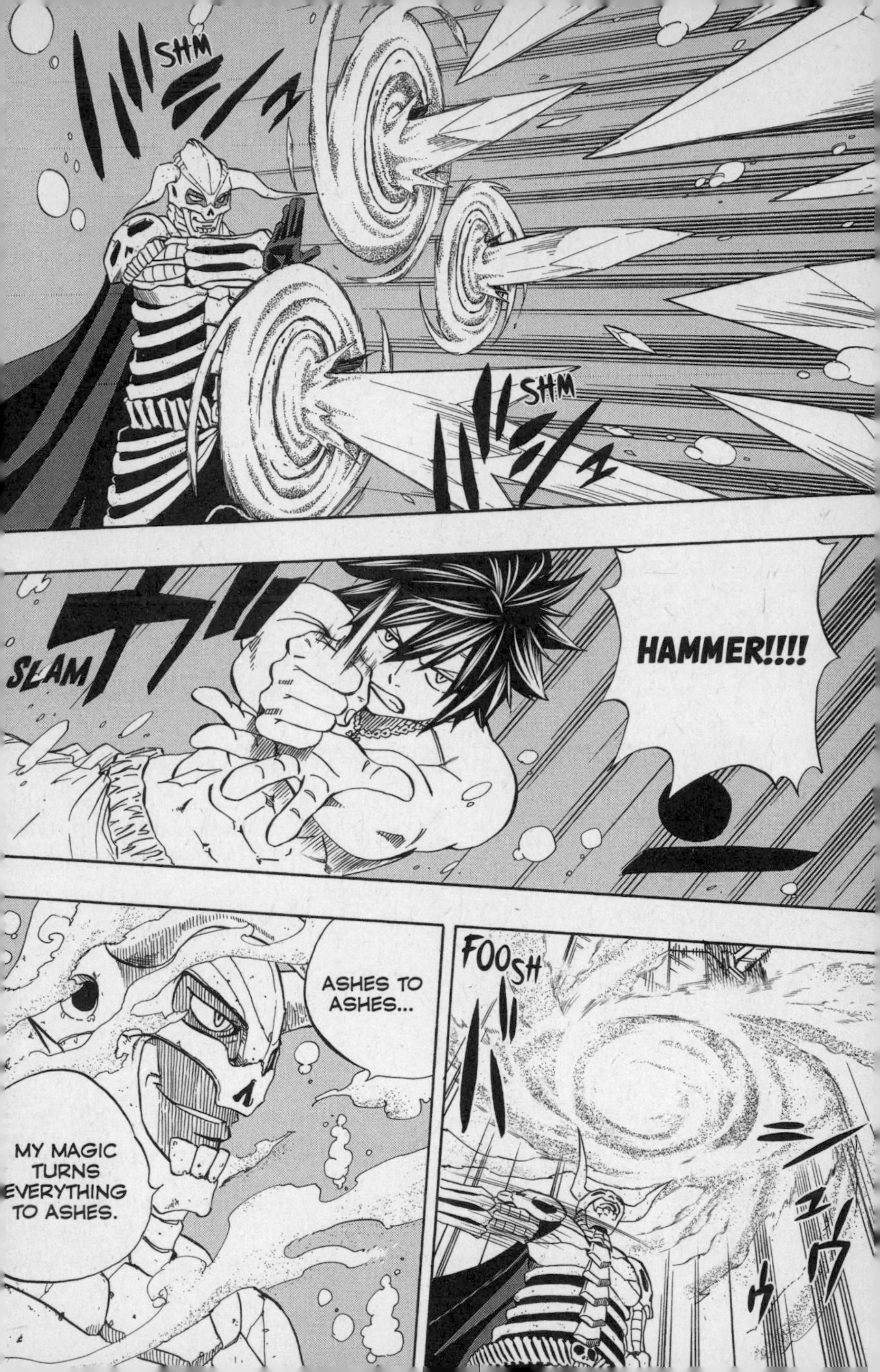
SHM
SHM
HAMMER!!!!
SLAM
FOOSH
ASHES TO ASHES...
MY MAGIC TURNS EVERYTHING TO ASHES.

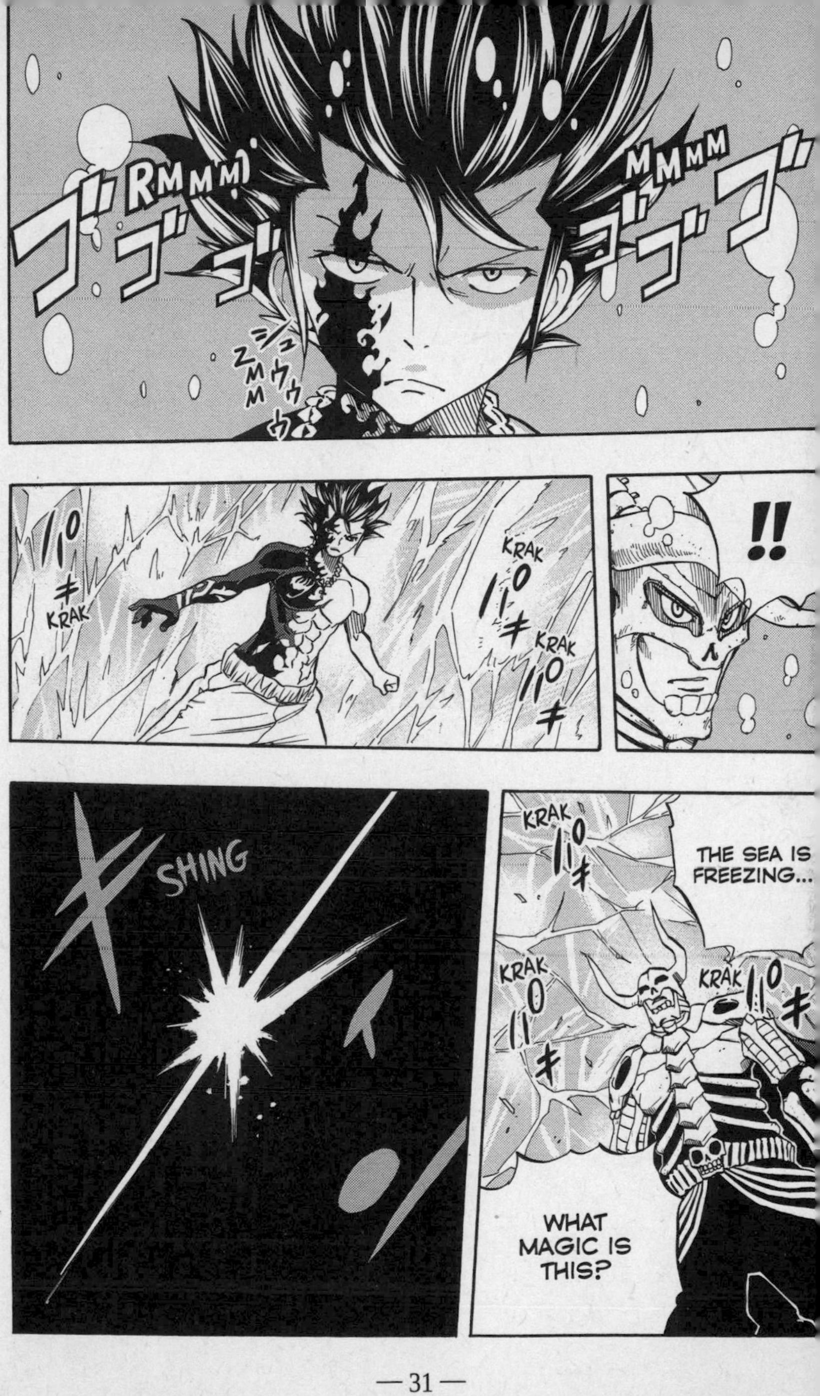
MMMM
RMMM
ZMMM
!!
KRAK
KRAK
KRAK
THE SEA IS FREEZING...
KRAK
KRAK
WHAT MAGIC IS THIS?
SHING

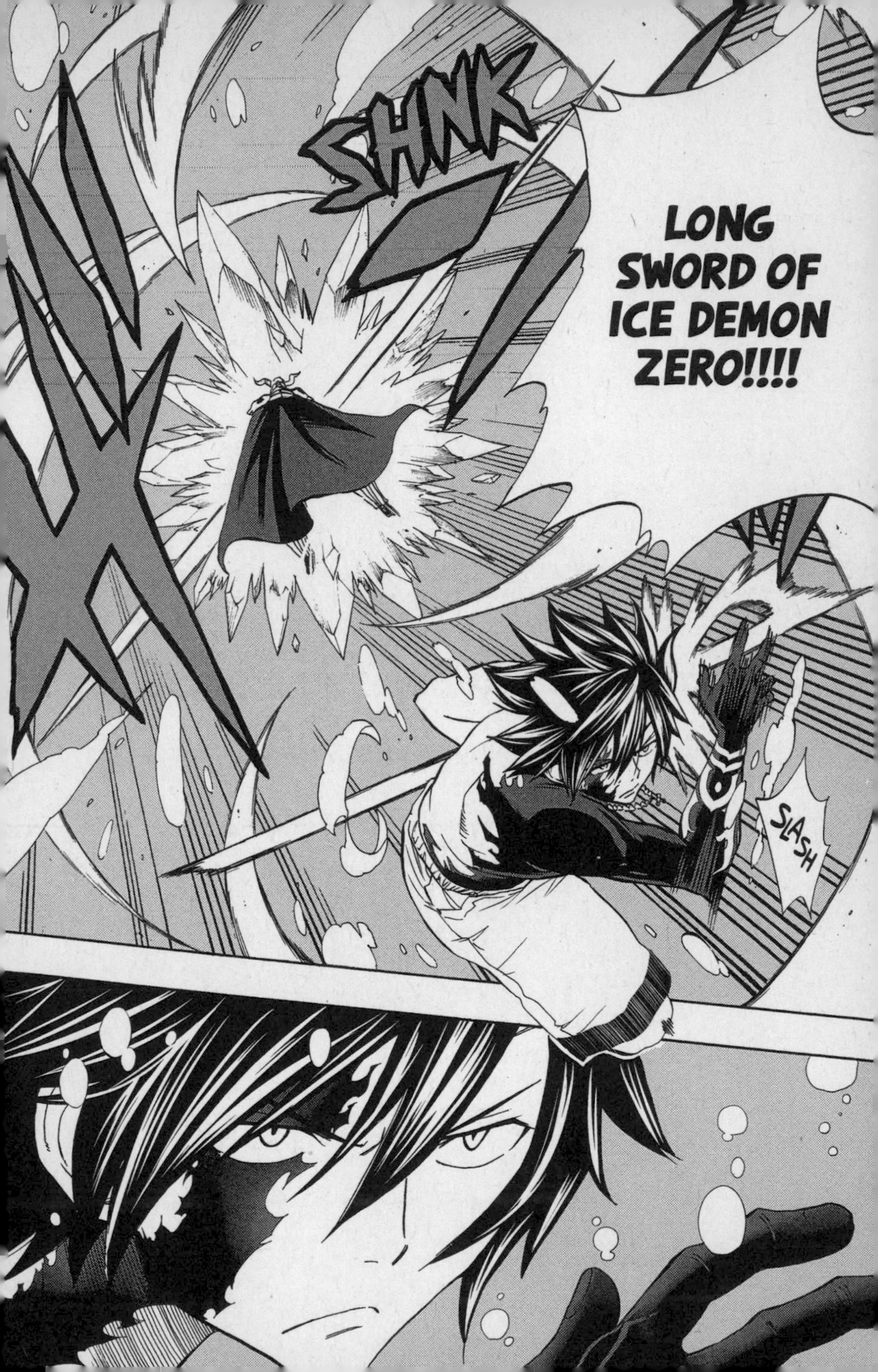
SHNK
LONG SWORD OF ICE DEMON ZERO!!!!
SLASH

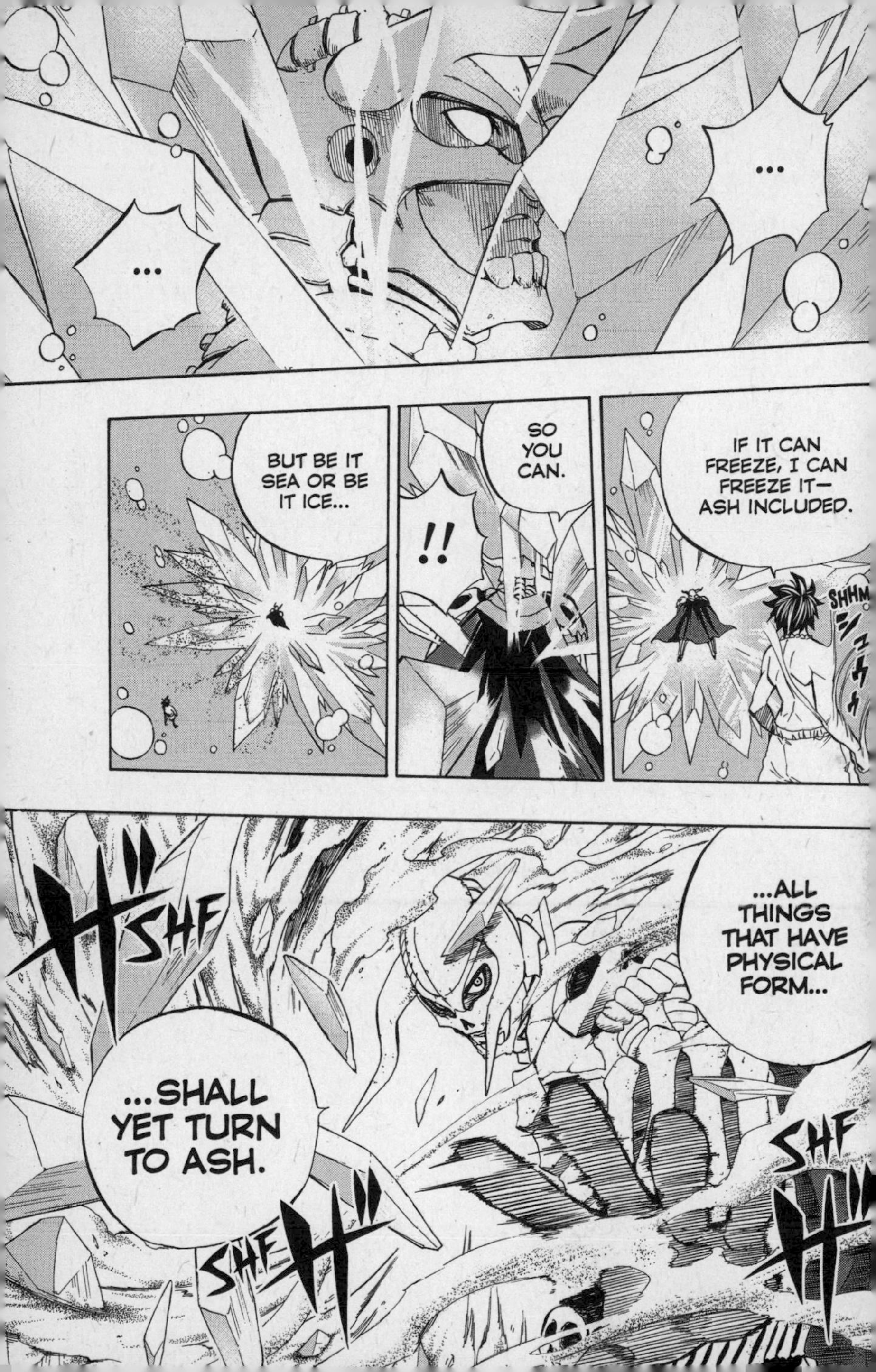
...
...
IF IT CAN FREEZE, I CAN FREEZE IT— ASH INCLUDED.
SHHM
SO YOU CAN.
!!
BUT BE IT SEA OR BE IT ICE...
...ALL THINGS THAT HAVE PHYSICAL FORM...
SHF
SHF
...SHALL YET TURN TO ASH.
SHF

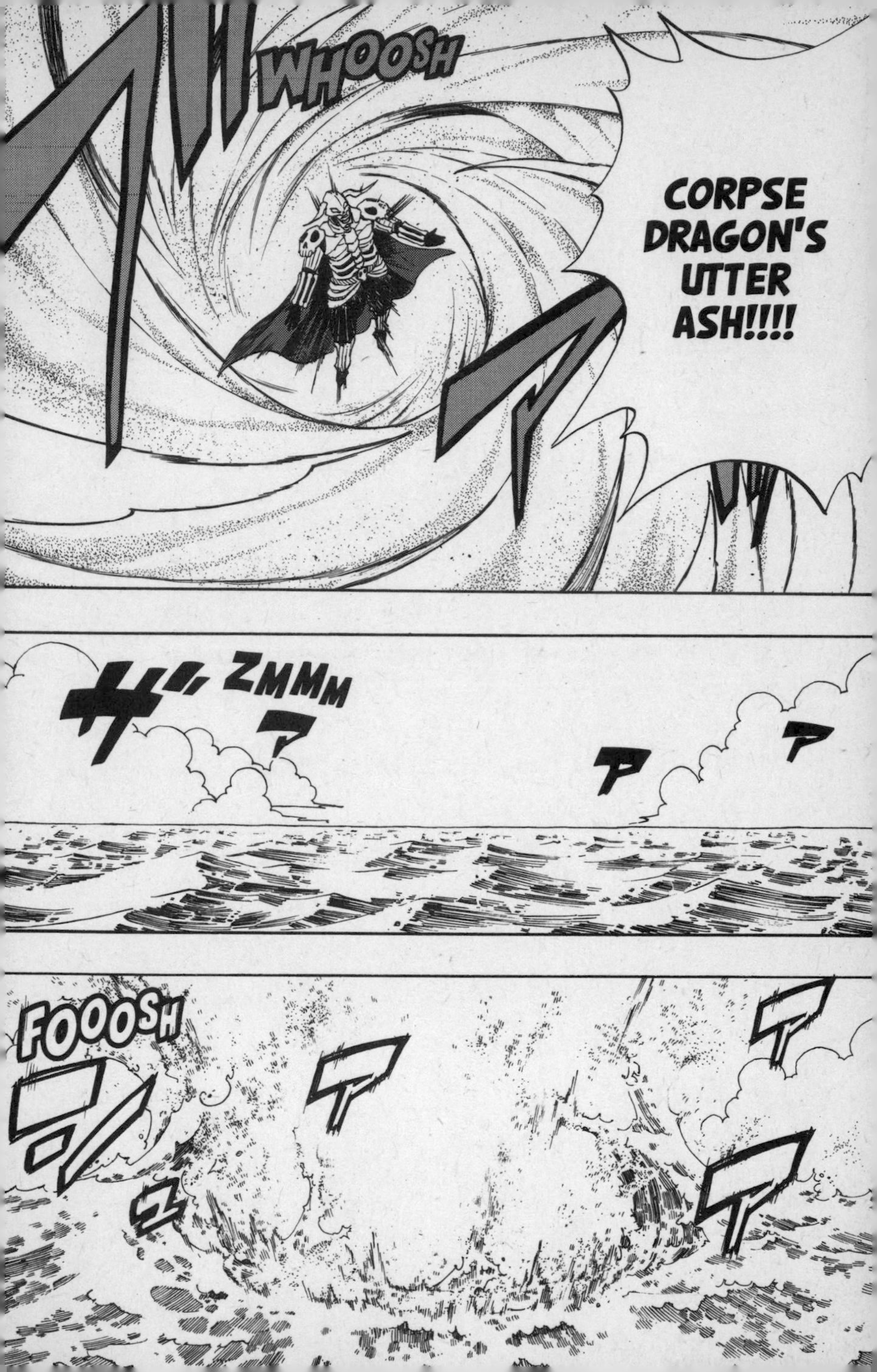
CORPSE DRAGON'S UTTER ASH!!!!
WHOOSH
ZMMM
FOOOSH

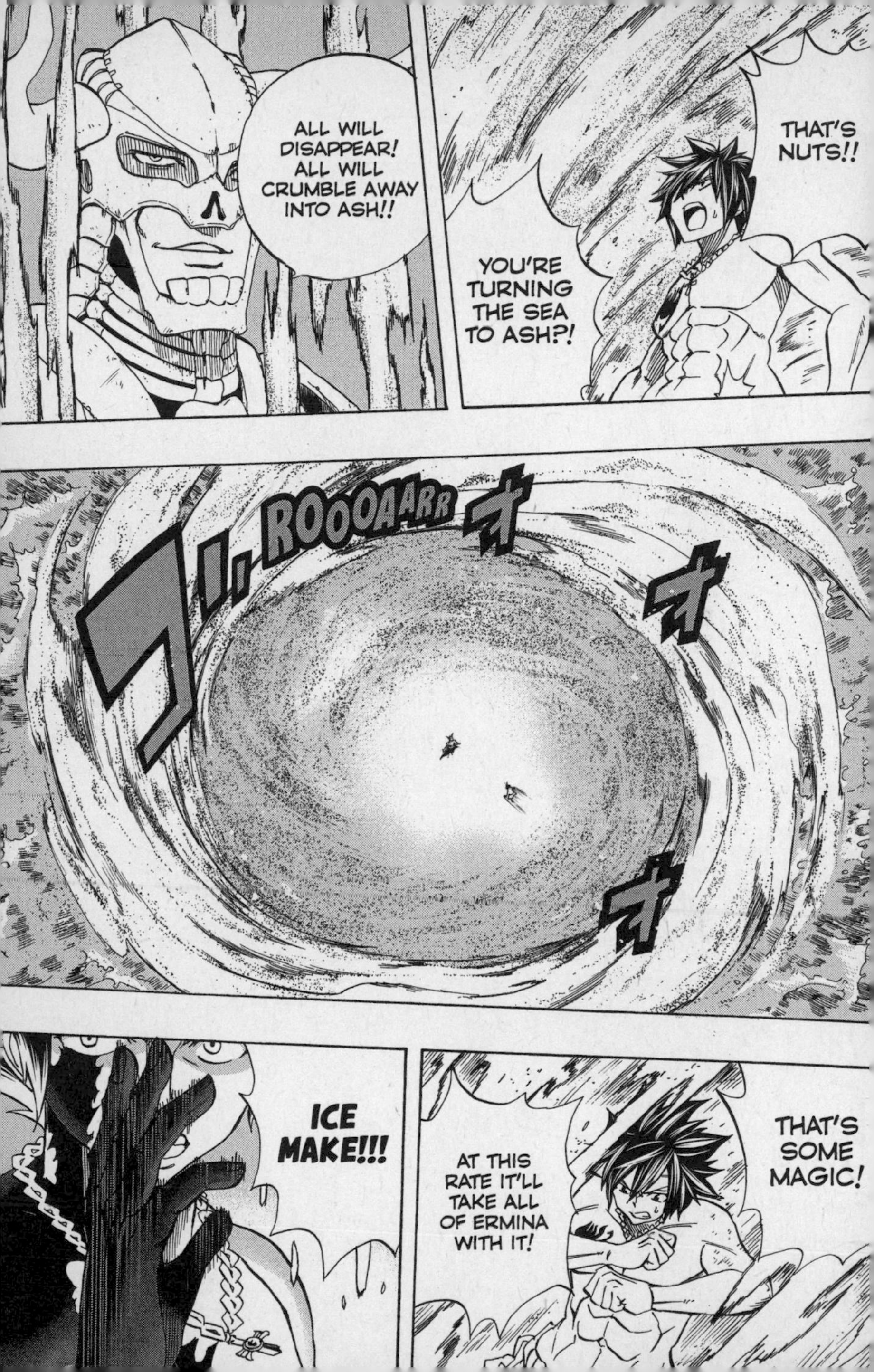
THAT'S NUTS!!
YOU'RE TURNING THE SEA TO ASH?!
ALL WILL DISAPPEAR! ALL WILL CRUMBLE AWAY INTO ASH!!
ROOOAARR
THAT'S SOME MAGIC!
AT THIS RATE IT'LL TAKE ALL OF ERMINA WITH IT!
ICE MAKE!!!

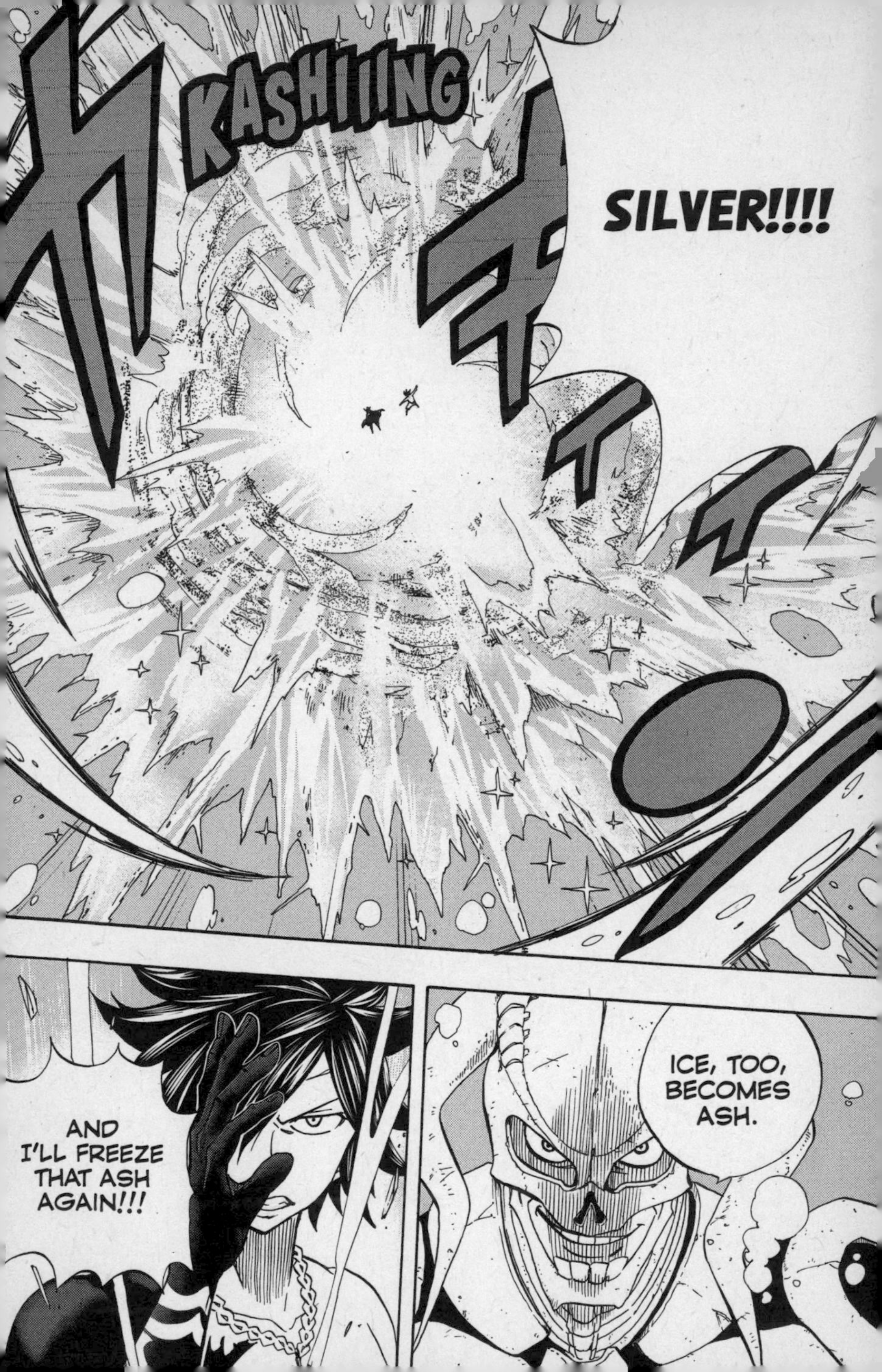
KASHIIING
SILVER!!!!
ICE, TOO, BECOMES ASH.
AND I'LL FREEZE THAT ASH AGAIN!!!

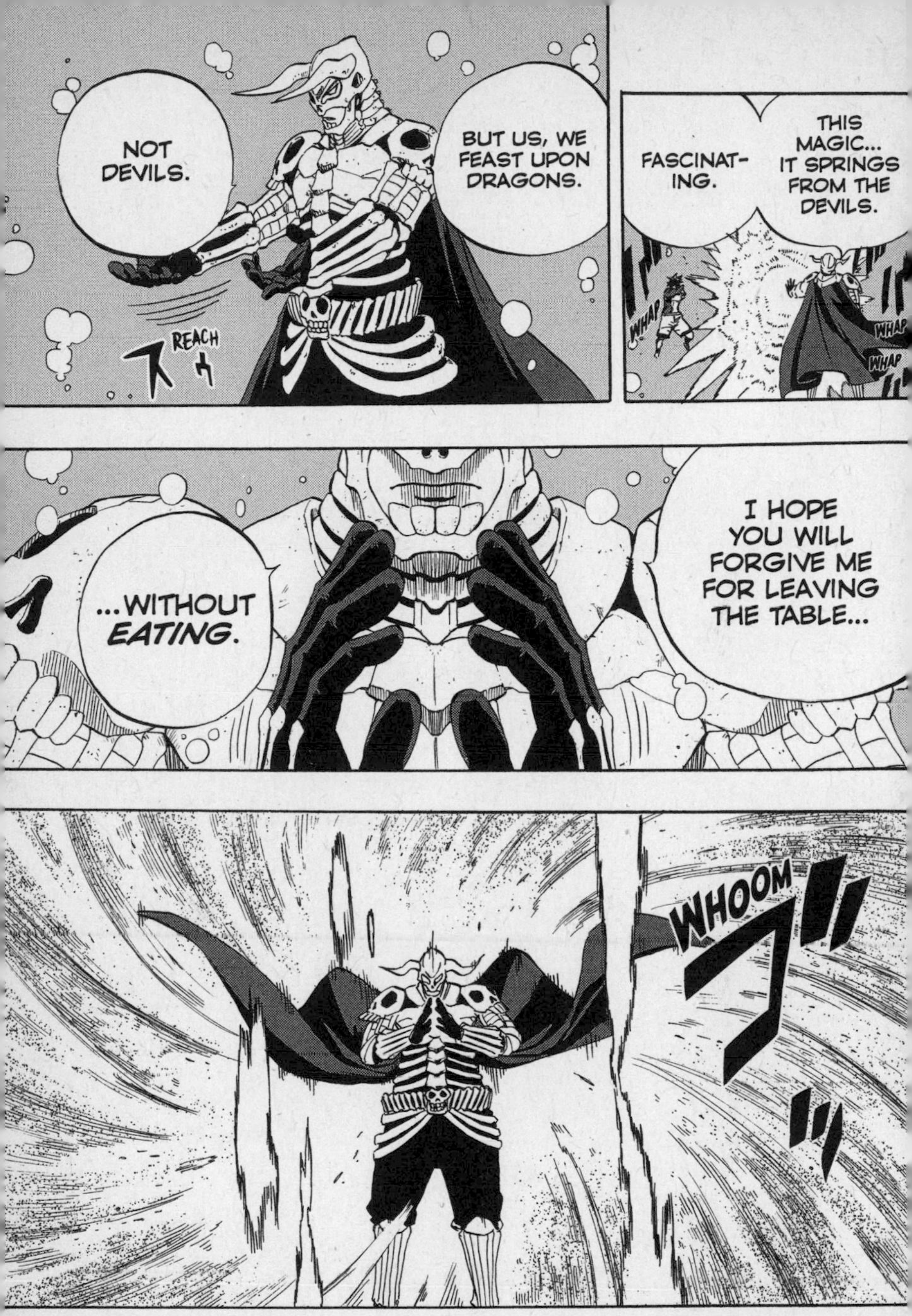
THIS MAGIC... IT SPRINGS FROM THE DEVILS.
FASCINATING.
WHAP
WHAP
WHAP
BUT US, WE FEAST UPON DRAGONS.
NOT DEVILS.
REACH
I HOPE YOU WILL FORGIVE ME FOR LEAVING THE TABLE...
...WITHOUT *EATING*.
WHOOM

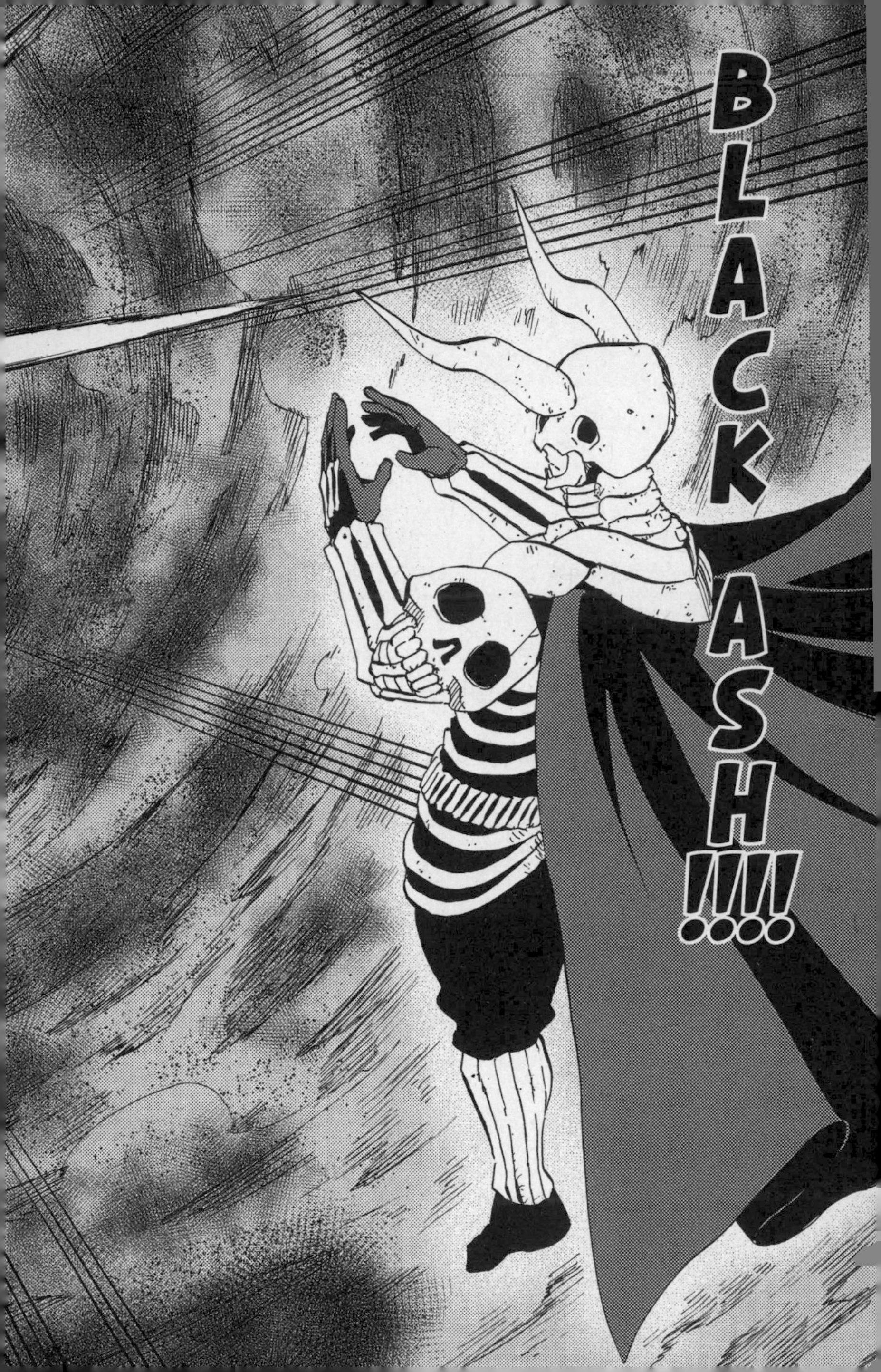
BLACK LASH!!!!!

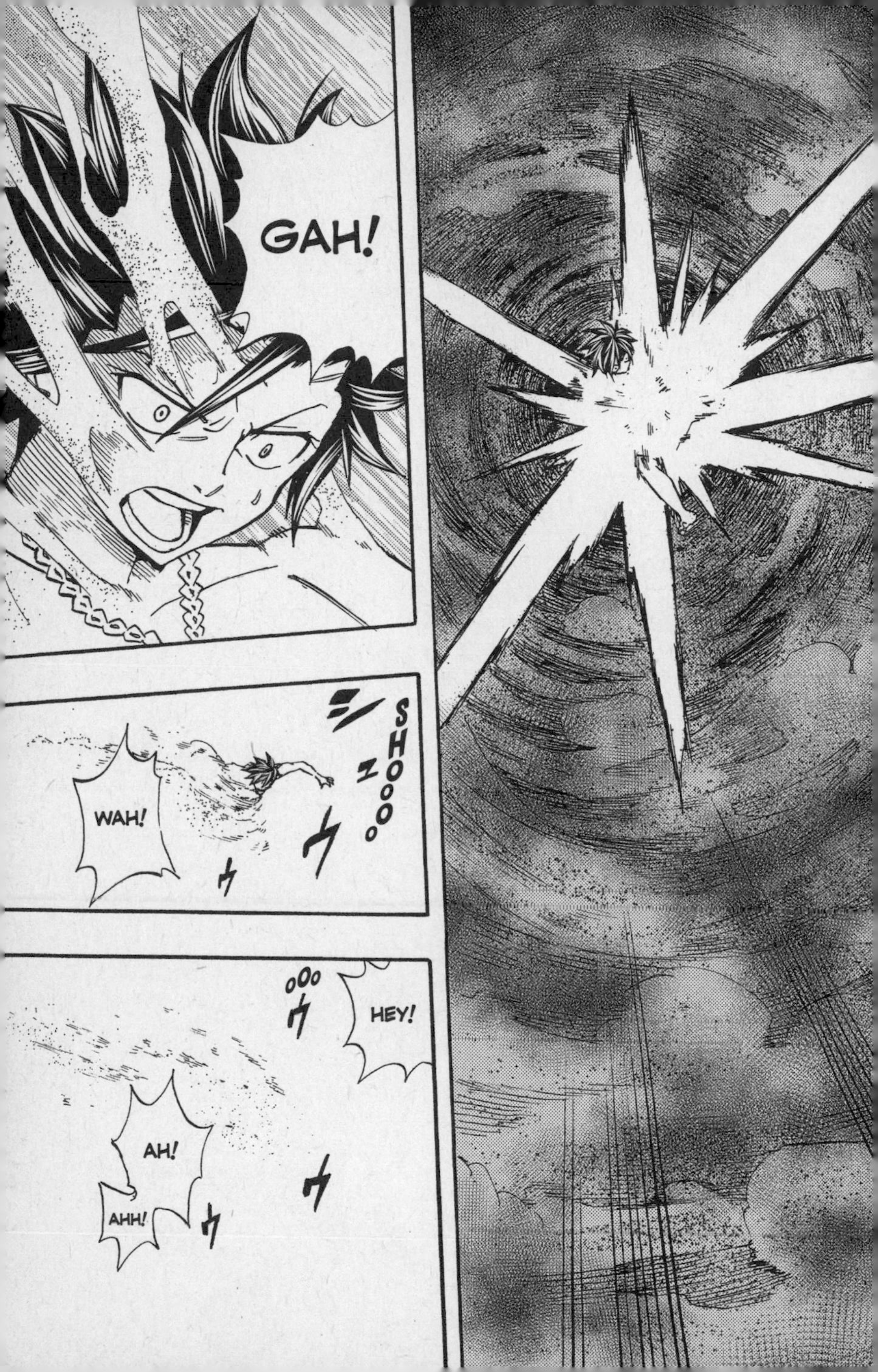
GAH!
SHOOOO
WAH!
OOO
HEY!
AH!
AHH!

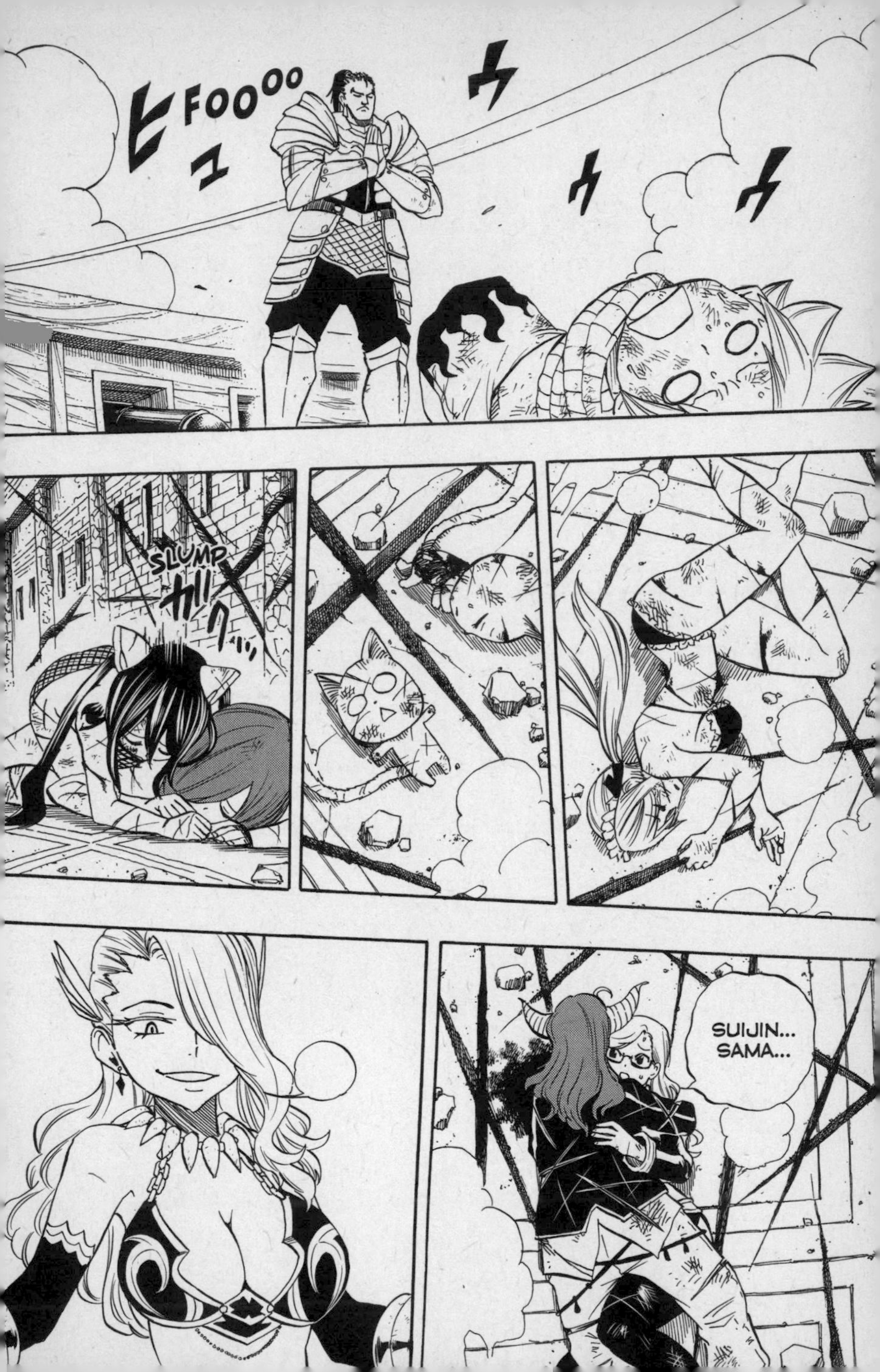
FOOOO
SLUMP
SUIJIN... SAMA...

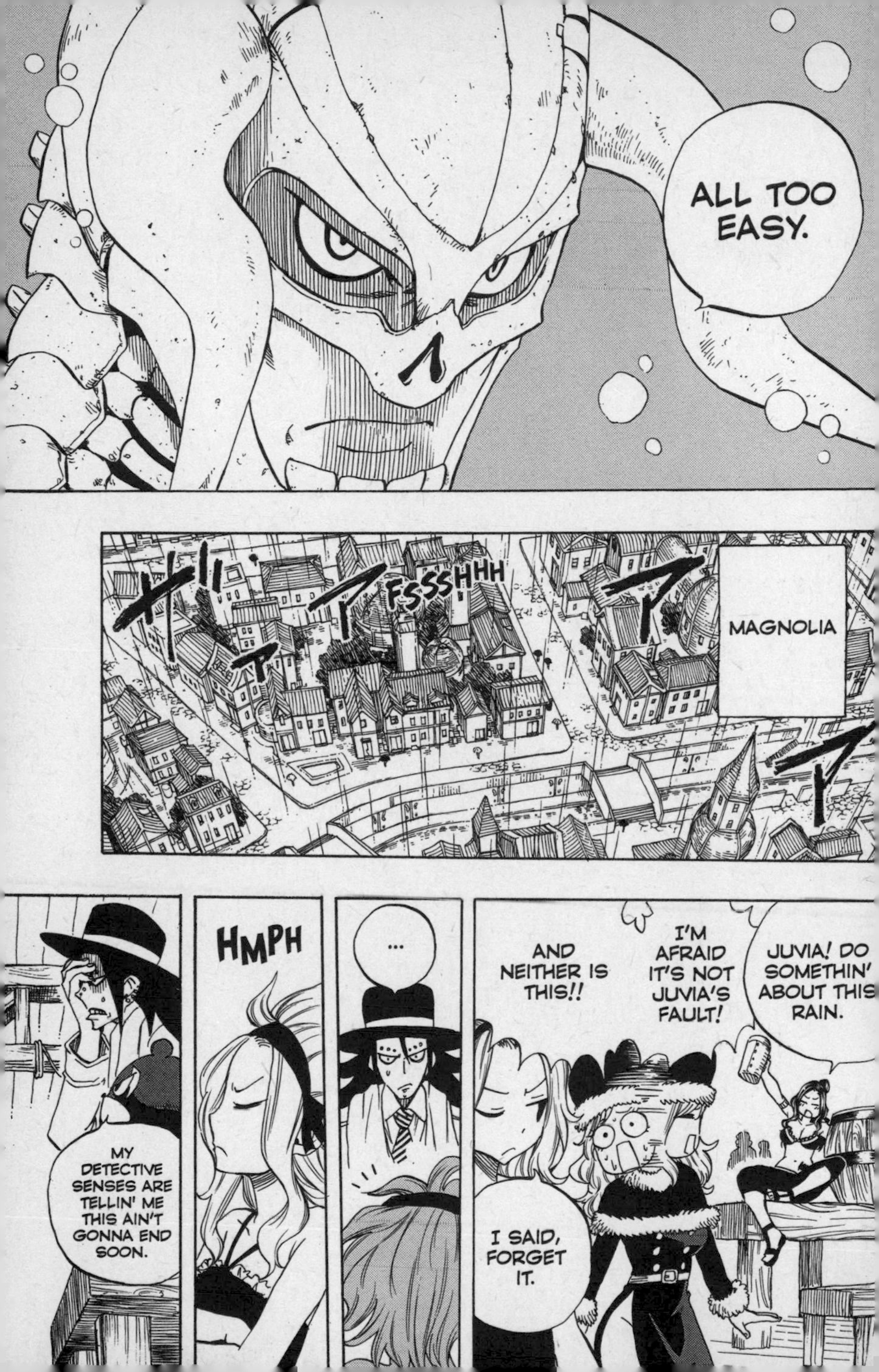
ALL TOO EASY.
MAGNOLIA
FSSSHHH
JUVIA! DO SOMETHIN' ABOUT THIS RAIN.
I'M AFRAID IT'S NOT JUVIA'S FAULT!
AND NEITHER IS THIS!!
I SAID, FORGET IT.
...
HMPH
MY DETECTIVE SENSES ARE TELLIN' ME THIS AIN'T GONNA END SOON.

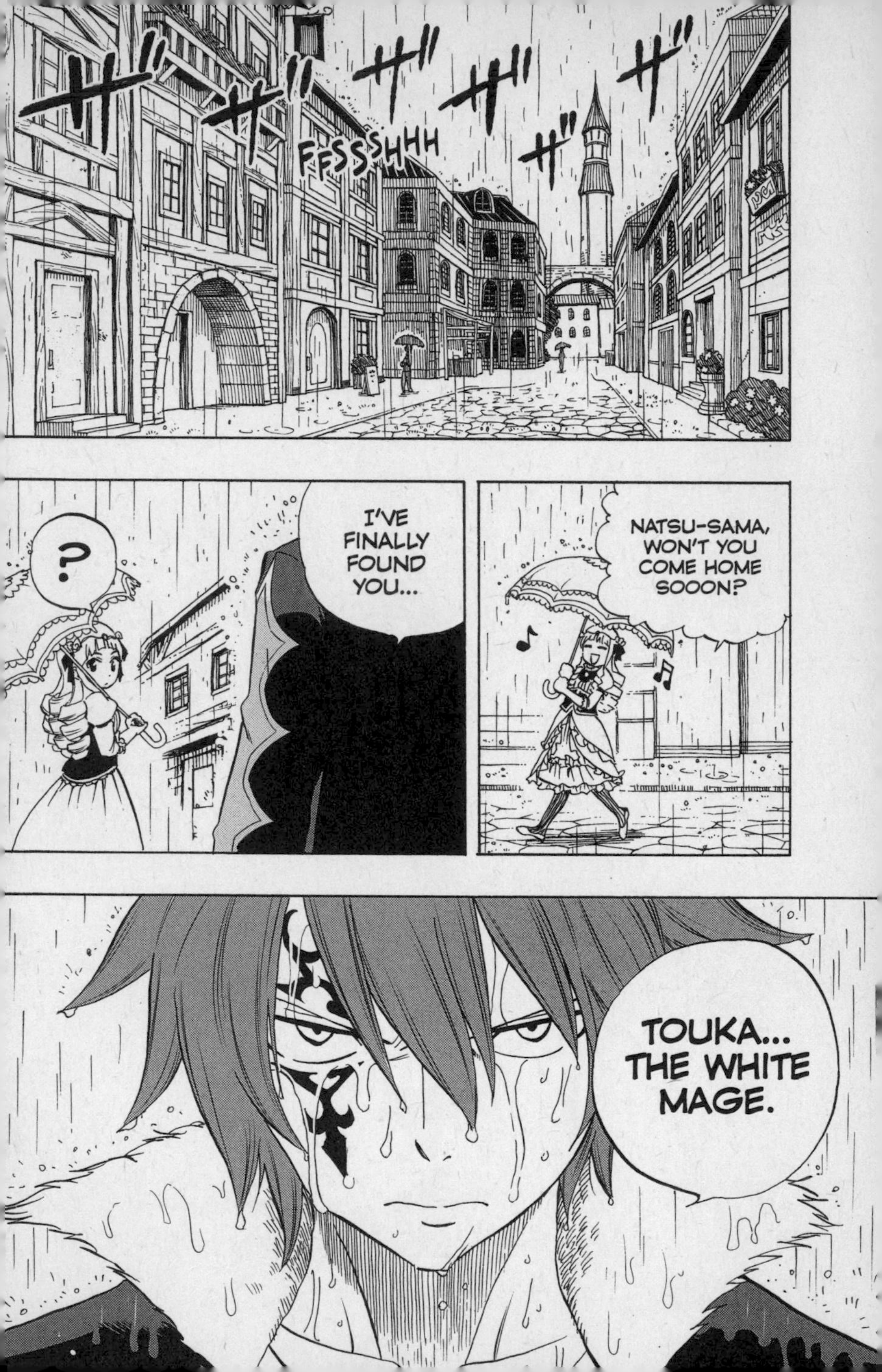
ザ ザ ザ ザ ザ ザ
FFSSSHHH
NATSU-SAMA, WON'T YOU COME HOME SOOON?
I'VE FINALLY FOUND YOU...
?
TOUKA... THE WHITE MAGE.

FAIRY TAIL 100 YEARS QUEST

Chapter 12: Stars and Lightning

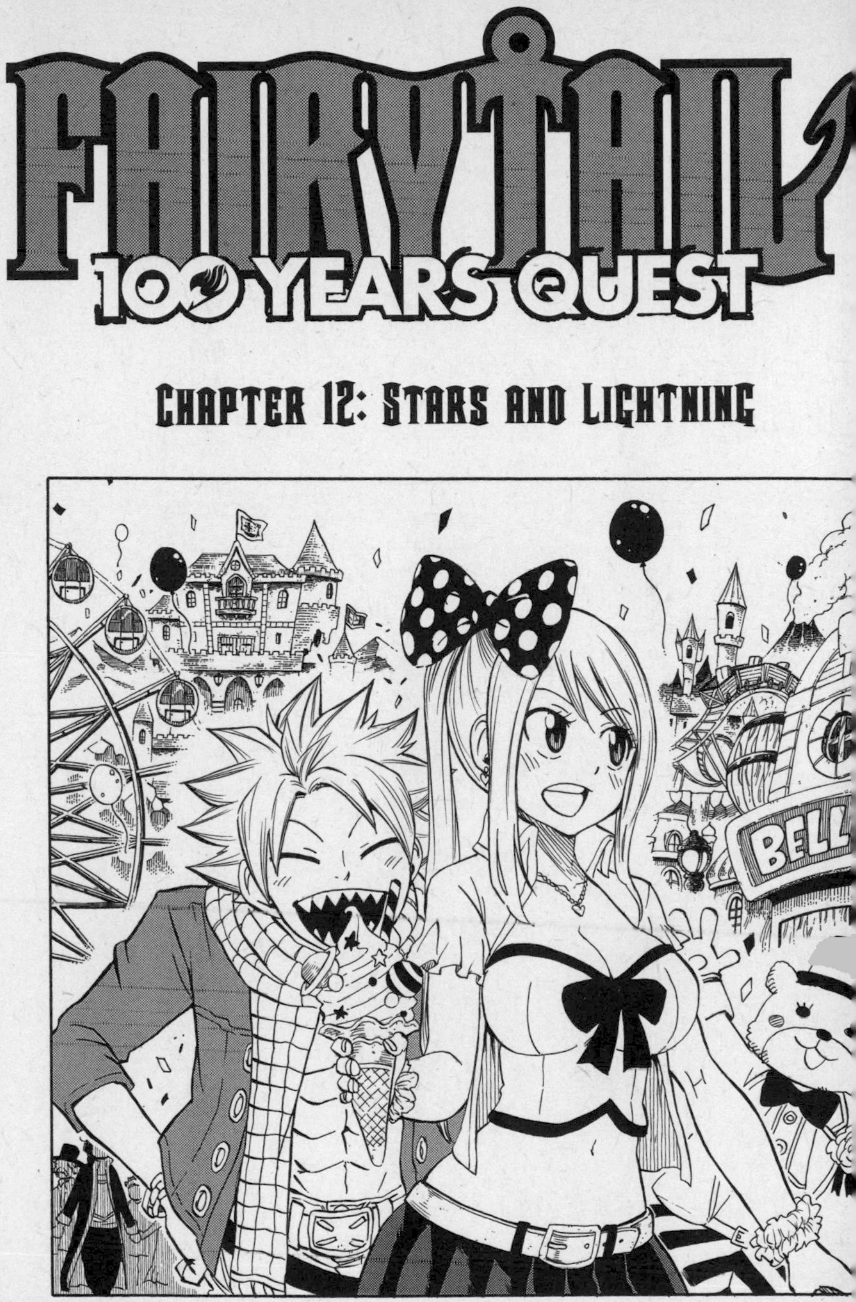
BELL

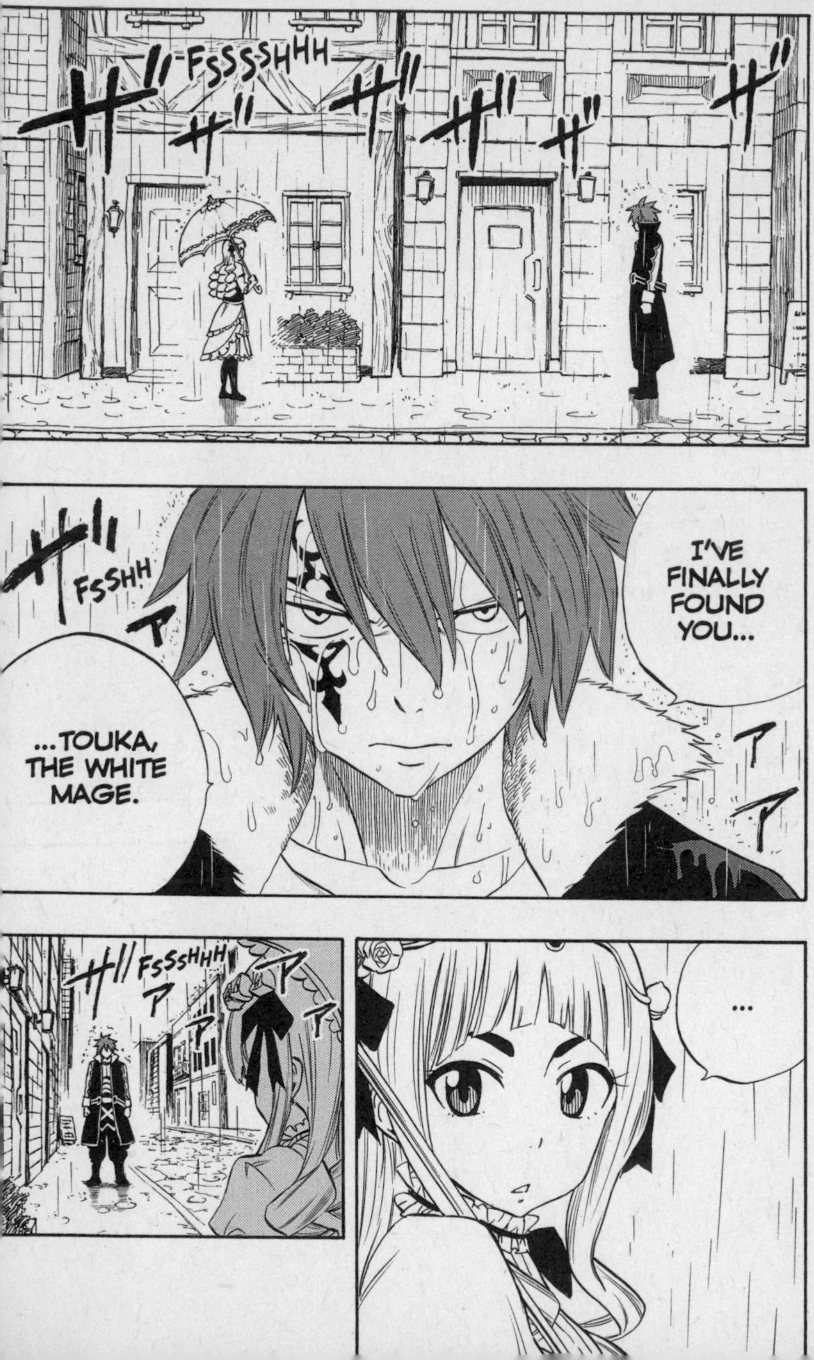
FSSSSHHH
FSSHH
I'VE FINALLY FOUND YOU...
...TOUKA, THE WHITE MAGE.
...
FSSSHHH

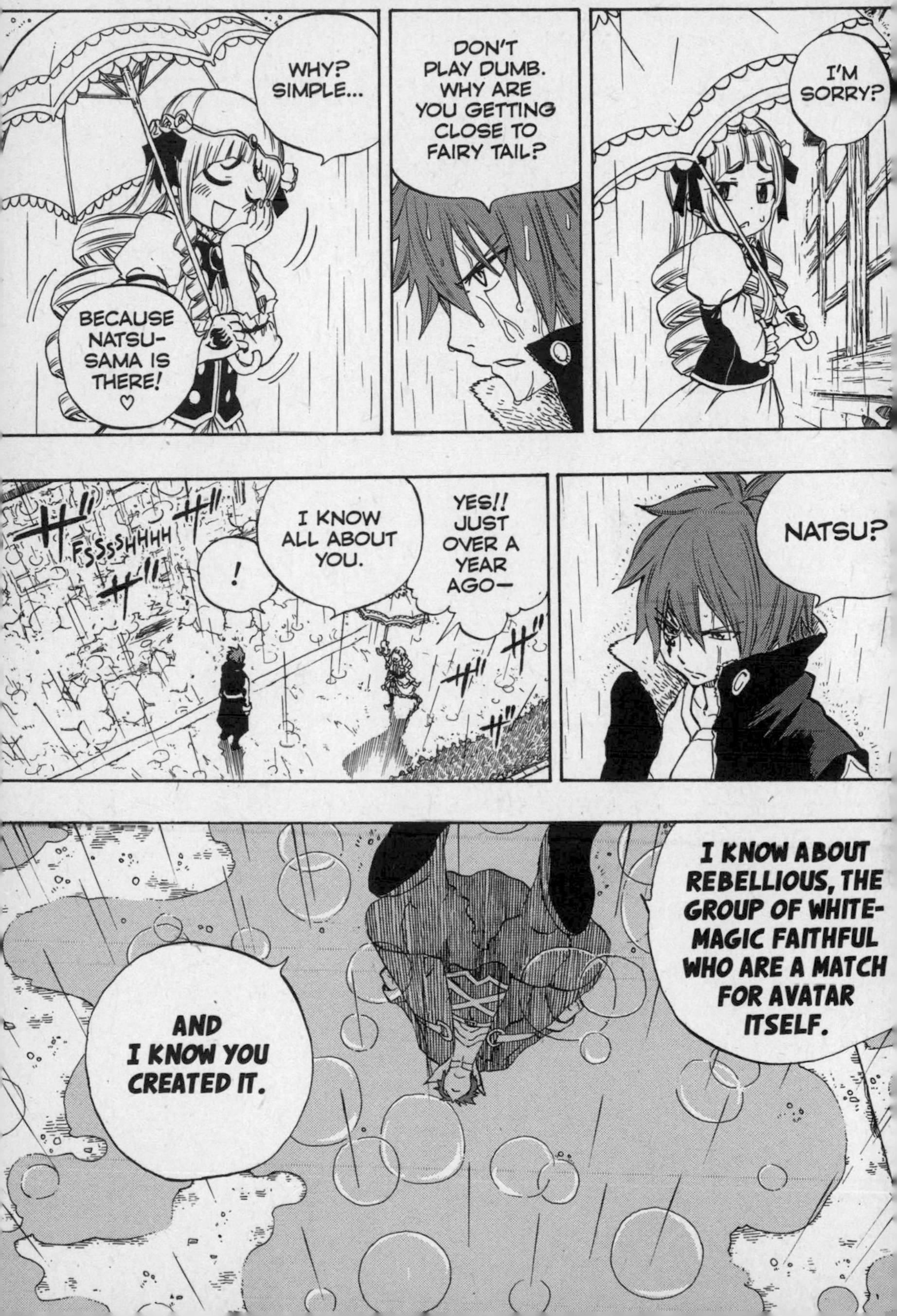
I'M SORRY?
DON'T PLAY DUMB. WHY ARE YOU GETTING CLOSE TO FAIRY TAIL?
WHY? SIMPLE...
BECAUSE NATSU-SAMA IS THERE! ♡
NATSU?
YES!! JUST OVER A YEAR AGO—
I KNOW ALL ABOUT YOU.
!
FSSSSHHHH
I KNOW ABOUT REBELLIOUS, THE GROUP OF WHITE-MAGIC FAITHFUL WHO ARE A MATCH FOR AVATAR ITSELF.
AND I KNOW YOU CREATED IT.

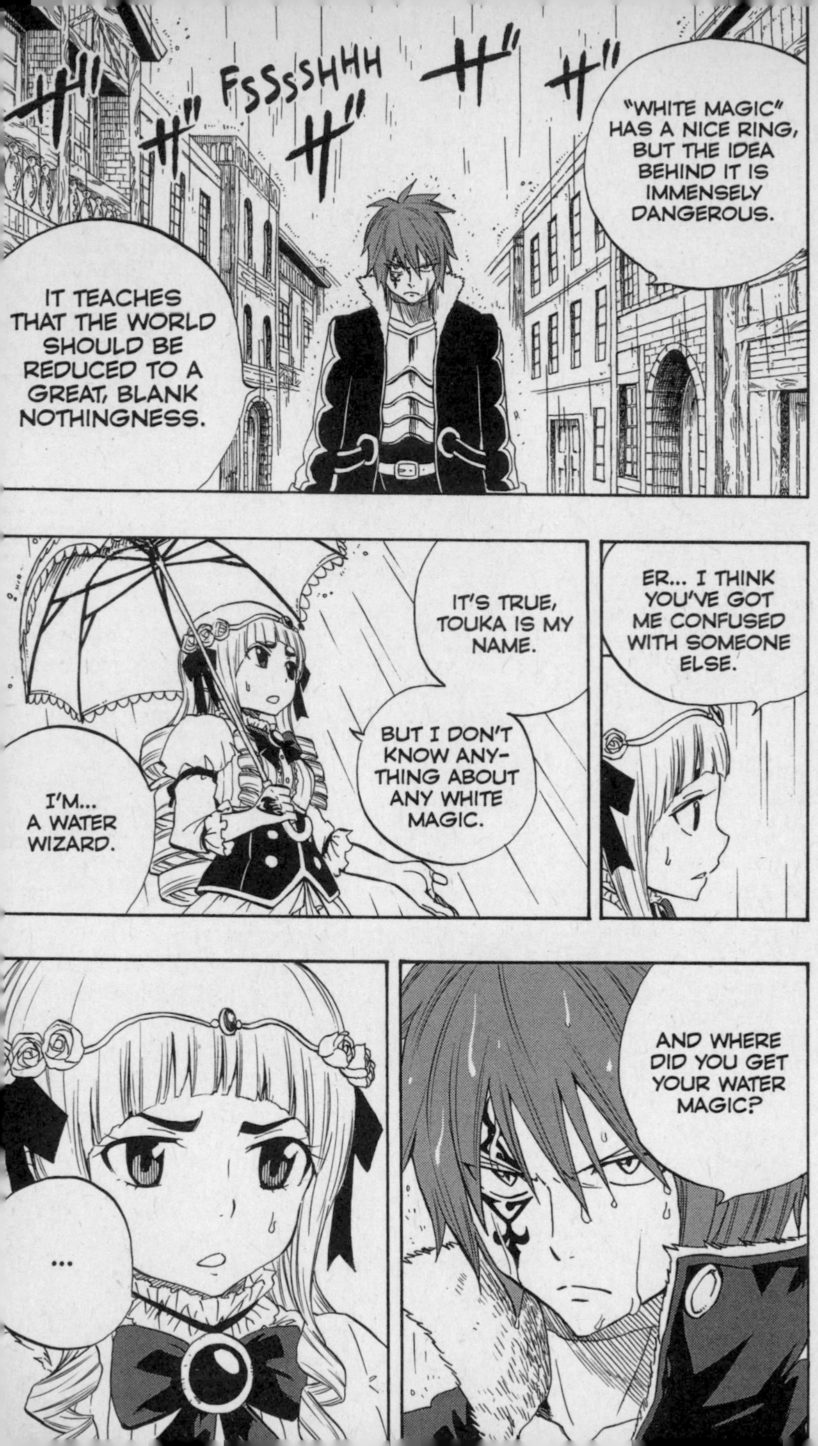
FSSSSHHH
"WHITE MAGIC" HAS A NICE RING, BUT THE IDEA BEHIND IT IS IMMENSELY DANGEROUS.
IT TEACHES THAT THE WORLD SHOULD BE REDUCED TO A GREAT, BLANK NOTHINGNESS.
ER... I THINK YOU'VE GOT ME CONFUSED WITH SOMEONE ELSE.
IT'S TRUE, TOUKA IS MY NAME.
BUT I DON'T KNOW ANY-THING ABOUT ANY WHITE MAGIC.
I'M... A WATER WIZARD.
AND WHERE DID YOU GET YOUR WATER MAGIC?
...

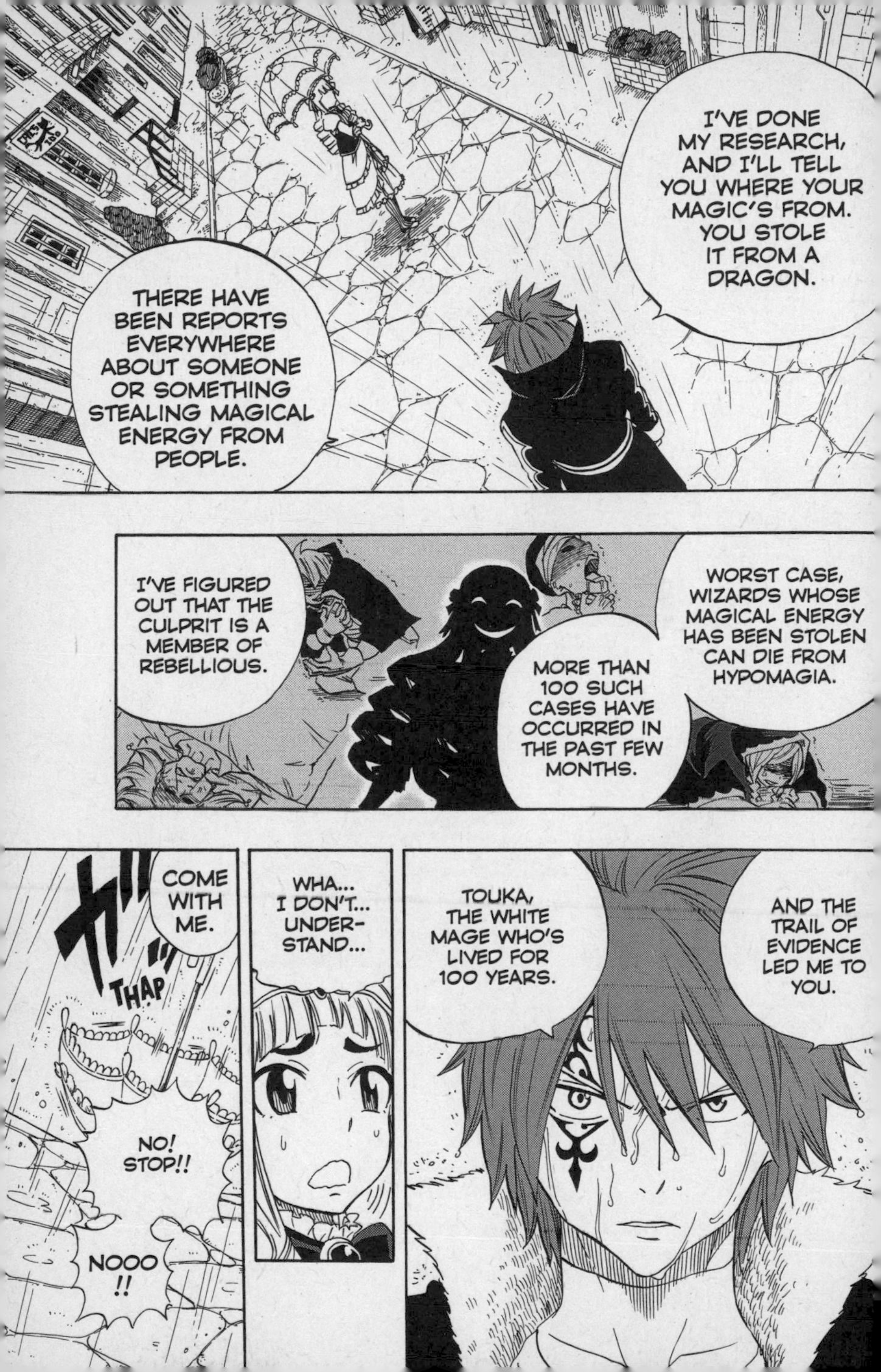
I'VE DONE MY RESEARCH, AND I'LL TELL YOU WHERE YOUR MAGIC'S FROM. YOU STOLE IT FROM A DRAGON.
THERE HAVE BEEN REPORTS EVERYWHERE ABOUT SOMEONE OR SOMETHING STEALING MAGICAL ENERGY FROM PEOPLE.
WORST CASE, WIZARDS WHOSE MAGICAL ENERGY HAS BEEN STOLEN CAN DIE FROM HYPOMAGIA.
MORE THAN 100 SUCH CASES HAVE OCCURRED IN THE PAST FEW MONTHS.
I'VE FIGURED OUT THAT THE CULPRIT IS A MEMBER OF REBELLIOUS.
AND THE TRAIL OF EVIDENCE LED ME TO YOU.
TOUKA, THE WHITE MAGE WHO'S LIVED FOR 100 YEARS.
WHA... I DON'T... UNDER-STAND...
COME WITH ME.
THAP
NO! STOP!!
NOOO !!

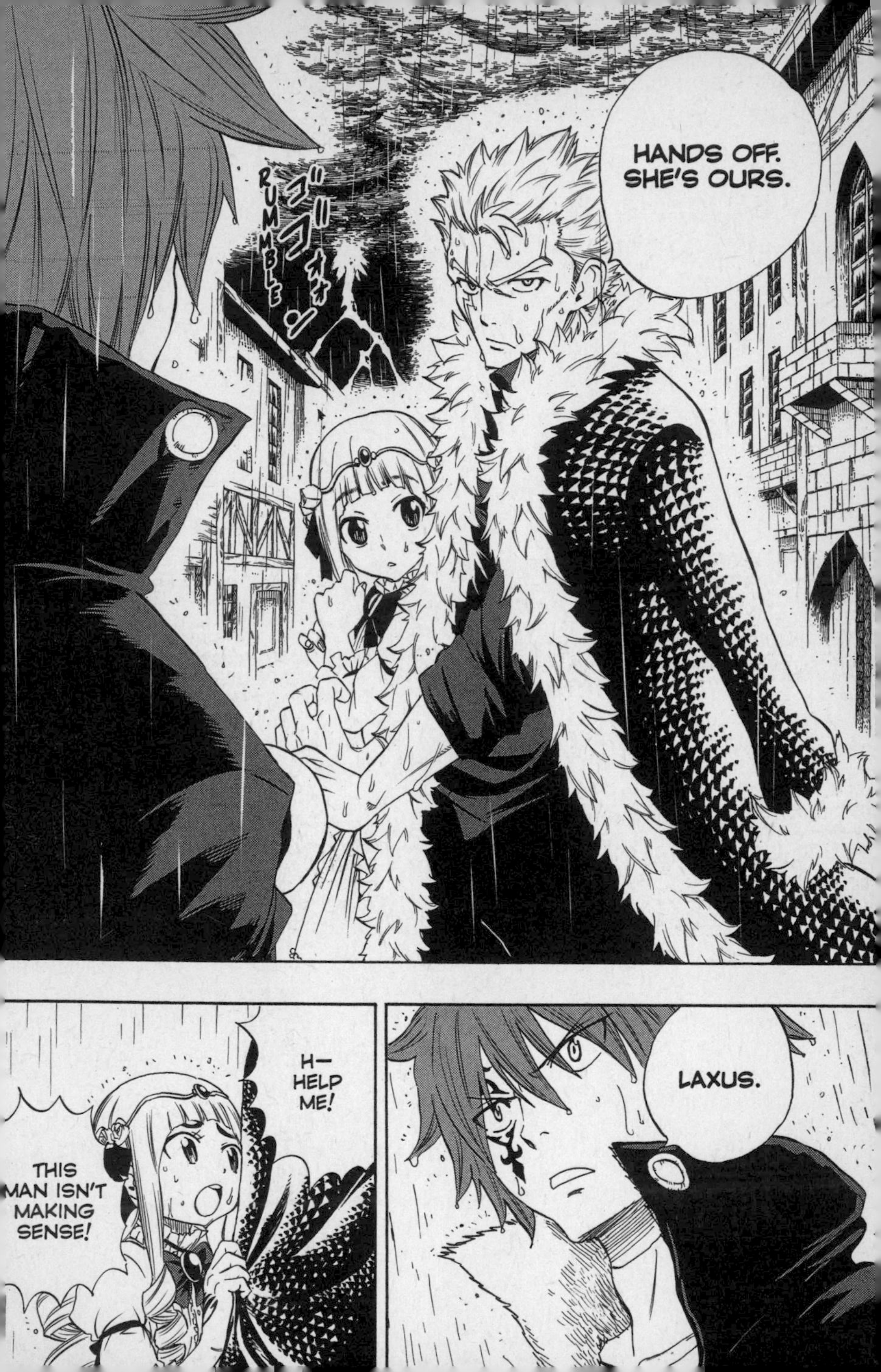
HANDS OFF. SHE'S OURS.
RUMBLE
LAXUS.
H— HELP ME!
THIS MAN ISN'T MAKING SENSE!

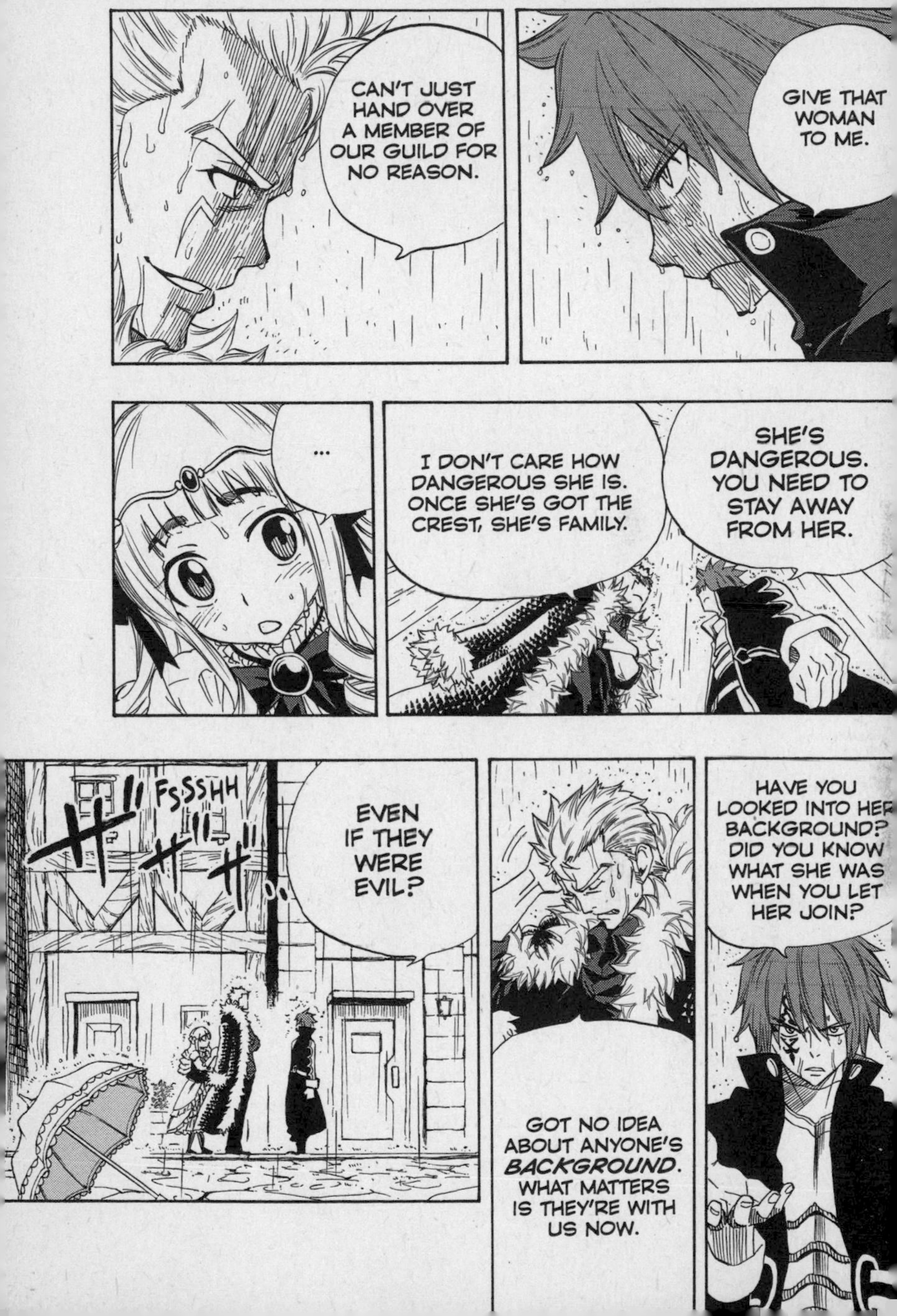
GIVE THAT WOMAN TO ME.
CAN'T JUST HAND OVER A MEMBER OF OUR GUILD FOR NO REASON.
SHE'S DANGEROUS. YOU NEED TO STAY AWAY FROM HER.
I DON'T CARE HOW DANGEROUS SHE IS. ONCE SHE'S GOT THE CREST, SHE'S FAMILY.
...
HAVE YOU LOOKED INTO HER BACKGROUND? DID YOU KNOW WHAT SHE WAS WHEN YOU LET HER JOIN?
GOT NO IDEA ABOUT ANYONE'S *BACKGROUND*. WHAT MATTERS IS THEY'RE WITH US NOW.
EVEN IF THEY WERE EVIL?
FSSSHH

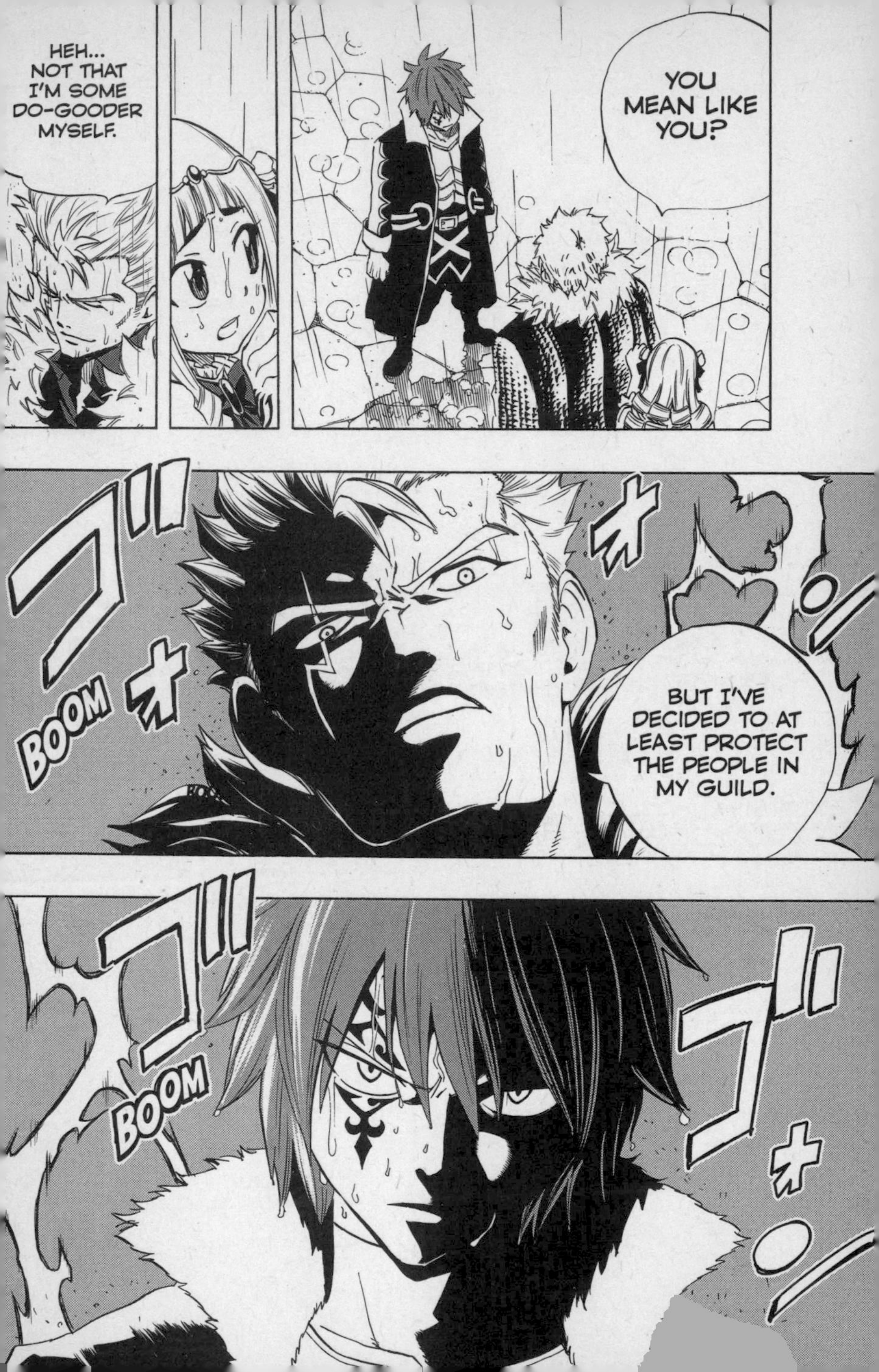
YOU MEAN LIKE YOU?
HEH... NOT THAT I'M SOME DO-GOODER MYSELF.
BUT I'VE DECIDED TO AT LEAST PROTECT THE PEOPLE IN MY GUILD.
BOOM
BOOM

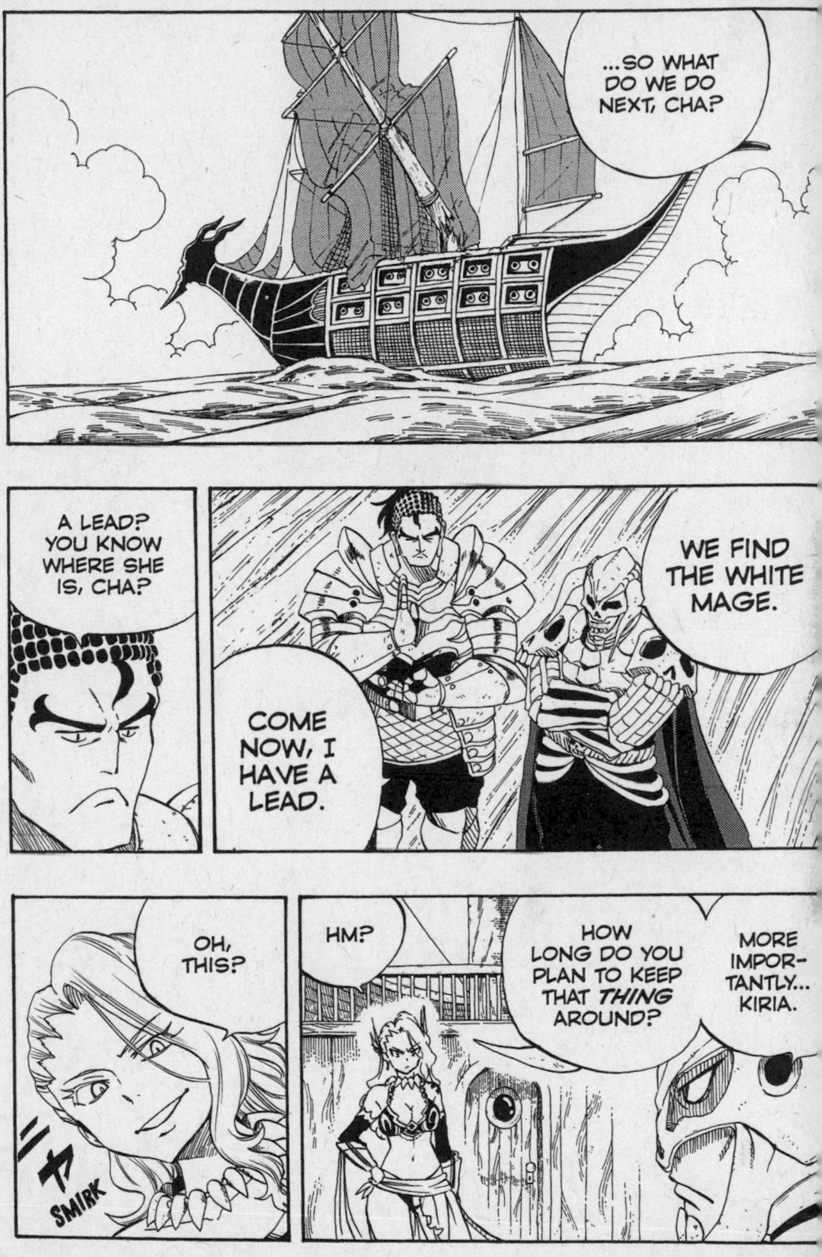
...SO WHAT DO WE DO NEXT, CHA?
WE FIND THE WHITE MAGE.
COME NOW, I HAVE A LEAD.
A LEAD? YOU KNOW WHERE SHE IS, CHA?
MORE IMPOR-TANTLY... KIRIA.
HOW LONG DO YOU PLAN TO KEEP THAT *THING* AROUND?
HM?
OH, THIS?
SMIRK

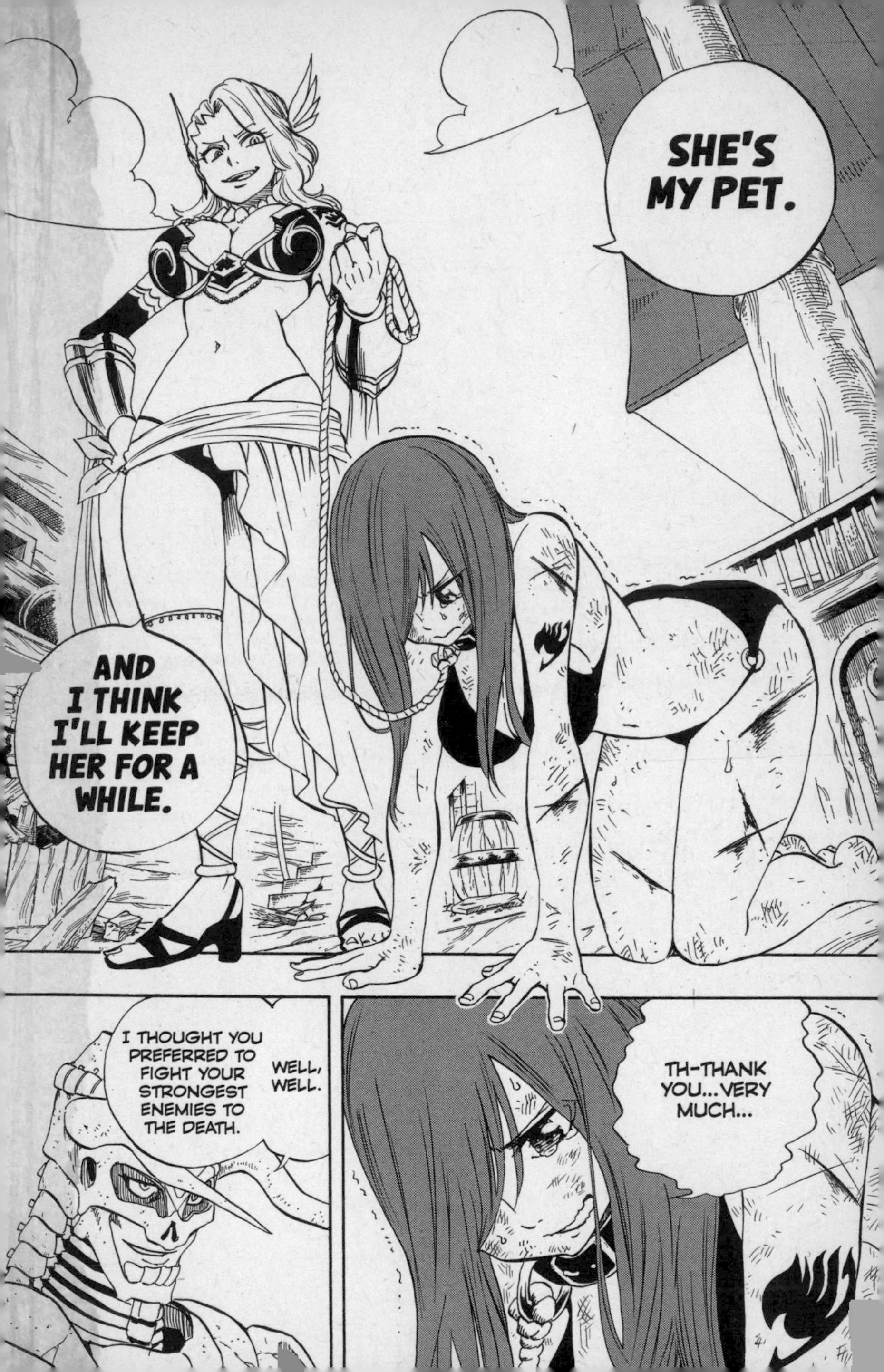
SHE'S MY PET.
AND I THINK I'LL KEEP HER FOR A WHILE.
TH-THANK YOU...VERY MUCH...
WELL, WELL.
I THOUGHT YOU PREFERRED TO FIGHT YOUR STRONGEST ENEMIES TO THE DEATH.

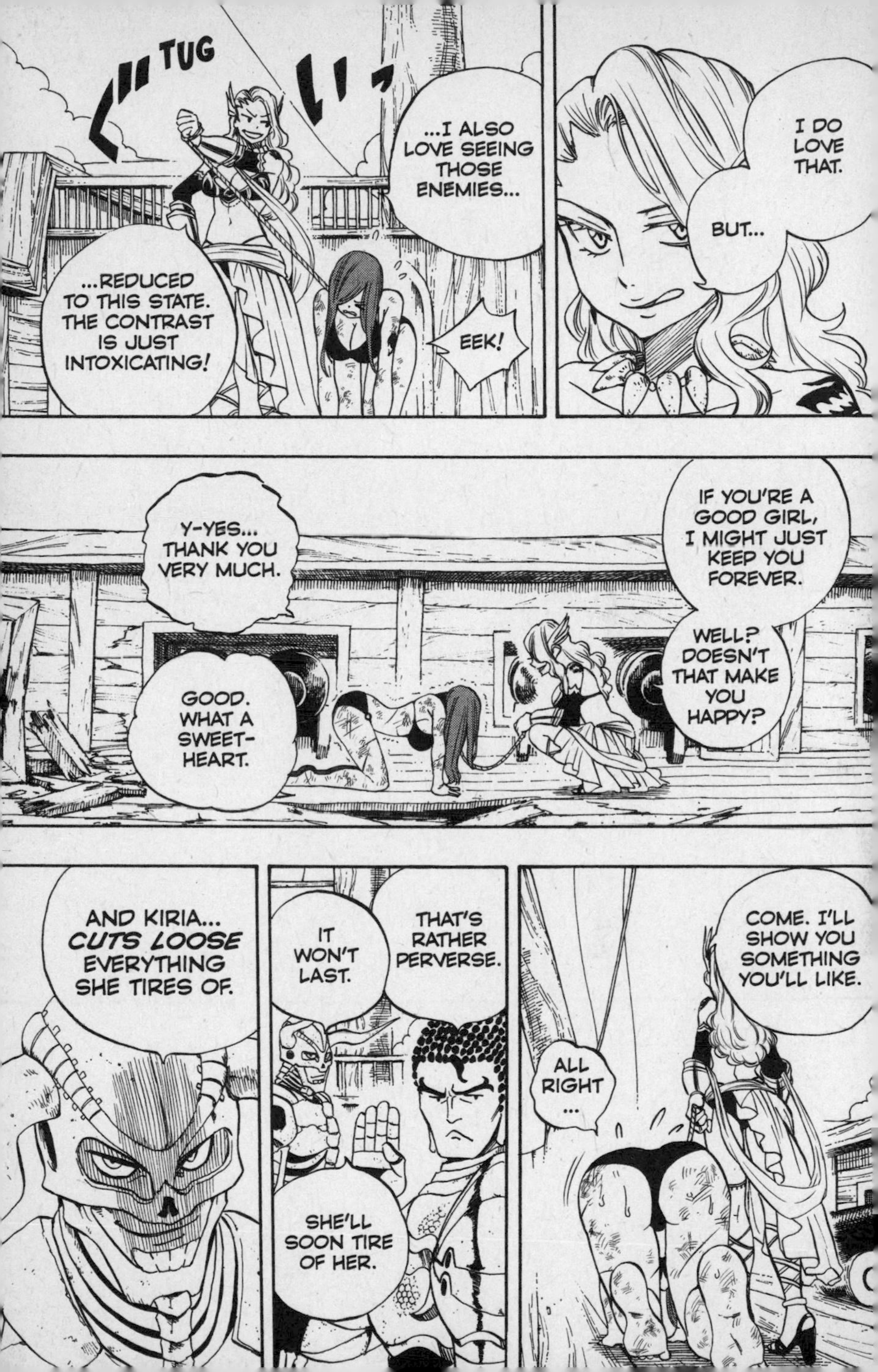
I DO LOVE THAT.
BUT...
...I ALSO LOVE SEEING THOSE ENEMIES...
TUG
...REDUCED TO THIS STATE. THE CONTRAST IS JUST INTOXICATING!
EEK!
IF YOU'RE A GOOD GIRL, I MIGHT JUST KEEP YOU FOREVER.
WELL? DOESN'T THAT MAKE YOU HAPPY?
Y-YES... THANK YOU VERY MUCH.
GOOD. WHAT A SWEET-HEART.
COME. I'LL SHOW YOU SOMETHING YOU'LL LIKE.
ALL RIGHT...
THAT'S RATHER PERVERSE.
IT WON'T LAST.
SHE'LL SOON TIRE OF HER.
AND KIRIA... *CUTS LOOSE* EVERYTHING SHE TIRES OF.

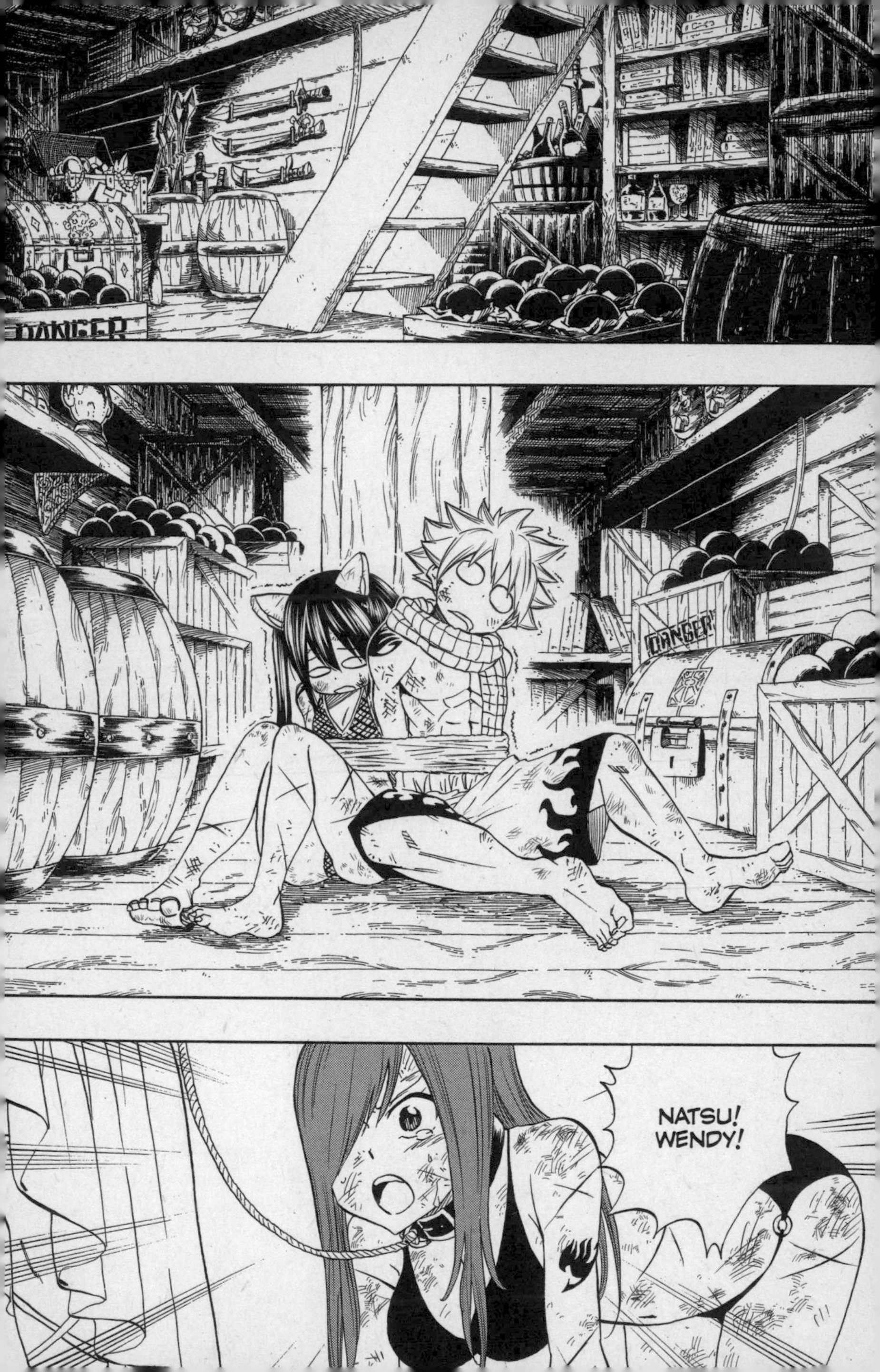
DANGER
DANGER
NATSU!
WENDY!

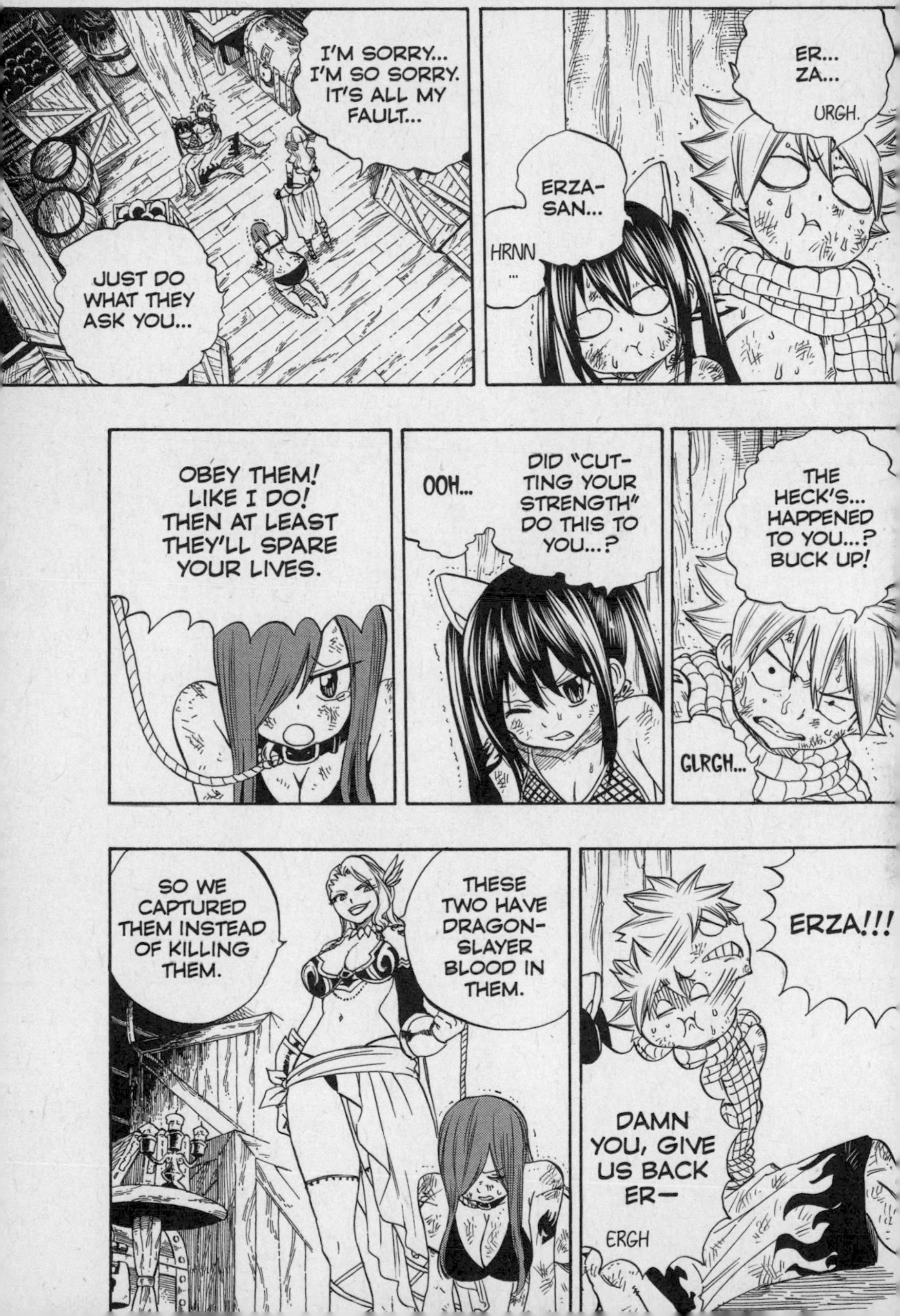
ER... ZA...
URGH.
ERZA-SAN...
HRNN...
I'M SORRY... I'M SO SORRY. IT'S ALL MY FAULT...
JUST DO WHAT THEY ASK YOU...
THE HECK'S... HAPPENED TO YOU...? BUCK UP!
GLRGH...
DID "CUTTING YOUR STRENGTH" DO THIS TO YOU...?
OOH...
OBEY THEM! LIKE I DO! THEN AT LEAST THEY'LL SPARE YOUR LIVES.
ERZA!!!
DAMN YOU, GIVE US BACK ER—
ERGH
THESE TWO HAVE DRAGON-SLAYER BLOOD IN THEM.
SO WE CAPTURED THEM INSTEAD OF KILLING THEM.

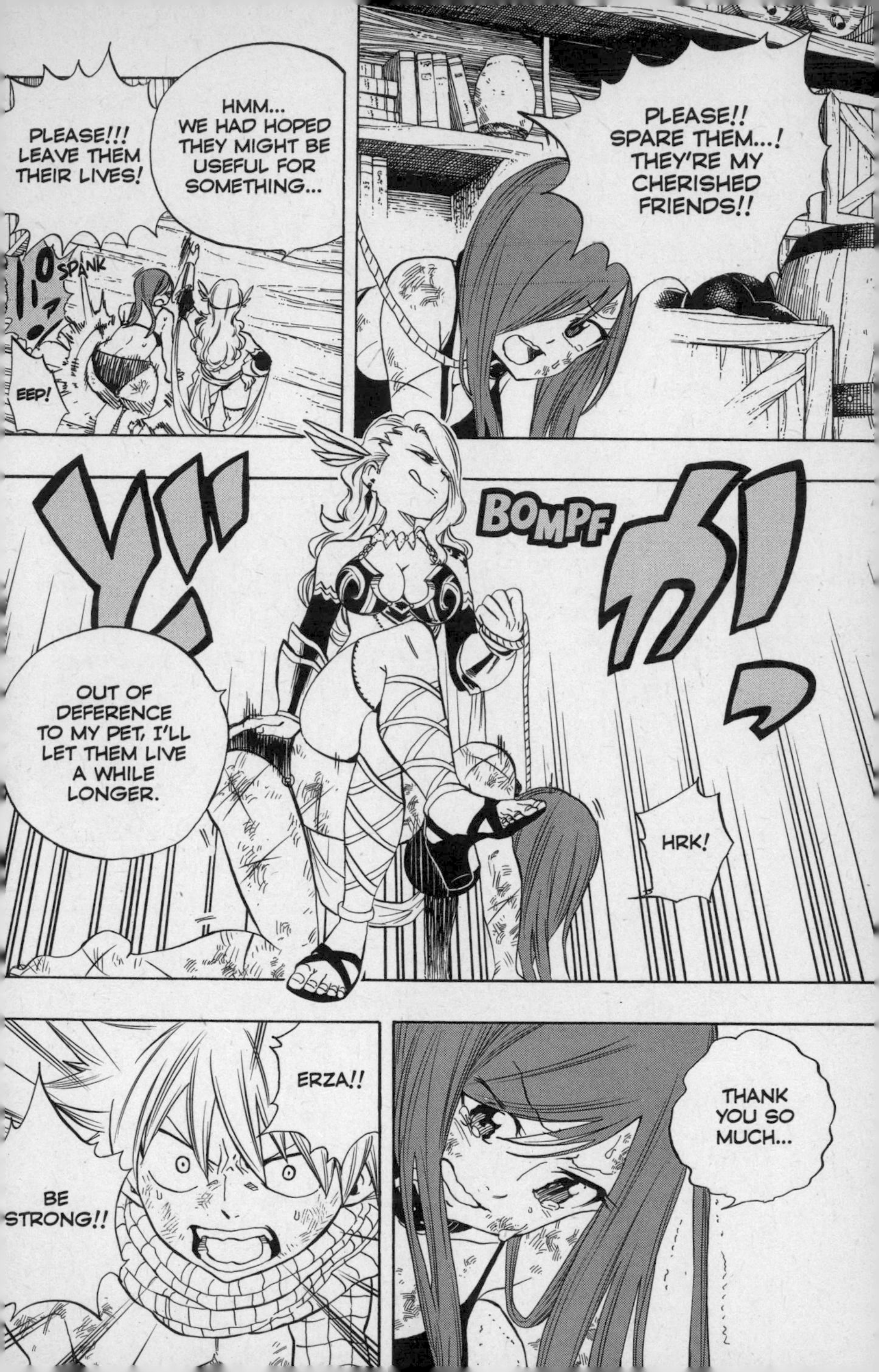
PLEASE!! SPARE THEM...! THEY'RE MY CHERISHED FRIENDS!!
HMM... WE HAD HOPED THEY MIGHT BE USEFUL FOR SOMETHING...
PLEASE!!! LEAVE THEM THEIR LIVES!
SPANK
EEP!
BOMPF
HRK!
OUT OF DEFERENCE TO MY PET, I'LL LET THEM LIVE A WHILE LONGER.
THANK YOU SO MUCH...
ERZA!!
BE STRONG!!

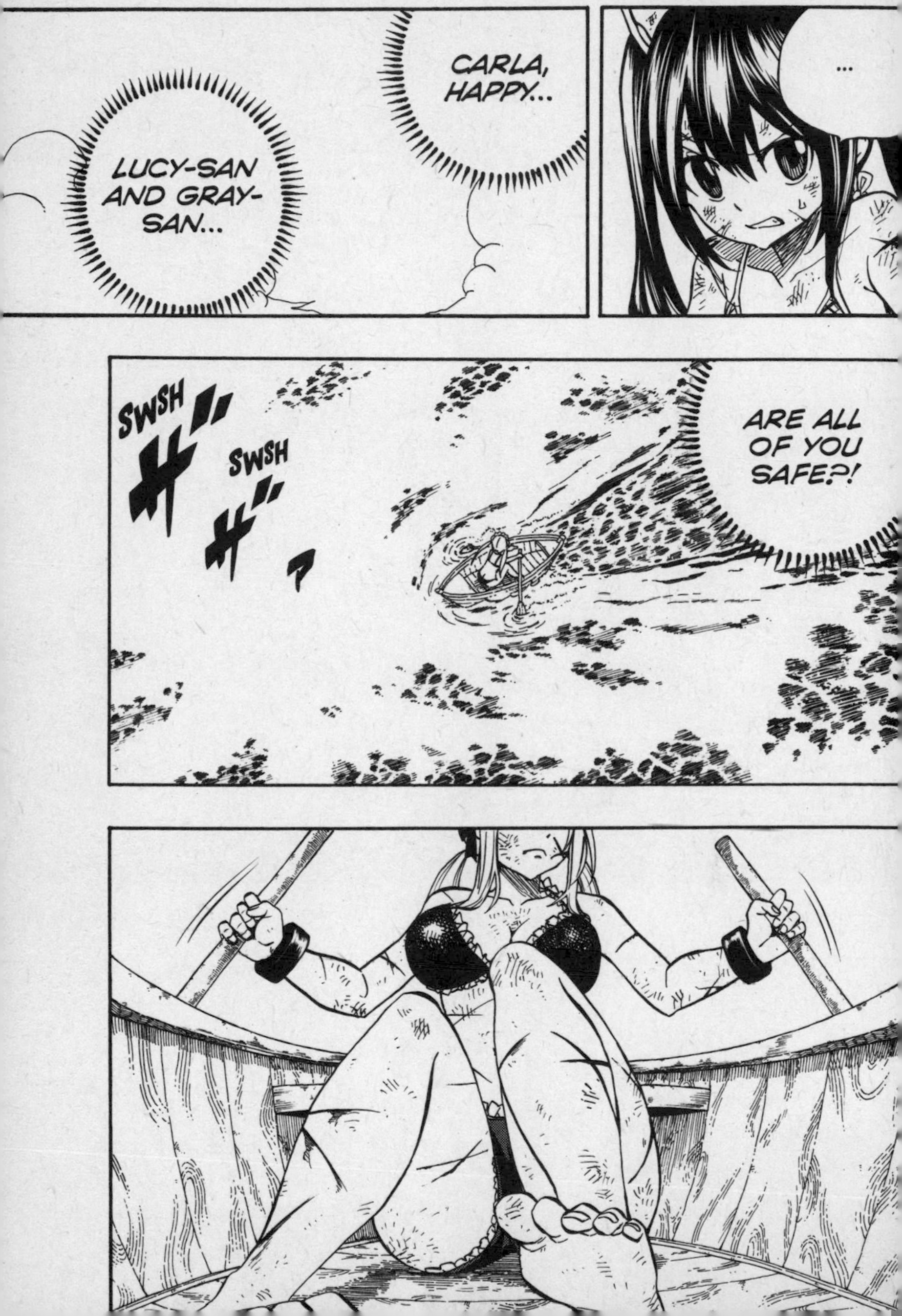
...
CARLA, HAPPY...
LUCY-SAN AND GRAY-SAN...
ARE ALL OF YOU SAFE?!
SWSH
SWSH

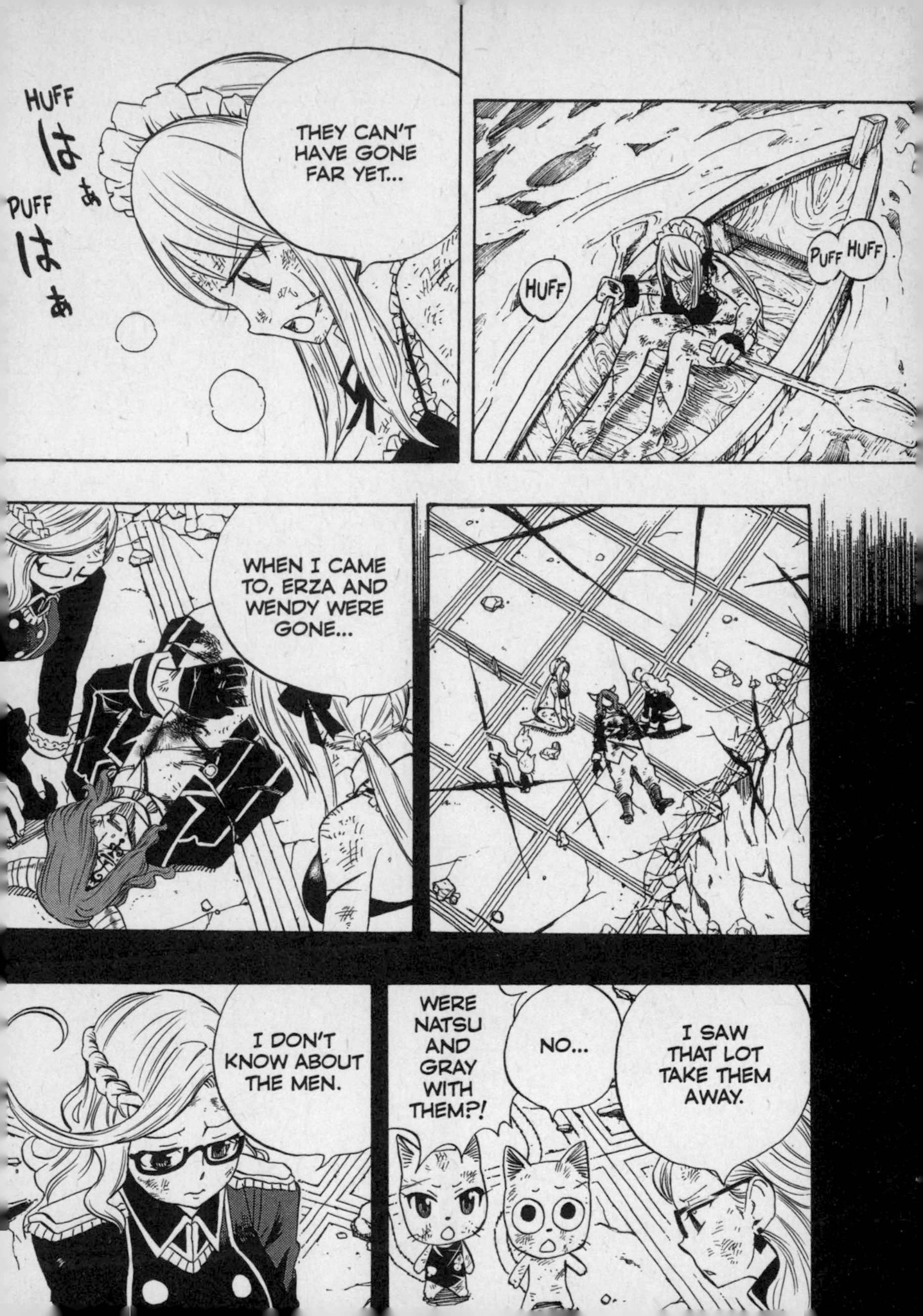
PUFF HUFF
HUFF
THEY CAN'T HAVE GONE FAR YET...
HUFF はぁ
PUFF はぁ
WHEN I CAME TO, ERZA AND WENDY WERE GONE...
I SAW THAT LOT TAKE THEM AWAY.
NO...
WERE NATSU AND GRAY WITH THEM?!
I DON'T KNOW ABOUT THE MEN.

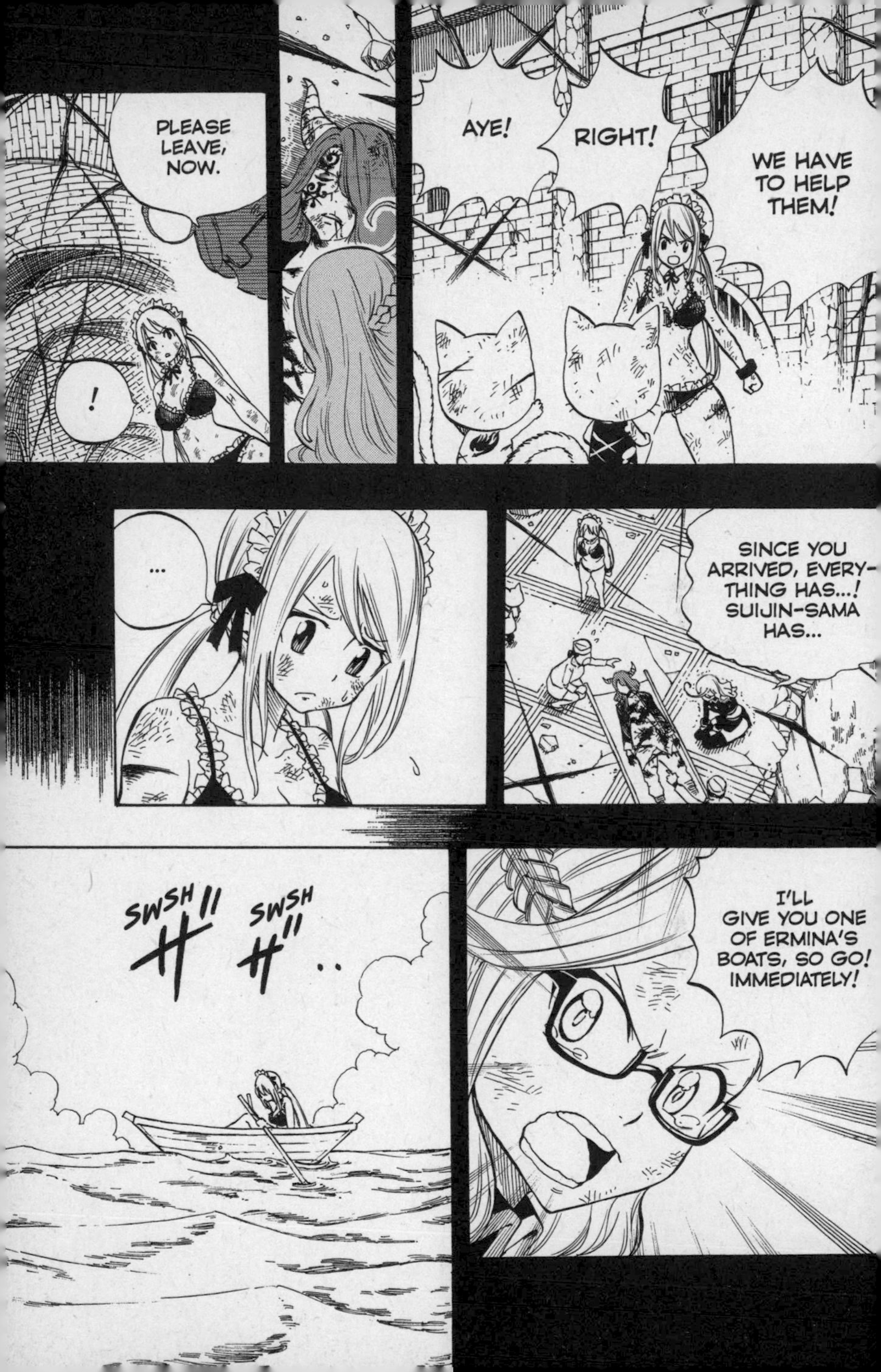
WE HAVE TO HELP THEM!
RIGHT!
AYE!
PLEASE LEAVE, NOW.
!
SINCE YOU ARRIVED, EVERY-THING HAS...! SUIJIN-SAMA HAS...
...
I'LL GIVE YOU ONE OF ERMINA'S BOATS, SO GO! IMMEDIATELY!
SWSH
SWSH
..

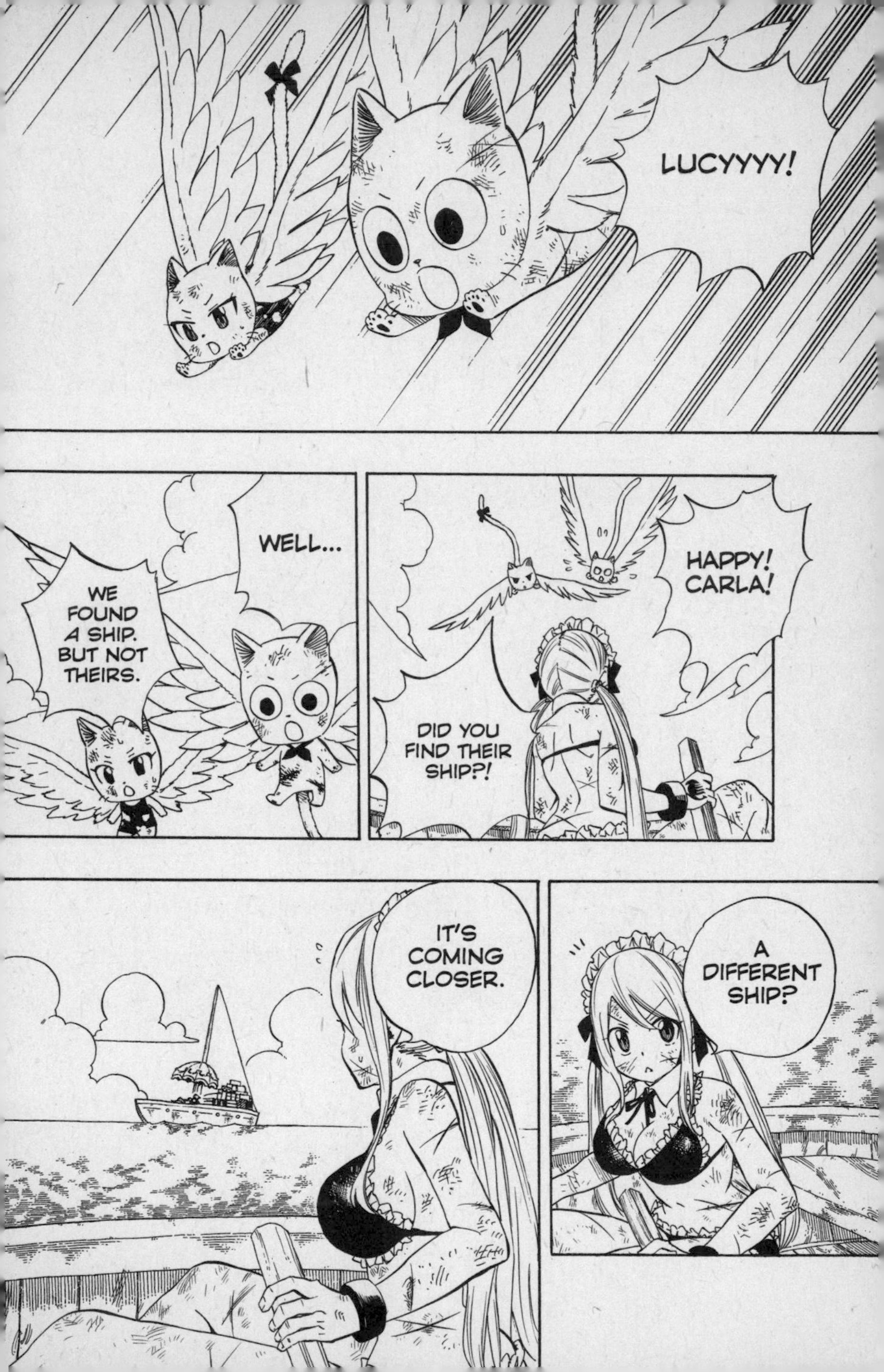
LUCYYY!
HAPPY! CARLA!
DID YOU FIND THEIR SHIP?!
WELL...
WE FOUND A SHIP. BUT NOT THEIRS.
A DIFFERENT SHIP?
IT'S COMING CLOSER.

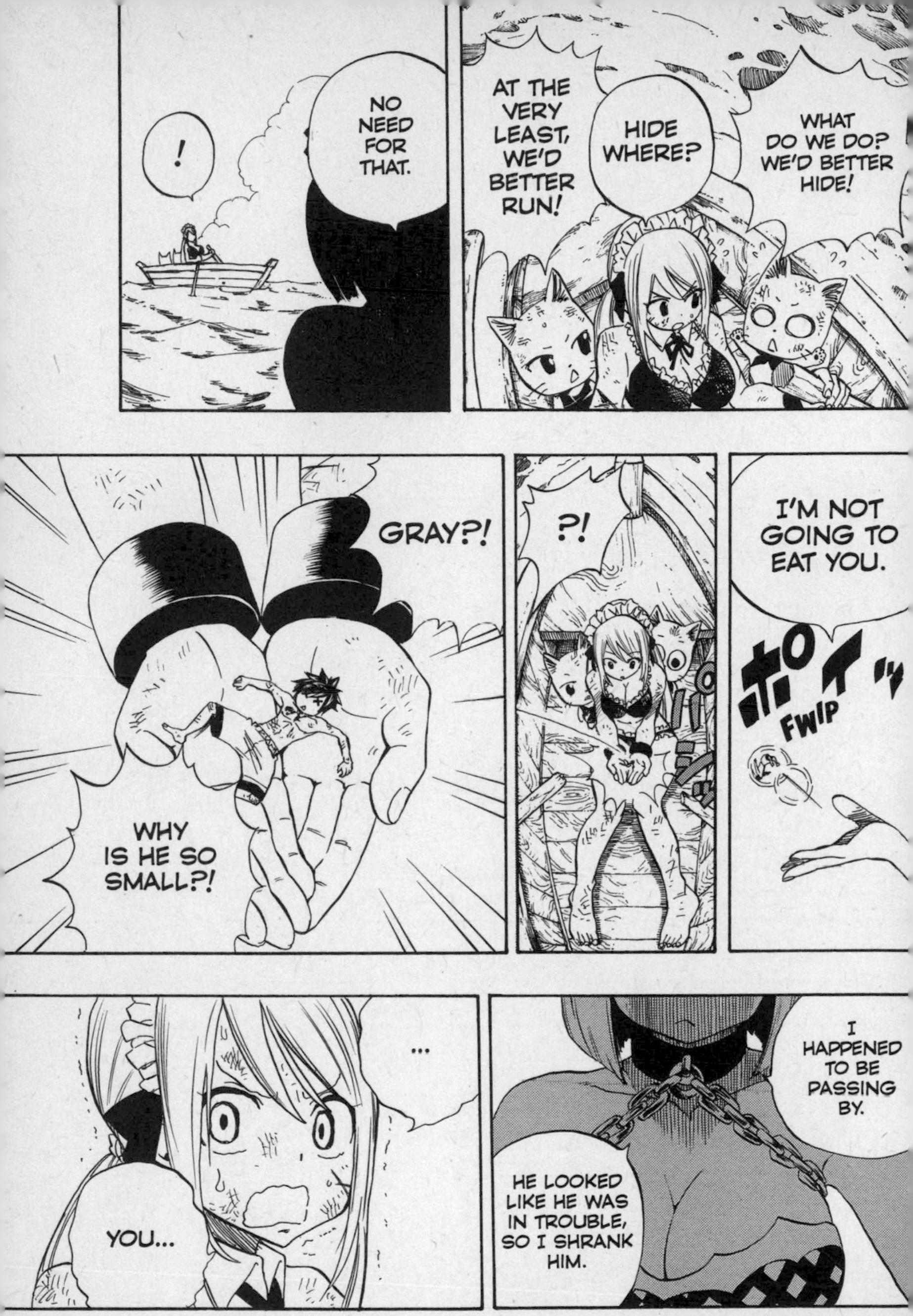
WHAT DO WE DO? WE'D BETTER HIDE!
HIDE WHERE?
AT THE VERY LEAST, WE'D BETTER RUN!
NO NEED FOR THAT.
!
I'M NOT GOING TO EAT YOU.
ポイッ
FWIP
?!
GRAY?!
WHY IS HE SO SMALL?!
I HAPPENED TO BE PASSING BY.
HE LOOKED LIKE HE WAS IN TROUBLE, SO I SHRANK HIM.
...
YOU...

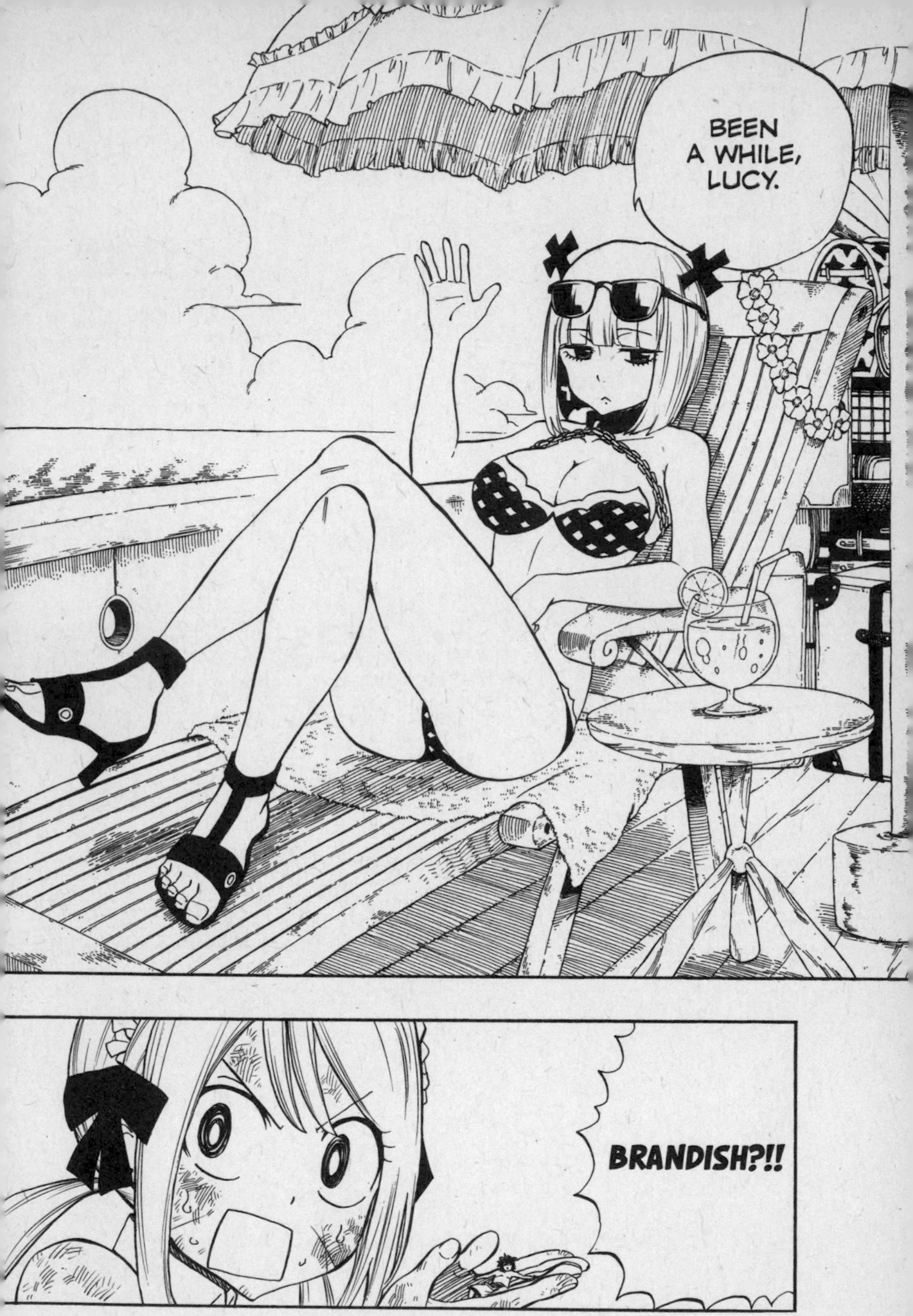
BEEN A WHILE, LUCY.
BRANDISH?!!

FAIRY TAIL 100 YEARS QUEST

Chapter 13: A Maritime Meeting

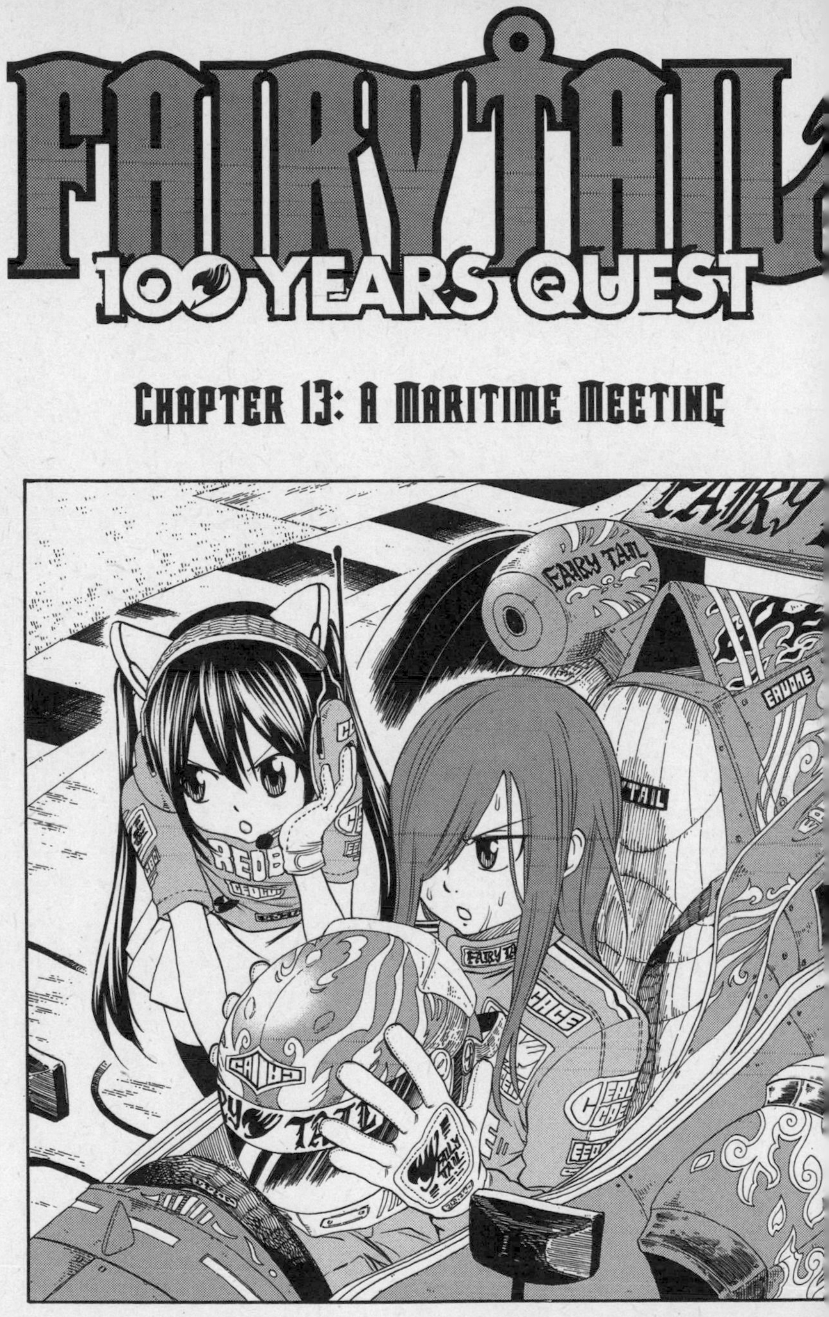

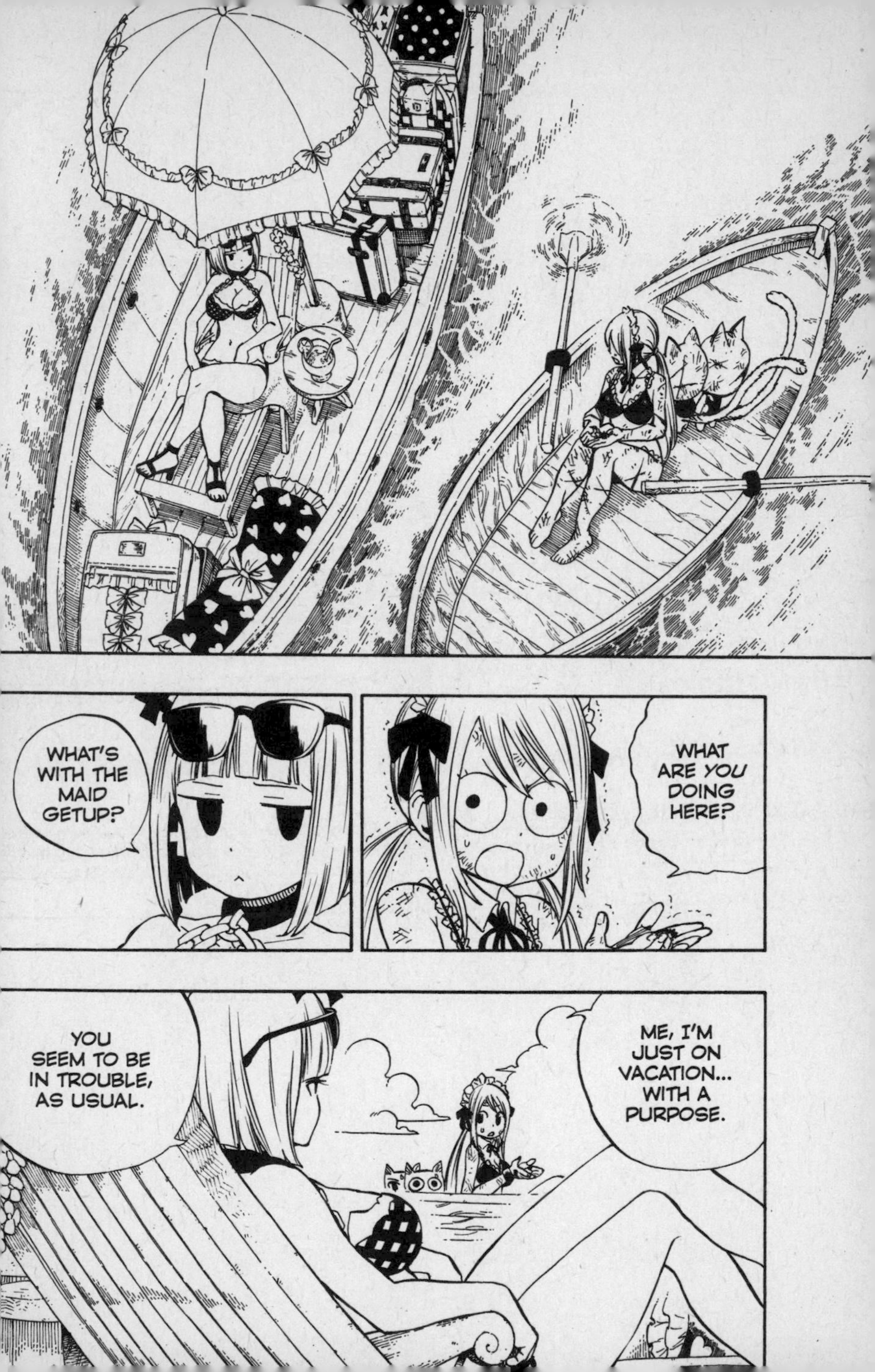
WHAT ARE *YOU* DOING HERE?
WHAT'S WITH THE MAID GETUP?
ME, I'M JUST ON VACATION... WITH A PURPOSE.
YOU SEEM TO BE IN TROUBLE, AS USUAL.

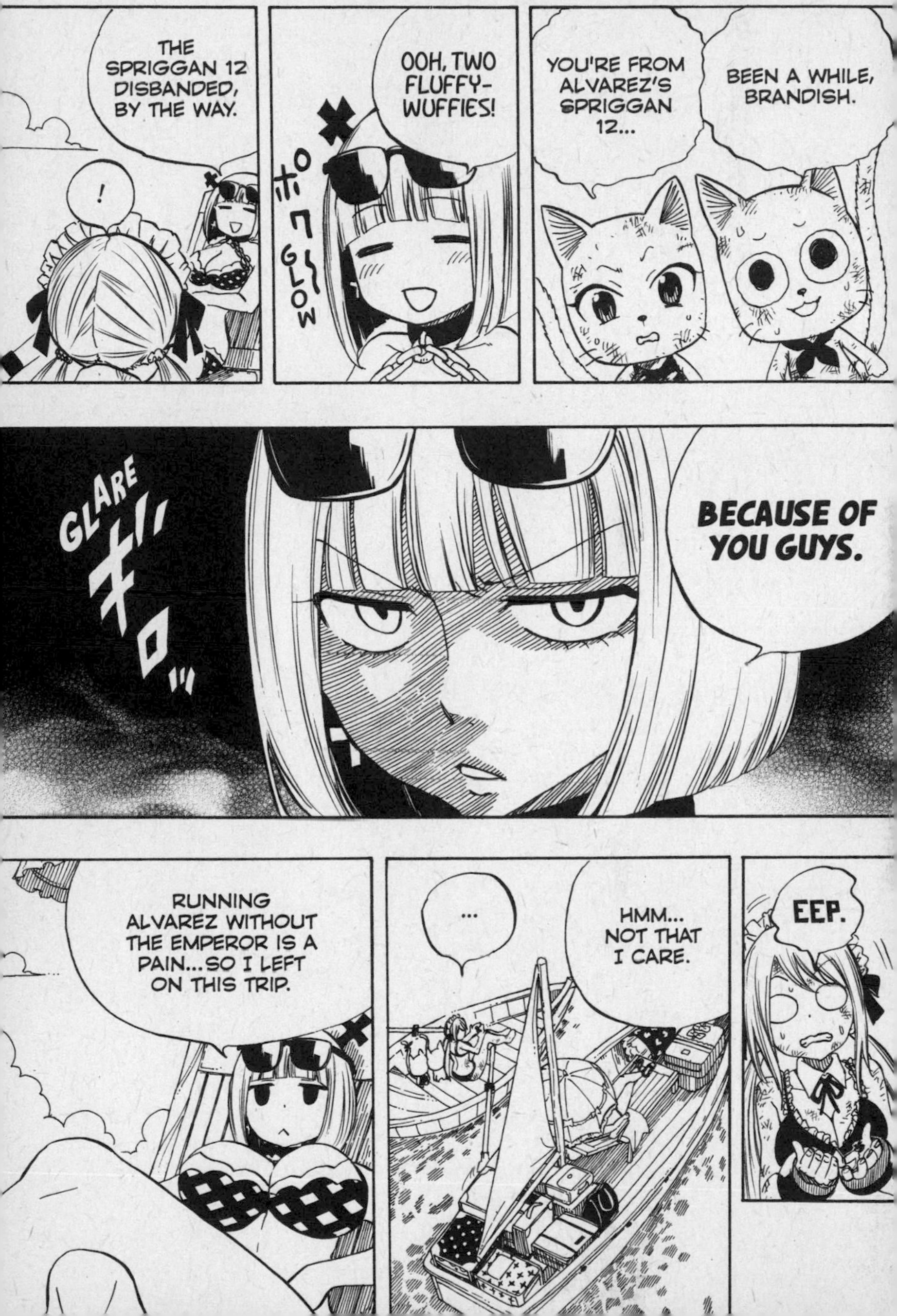
BEEN A WHILE, BRANDISH.
YOU'RE FROM ALVAREZ'S SPRIGGAN 12...
OOH, TWO FLUFFY-WUFFIES!
GLOW
THE SPRIGGAN 12 DISBANDED, BY THE WAY.
!
BECAUSE OF YOU GUYS.
GLARE
EEP.
HMM... NOT THAT I CARE.
...
RUNNING ALVAREZ WITHOUT THE EMPEROR IS A PAIN...SO I LEFT ON THIS TRIP.

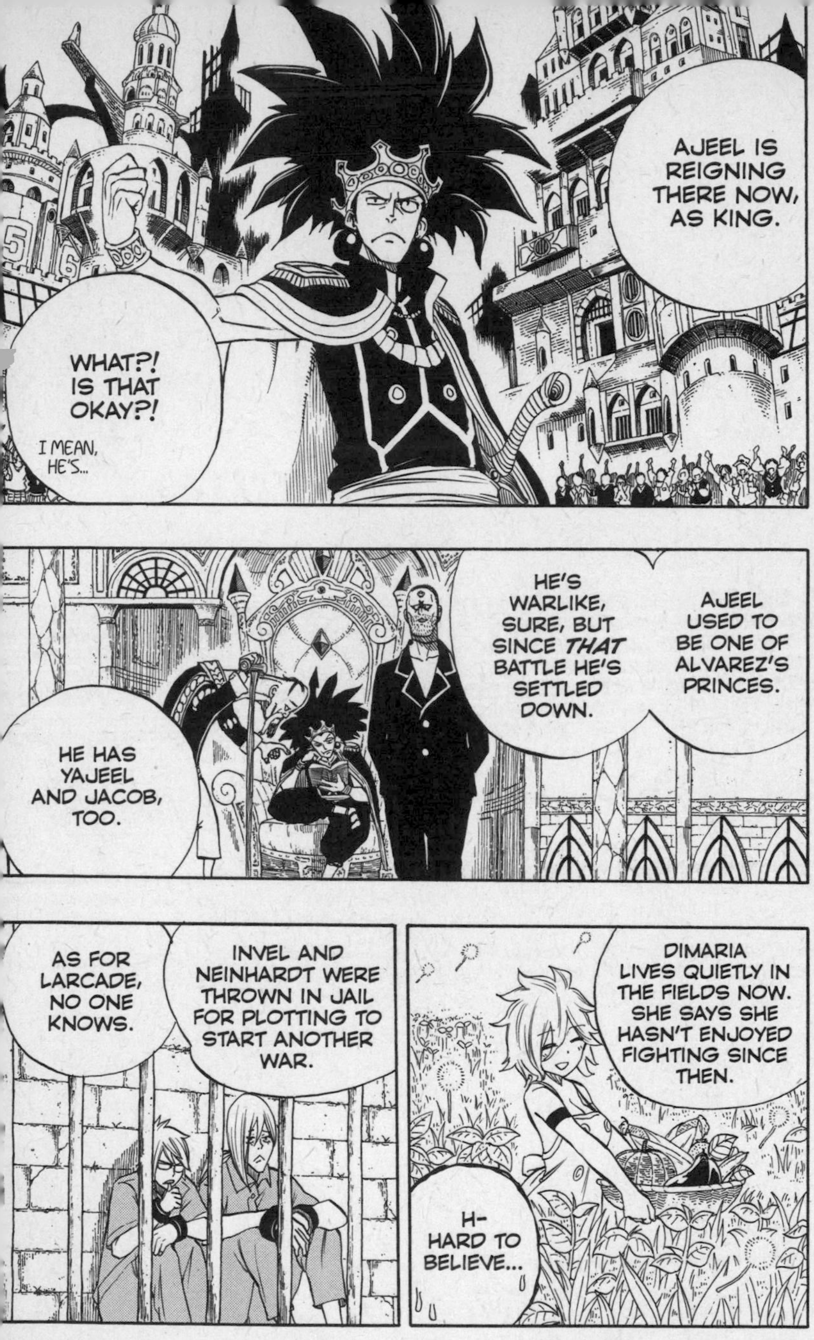
AJEEL IS REIGNING THERE NOW, AS KING.
WHAT?! IS THAT OKAY?!
I MEAN, HE'S...
AJEEL USED TO BE ONE OF ALVAREZ'S PRINCES.
HE'S WARLIKE, SURE, BUT SINCE *THAT* BATTLE HE'S SETTLED DOWN.
HE HAS YAJEEL AND JACOB, TOO.
DIMARIA LIVES QUIETLY IN THE FIELDS NOW. SHE SAYS SHE HASN'T ENJOYED FIGHTING SINCE THEN.
H- HARD TO BELIEVE...
INVEL AND NEINHARDT WERE THROWN IN JAIL FOR PLOTTING TO START ANOTHER WAR.
AS FOR LARCADE, NO ONE KNOWS.

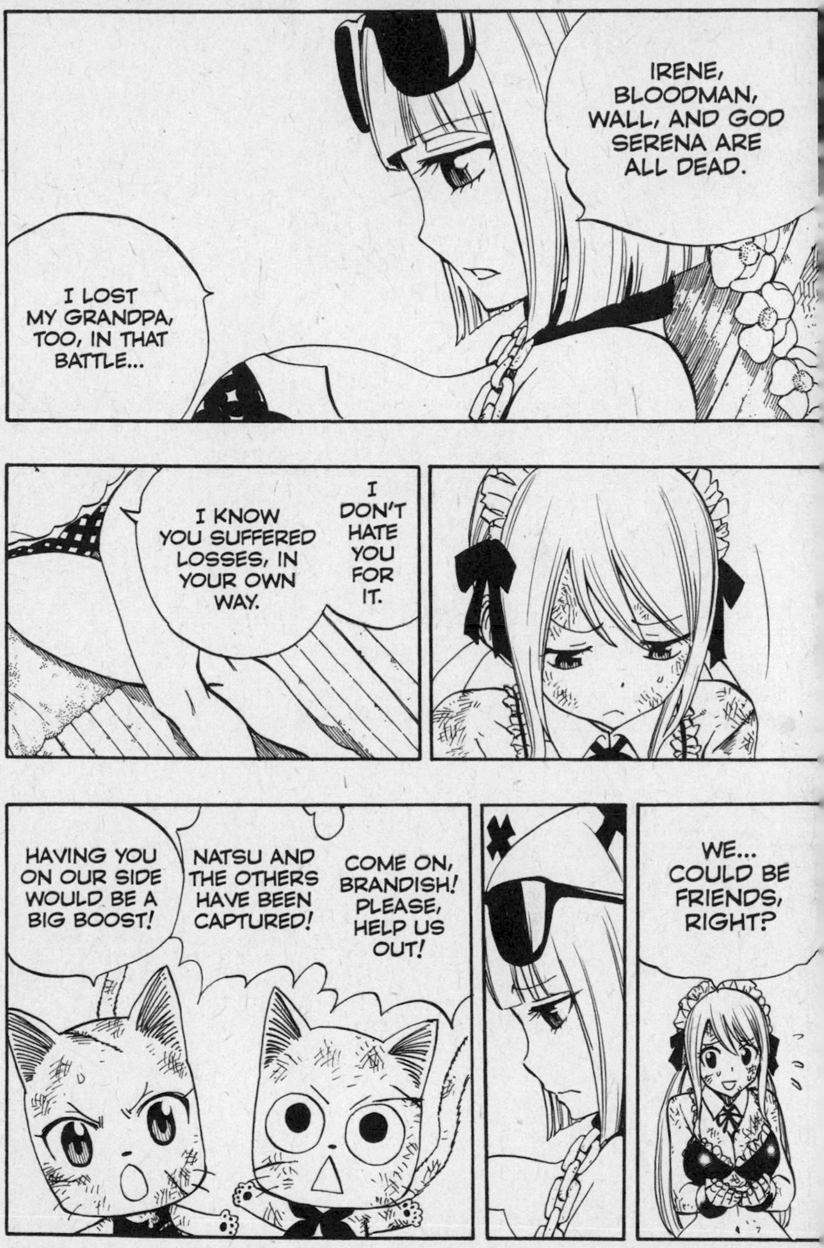
IRENE, BLOODMAN, WALL, AND GOD SERENA ARE ALL DEAD.
I LOST MY GRANDPA, TOO, IN THAT BATTLE...
I DON'T HATE YOU FOR IT.
I KNOW YOU SUFFERED LOSSES, IN YOUR OWN WAY.
WE... COULD BE FRIENDS, RIGHT?
COME ON, BRANDISH! PLEASE, HELP US OUT!
NATSU AND THE OTHERS HAVE BEEN CAPTURED!
HAVING YOU ON OUR SIDE WOULD BE A BIG BOOST!

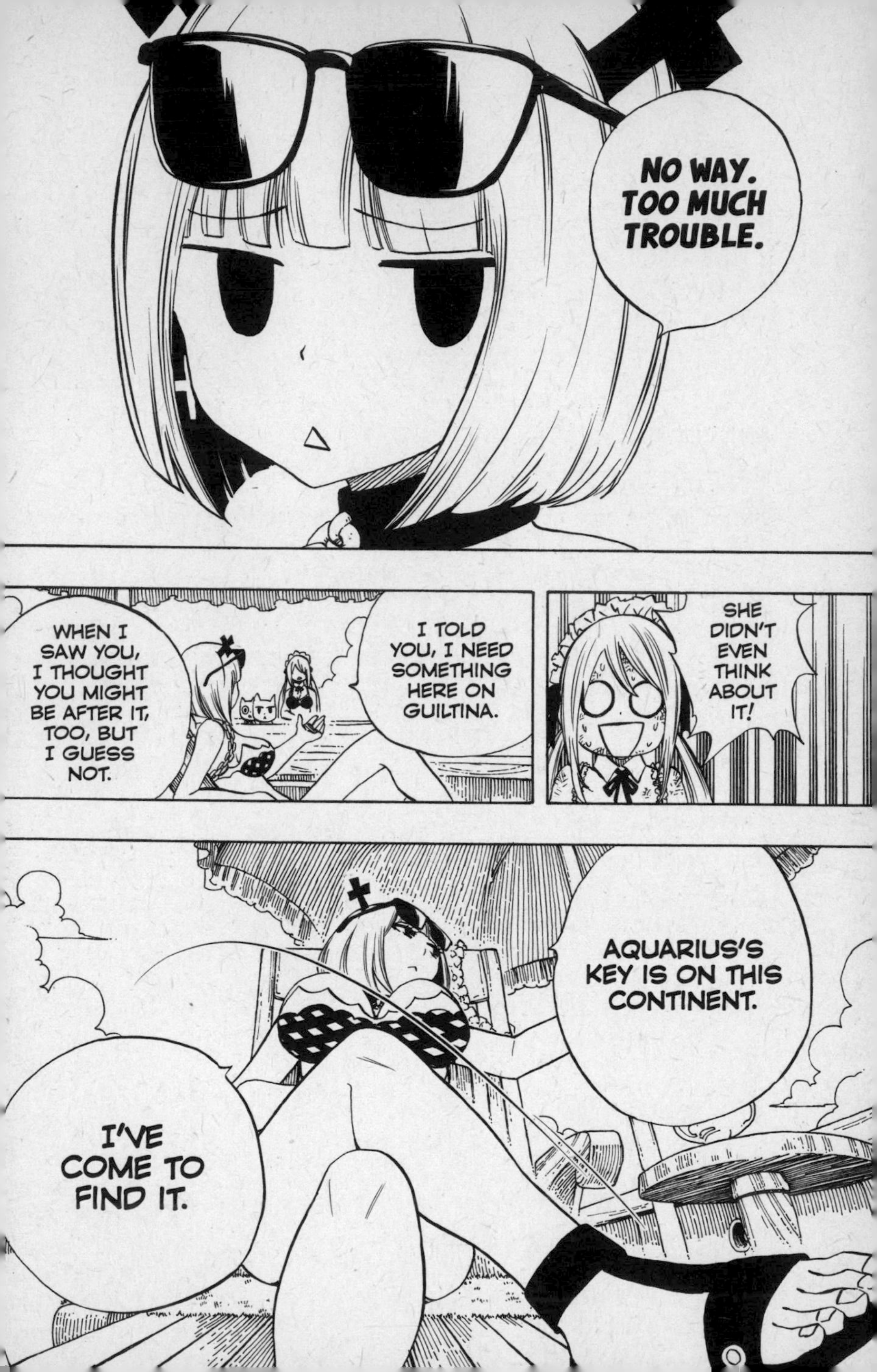
NO WAY. TOO MUCH TROUBLE.
SHE DIDN'T EVEN THINK ABOUT IT!
I TOLD YOU, I NEED SOMETHING HERE ON GUILTINA.
WHEN I SAW YOU, I THOUGHT YOU MIGHT BE AFTER IT, TOO, BUT I GUESS NOT.
AQUARIUS'S KEY IS ON THIS CONTINENT.
I'VE COME TO FIND IT.

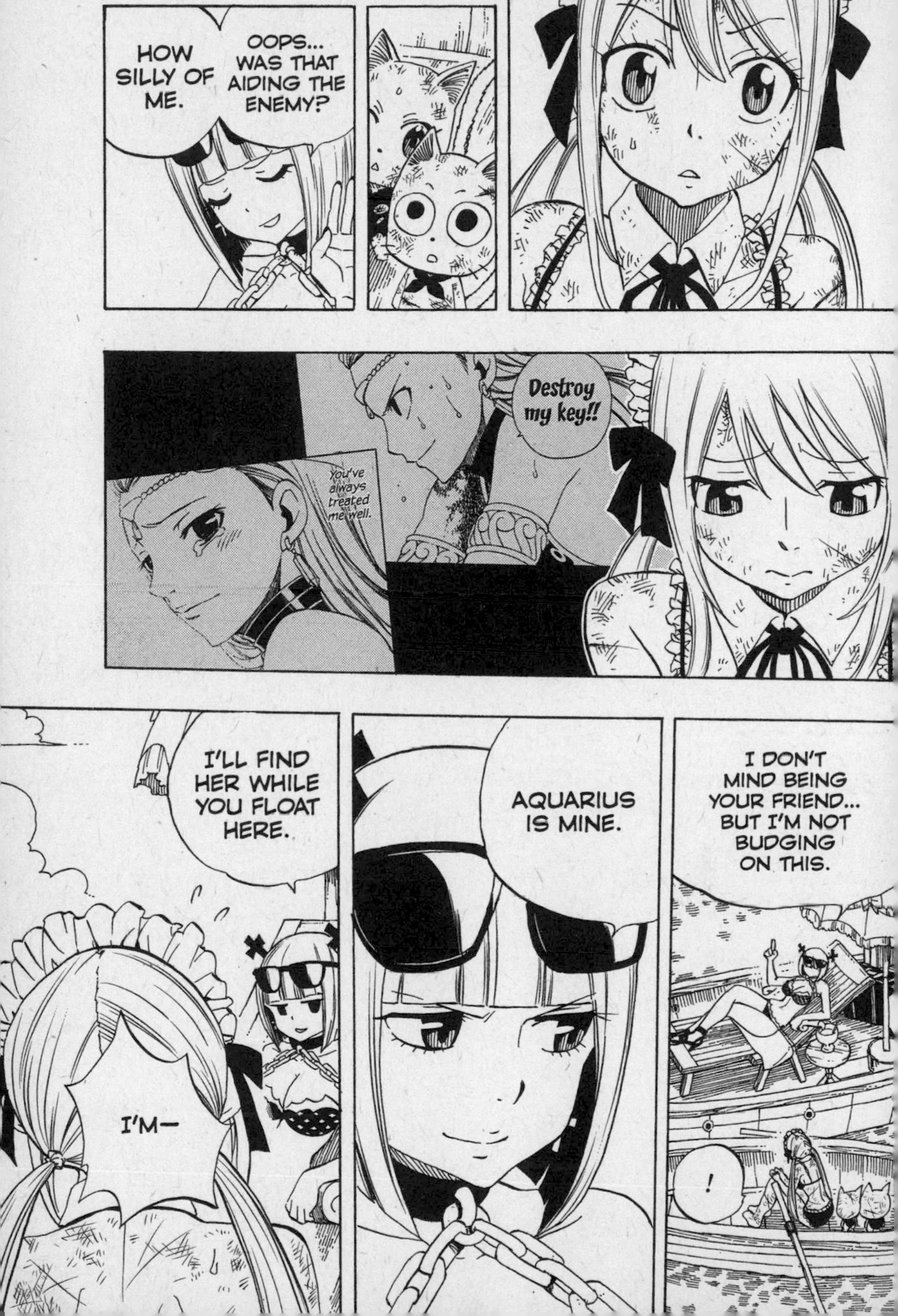
OOPS... WAS THAT AIDING THE ENEMY?
HOW SILLY OF ME.
Destroy my key!!
You've always treated me well.
I DON'T MIND BEING YOUR FRIEND... BUT I'M NOT BUDGING ON THIS.
!
AQUARIUS IS MINE.
I'LL FIND HER WHILE YOU FLOAT HERE.
I'M—

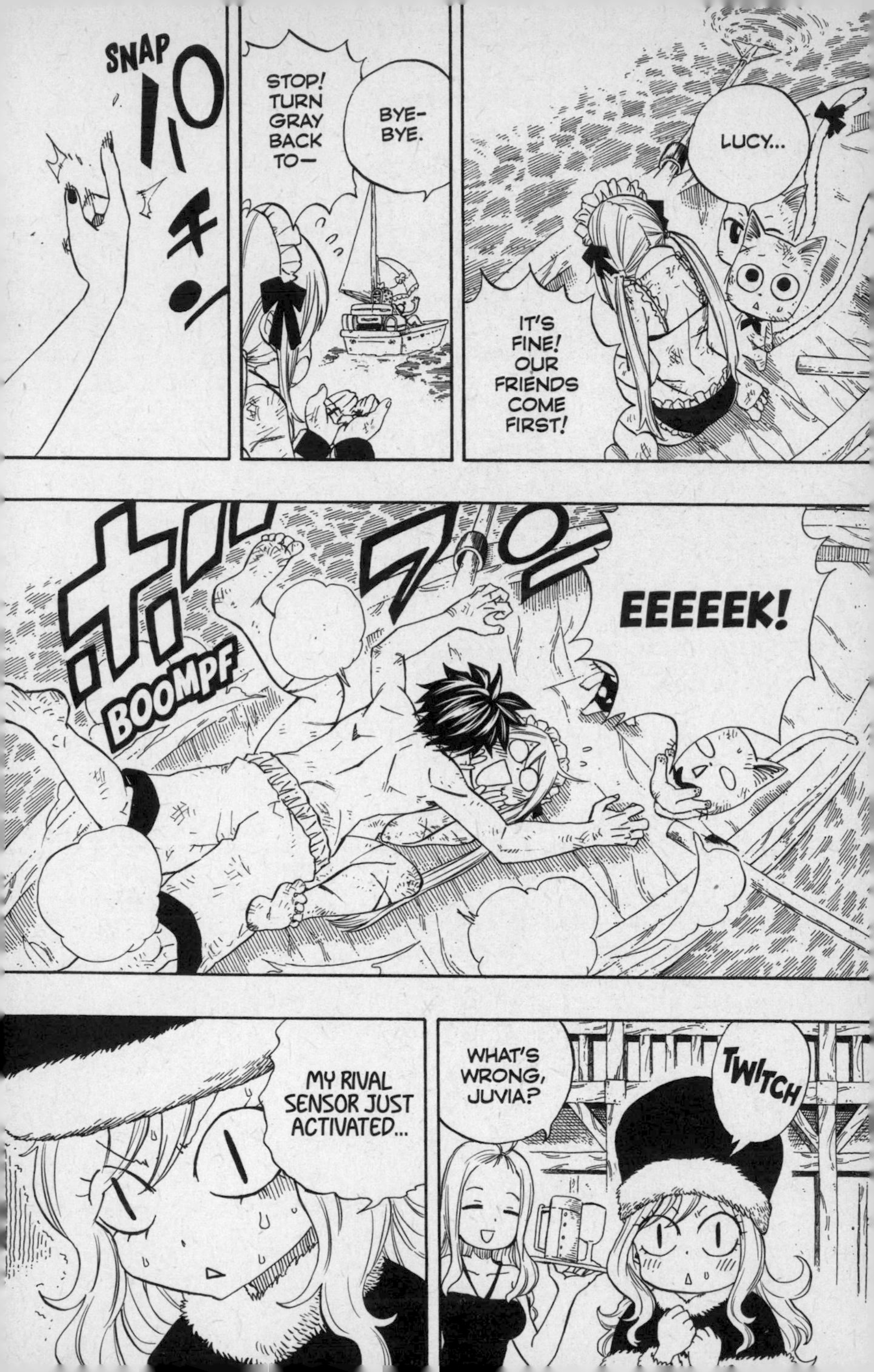
LUCY...
IT'S FINE! OUR FRIENDS COME FIRST!
STOP! TURN GRAY BACK TO—
BYE-BYE.
SNAP
パチン
EEEEEK!
BOOMPF
WHAT'S WRONG, JUVIA?
TWITCH
MY RIVAL SENSOR JUST ACTIVATED...

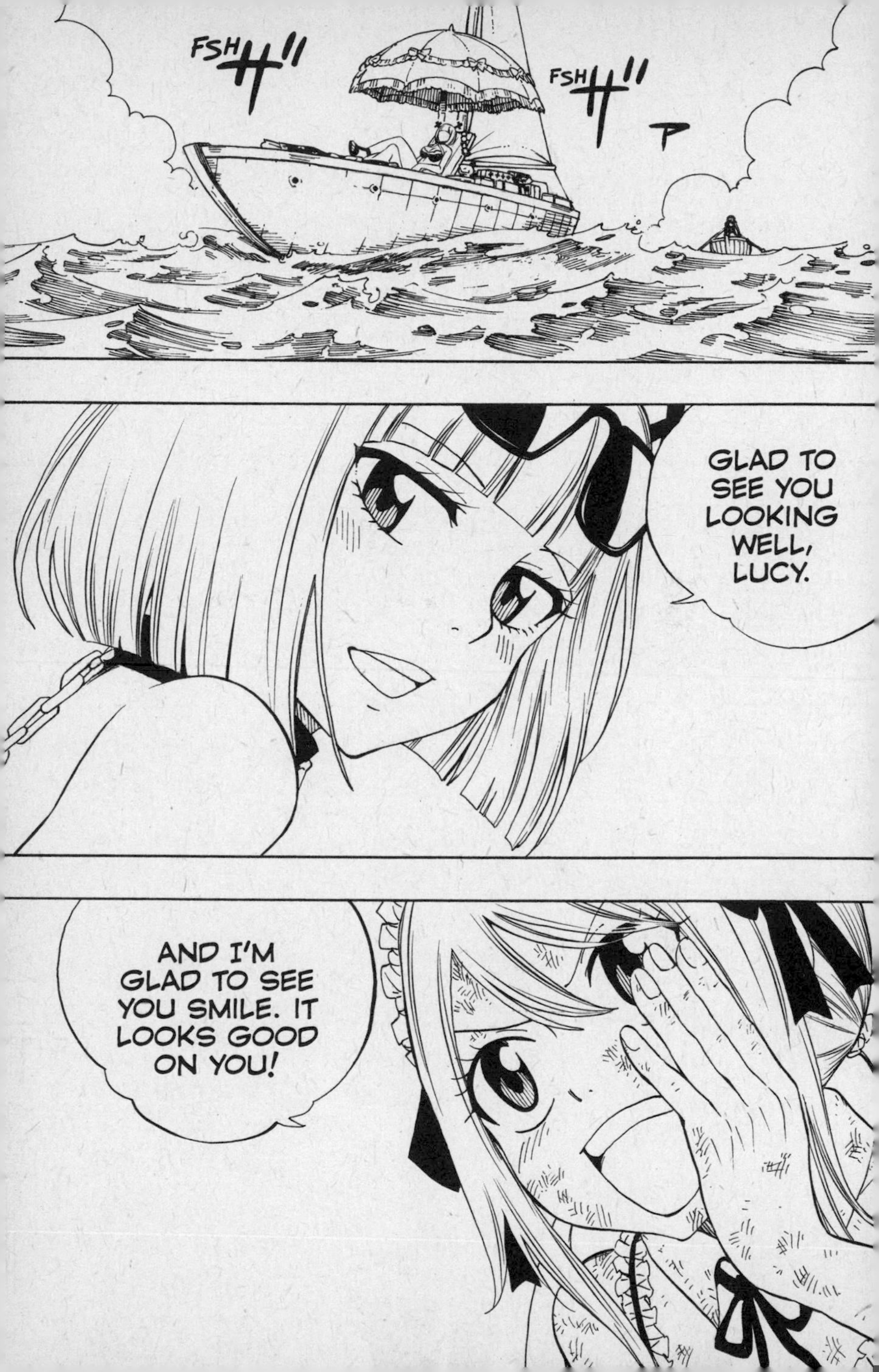
FSH
FSH
P
GLAD TO SEE YOU LOOKING WELL, LUCY.
AND I'M GLAD TO SEE YOU SMILE. IT LOOKS GOOD ON YOU!

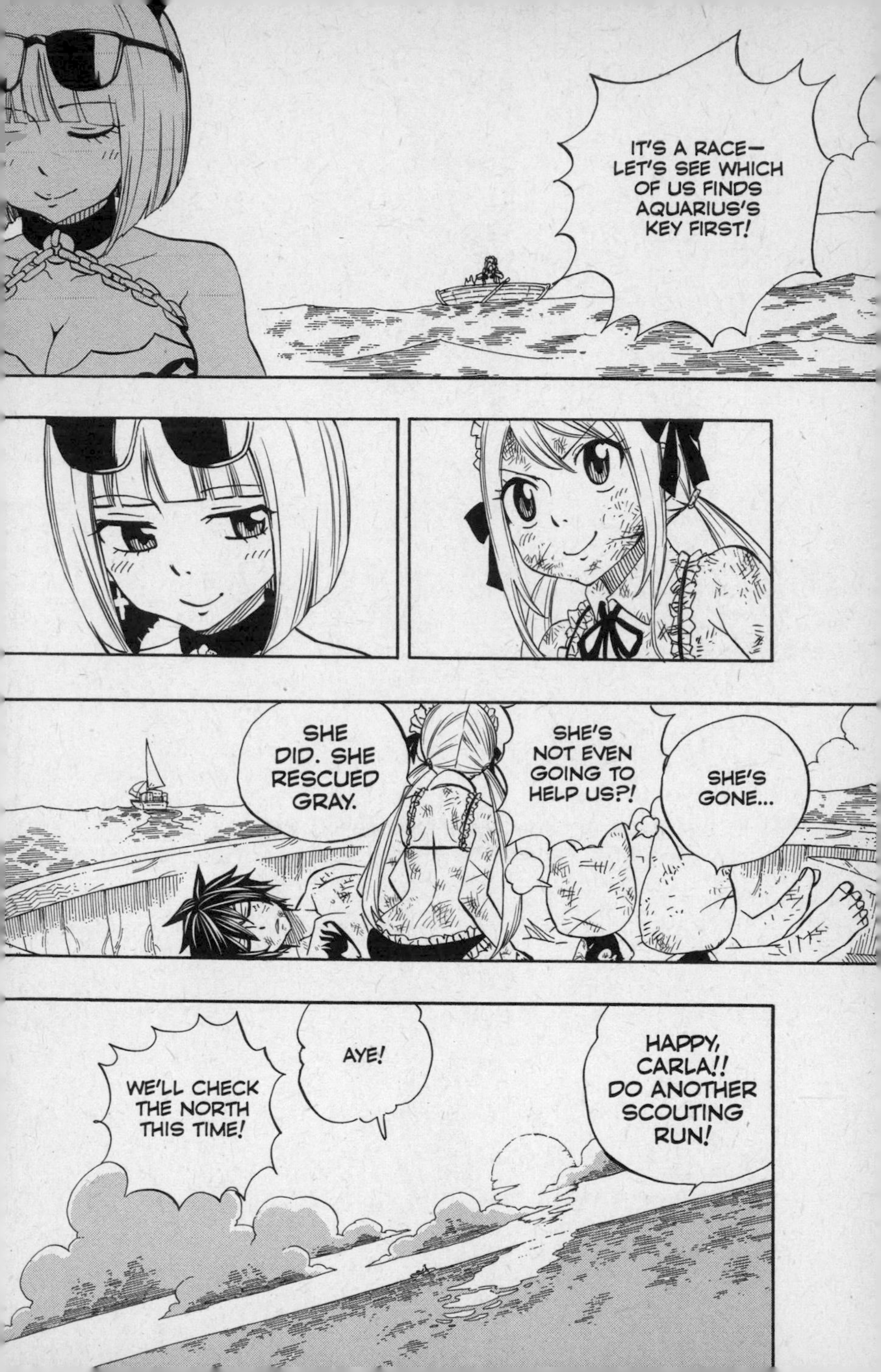
IT'S A RACE—LET'S SEE WHICH OF US FINDS AQUARIUS'S KEY FIRST!
SHE'S GONE...
SHE'S NOT EVEN GOING TO HELP US?!
SHE DID. SHE RESCUED GRAY.
HAPPY, CARLA!! DO ANOTHER SCOUTING RUN!
AYE!
WE'LL CHECK THE NORTH THIS TIME!

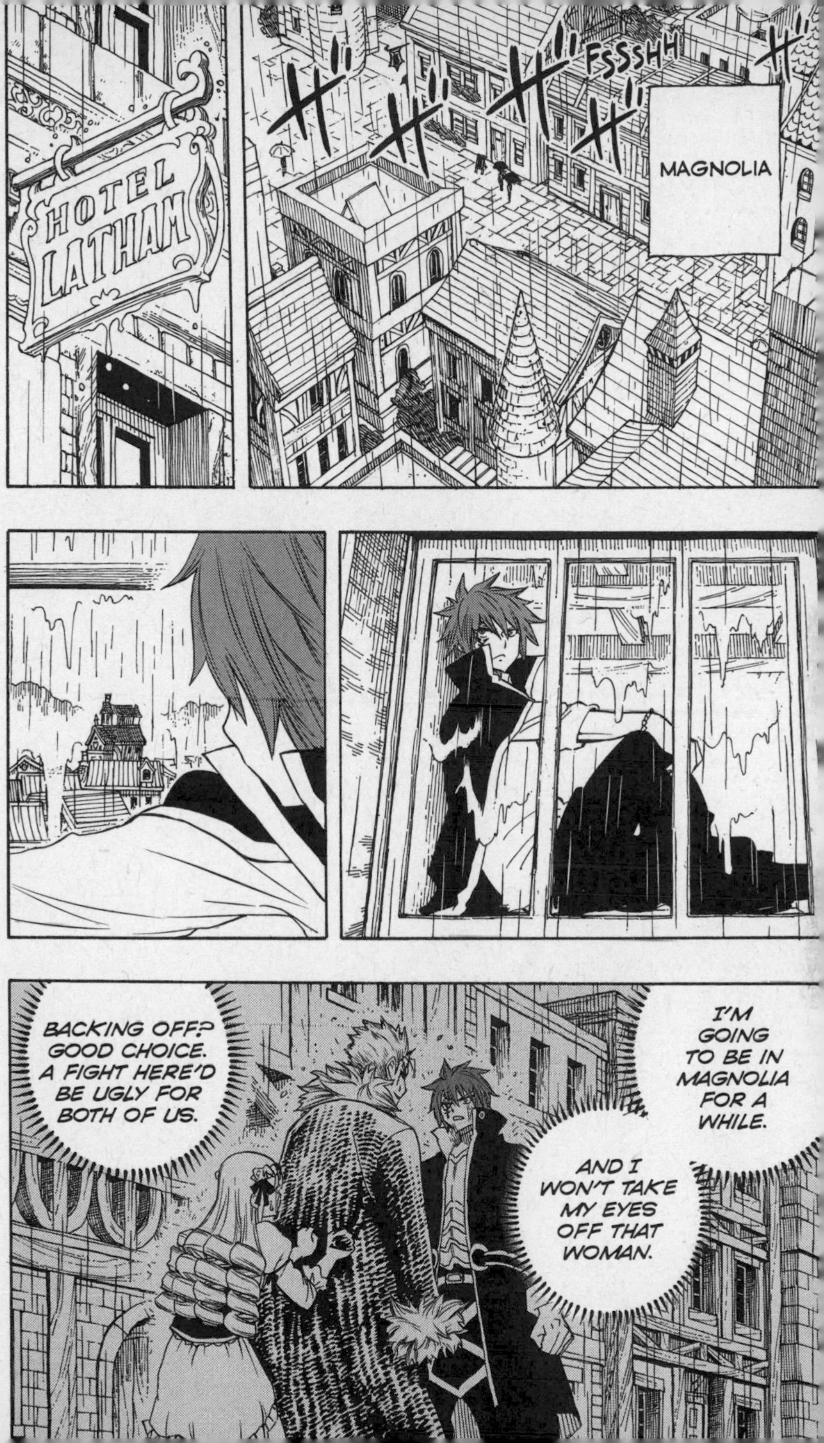
FSSSHH
MAGNOLIA
HOTEL LATHAM
I'M GOING TO BE IN MAGNOLIA FOR A WHILE.
AND I WON'T TAKE MY EYES OFF THAT WOMAN.
BACKING OFF? GOOD CHOICE. A FIGHT HERE'D BE UGLY FOR BOTH OF US.

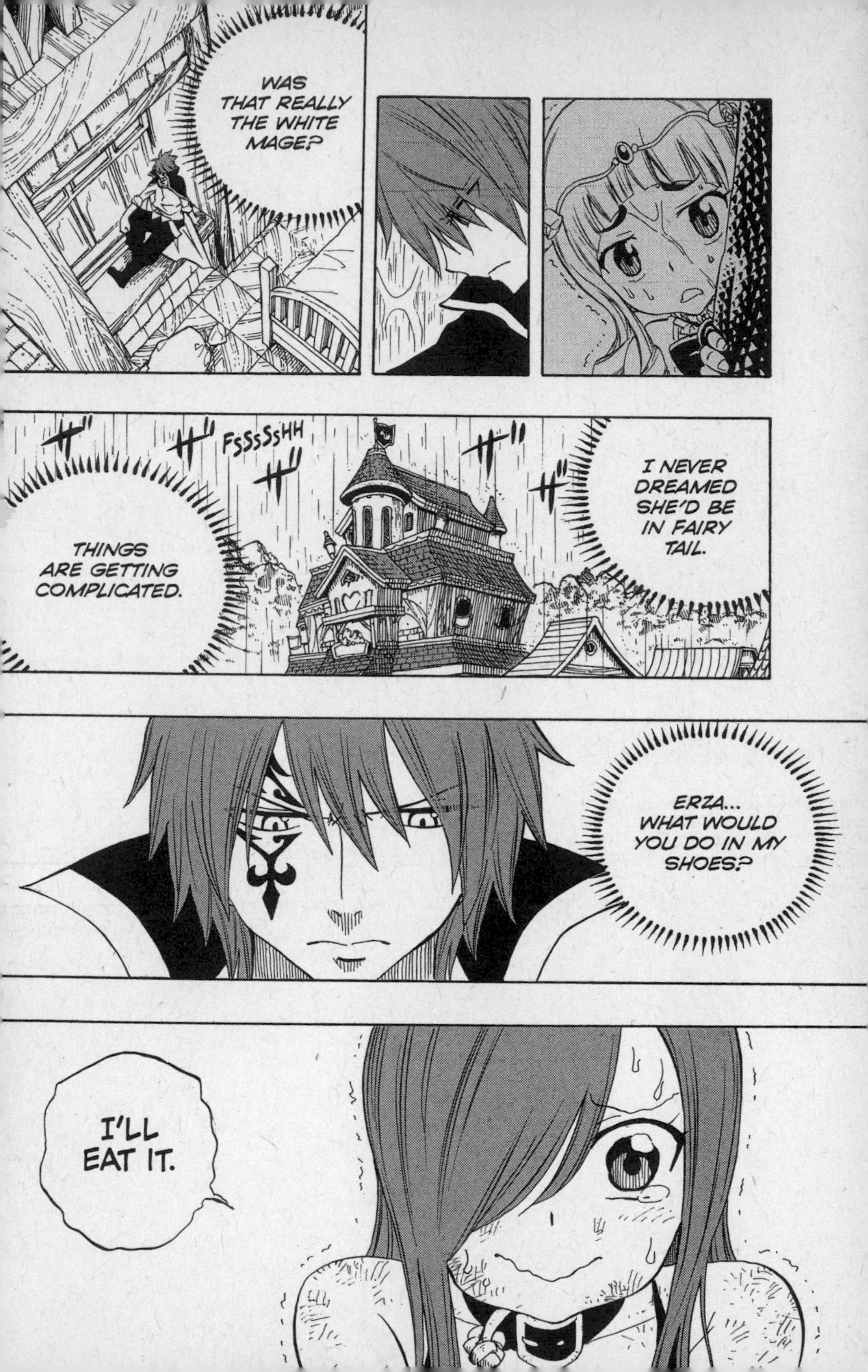
WAS THAT REALLY THE WHITE MAGE?
I NEVER DREAMED SHE'D BE IN FAIRY TAIL.
FSSSSSHH
THINGS ARE GETTING COMPLICATED.
ERZA... WHAT WOULD YOU DO IN MY SHOES?
I'LL EAT IT.

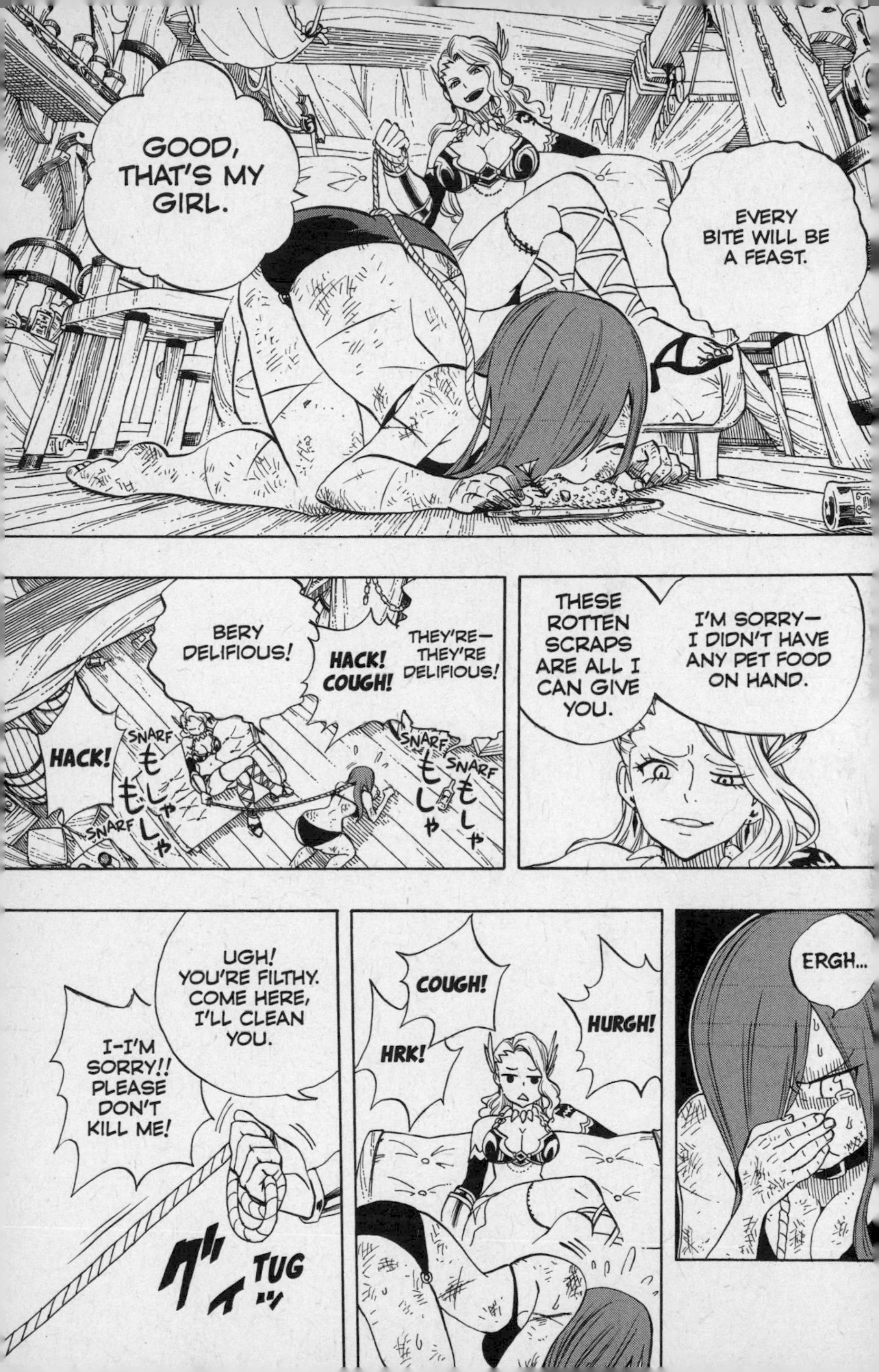
EVERY BITE WILL BE A FEAST.
GOOD, THAT'S MY GIRL.
I'M SORRY— I DIDN'T HAVE ANY PET FOOD ON HAND.
THESE ROTTEN SCRAPS ARE ALL I CAN GIVE YOU.
THEY'RE— THEY'RE DELIFIOUS!
HACK! COUGH!
BERY DELIFIOUS!
SNARF もしゃもしゃ SNARF
SNARF もしゃもしゃ SNARF
HACK!
ERGH...
HURGH!
COUGH!
HRK!
UGH! YOU'RE FILTHY. COME HERE, I'LL CLEAN YOU.
I-I'M SORRY!! PLEASE DON'T KILL ME!
グイッ TUG

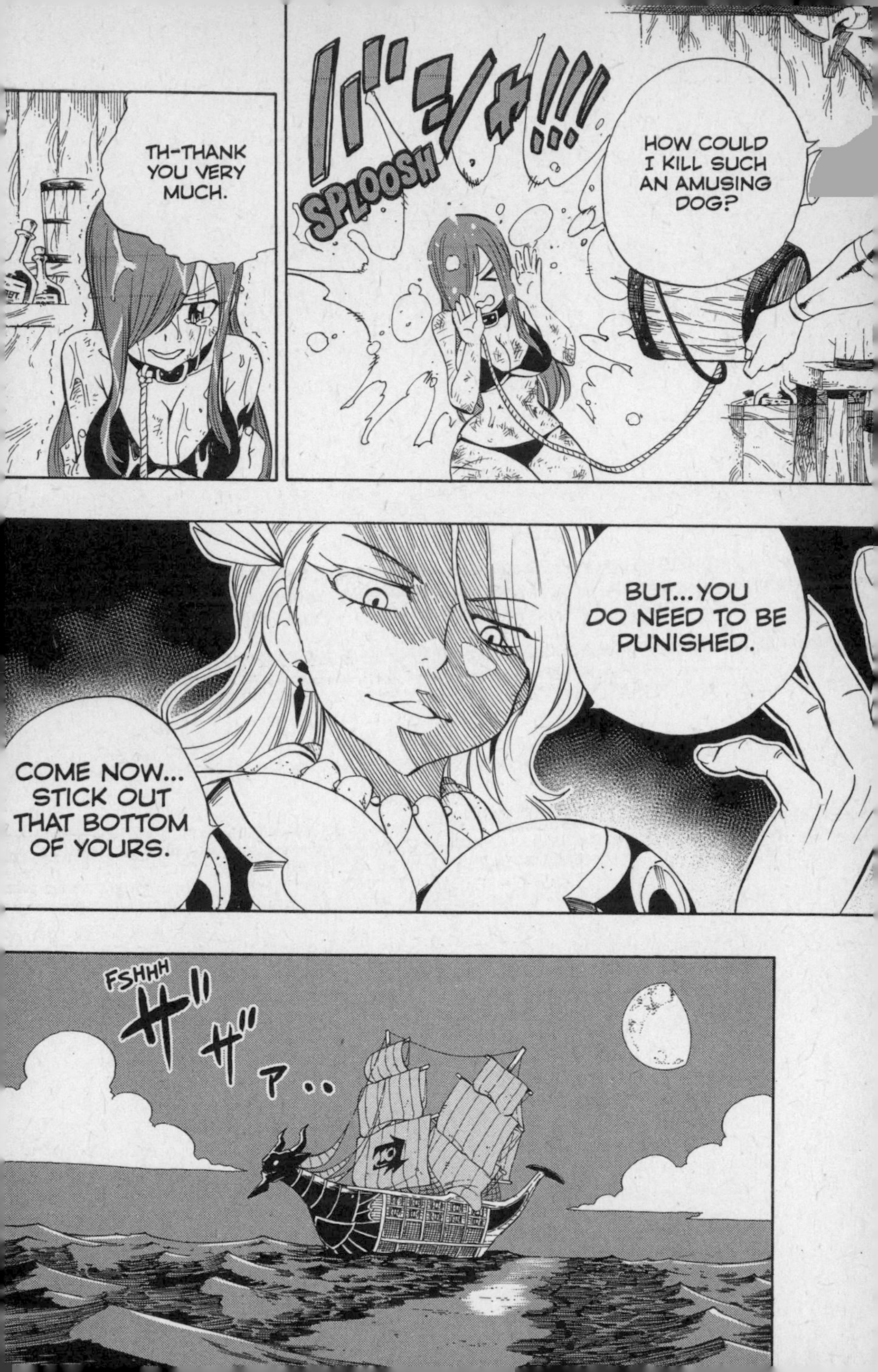
HOW COULD I KILL SUCH AN AMUSING DOG?
SPLOOSH
TH-THANK YOU VERY MUCH.
BUT...YOU DO NEED TO BE PUNISHED.
COME NOW... STICK OUT THAT BOTTOM OF YOURS.
FSHHH

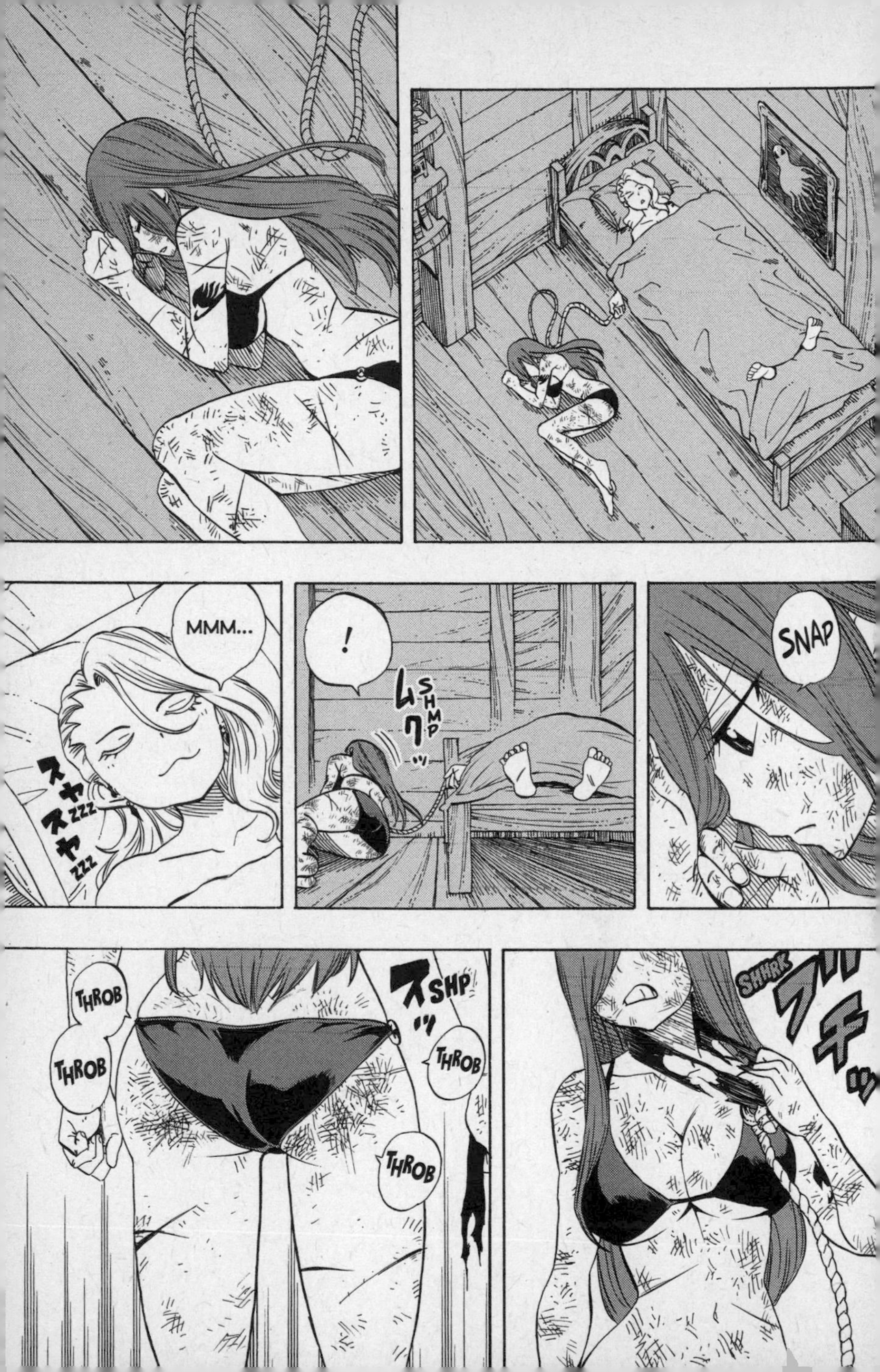
SNAP
!
ムクッ
SHMP
MMM...
スヤスヤ
zzz
zzz
SHHRK
スッ
SHP
THROB
THROB
THROB
THROB

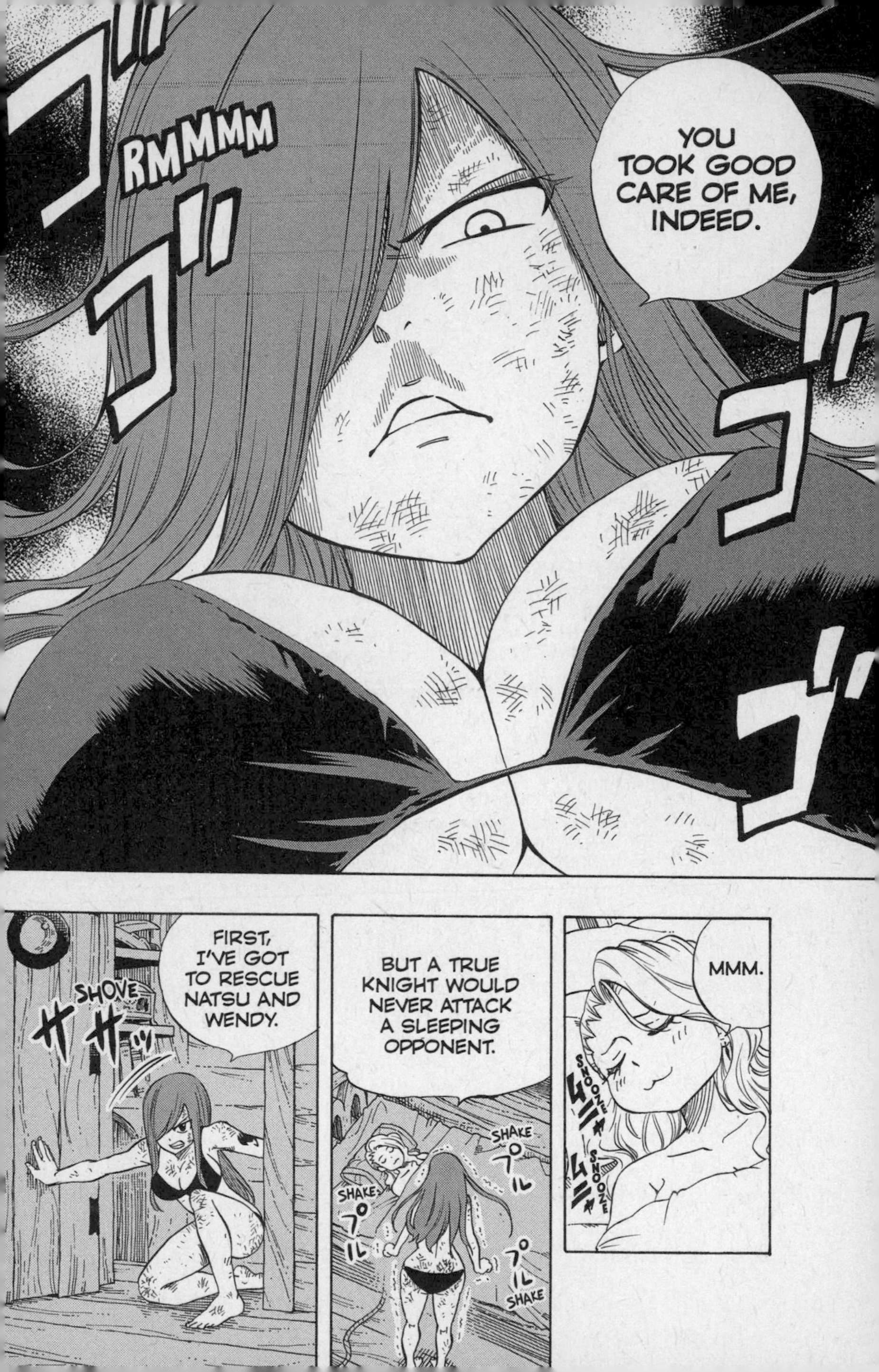
RMMMM
YOU TOOK GOOD CARE OF ME, INDEED.
MMM.
SNOOZE
SNOOZE
BUT A TRUE KNIGHT WOULD NEVER ATTACK A SLEEPING OPPONENT.
SHAKE
SHAKE
SHAKE
FIRST, I'VE GOT TO RESCUE NATSU AND WENDY.
SHOVE

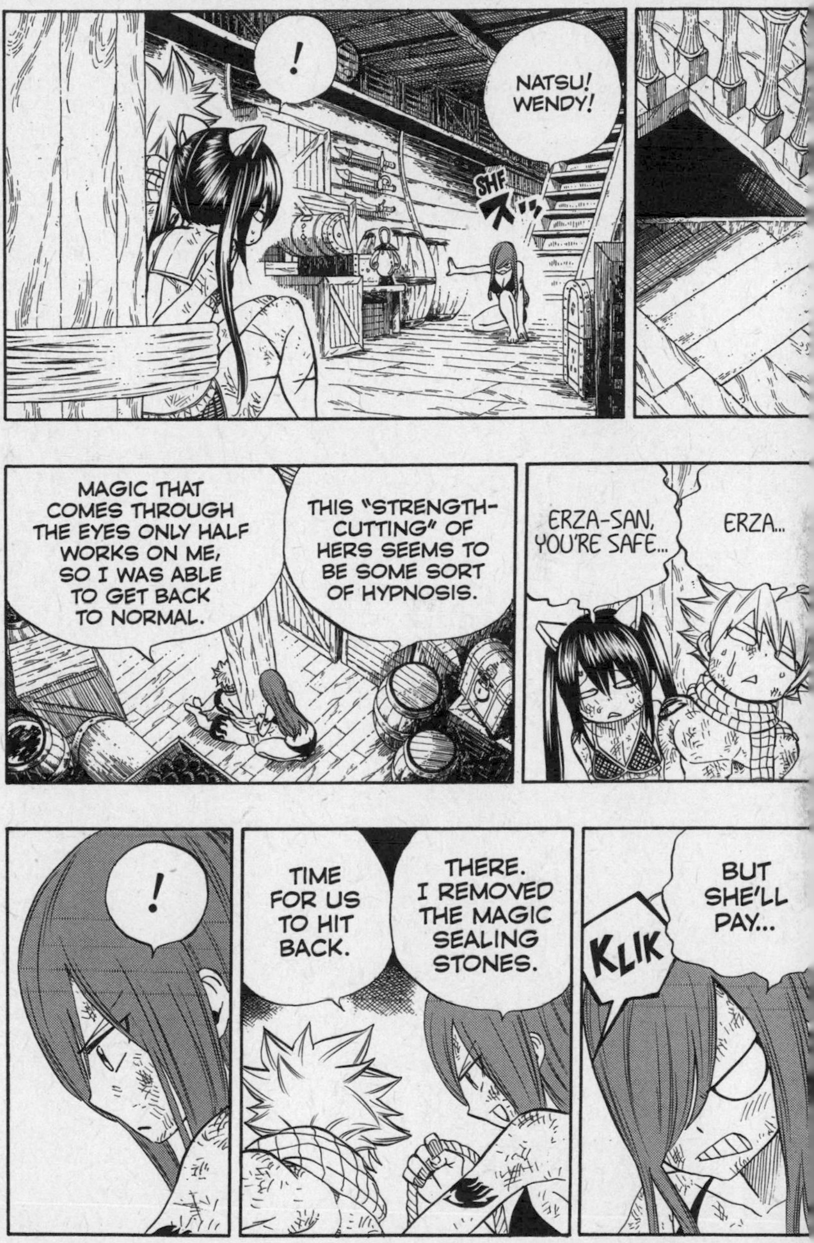
NATSU! WENDY!
SHF
!
ERZA...
ERZA-SAN, YOU'RE SAFE...
THIS "STRENGTH-CUTTING" OF HERS SEEMS TO BE SOME SORT OF HYPNOSIS.
MAGIC THAT COMES THROUGH THE EYES ONLY HALF WORKS ON ME, SO I WAS ABLE TO GET BACK TO NORMAL.
BUT SHE'LL PAY...
KLIK
THERE. I REMOVED THE MAGIC SEALING STONES.
TIME FOR US TO HIT BACK.
!

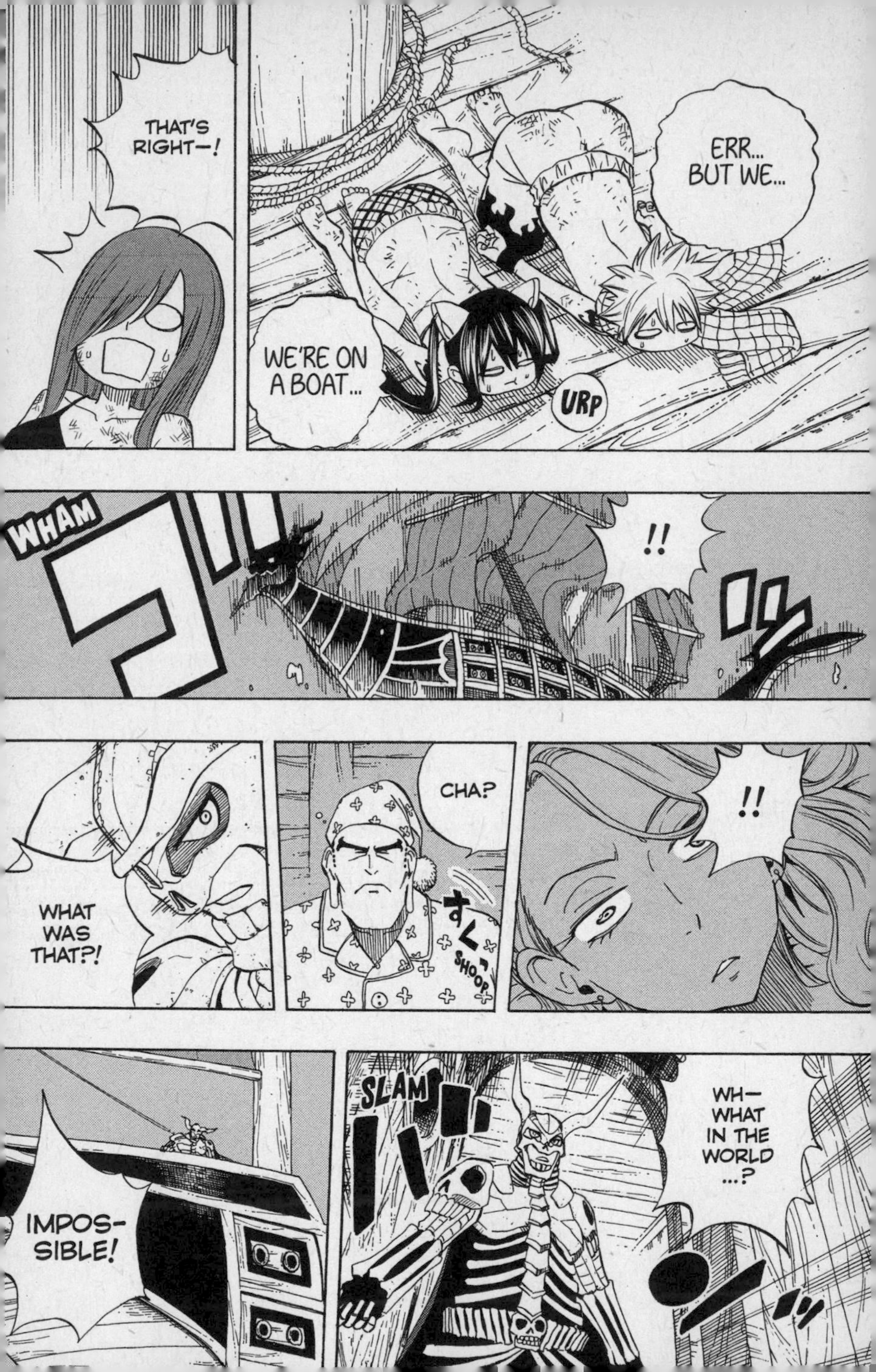
ERR... BUT WE...
WE'RE ON A BOAT...
URP
THAT'S RIGHT—!
!!
WHAM
!!
CHA?
SHOOP
WHAT WAS THAT?!
WH— WHAT IN THE WORLD ...?
SLAM
IMPOS-SIBLE!

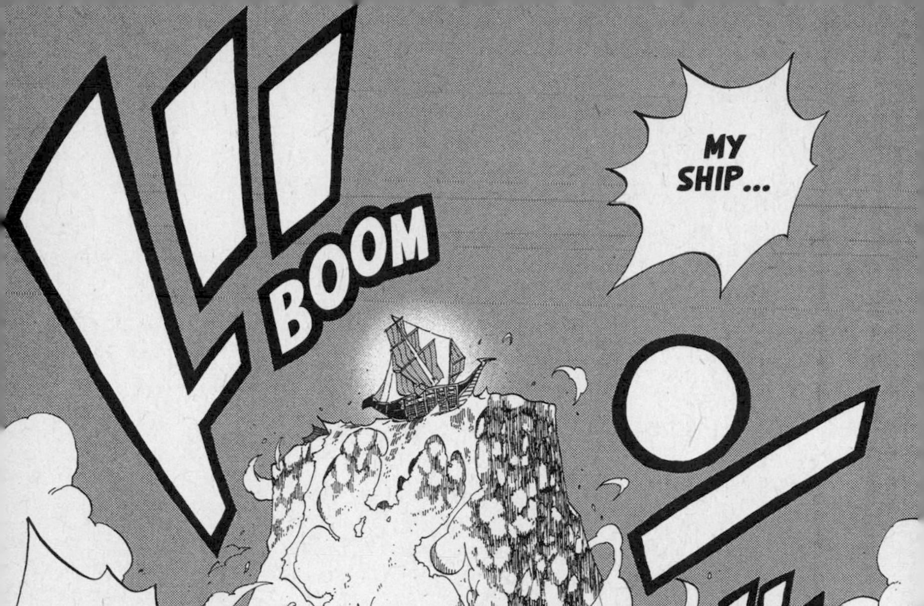
MY SHIP...
BOOM
IT'S ON A HILL-TOP?!

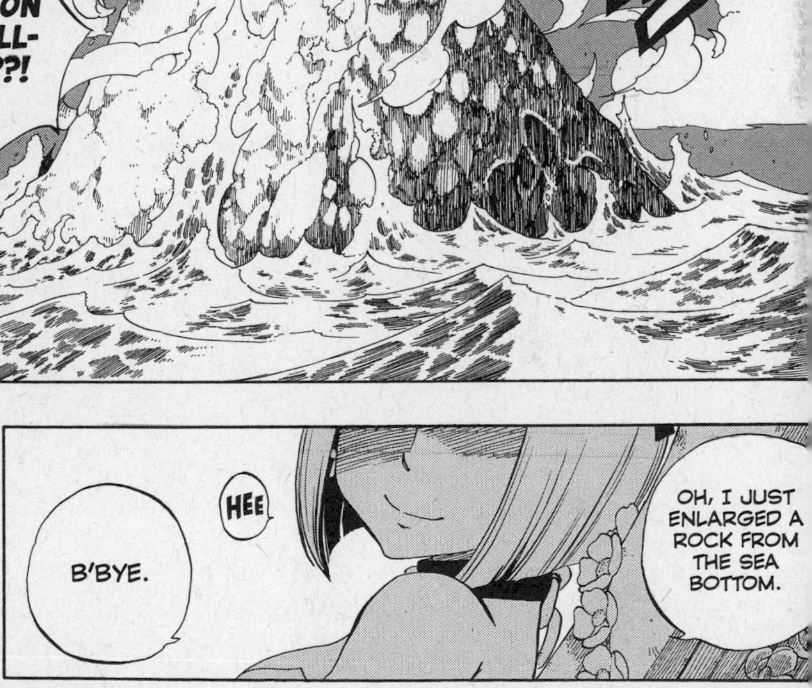
OH, I JUST ENLARGED A ROCK FROM THE SEA BOTTOM.
HEE
B'BYE.

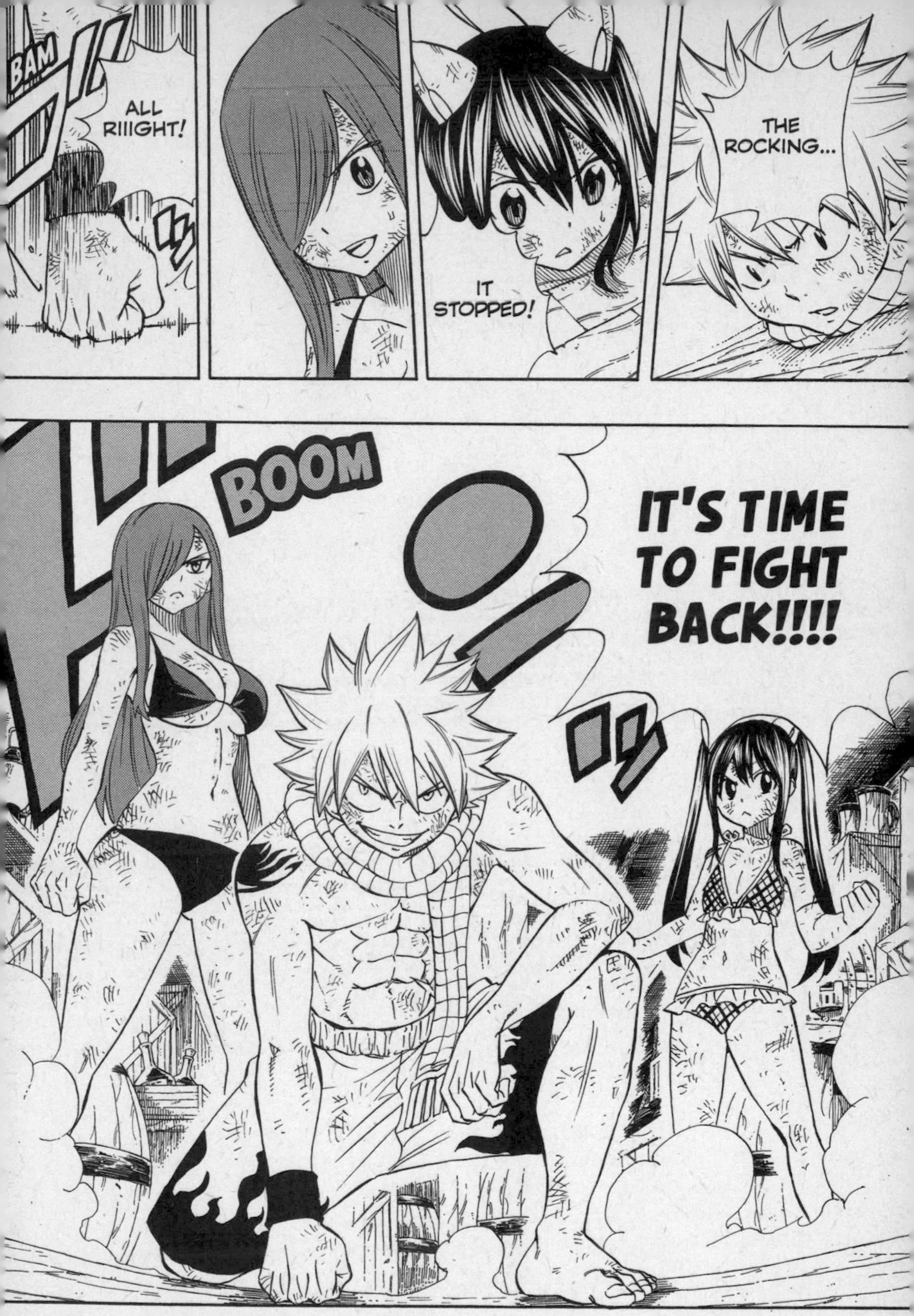
THE ROCKING...
IT STOPPED!
BAM
ALL RIIIGHT!
IT'S TIME TO FIGHT BACK!!!!
BOOM

FAIRY TAIL 100 YEARS QUEST

Chapter 14: Rain and Shadow

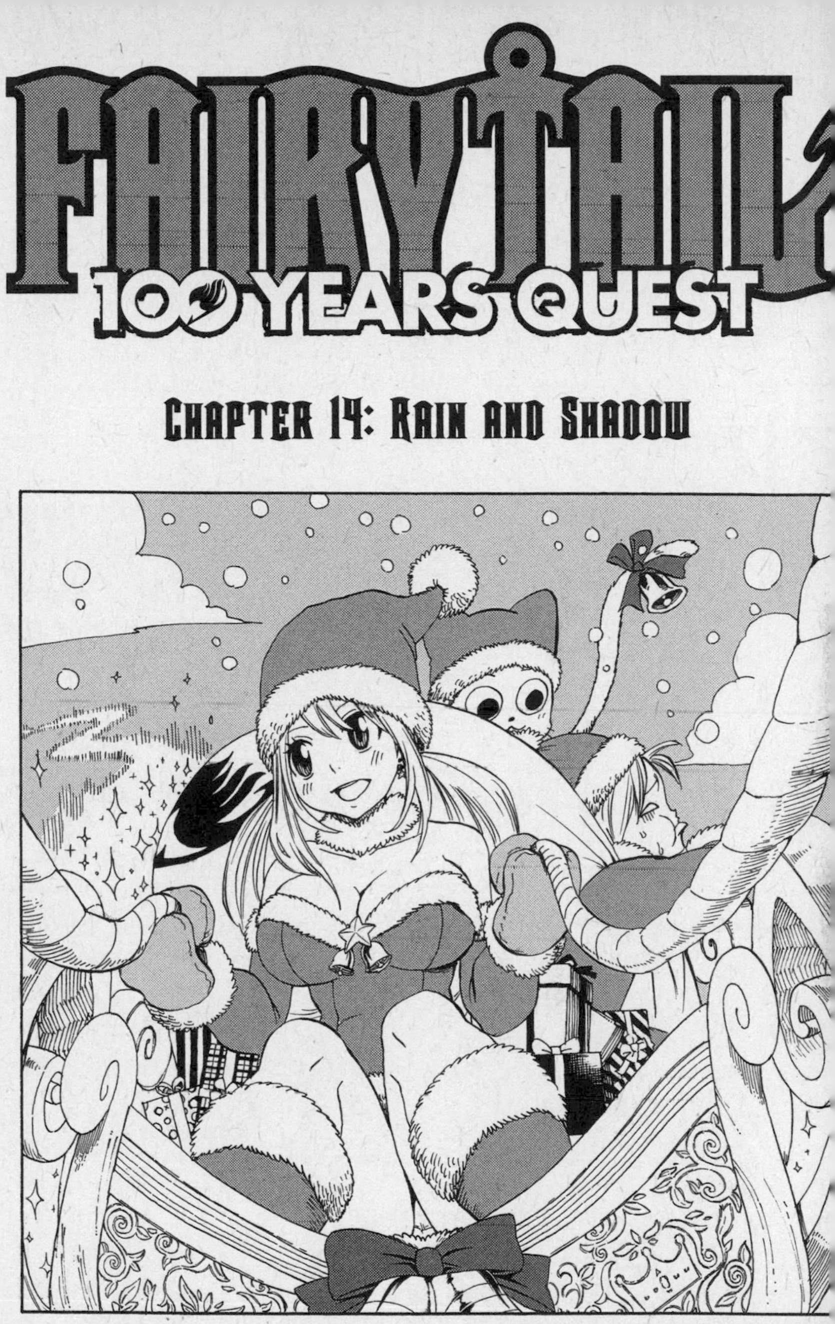

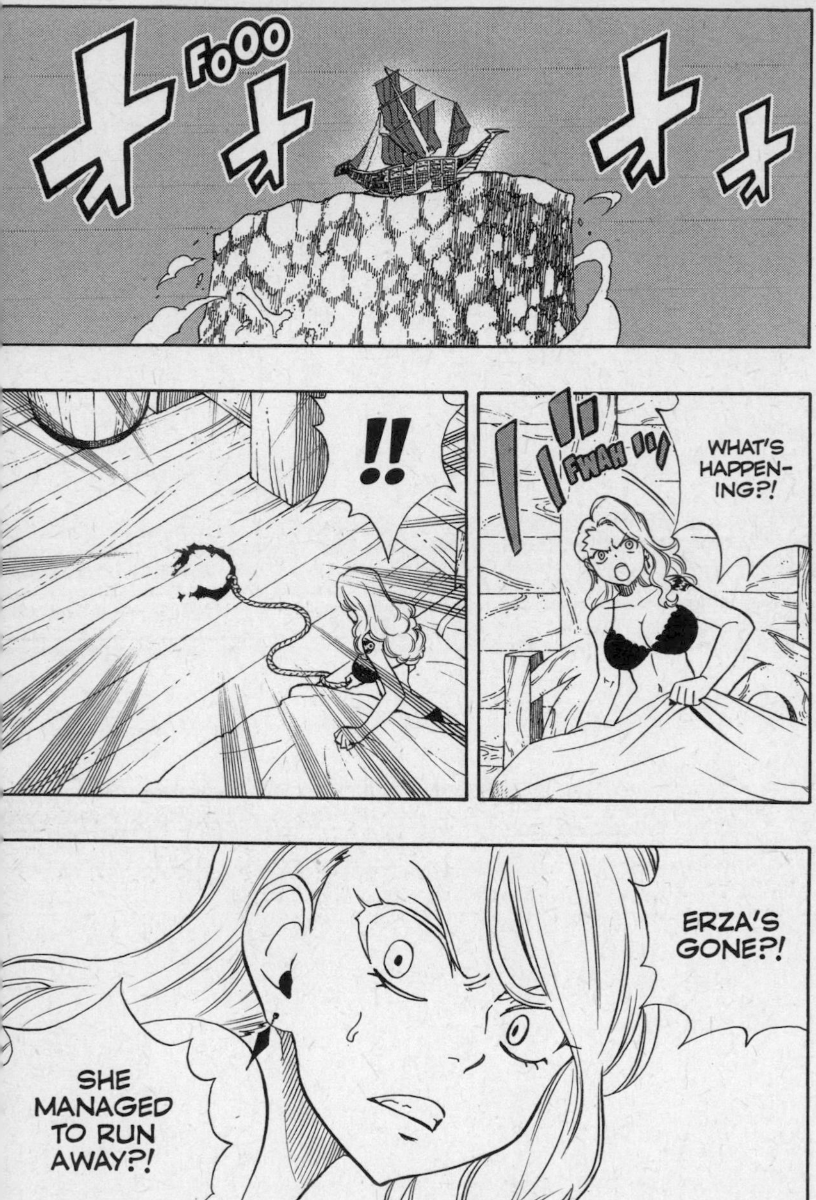
FoOO
FWAH!!
WHAT'S HAPPEN-ING?!
!!
ERZA'S GONE?!
SHE MANAGED TO RUN AWAY?!

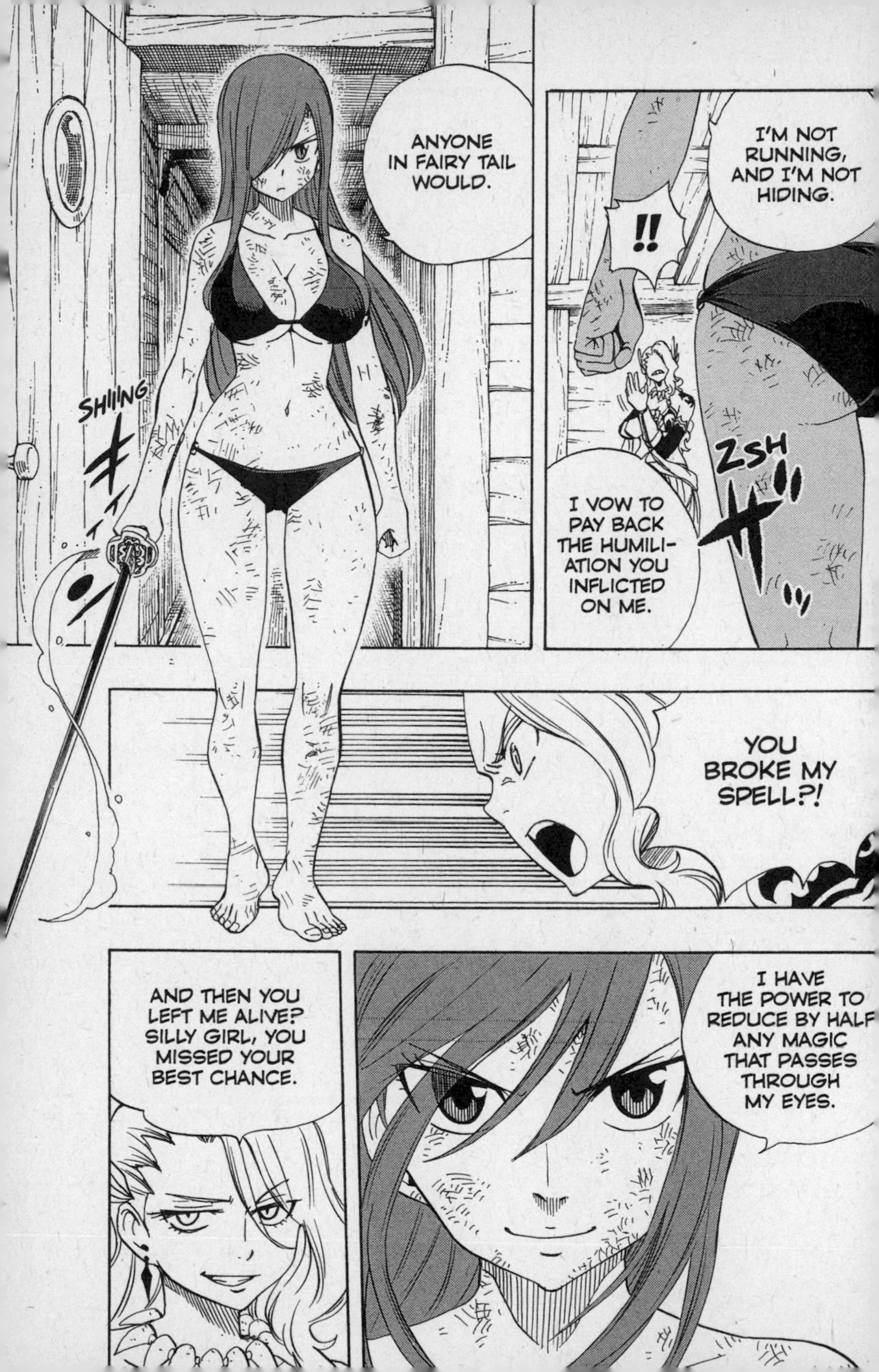
I'M NOT RUNNING, AND I'M NOT HIDING.
!!
ZSH
I VOW TO PAY BACK THE HUMILI-ATION YOU INFLICTED ON ME.
YOU BROKE MY SPELL?!
ANYONE IN FAIRY TAIL WOULD.
SHIING
I HAVE THE POWER TO REDUCE BY HALF ANY MAGIC THAT PASSES THROUGH MY EYES.
AND THEN YOU LEFT ME ALIVE? SILLY GIRL, YOU MISSED YOUR BEST CHANCE.

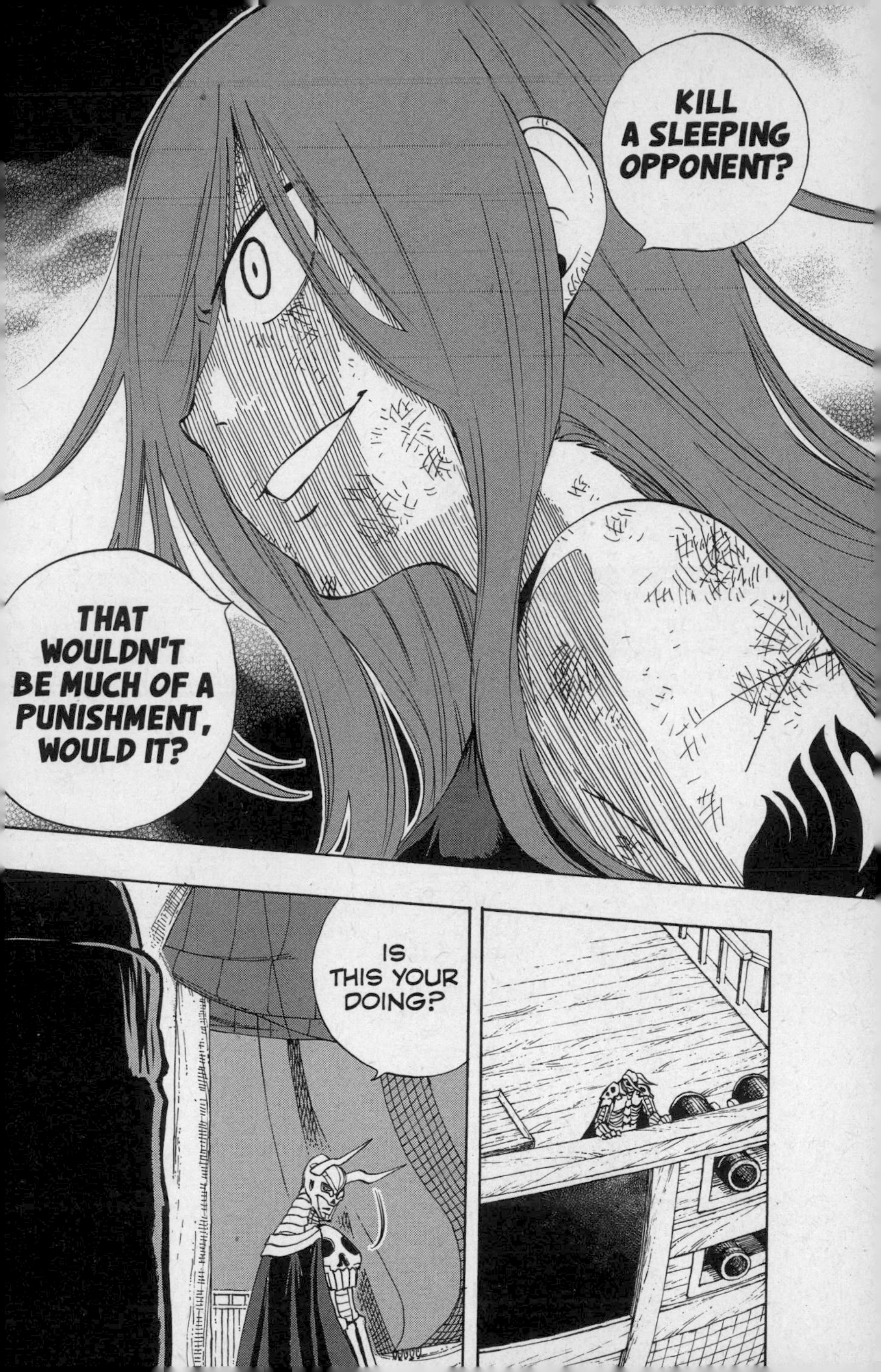
KILL A SLEEPING OPPONENT?
THAT WOULDN'T BE MUCH OF A PUNISHMENT, WOULD IT?
IS THIS YOUR DOING?

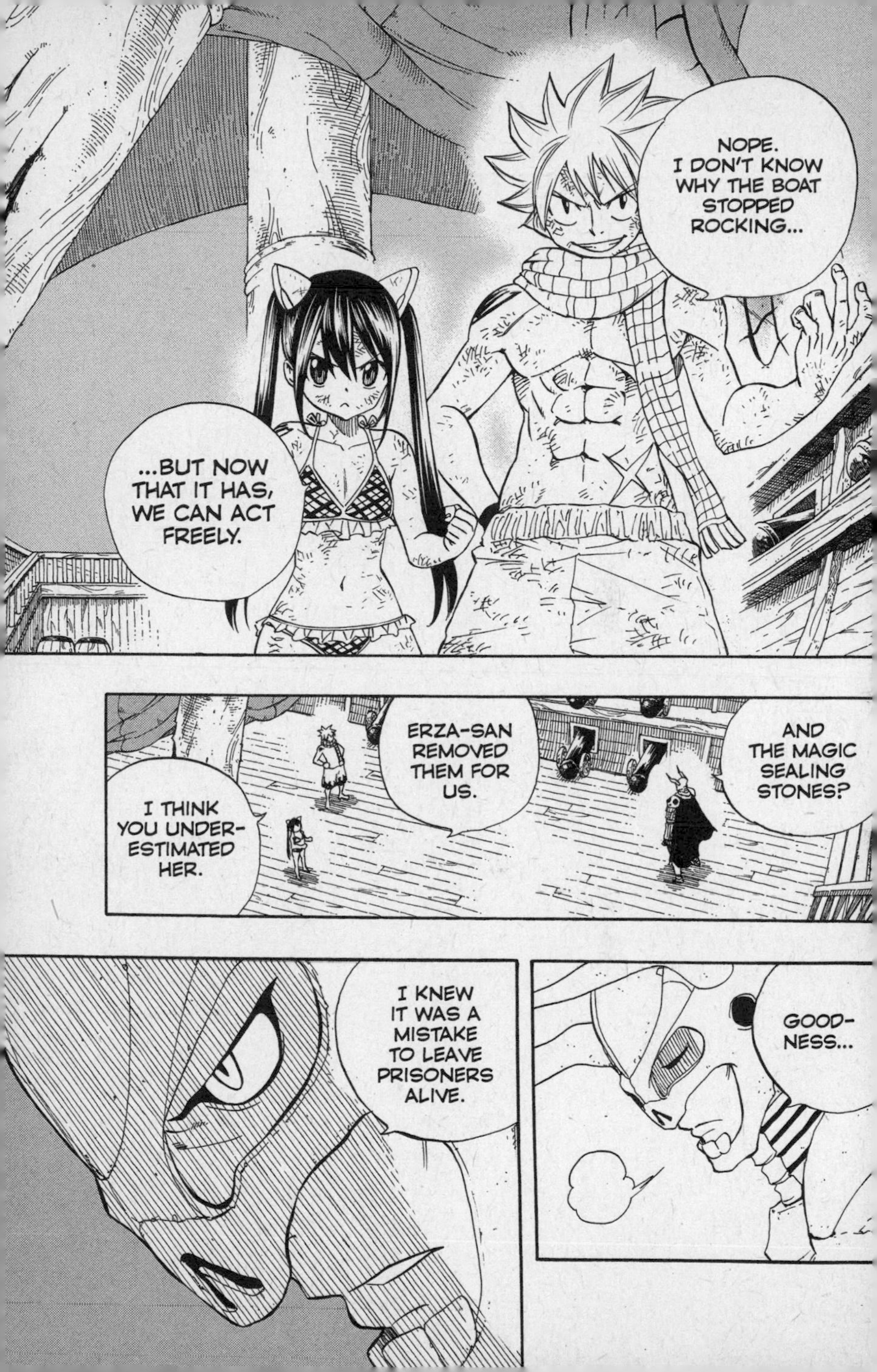
NOPE. I DON'T KNOW WHY THE BOAT STOPPED ROCKING...
...BUT NOW THAT IT HAS, WE CAN ACT FREELY.
AND THE MAGIC SEALING STONES?
ERZA-SAN REMOVED THEM FOR US.
I THINK YOU UNDER-ESTIMATED HER.
GOOD-NESS...
I KNEW IT WAS A MISTAKE TO LEAVE PRISONERS ALIVE.

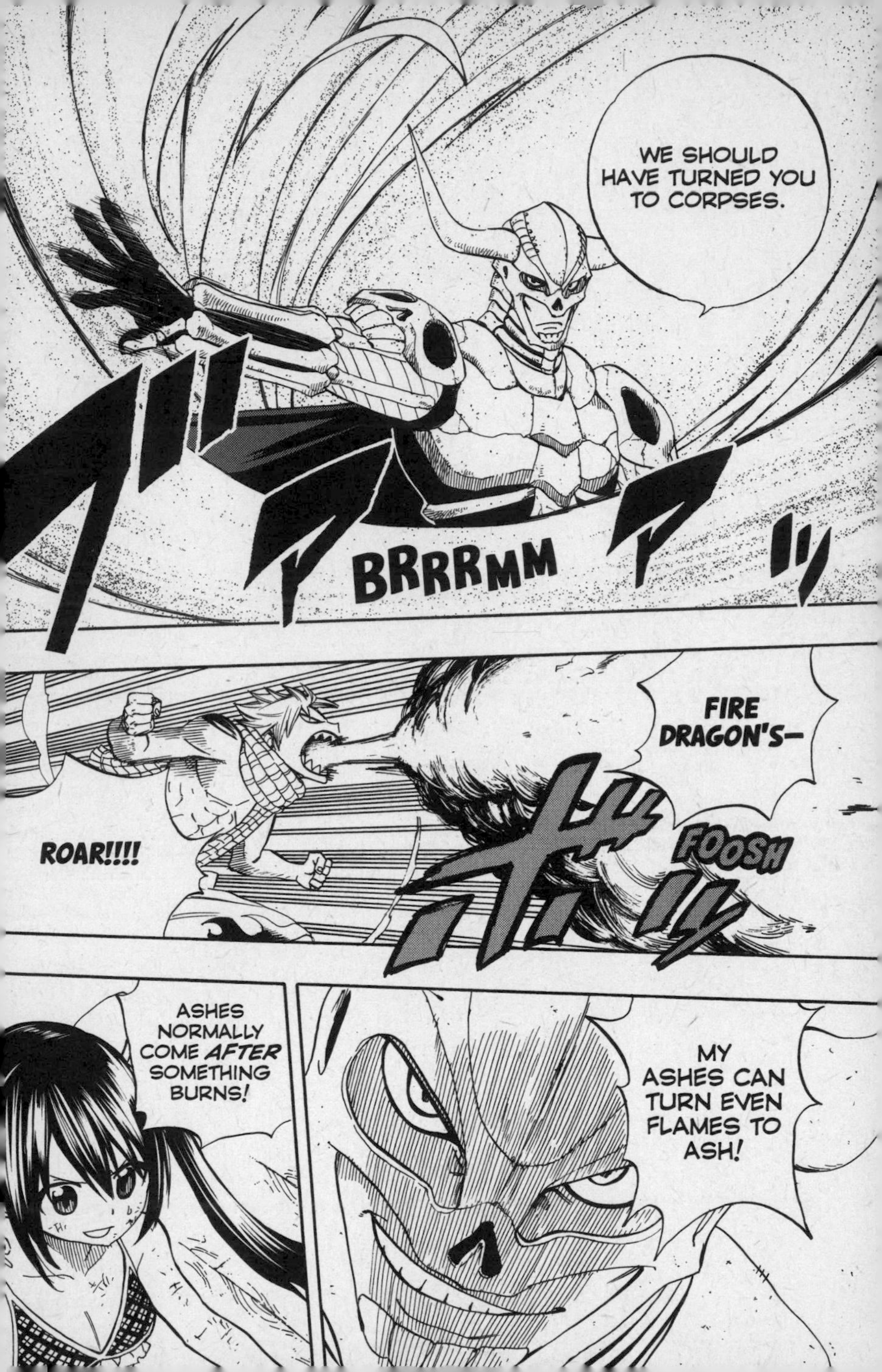
WE SHOULD HAVE TURNED YOU TO CORPSES.
BRRRMM
FIRE DRAGON'S—
FOOSH
ROAR!!!!
MY ASHES CAN TURN EVEN FLAMES TO ASH!
ASHES NORMALLY COME *AFTER* SOMETHING BURNS!

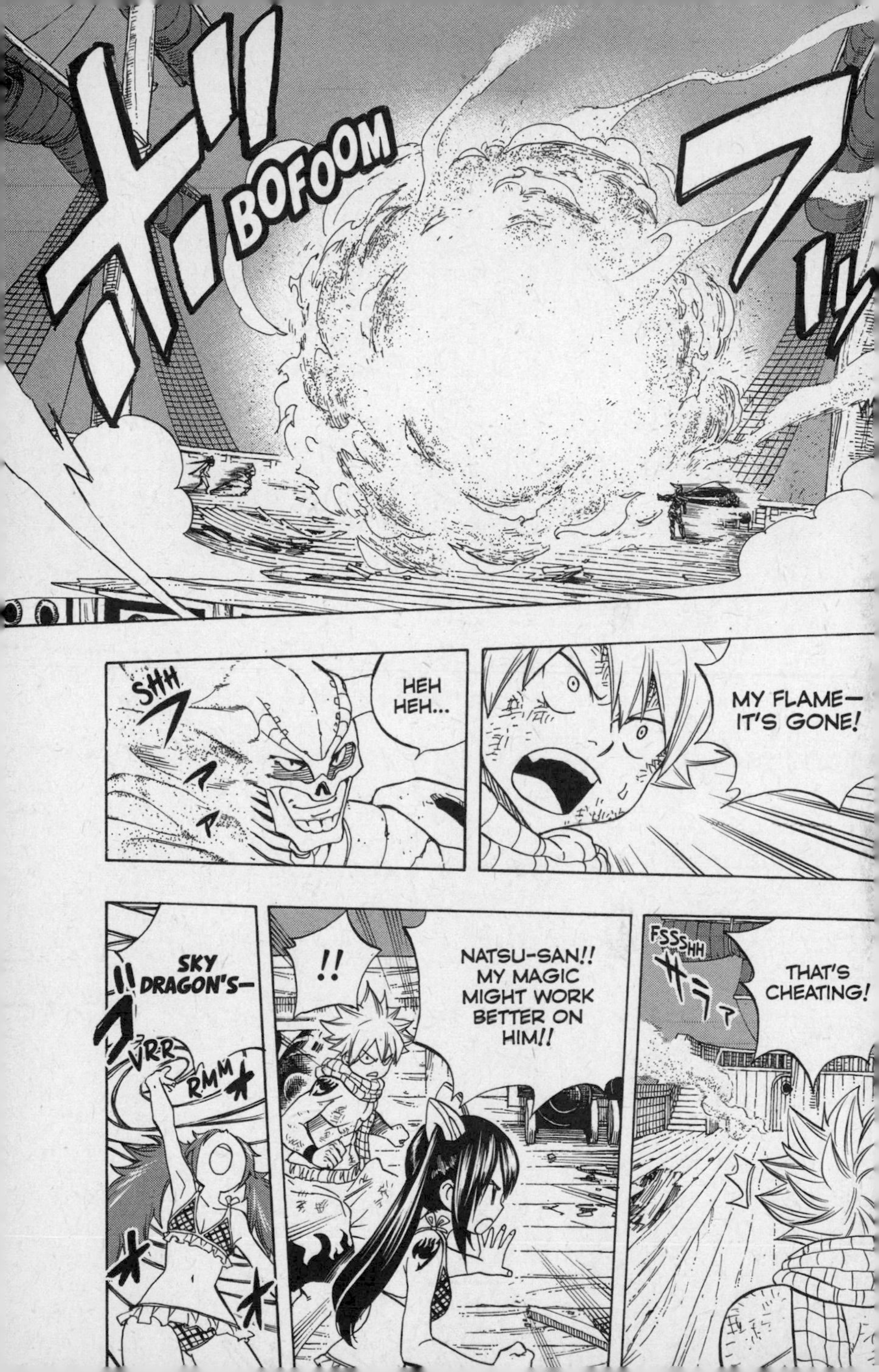
BOFOOM
MY FLAME—IT'S GONE!
HEH HEH...
SHH
FSSSHH
THAT'S CHEATING!
NATSU-SAN!! MY MAGIC MIGHT WORK BETTER ON HIM!!
!!
SKY DRAGON'S—
VRRRMM

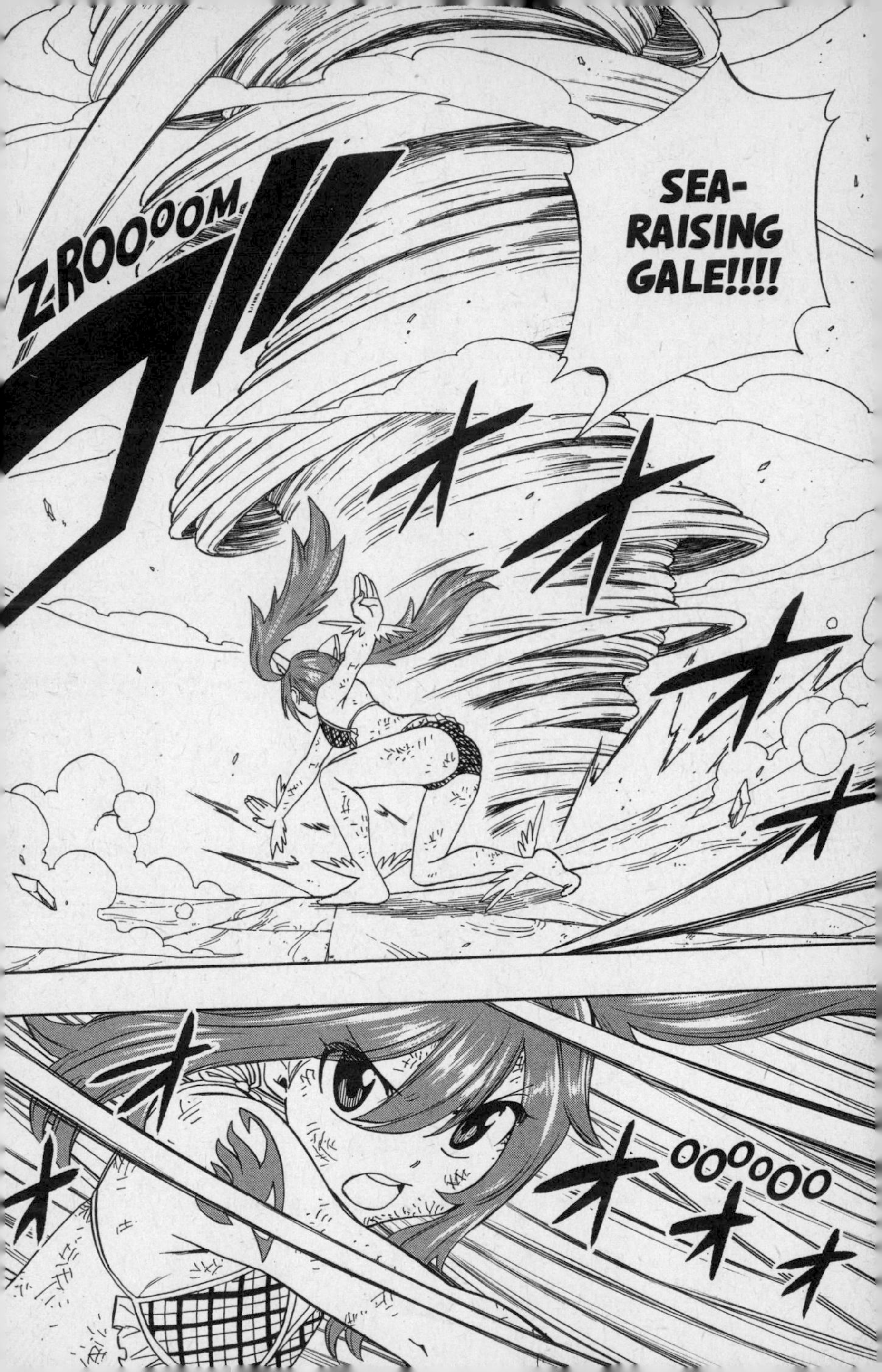
SEA-RAISING GALE!!!!
Z-ROOOOOM
OOOOOO

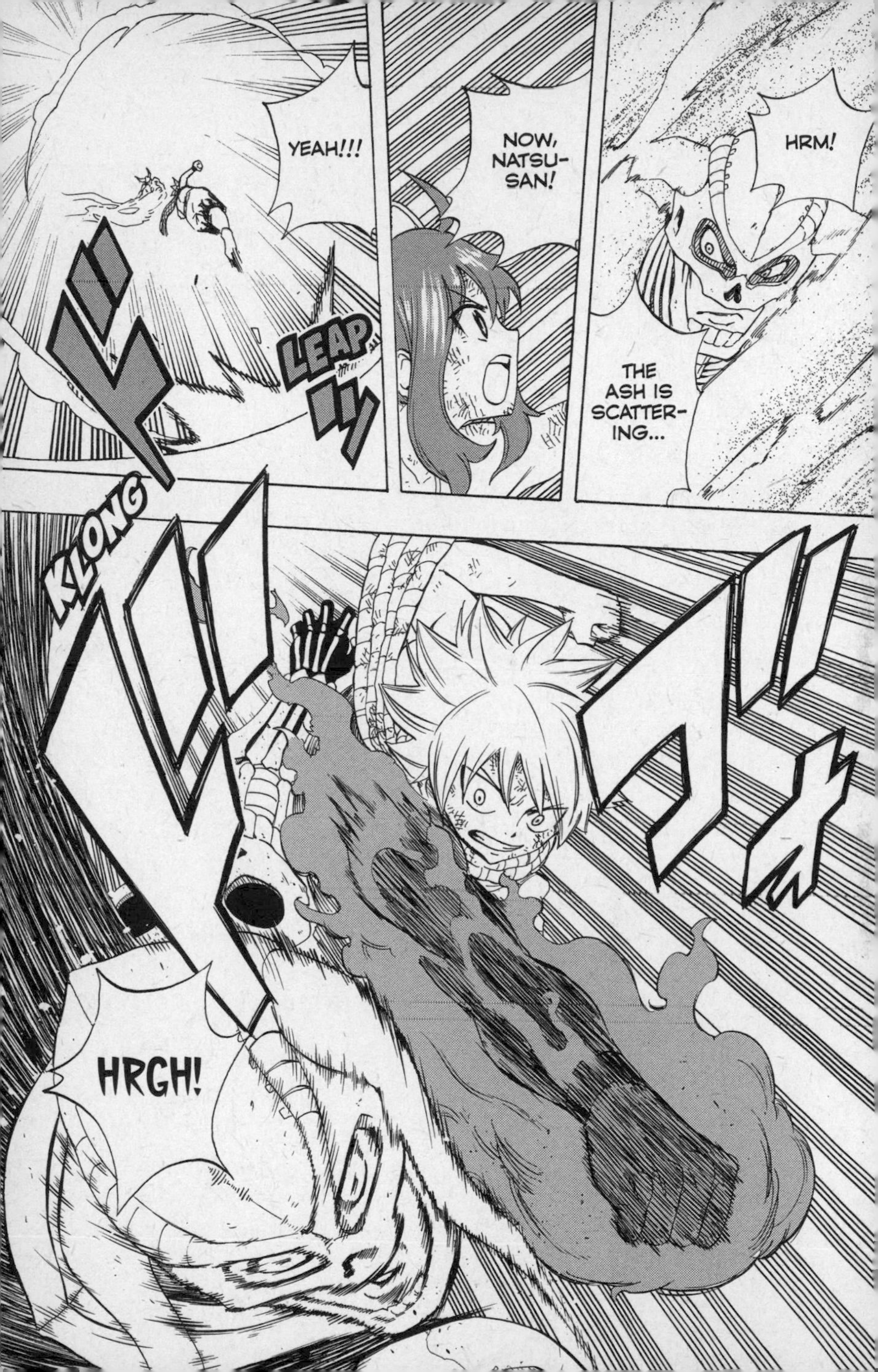
HRM!
THE ASH IS SCATTERING...
NOW, NATSU-SAN!
YEAH!!!
LEAP
KLONG
HRGH!

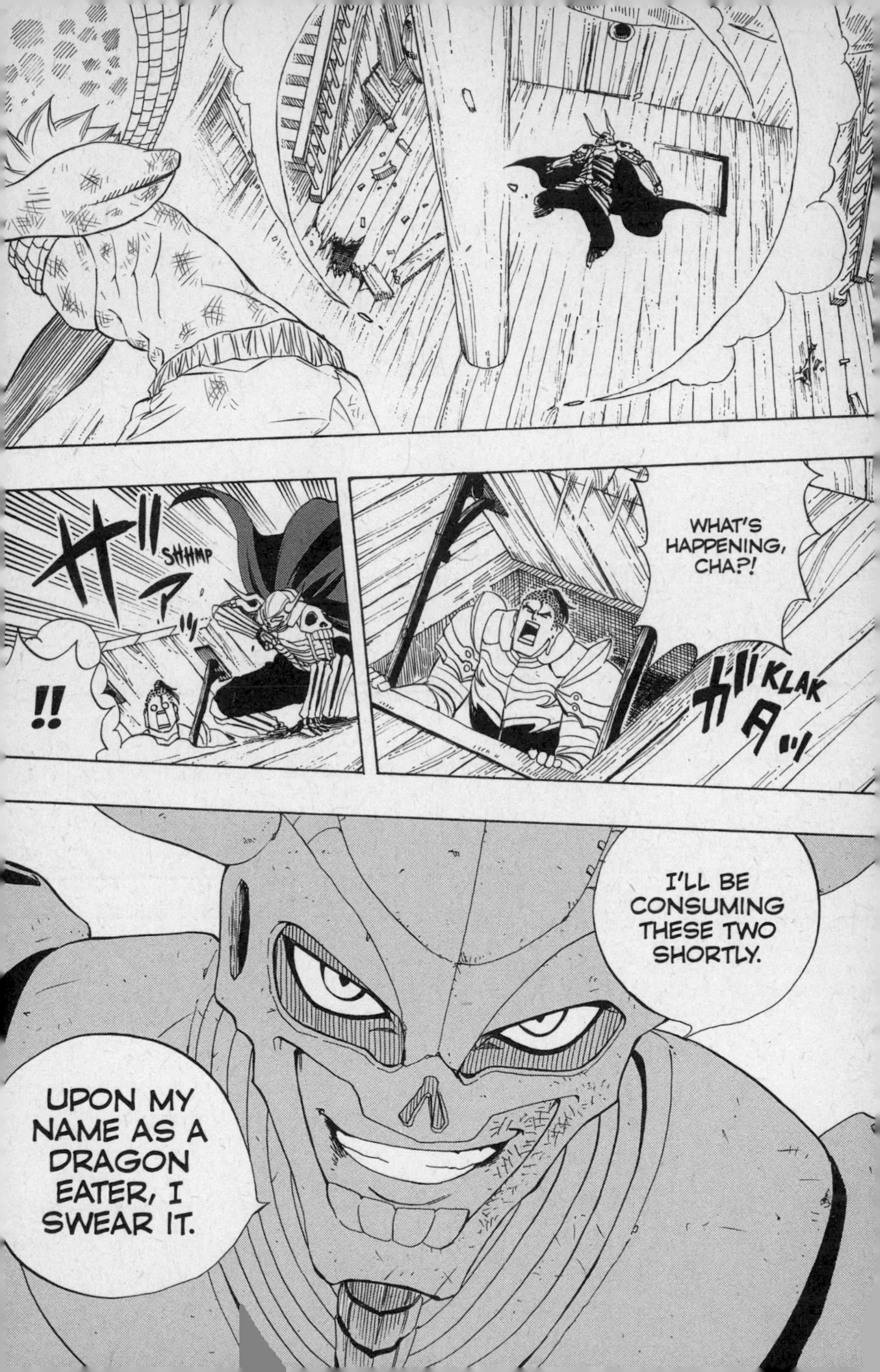
WHAT'S HAPPENING, CHA?!
KLAK
SHHMP
!!
I'LL BE CONSUMING THESE TWO SHORTLY.
UPON MY NAME AS A DRAGON EATER, I SWEAR IT.

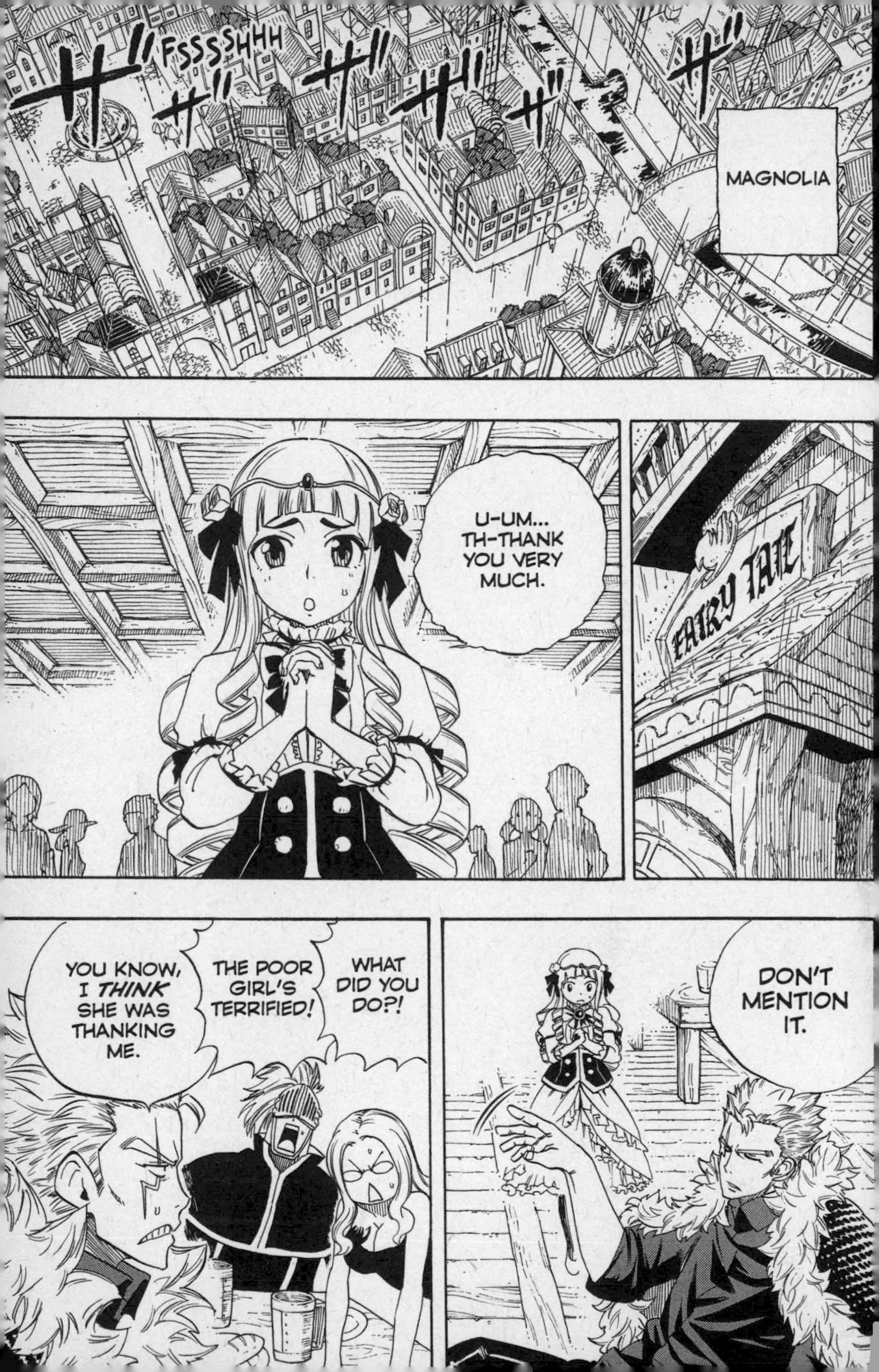
FSSSSHHH
MAGNOLIA
FAIRY TAIL
U-UM... TH-THANK YOU VERY MUCH.
DON'T MENTION IT.
WHAT DID YOU DO?!
THE POOR GIRL'S TERRIFIED!
YOU KNOW, I *THINK* SHE WAS THANKING ME.

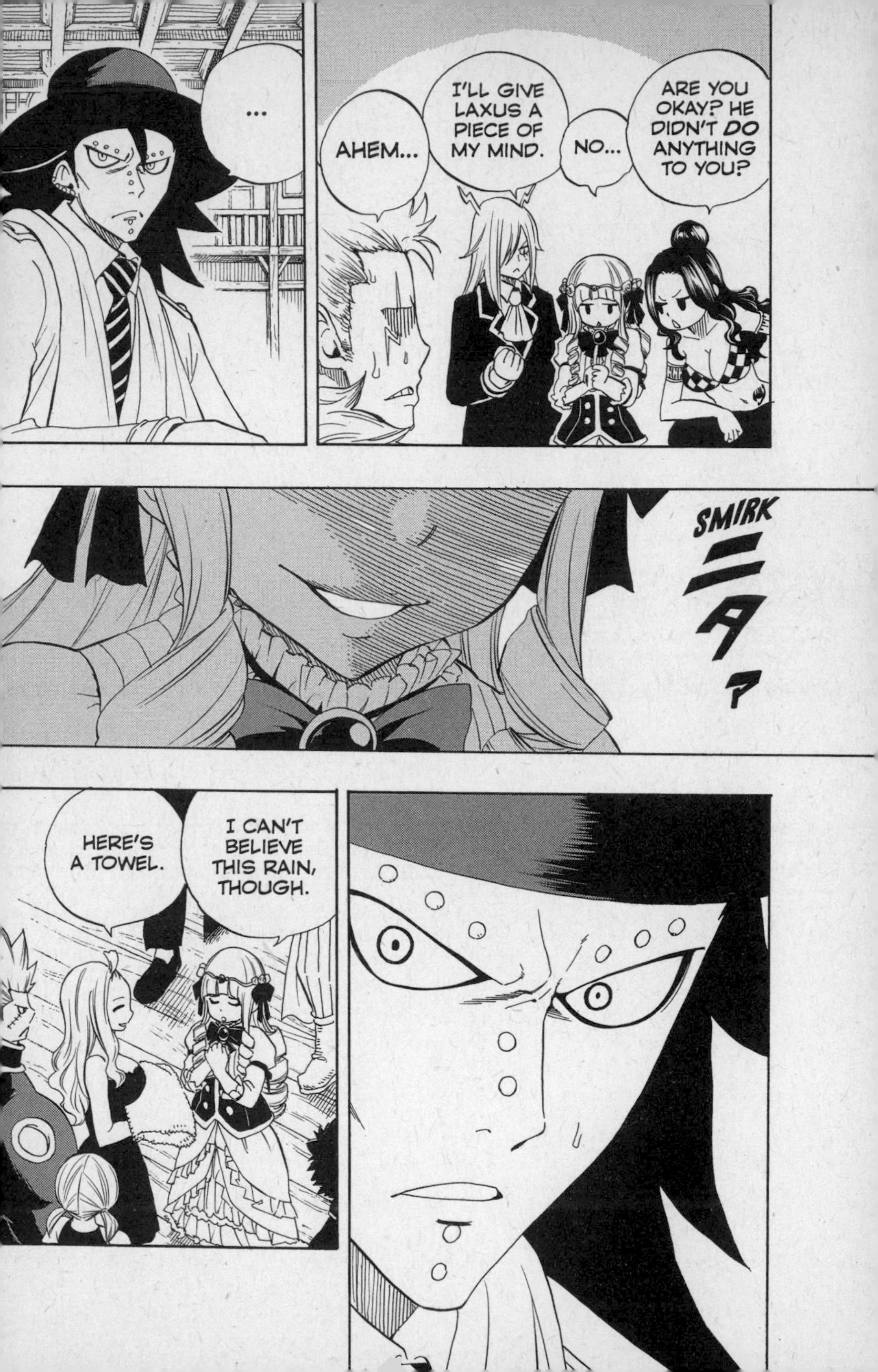
ARE YOU OKAY? HE DIDN'T *DO* ANYTHING TO YOU?
NO...
I'LL GIVE LAXUS A PIECE OF MY MIND.
AHEM...
...
SMIRK
ニタァ
I CAN'T BELIEVE THIS RAIN, THOUGH.
HERE'S A TOWEL.

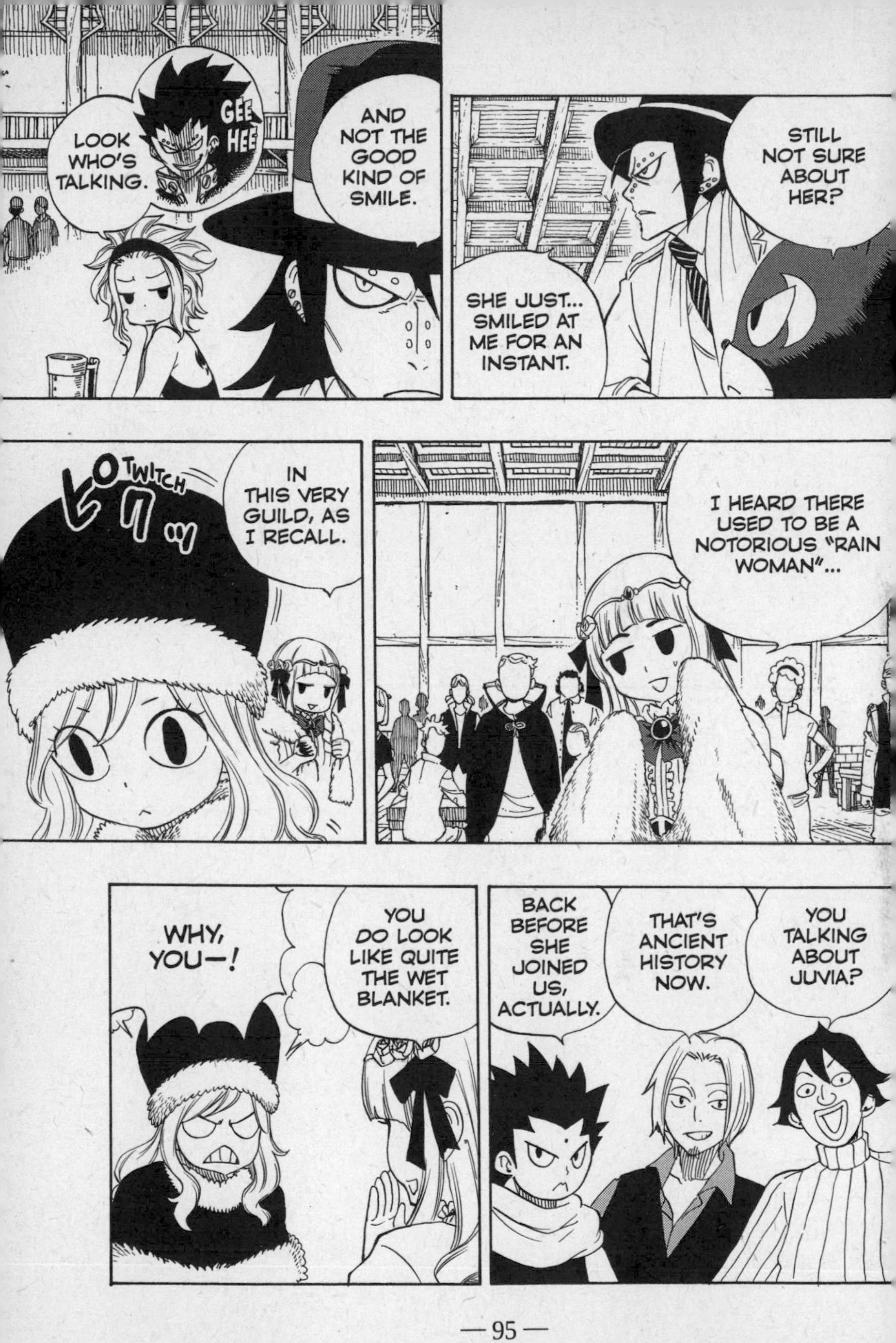
STILL NOT SURE ABOUT HER?
SHE JUST... SMILED AT ME FOR AN INSTANT.
AND NOT THE GOOD KIND OF SMILE.
LOOK WHO'S TALKING.
GEE HEE
I HEARD THERE USED TO BE A NOTORIOUS "RAIN WOMAN"...
IN THIS VERY GUILD, AS I RECALL.
TWITCH
YOU TALKING ABOUT JUVIA?
THAT'S ANCIENT HISTORY NOW.
BACK BEFORE SHE JOINED US, ACTUALLY.
YOU DO LOOK LIKE QUITE THE WET BLANKET.
WHY, YOU—!

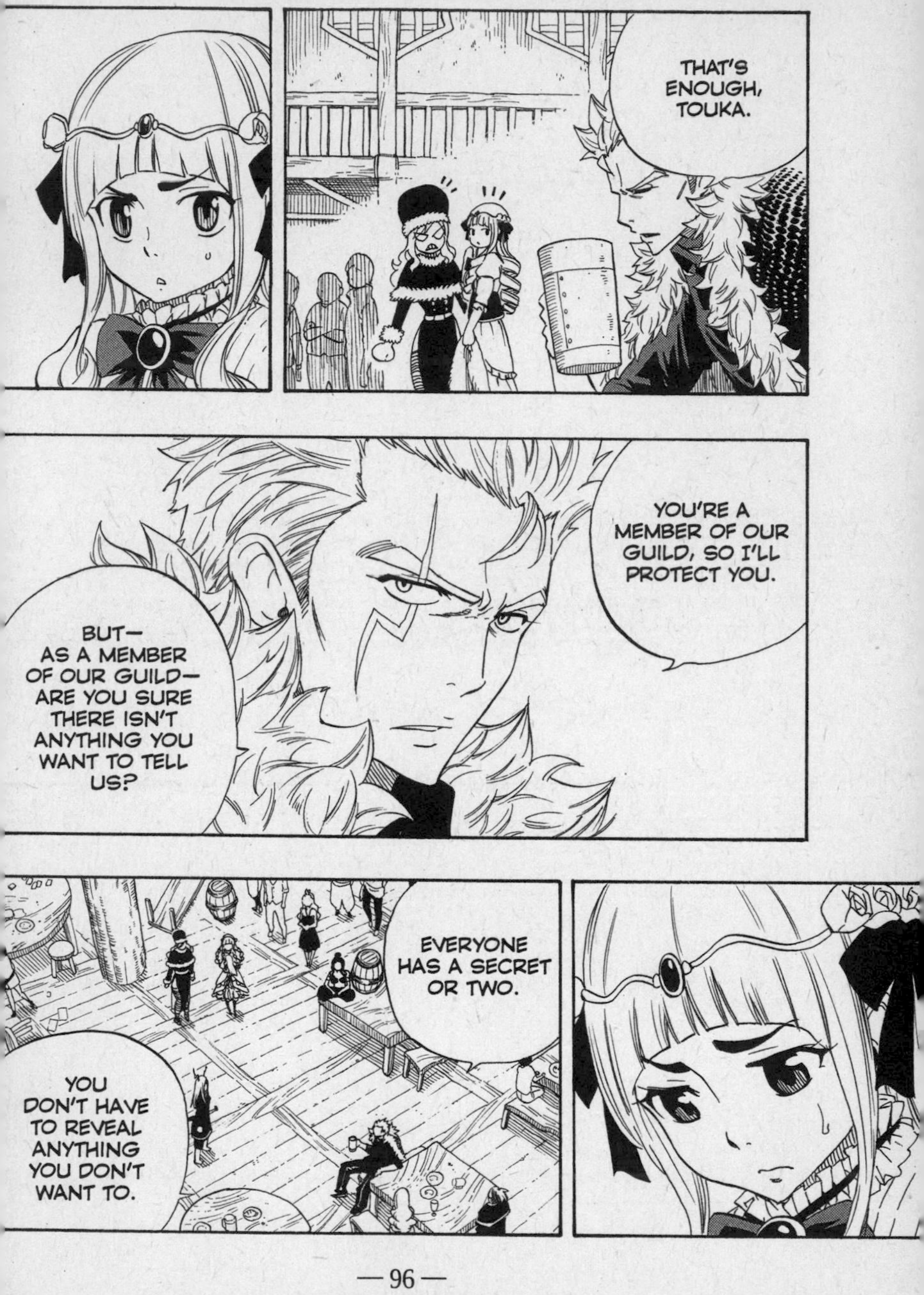
THAT'S ENOUGH, TOUKA.
YOU'RE A MEMBER OF OUR GUILD, SO I'LL PROTECT YOU.
BUT— AS A MEMBER OF OUR GUILD— ARE YOU SURE THERE ISN'T ANYTHING YOU WANT TO TELL US?
EVERYONE HAS A SECRET OR TWO.
YOU DON'T HAVE TO REVEAL ANYTHING YOU DON'T WANT TO.

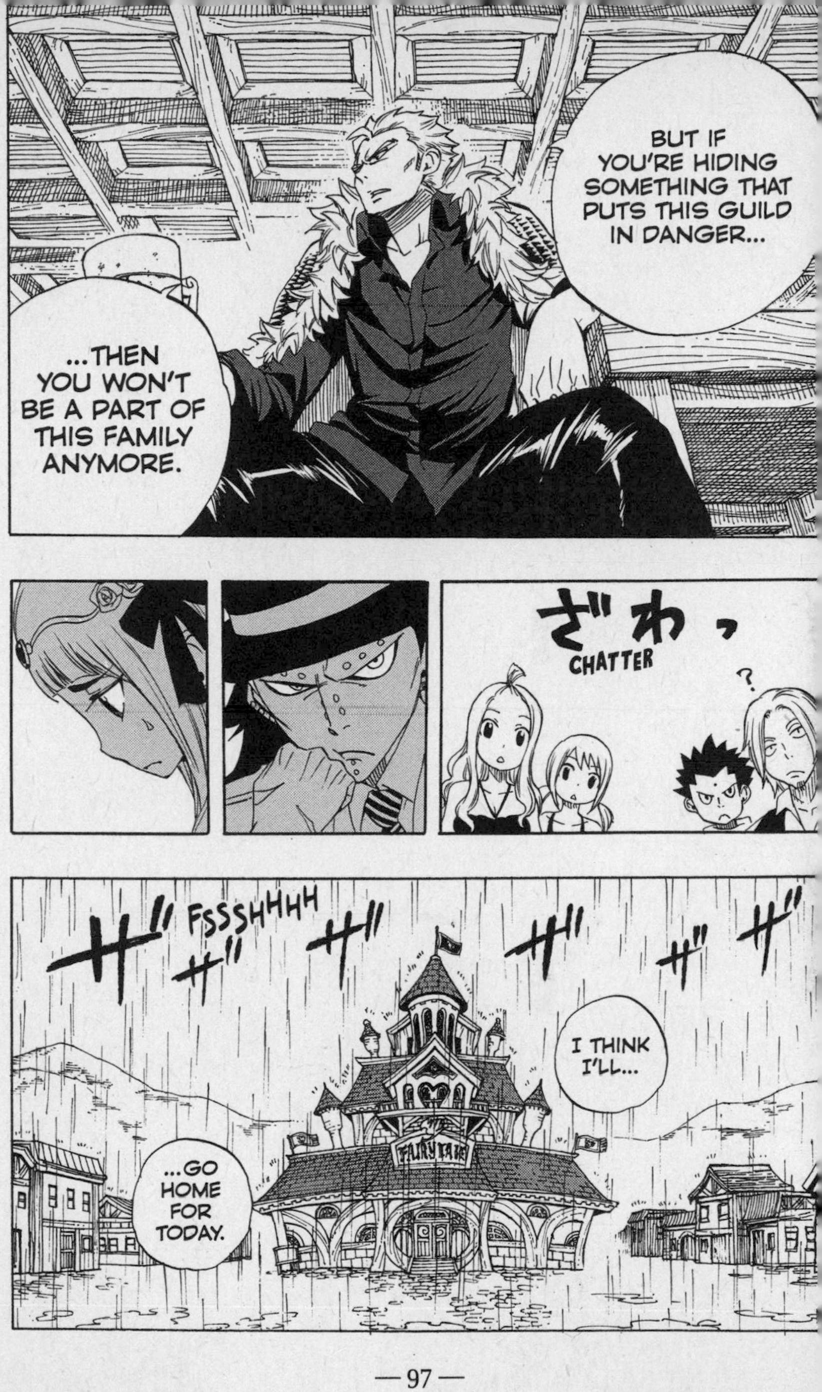
BUT IF YOU'RE HIDING SOMETHING THAT PUTS THIS GUILD IN DANGER...
...THEN YOU WON'T BE A PART OF THIS FAMILY ANYMORE.
ざわっ
CHATTER
?
ザ
FSSSHHHH
I THINK I'LL...
...GO HOME FOR TODAY.

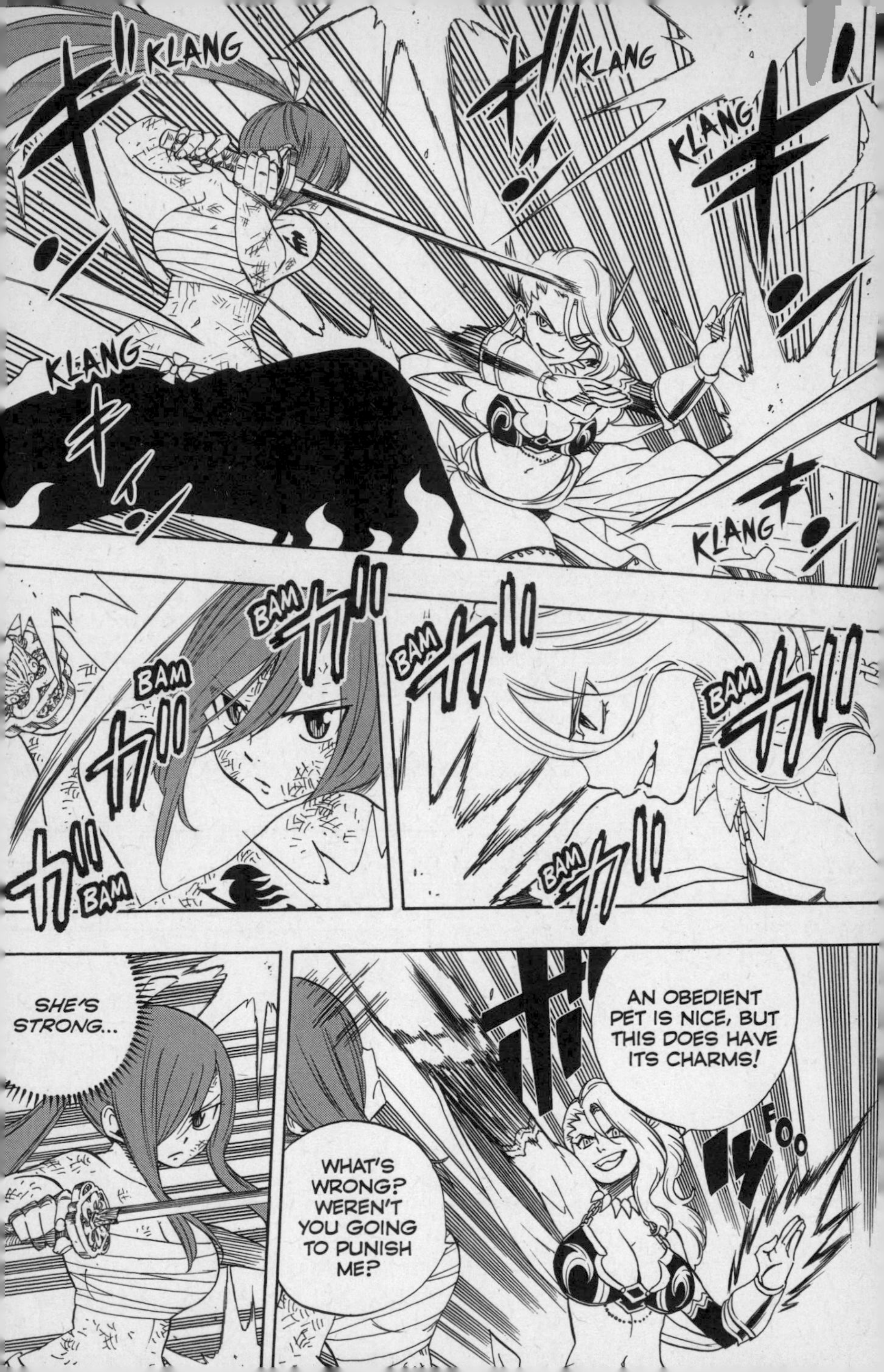
KLANG
KLANG
KLANG
KLANG
KLANG
KLANG
BAM
BAM
BAM
BAM
BAM
BAM
AN OBEDIENT PET IS NICE, BUT THIS DOES HAVE ITS CHARMS!
FOO
WHAT'S WRONG? WEREN'T YOU GOING TO PUNISH ME?
SHE'S STRONG...

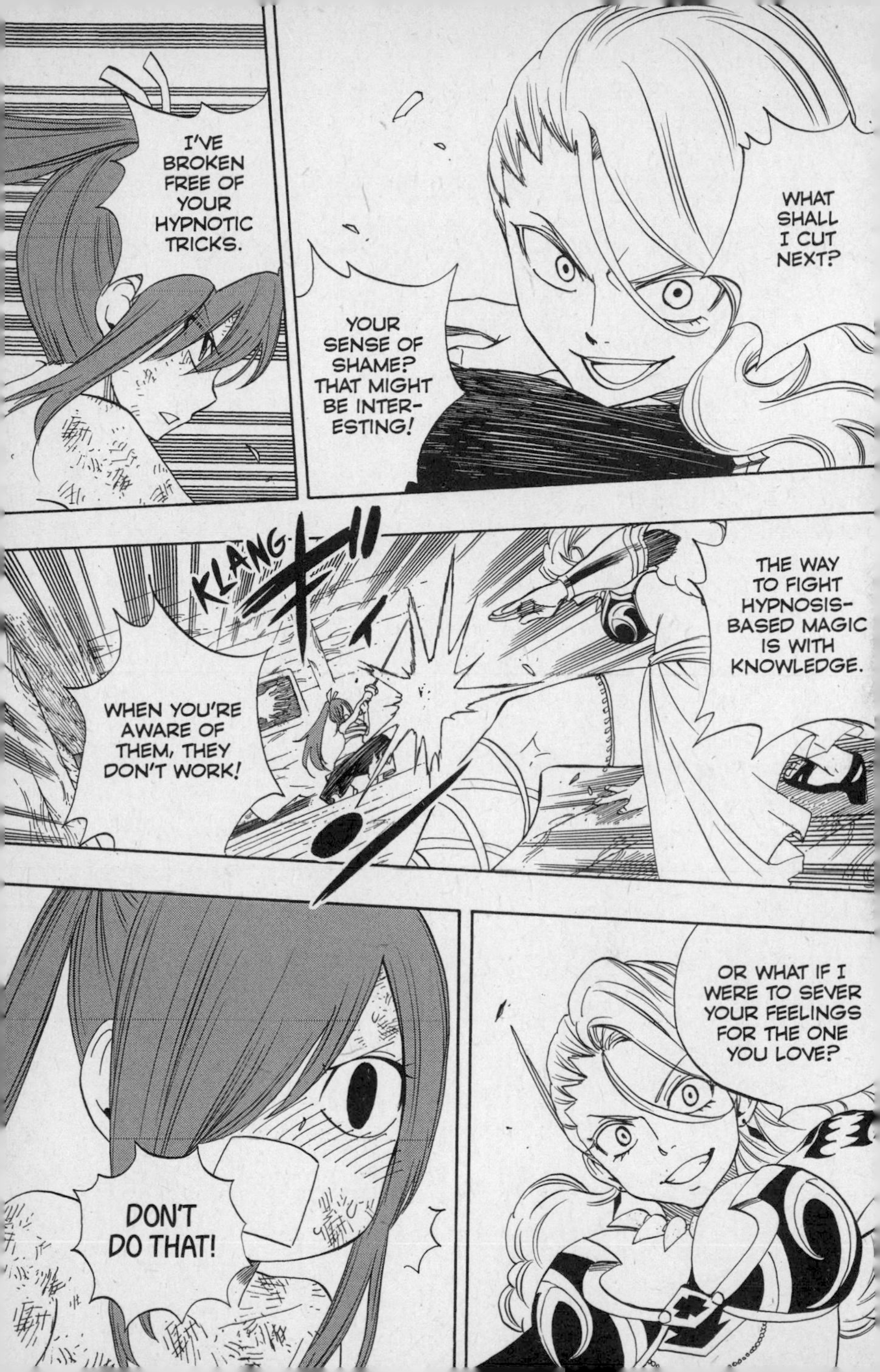
WHAT SHALL I CUT NEXT?
YOUR SENSE OF SHAME? THAT MIGHT BE INTER-ESTING!
I'VE BROKEN FREE OF YOUR HYPNOTIC TRICKS.
THE WAY TO FIGHT HYPNOSIS-BASED MAGIC IS WITH KNOWLEDGE.
KLANG
WHEN YOU'RE AWARE OF THEM, THEY DON'T WORK!
OR WHAT IF I WERE TO SEVER YOUR FEELINGS FOR THE ONE YOU LOVE?
DON'T DO THAT!

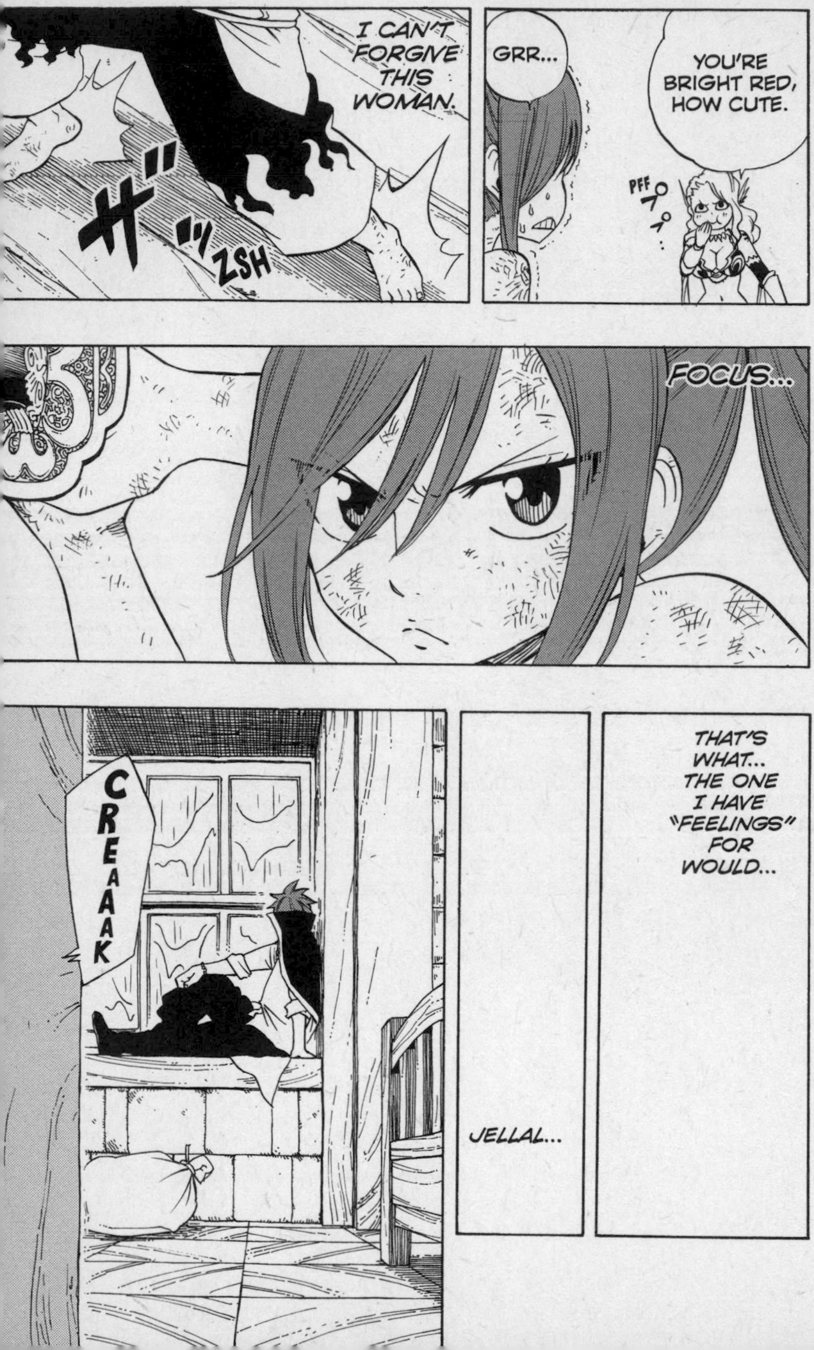
YOU'RE BRIGHT RED, HOW CUTE.
GRR...
PFF
I CAN'T FORGIVE THIS WOMAN.
ZSH
FOCUS...
THAT'S WHAT... THE ONE I HAVE "FEELINGS" FOR WOULD...
JELLAL...
CREAAAK

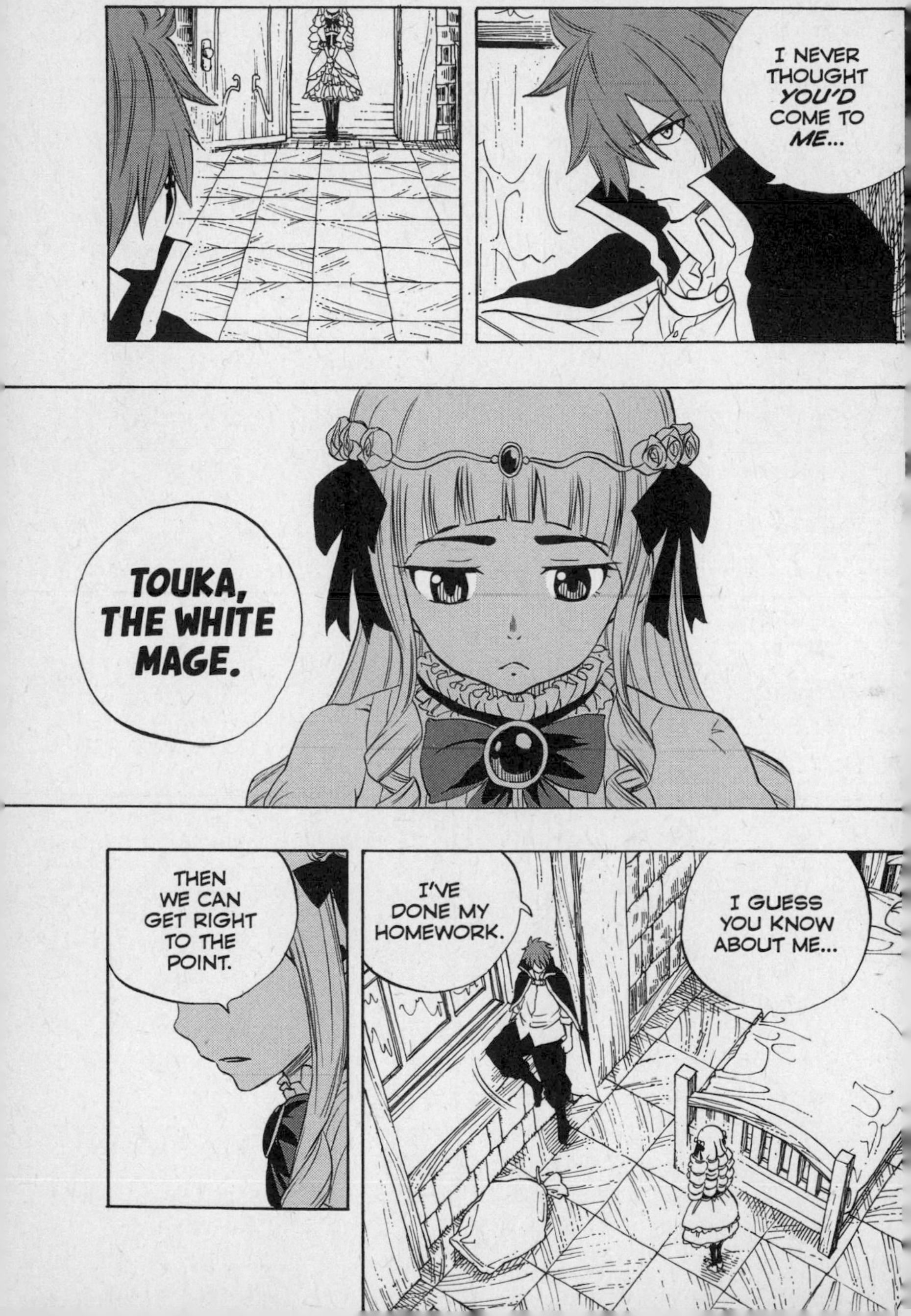
I NEVER THOUGHT *YOU'D* COME TO *ME*...
TOUKA, THE WHITE MAGE.
I GUESS YOU KNOW ABOUT ME...
I'VE DONE MY HOMEWORK.
THEN WE CAN GET RIGHT TO THE POINT.

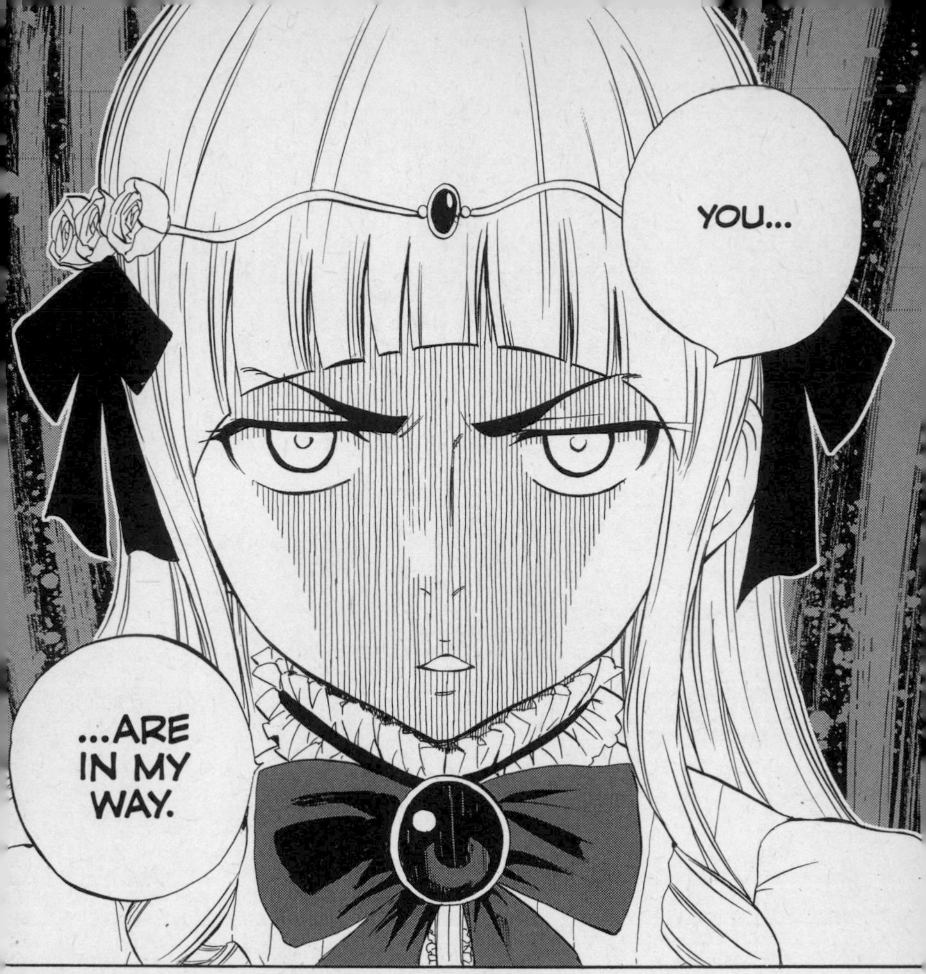
YOU...
...ARE IN MY WAY.
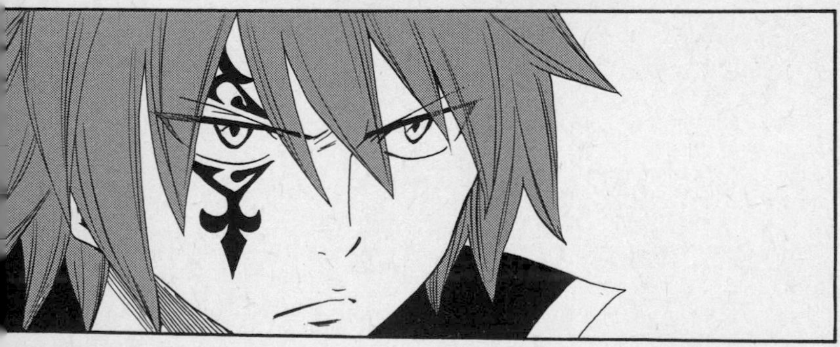

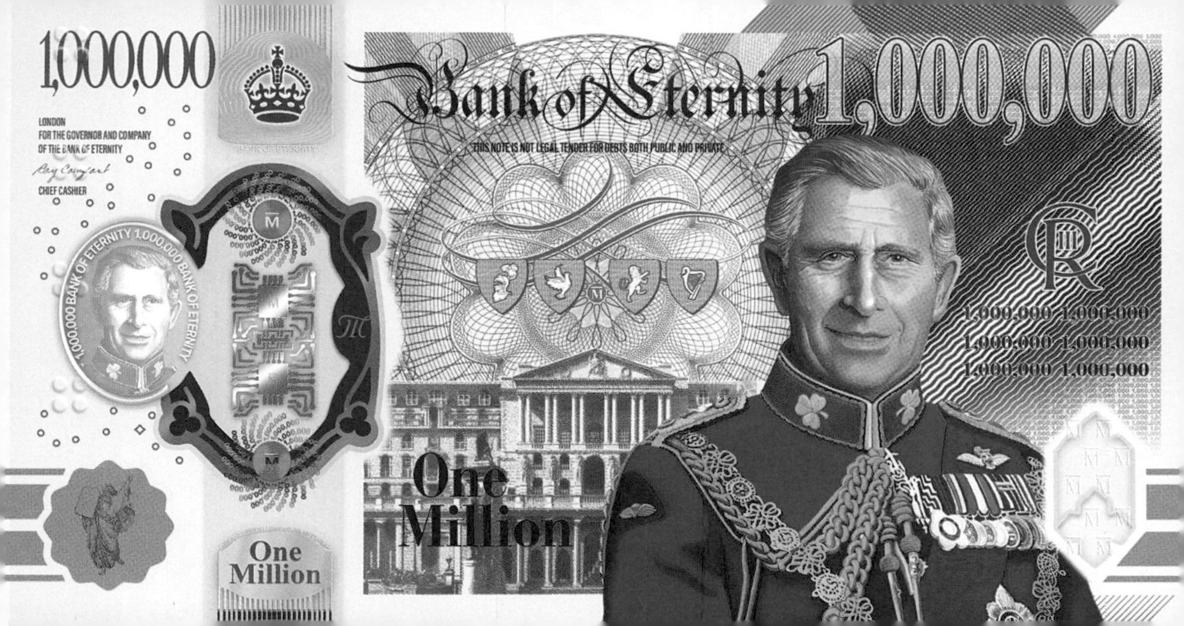
1,000,000
LONDON
FOR THE GOVERNOR AND COMPANY
OF THE BANK OF ETERNITY
CHIEF CASHIER
1,000,000 BANK OF ETERNITY 1,000,000 BANK OF ETERNITY
One
Million
Bank of Eternity
1,000,000
THIS NOTE IS NOT LEGAL TENDER FOR DEBTS BOTH PUBLIC AND PRIVATE
1,000,000 1,000,000
1,000,000 1,000,000
1,000,000 1,000,000
One
Million

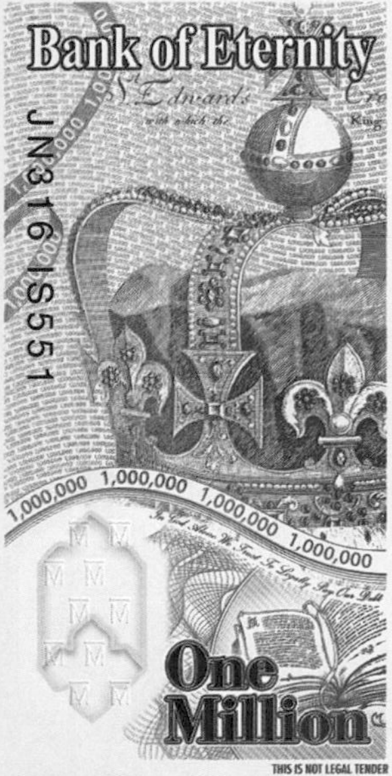
Bank of Eternity
JN316 IS551
1,000,000
One Million
THIS IS NOT LEGAL TENDER

During the coronation, King Charles honours the Bible—in which God promised to destroy death. To understand how He destroyed death, answer these questions: Have you ever lied, stolen, or used God's name in vain? Jesus said, "Whoever looks at a woman to lust for her has already committed adultery with her in his heart." If you have done these things, God sees you as a lying, thieving, blasphemous adulterer at heart, and He will punish you in a terrible place called Hell. But He is not willing that any should perish. Sinners broke God's Law but here's the gospel (good news)—Jesus paid their fine. This means their case can be dismissed: "God so loved the world that He gave His only begotten Son, that whoever believes in Him should not perish but have everlasting life." Then Jesus rose from the dead, defeating death. Today, repent and trust Jesus, and God will give you eternal life. Then read the Bible daily and obey it. God will never fail you. Don't miss the Living Waters podcast and YouTube channel (over 200,000,000 views). LivingWaters.com

1,000,000

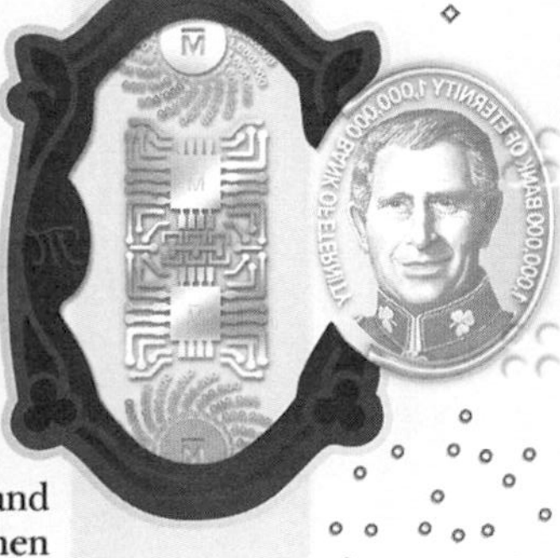
1,000,000 BANK OF ETERNITY

JN316 IS551

FAIRY TAIL 100 YEARS QUEST

Chapter 15: Dyed White

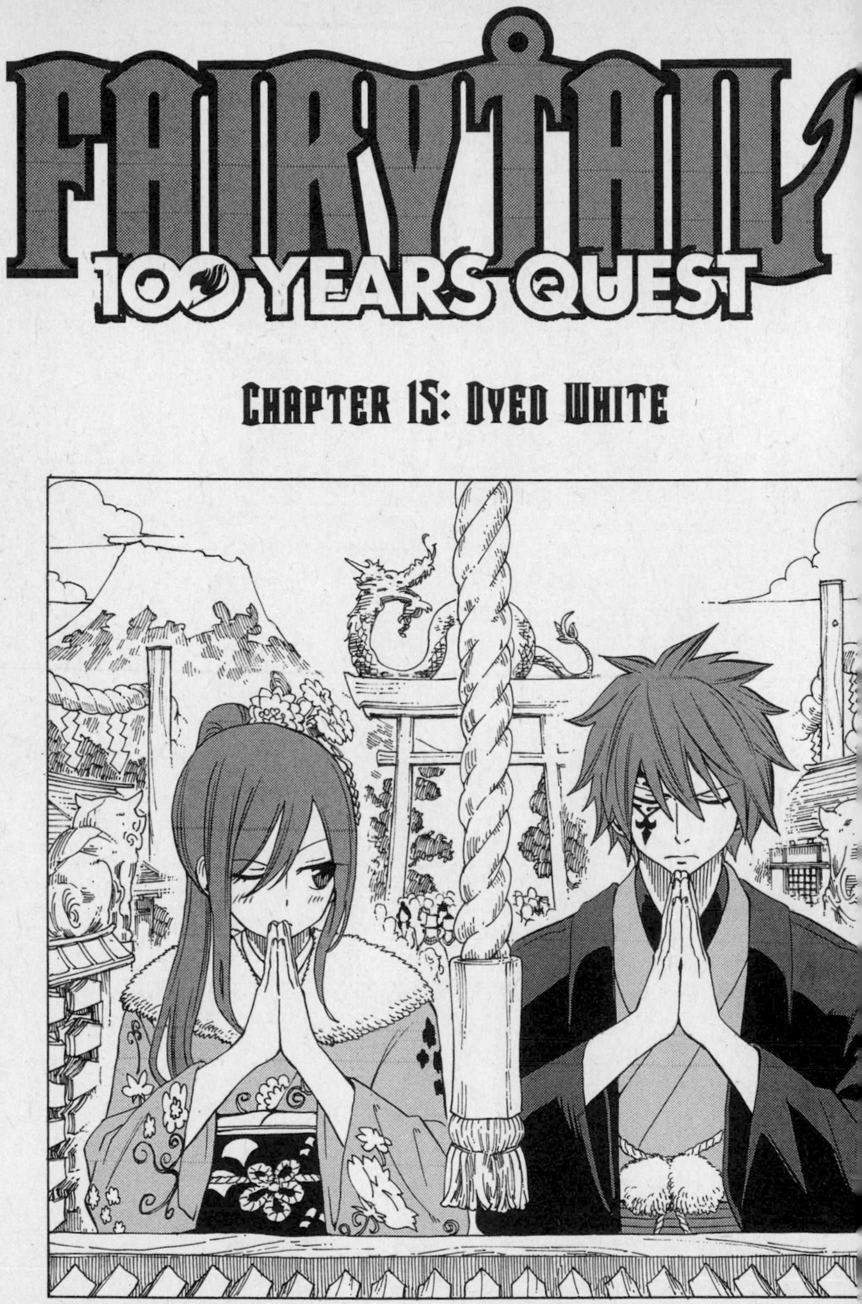

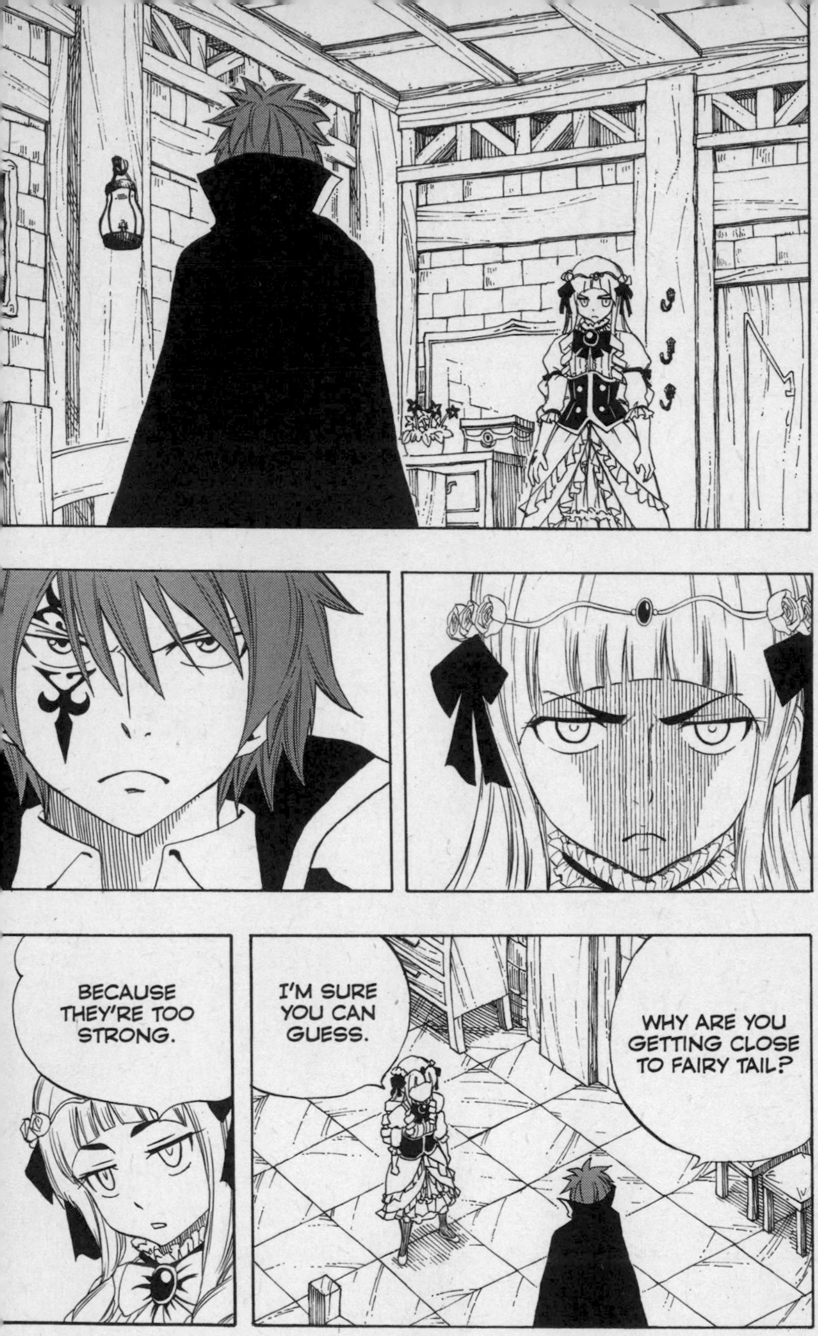
WHY ARE YOU GETTING CLOSE TO FAIRY TAIL?
I'M SURE YOU CAN GUESS.
BECAUSE THEY'RE TOO STRONG.

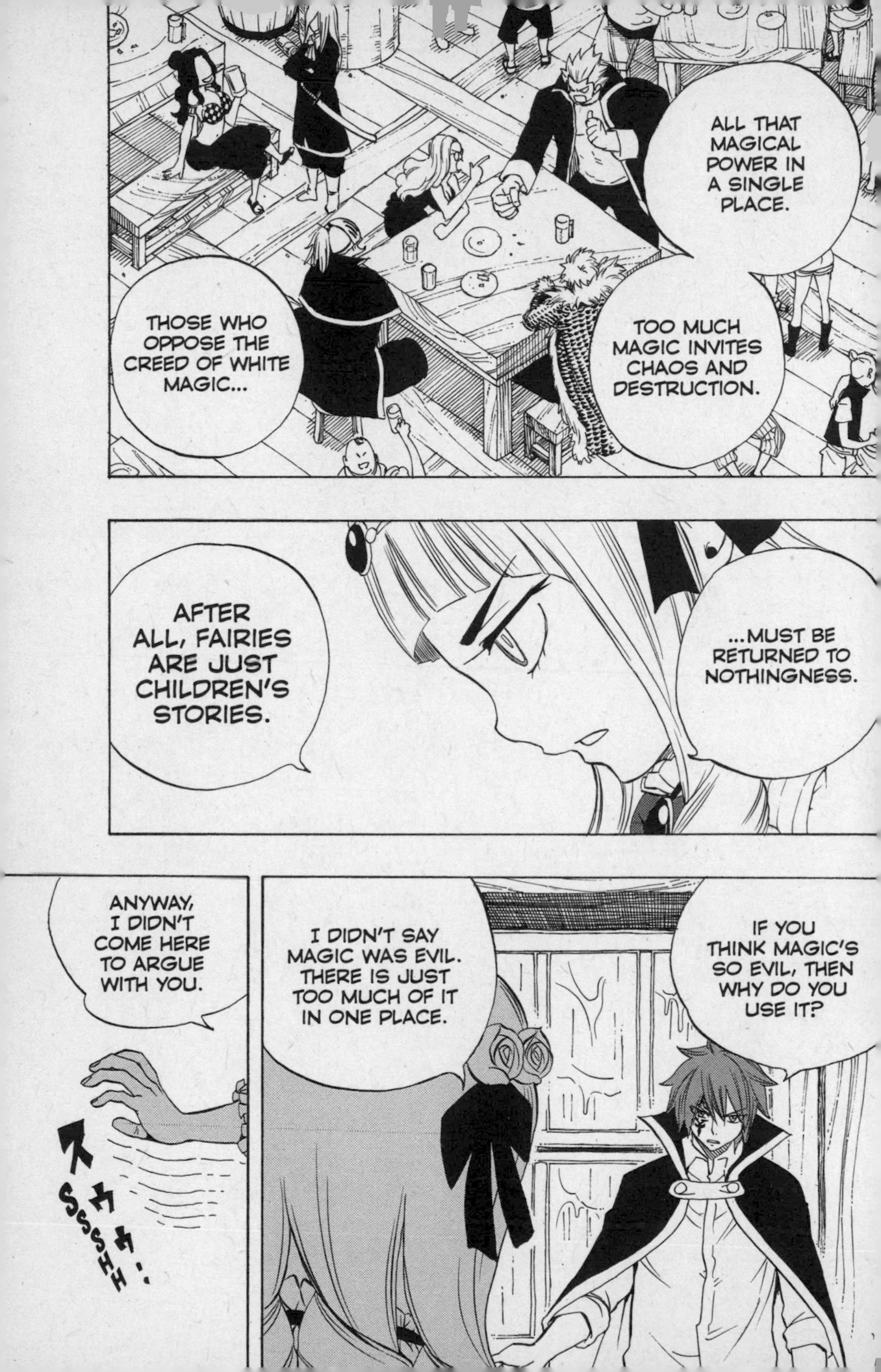
ALL THAT MAGICAL POWER IN A SINGLE PLACE.
TOO MUCH MAGIC INVITES CHAOS AND DESTRUCTION.
THOSE WHO OPPOSE THE CREED OF WHITE MAGIC...
...MUST BE RETURNED TO NOTHINGNESS.
AFTER ALL, FAIRIES ARE JUST CHILDREN'S STORIES.
IF YOU THINK MAGIC'S SO EVIL, THEN WHY DO YOU USE IT?
I DIDN'T SAY MAGIC WAS EVIL. THERE IS JUST TOO MUCH OF IT IN ONE PLACE.
ANYWAY, I DIDN'T COME HERE TO ARGUE WITH YOU.
SSSHH

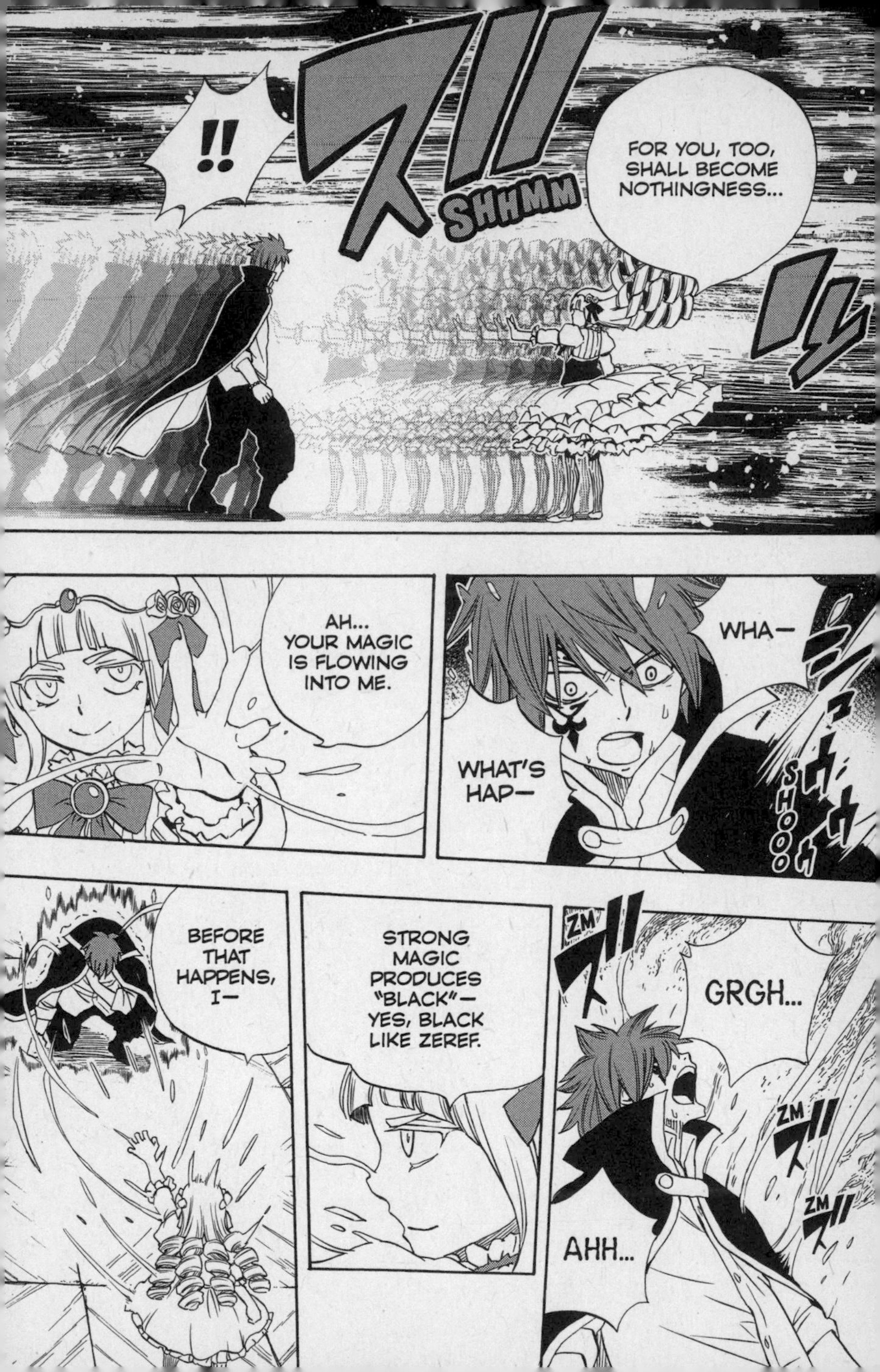
FOR YOU, TOO, SHALL BECOME NOTHINGNESS...
SHHMM
!!
WHA—
WHAT'S HAP—
SHOOO
AH... YOUR MAGIC IS FLOWING INTO ME.
ZM
GRGH...
ZM
ZM
AHH...
STRONG MAGIC PRODUCES "BLACK"— YES, BLACK LIKE ZEREF.
BEFORE THAT HAPPENS, I—

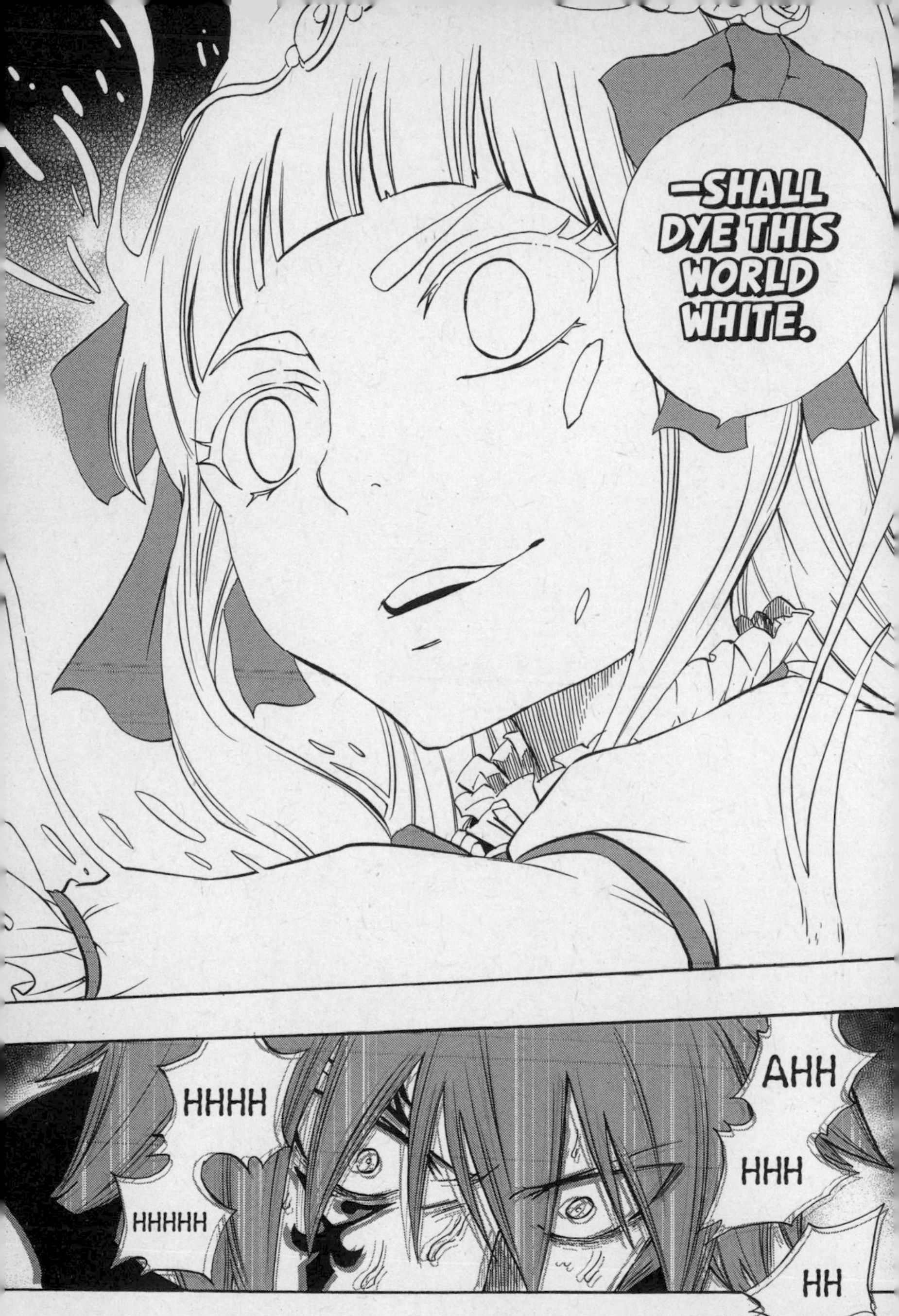
–SHALL DYE THIS WORLD WHITE.
AHH
HHH
HH
HHHH
HHHHH

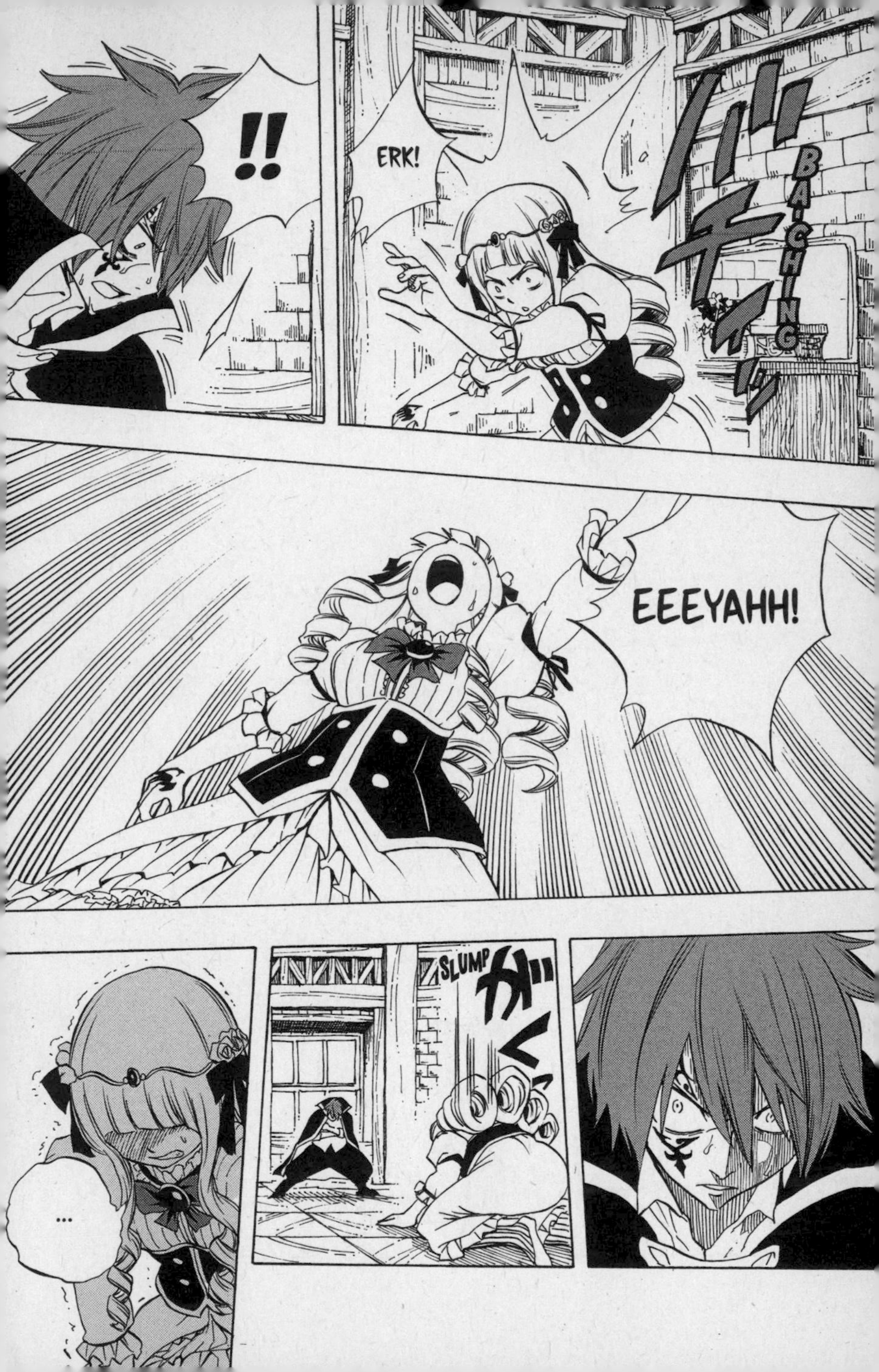
BAICHING
ERK!
!!
EEEYAHH!
SLUMP
...

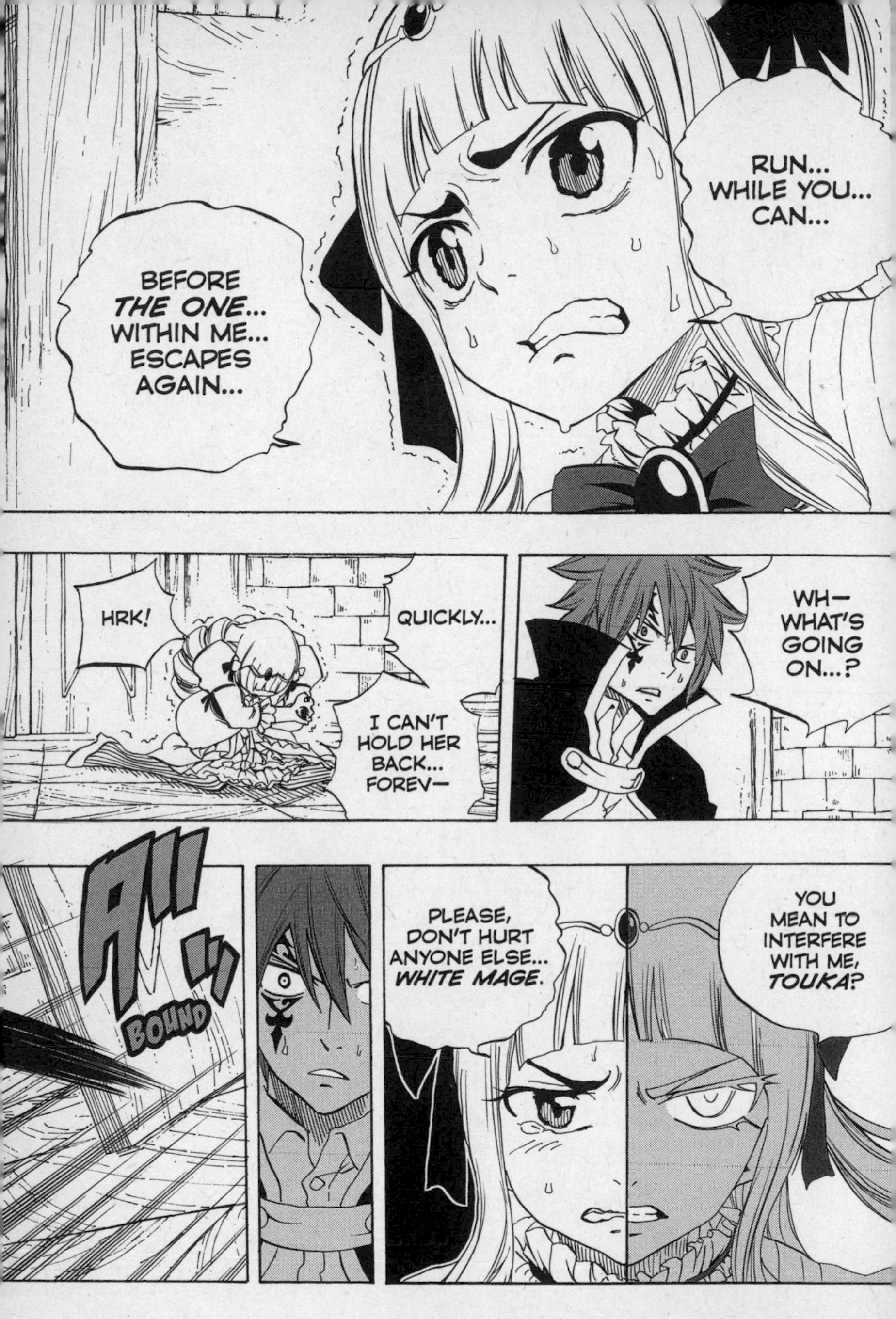
RUN... WHILE YOU... CAN...
BEFORE *THE ONE*... WITHIN ME... ESCAPES AGAIN...
WH— WHAT'S GOING ON...?
QUICKLY...
HRK!
I CAN'T HOLD HER BACK... FOREV—
YOU MEAN TO INTERFERE WITH ME, *TOUKA*?
PLEASE, DON'T HURT ANYONE ELSE... *WHITE MAGE*.
BOUND

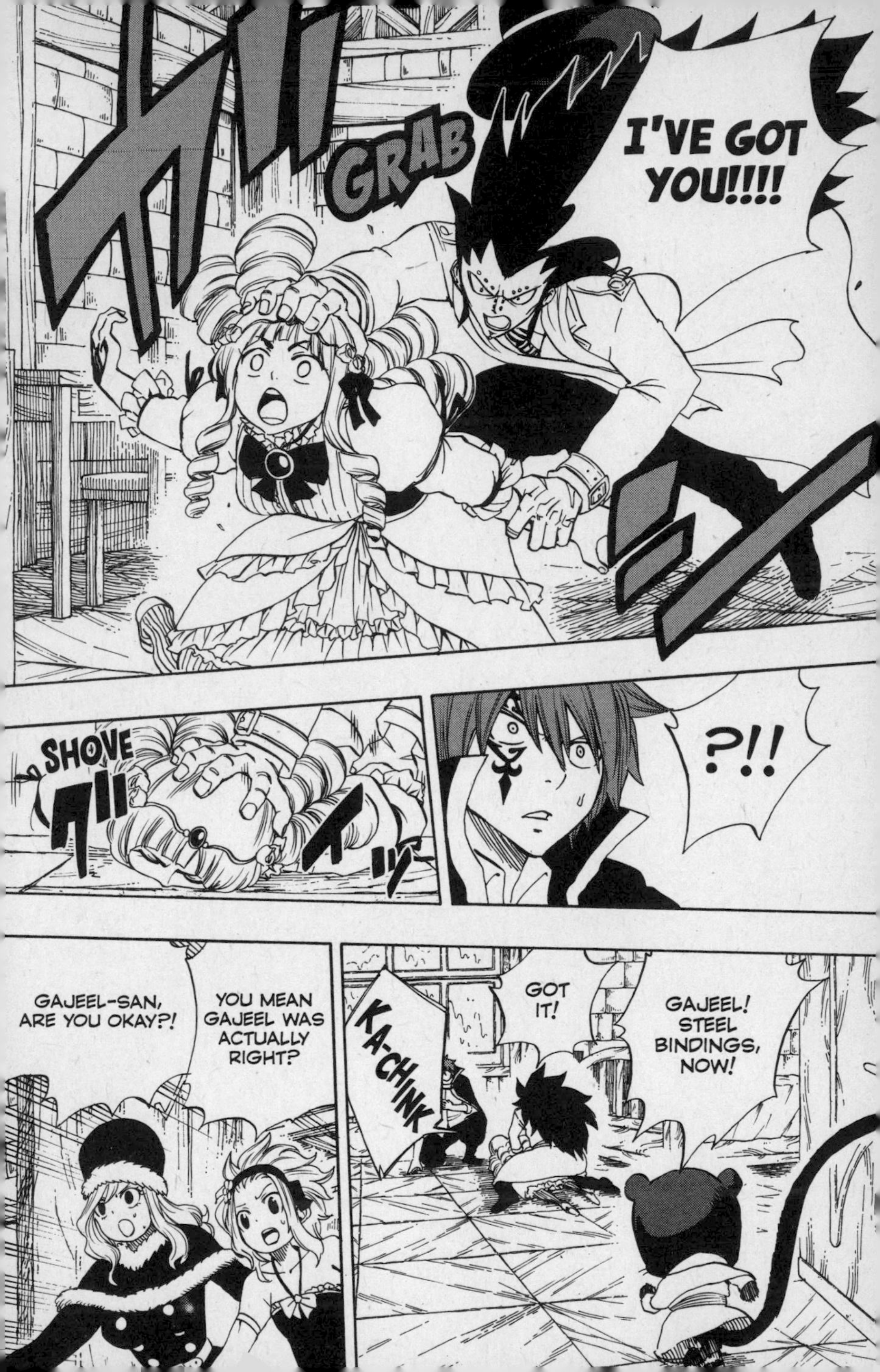
I'VE GOT YOU!!!!
GRAB
?!!
SHOVE
GAJEEL! STEEL BINDINGS, NOW!
GOT IT!
KA-CHINK
YOU MEAN GAJEEL WAS ACTUALLY RIGHT?
GAJEEL-SAN, ARE YOU OKAY?!

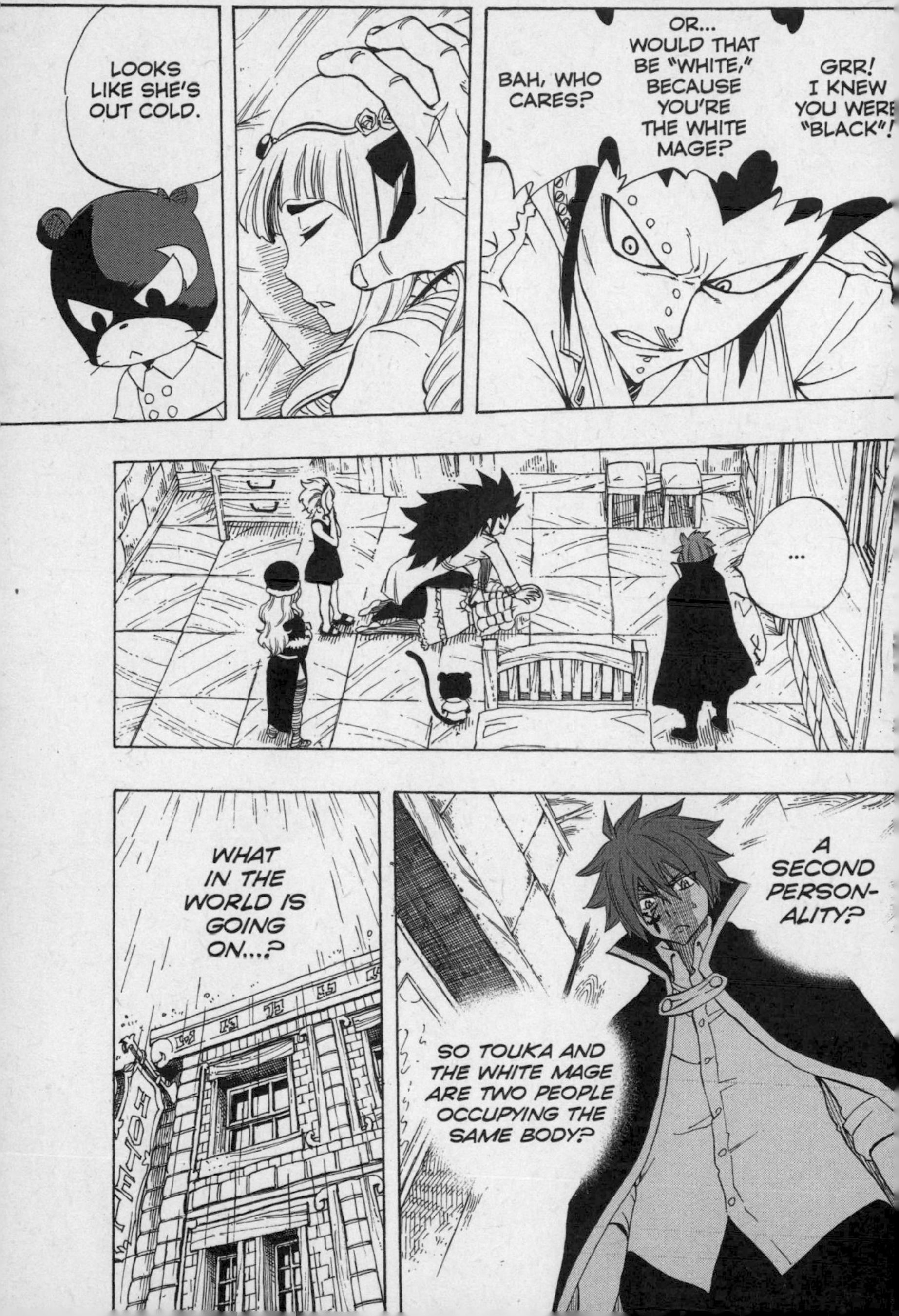
GRR! I KNEW YOU WERE "BLACK"!
OR... WOULD THAT BE "WHITE," BECAUSE YOU'RE THE WHITE MAGE?
BAH, WHO CARES?
LOOKS LIKE SHE'S OUT COLD.
...
A SECOND PERSON-ALITY?
SO TOUKA AND THE WHITE MAGE ARE TWO PEOPLE OCCUPYING THE SAME BODY?
WHAT IN THE WORLD IS GOING ON...?

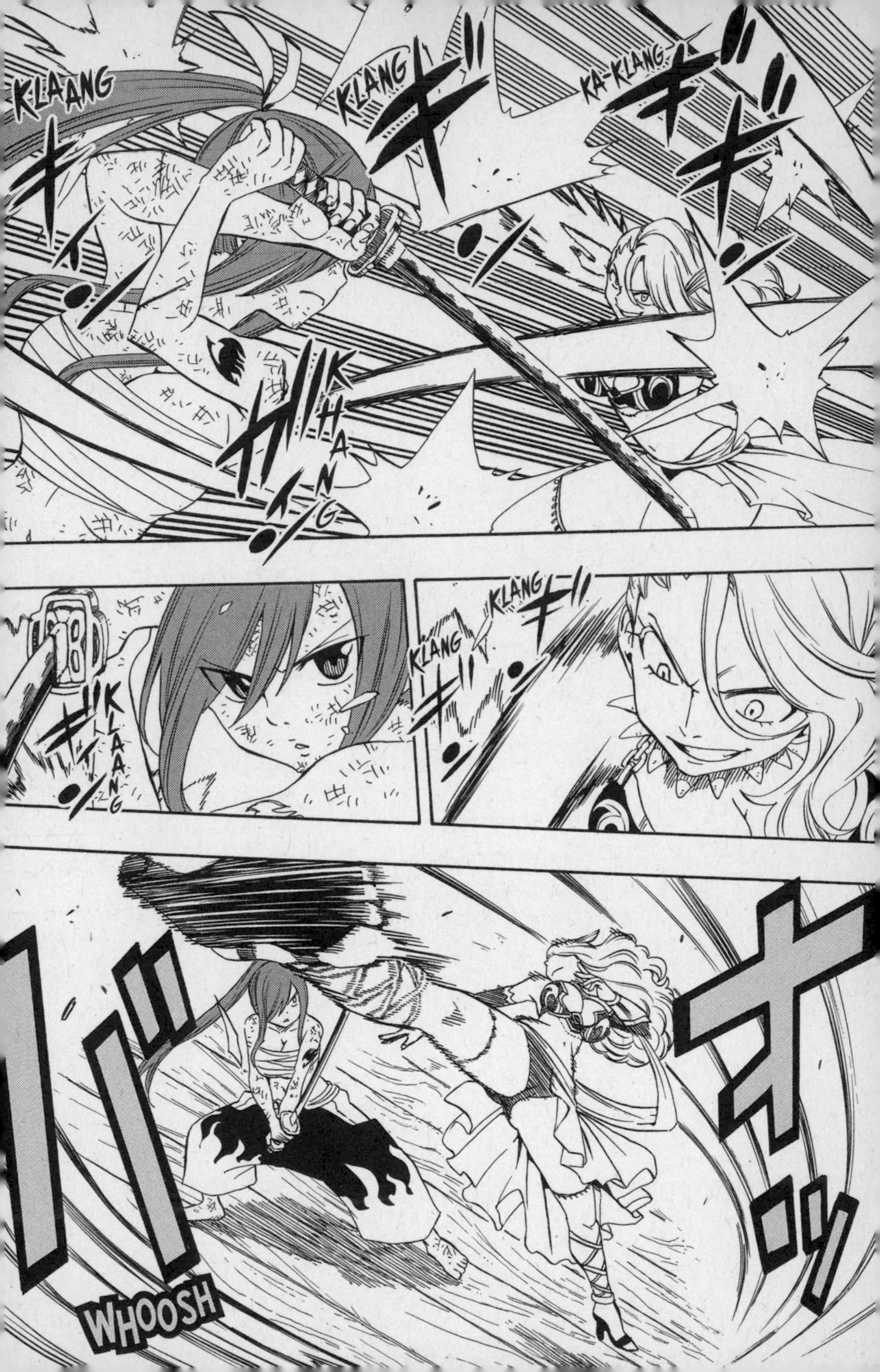
KA-KLANG
KLANG
KLAANG
KHANG
KLANG
KLANG
KLAANG
WHOOSH

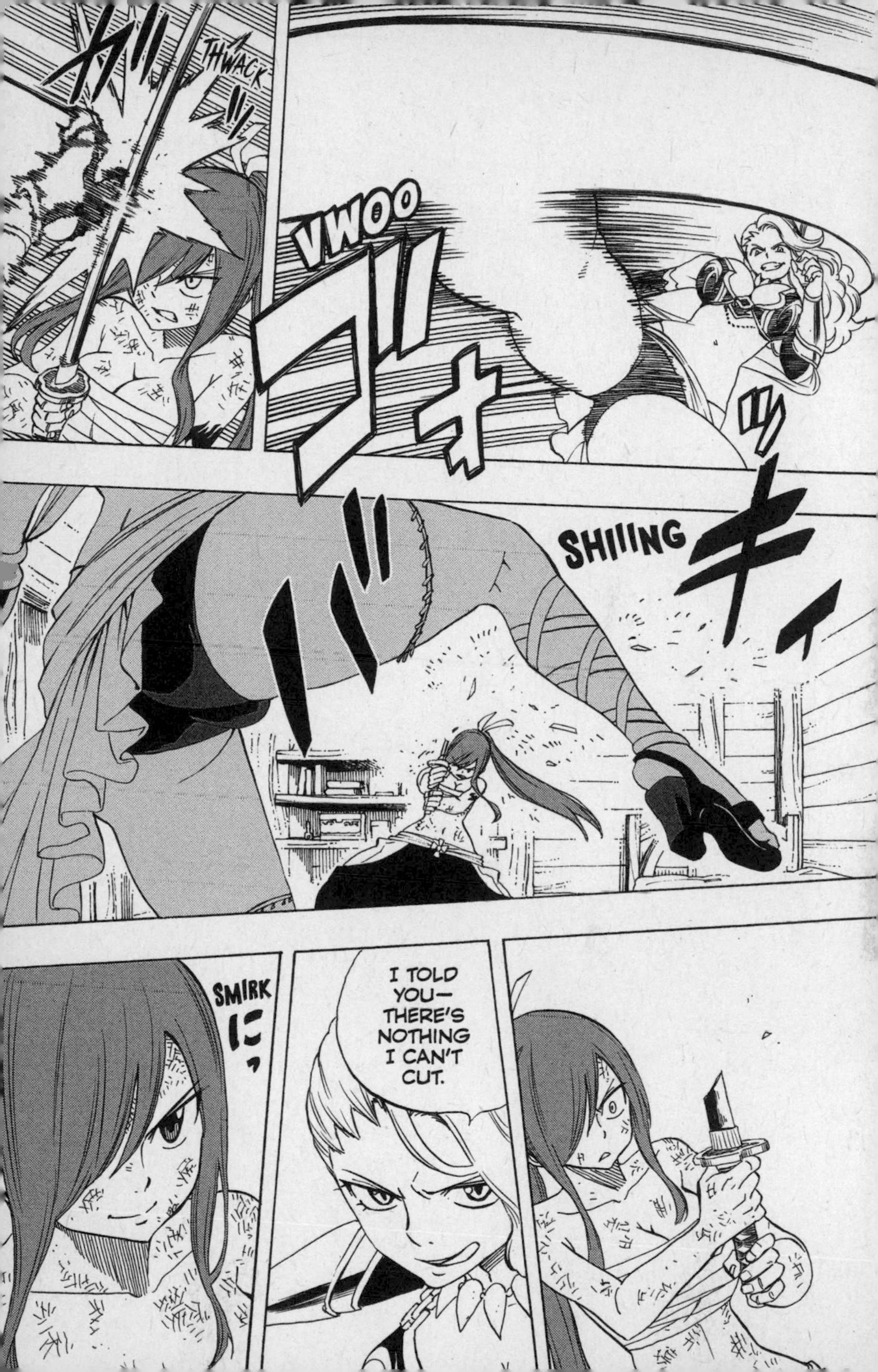
VWOO
THWACK
SHIIING
I TOLD YOU— THERE'S NOTHING I CAN'T CUT.
SMIRK

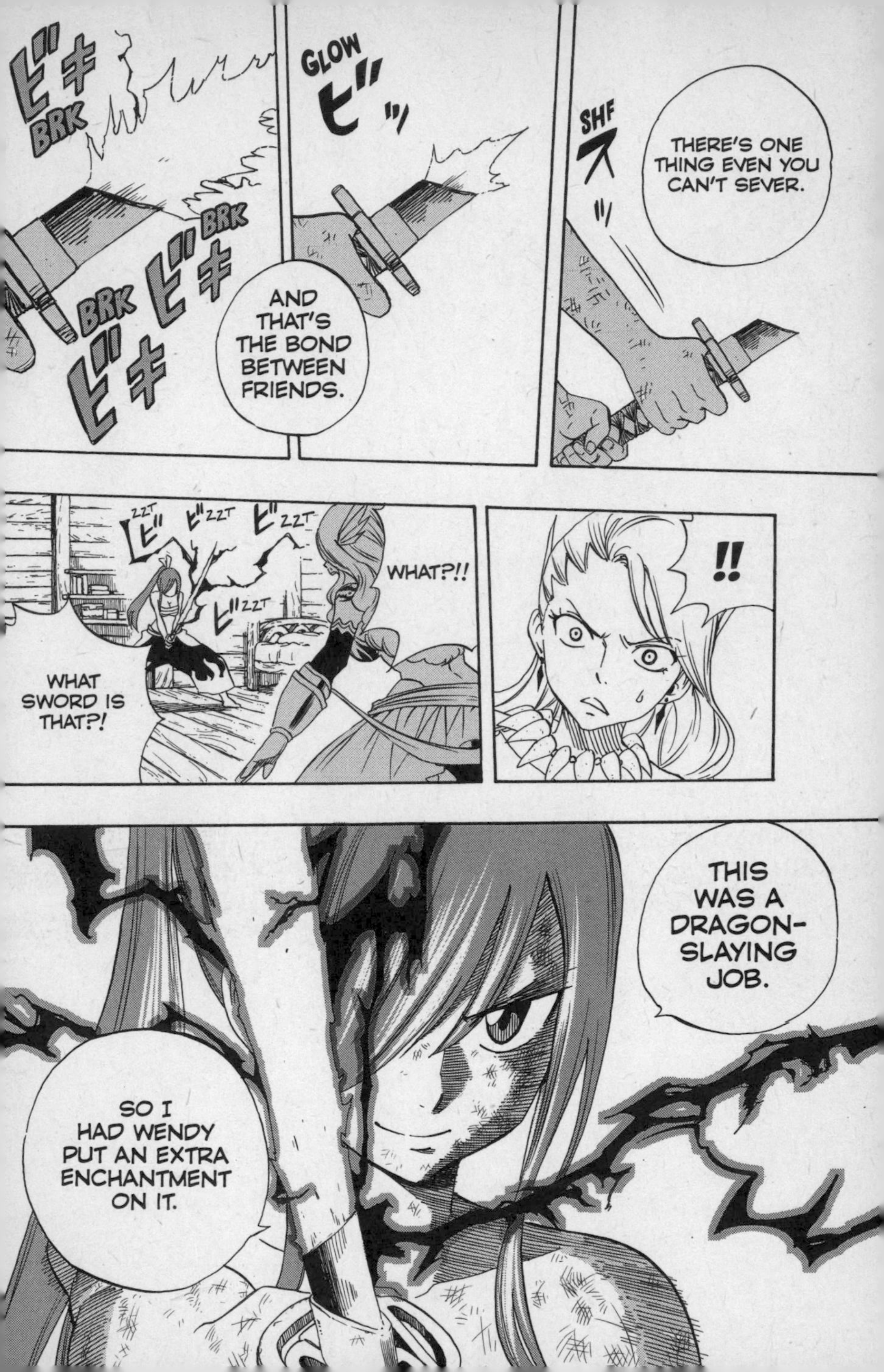
SHF
ス
THERE'S ONE THING EVEN YOU CAN'T SEVER.
GLOW
ビッ
AND THAT'S THE BOND BETWEEN FRIENDS.
ビキ
BRK
BRK
ビキ
BRK
ビキ
!!
ZZT
ビ
ZZT
ビ
ZZT
ビ
WHAT?!!
ビ
ZZT
WHAT SWORD IS THAT?!
THIS WAS A DRAGON-SLAYING JOB.
SO I HAD WENDY PUT AN EXTRA ENCHANTMENT ON IT.

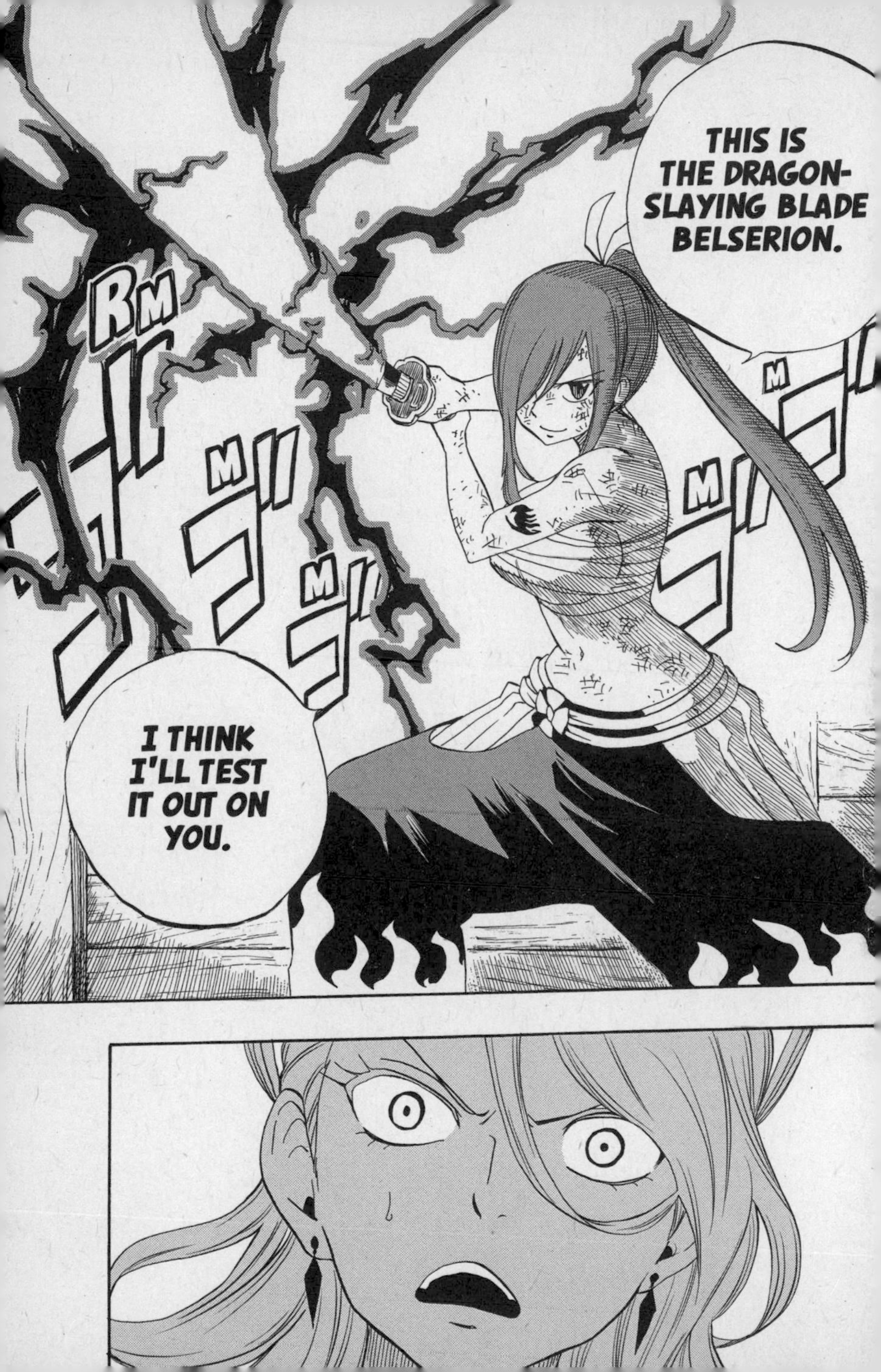
THIS IS THE DRAGON-SLAYING BLADE BELSERION.
M
M
M
M
RM
I THINK I'LL TEST IT OUT ON YOU.

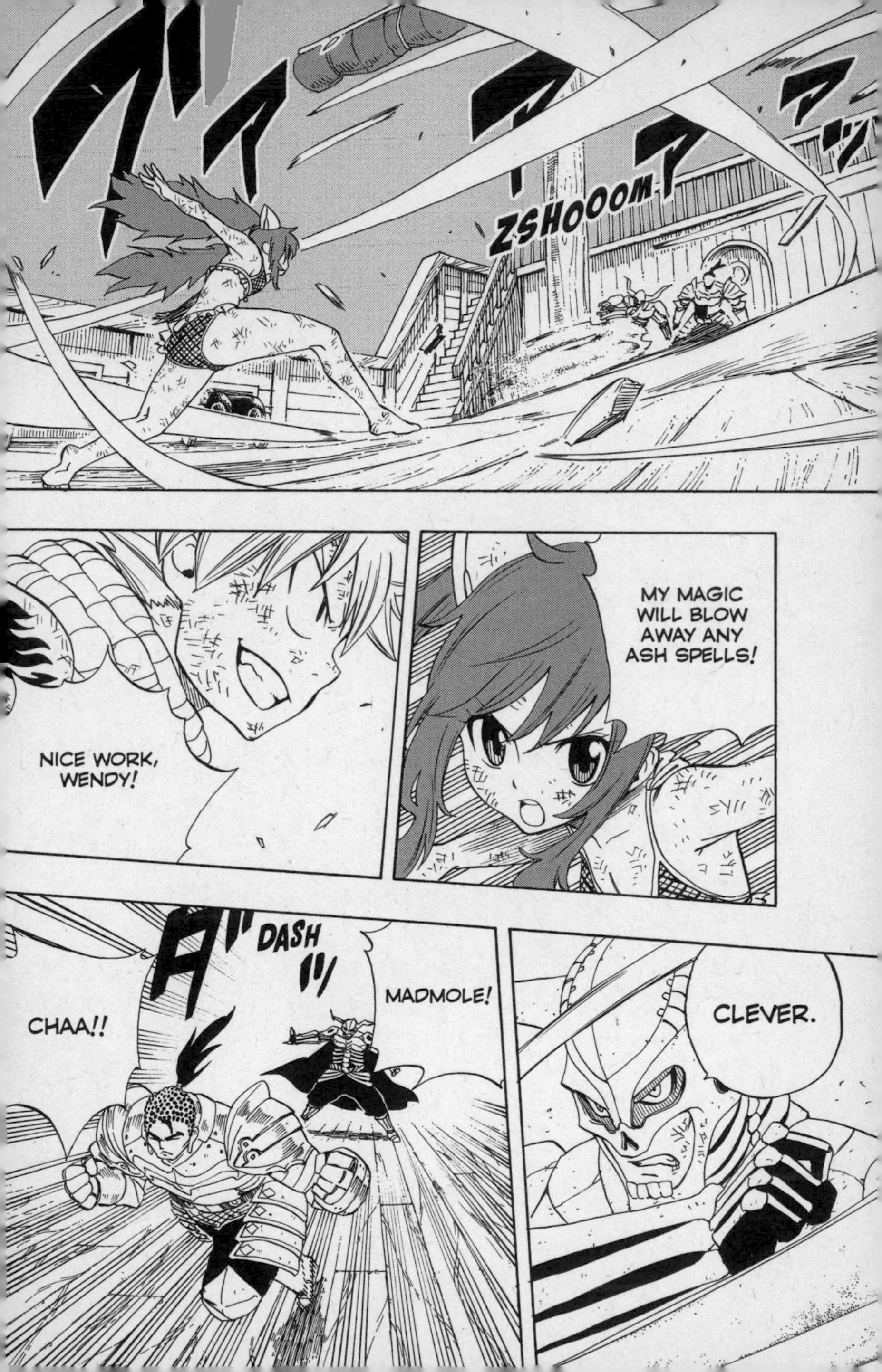
ZSHOOOM
MY MAGIC WILL BLOW AWAY ANY ASH SPELLS!
NICE WORK, WENDY!
CLEVER.
DASH
MADMOLE!
CHAA!!

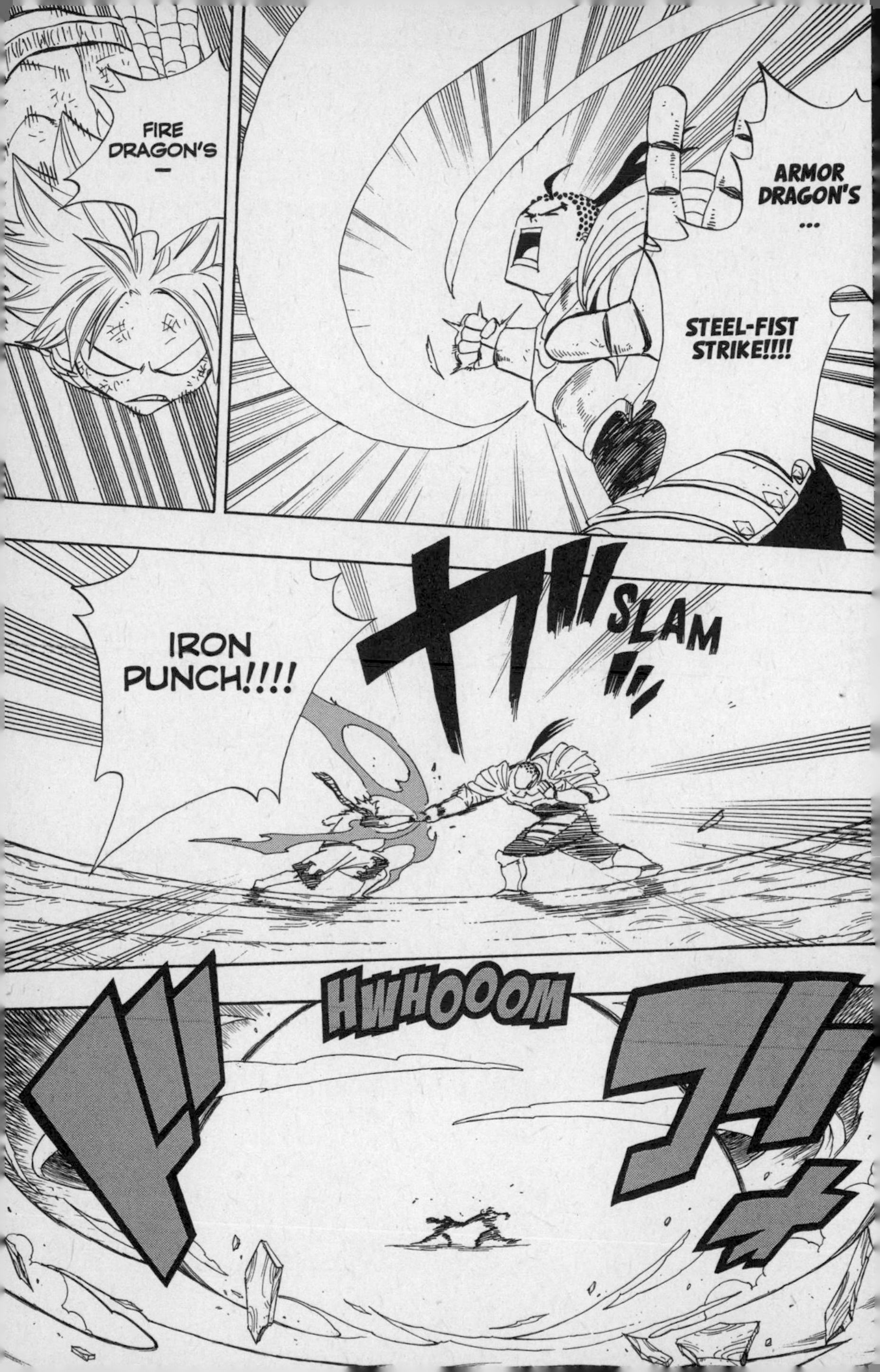
ARMOR DRAGON'S ...
STEEL-FIST STRIKE!!!!
FIRE DRAGON'S —
SLAM
IRON PUNCH!!!!
HWHOOOM

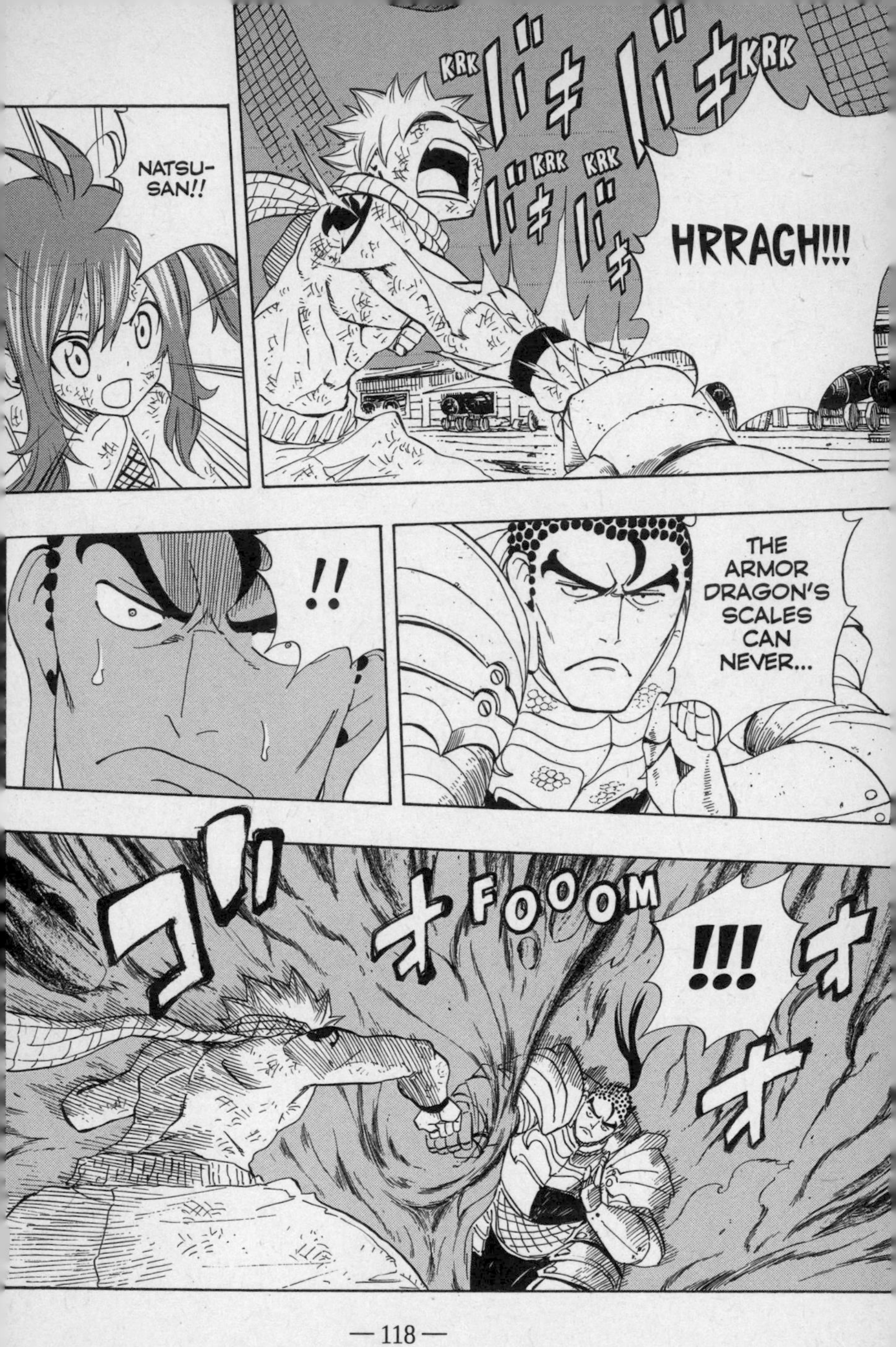
KRK
バキ
KRK
バキ
KRK
バキ
KRK
バキ
HRRAGH!!!
NATSU-SAN!!
THE ARMOR DRAGON'S SCALES CAN NEVER...
!!
ゴオ
FOOOM
!!!
オオ

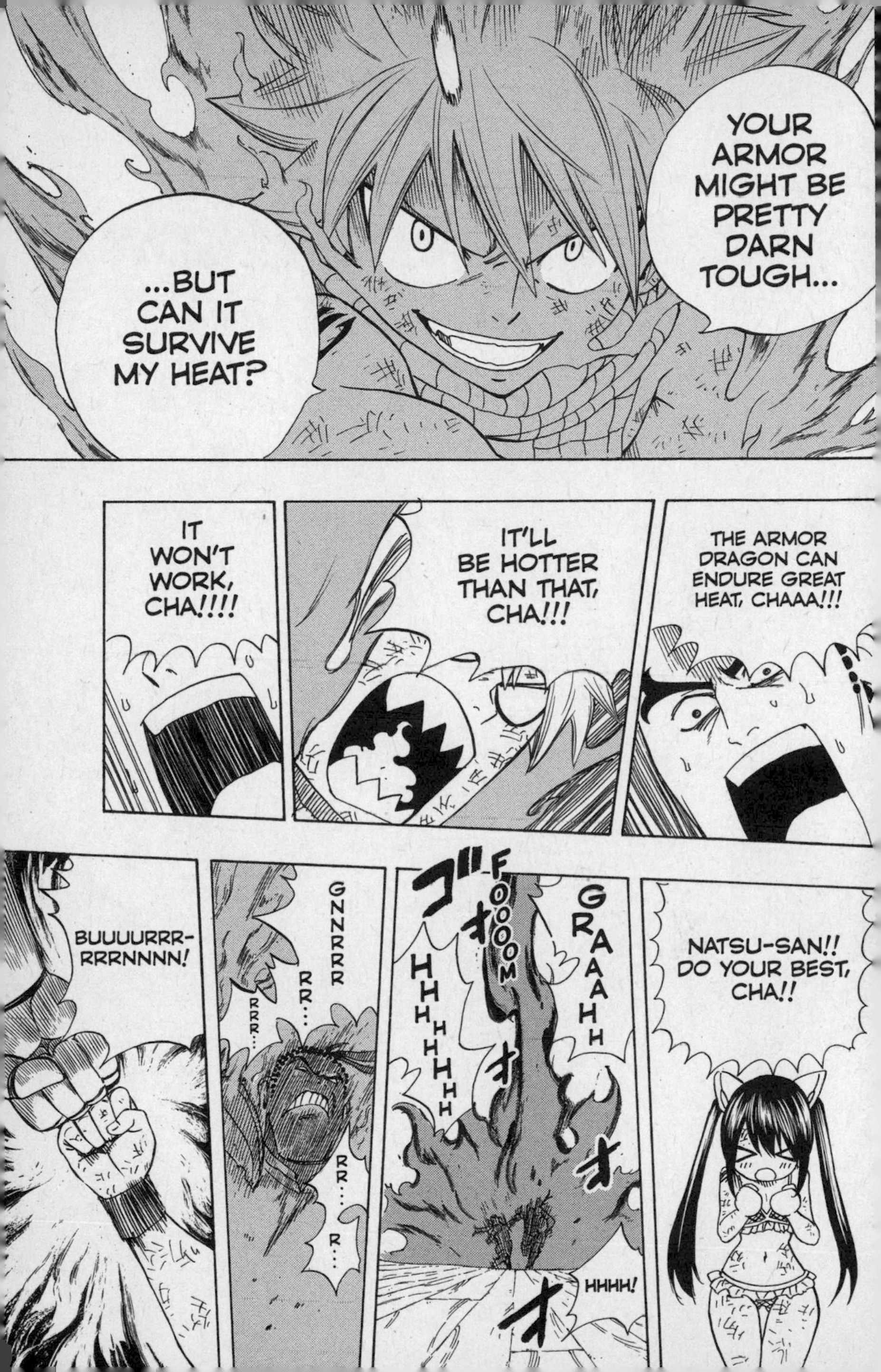
YOUR ARMOR MIGHT BE PRETTY DARN TOUGH...
...BUT CAN IT SURVIVE MY HEAT?
THE ARMOR DRAGON CAN ENDURE GREAT HEAT, CHAAA!!!
IT'LL BE HOTTER THAN THAT, CHA!!!
IT WON'T WORK, CHA!!!!
NATSU-SAN!! DO YOUR BEST, CHA!!
GRAAAHH
FOOOOM
HHHHHHHH
HHHH!
GNNRRR
RR...
RRR...
RR... R...
BUUUURRR-RRRNNNN!

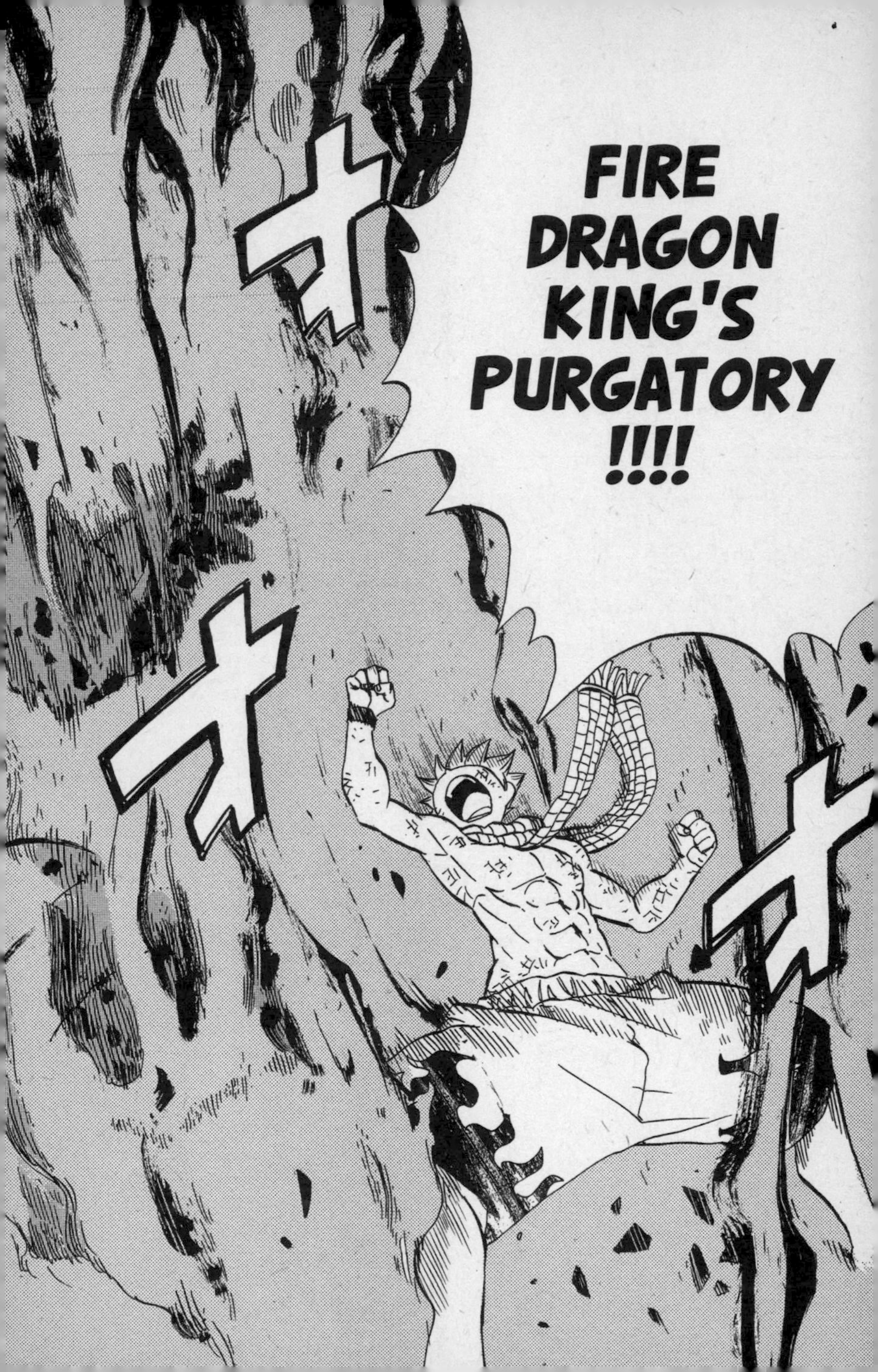
FIRE DRAGON KING'S PURGATORY !!!!

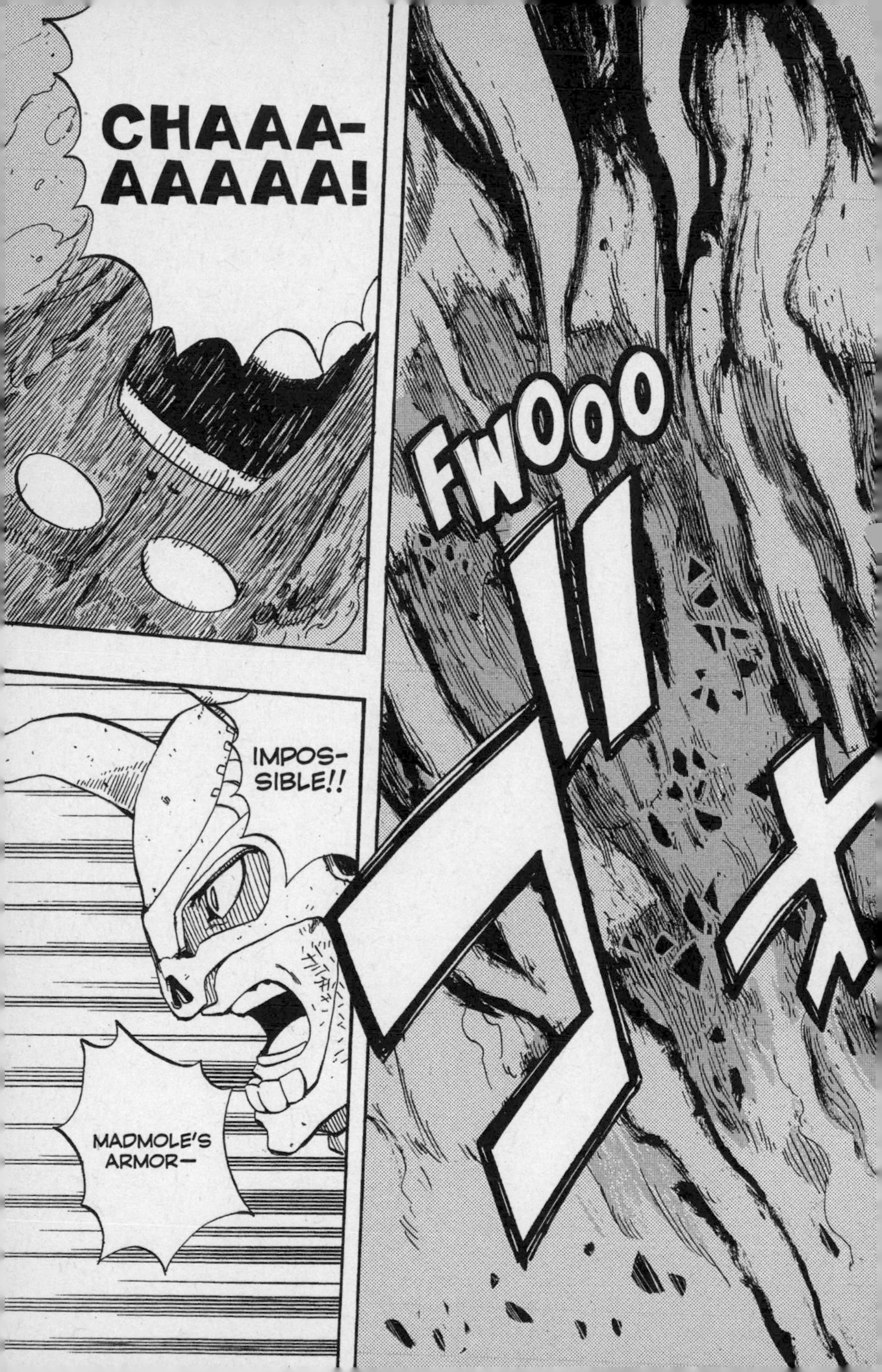
FWOOO
CHAAAAAAAAA!
IMPOSSIBLE!!
MADMOLE'S ARMOR—

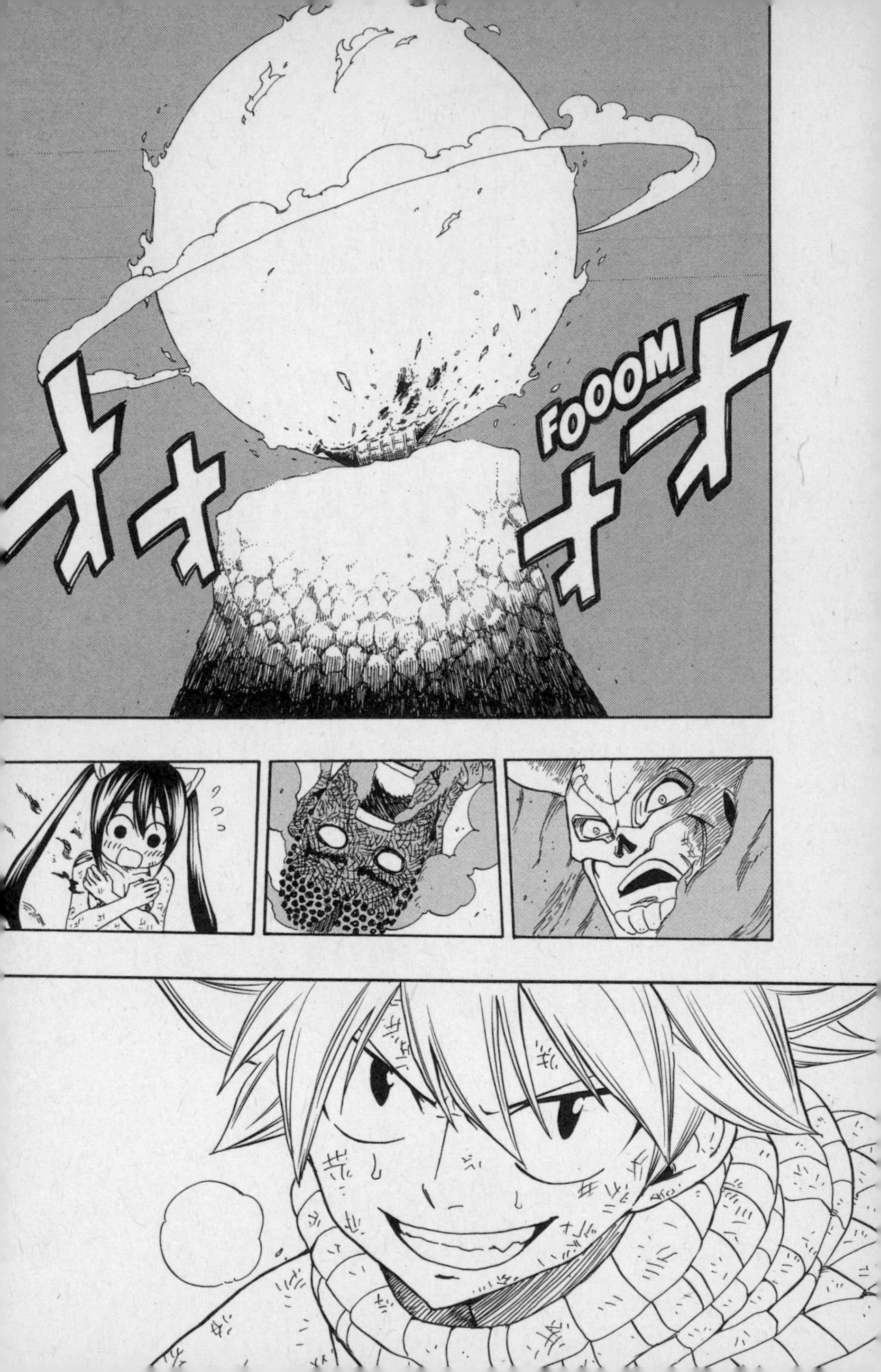
FOOOM
オオオオ

FAIRY TAIL 100 YEARS QUEST

Chapter 16: Ash and Dark Clouds

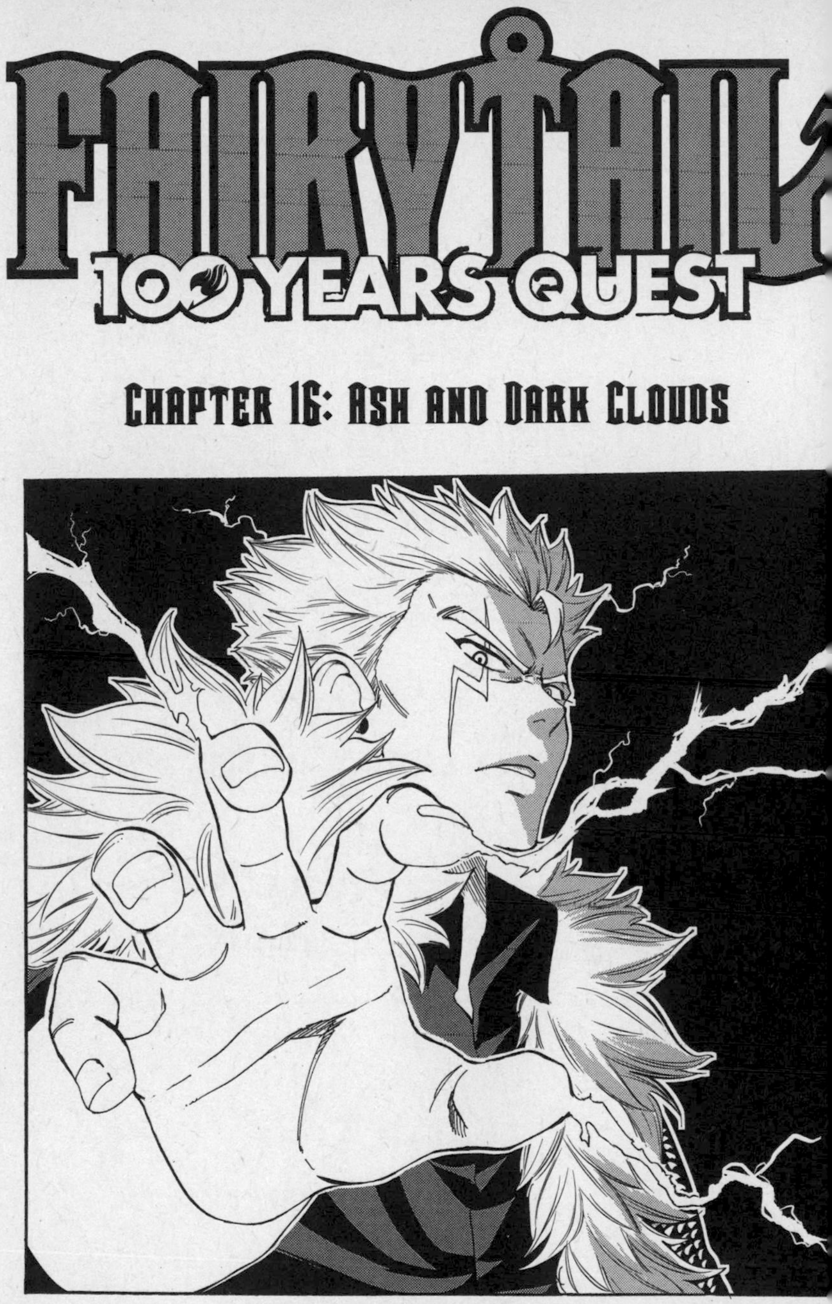

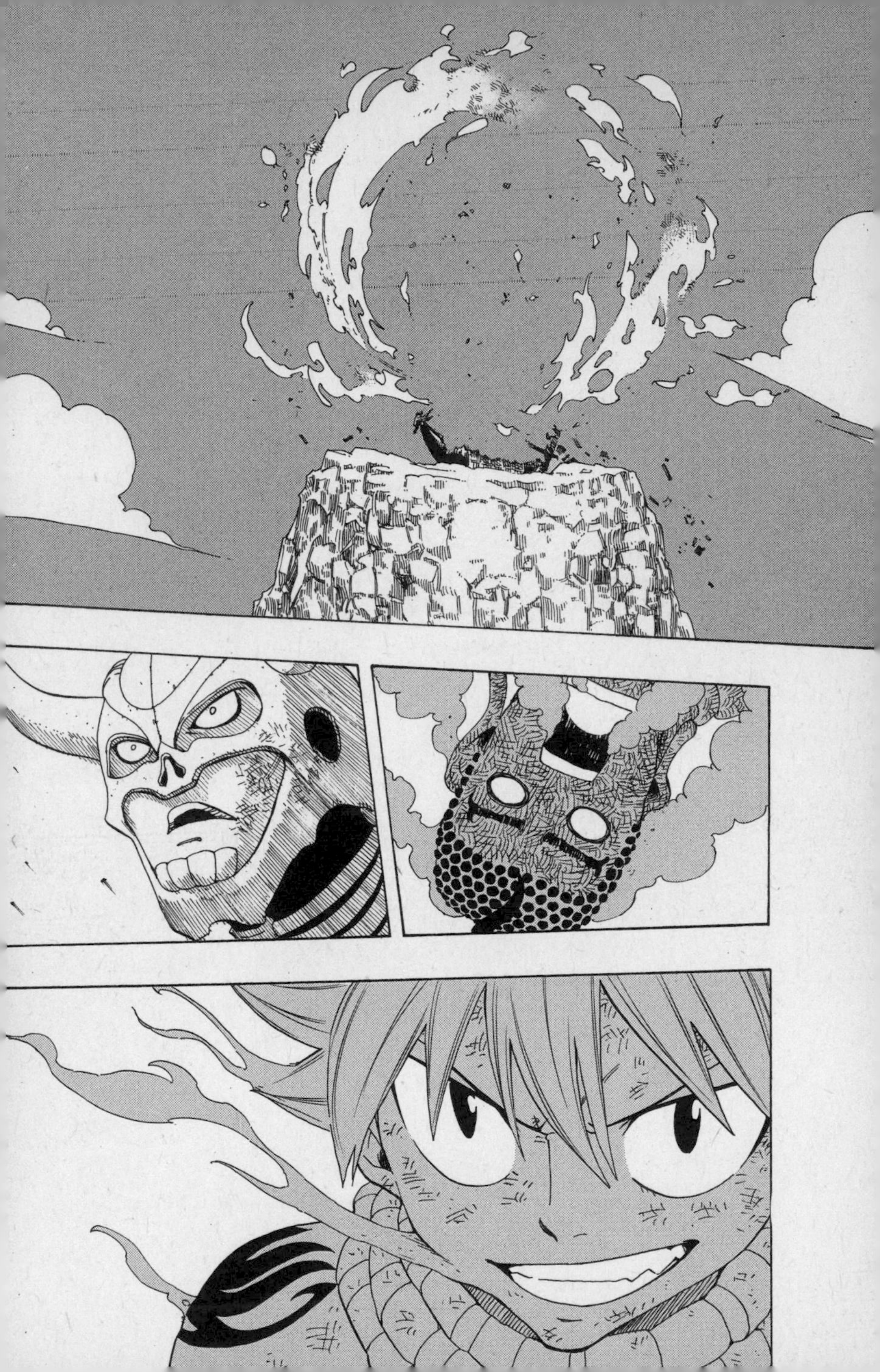

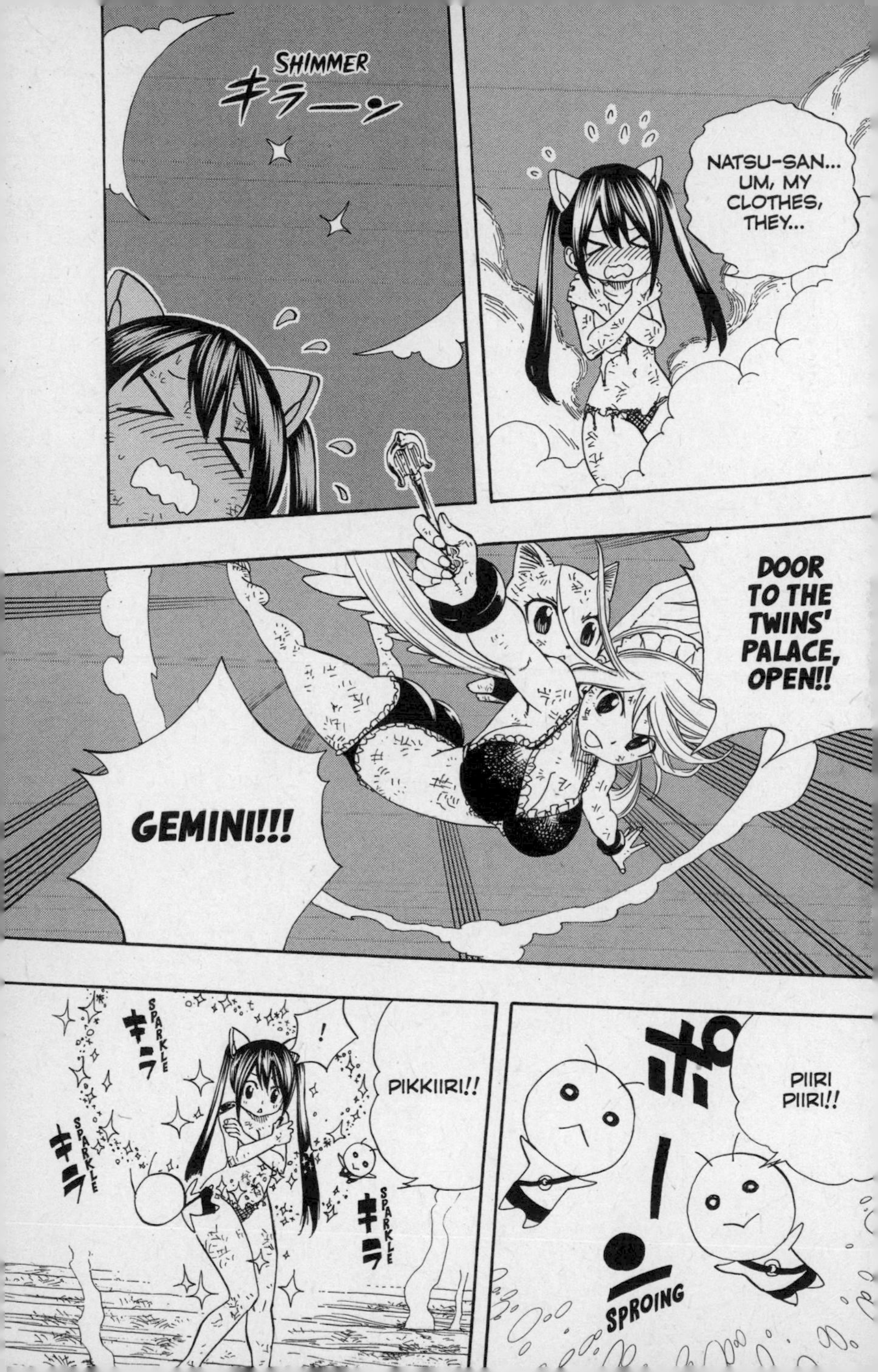

NATSU-SAN... UM, MY CLOTHES, THEY...
SHIMMER
キラーン
DOOR TO THE TWINS' PALACE, OPEN!!
GEMINI!!!
PIIRI PIIRI!!
SPROING
PIKKIIRI!!
!
SPARKLE
キラ
SPARKLE
キラ
SPARKLE
キラ

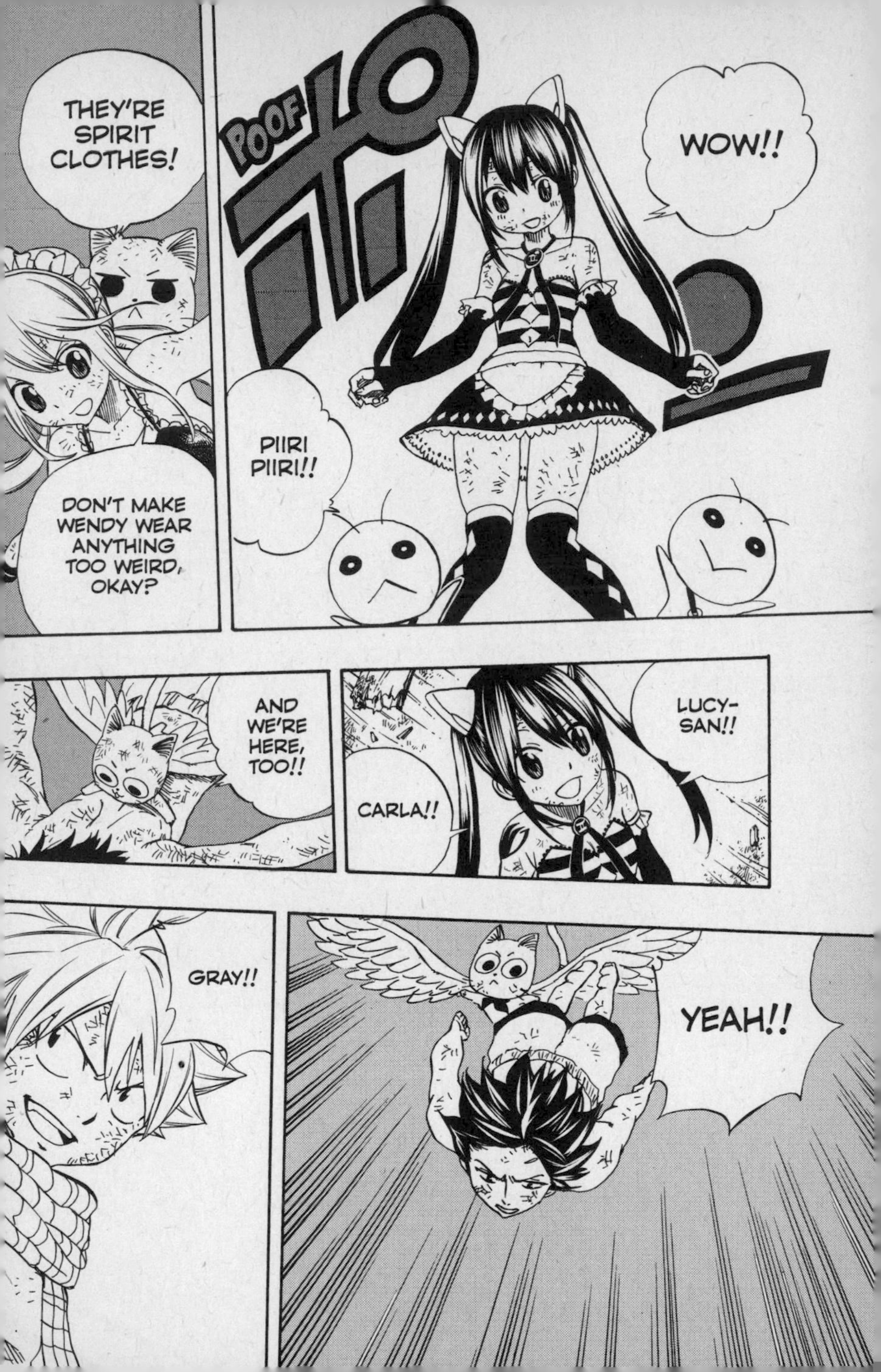
WOW!!
POOF
PIIRI PIIRI!!
THEY'RE SPIRIT CLOTHES!
DON'T MAKE WENDY WEAR ANYTHING TOO WEIRD, OKAY?
LUCY-SAN!!
CARLA!!
AND WE'RE HERE, TOO!!
YEAH!!
GRAY!!

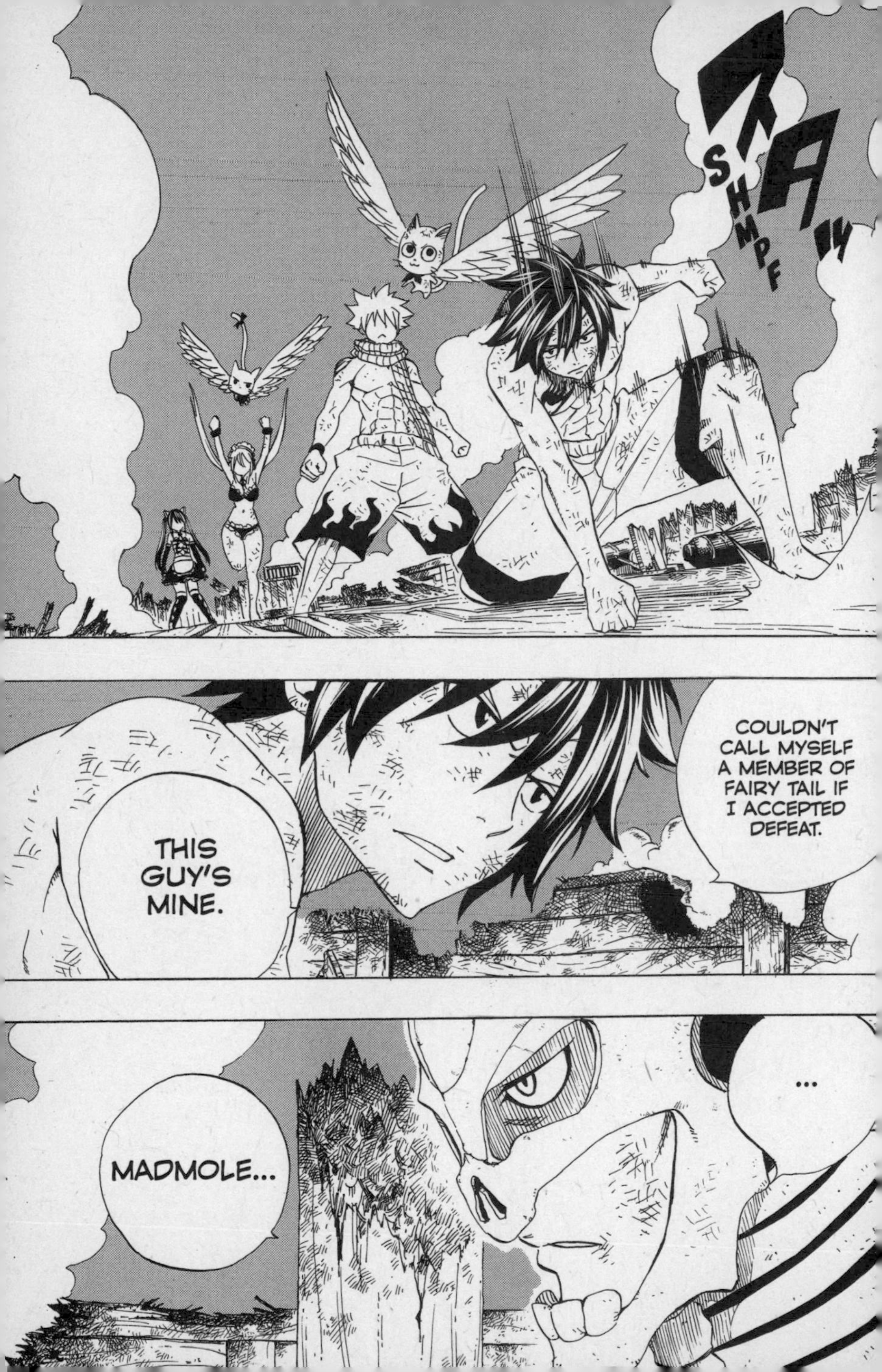
SHMPF
COULDN'T CALL MYSELF A MEMBER OF FAIRY TAIL IF I ACCEPTED DEFEAT.
THIS GUY'S MINE.
...
MADMOLE...

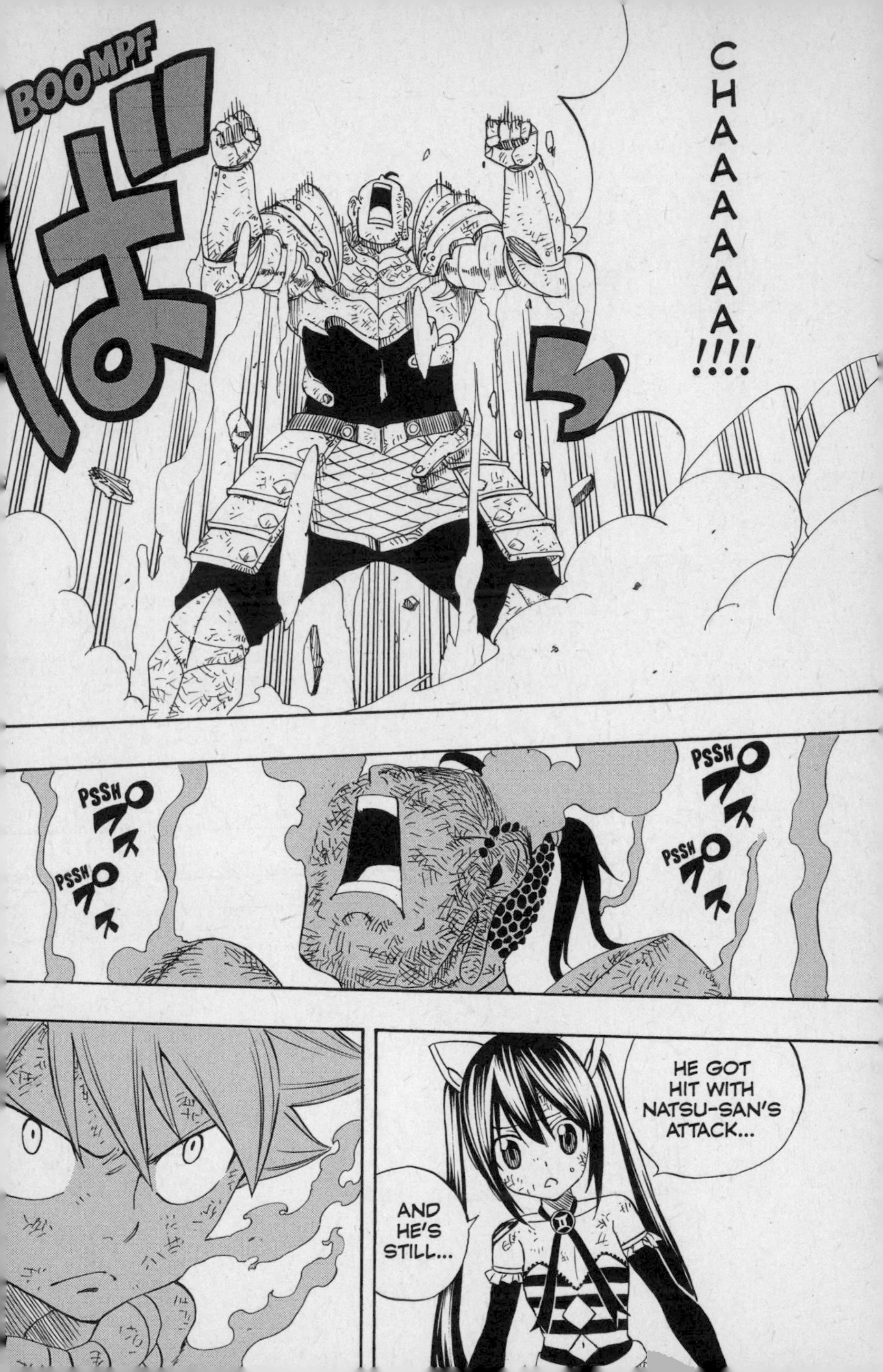
CHAAAAAA!!!!
BOOMPF
PSSH
PSSH
PSSH
PSSH
HE GOT HIT WITH NATSU-SAN'S ATTACK...
AND HE'S STILL...

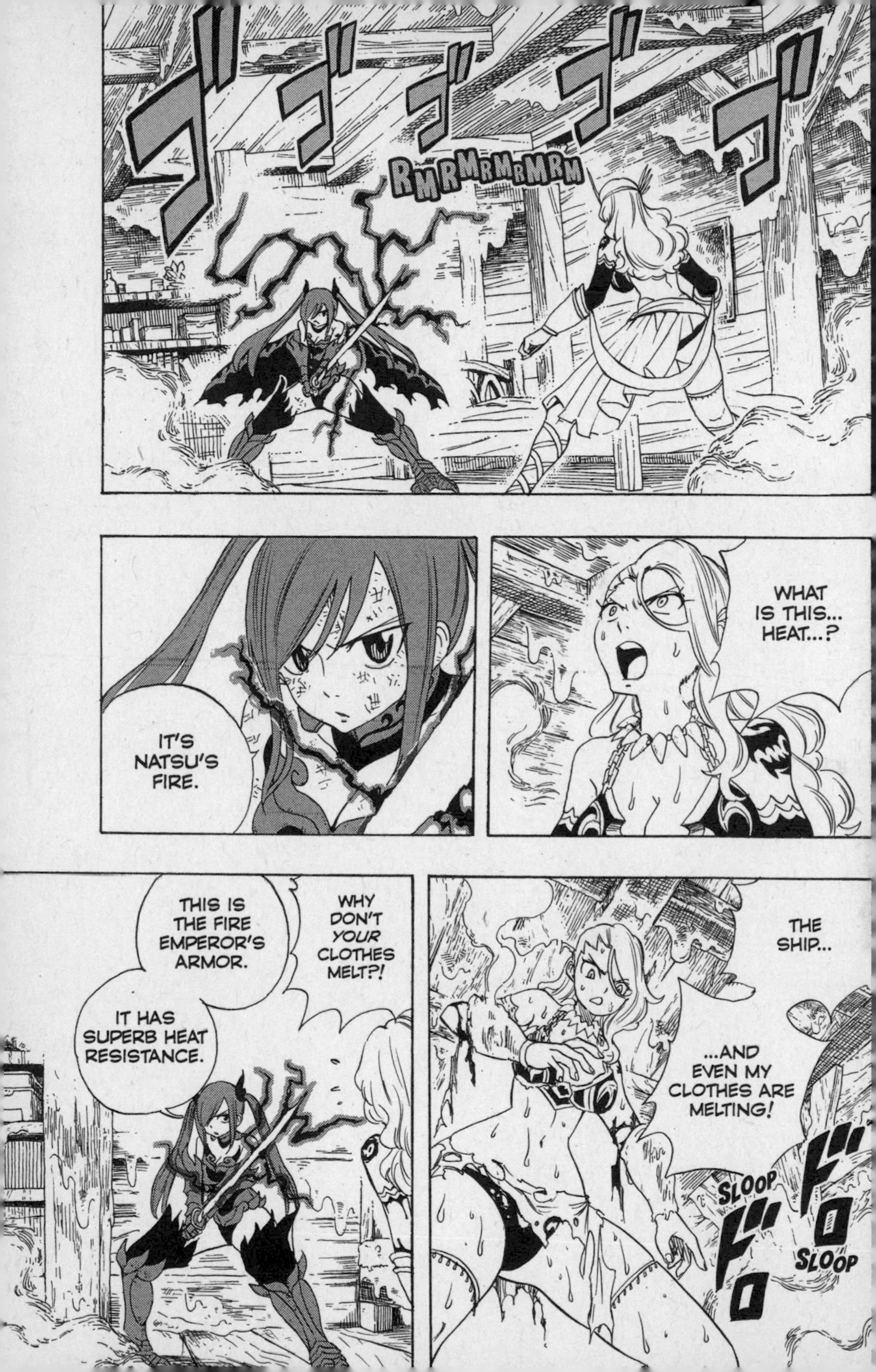
RMRMRMRMRM
WHAT IS THIS... HEAT...?
IT'S NATSU'S FIRE.
THE SHIP...
...AND EVEN MY CLOTHES ARE MELTING!
SLOOP
SLOOP
WHY DON'T *YOUR* CLOTHES MELT?!
THIS IS THE FIRE EMPEROR'S ARMOR.
IT HAS SUPERB HEAT RESISTANCE.

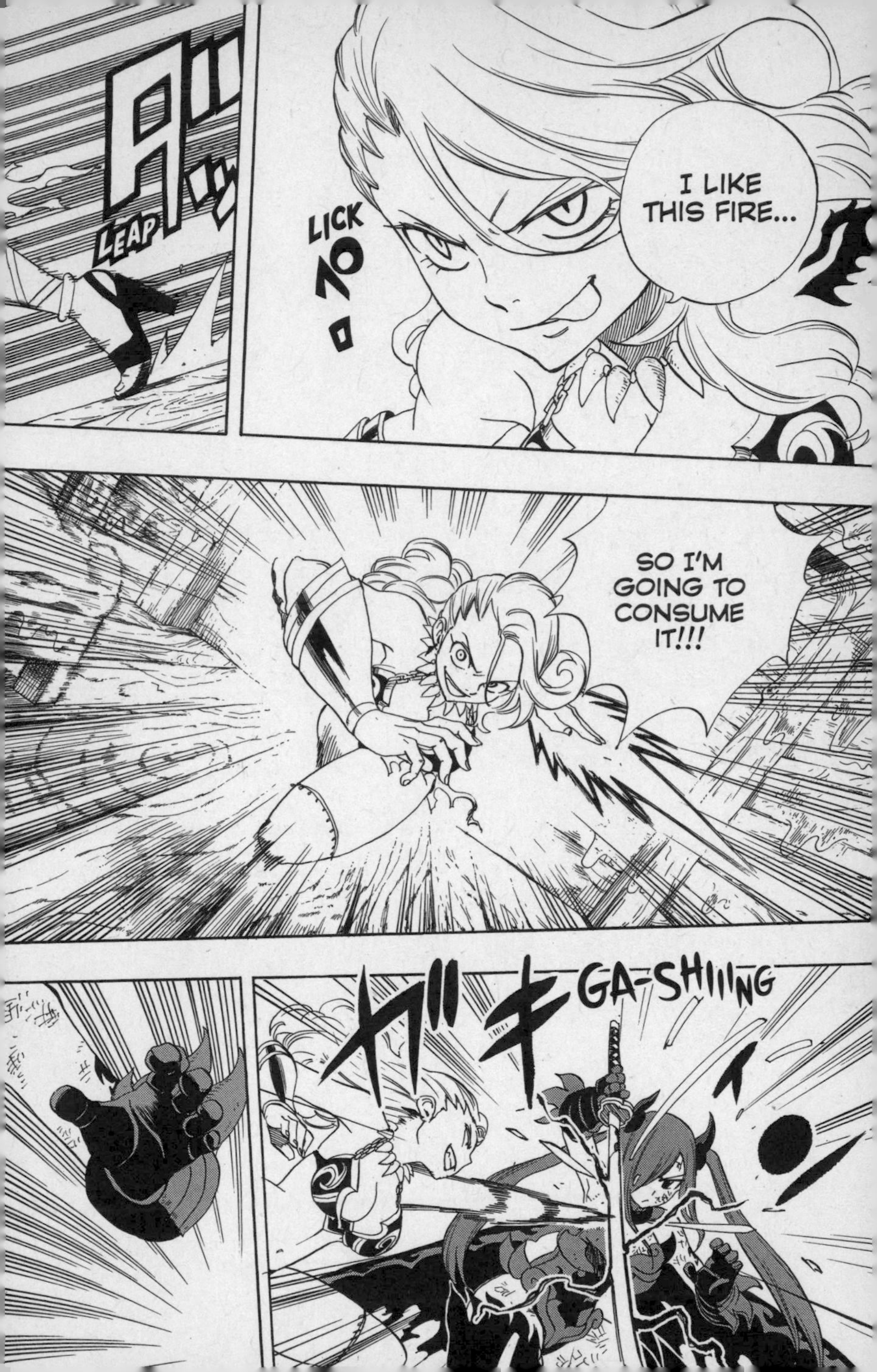
LICK
I LIKE THIS FIRE...
LEAP
SO I'M GOING TO CONSUME IT!!!
GA-SHIIING

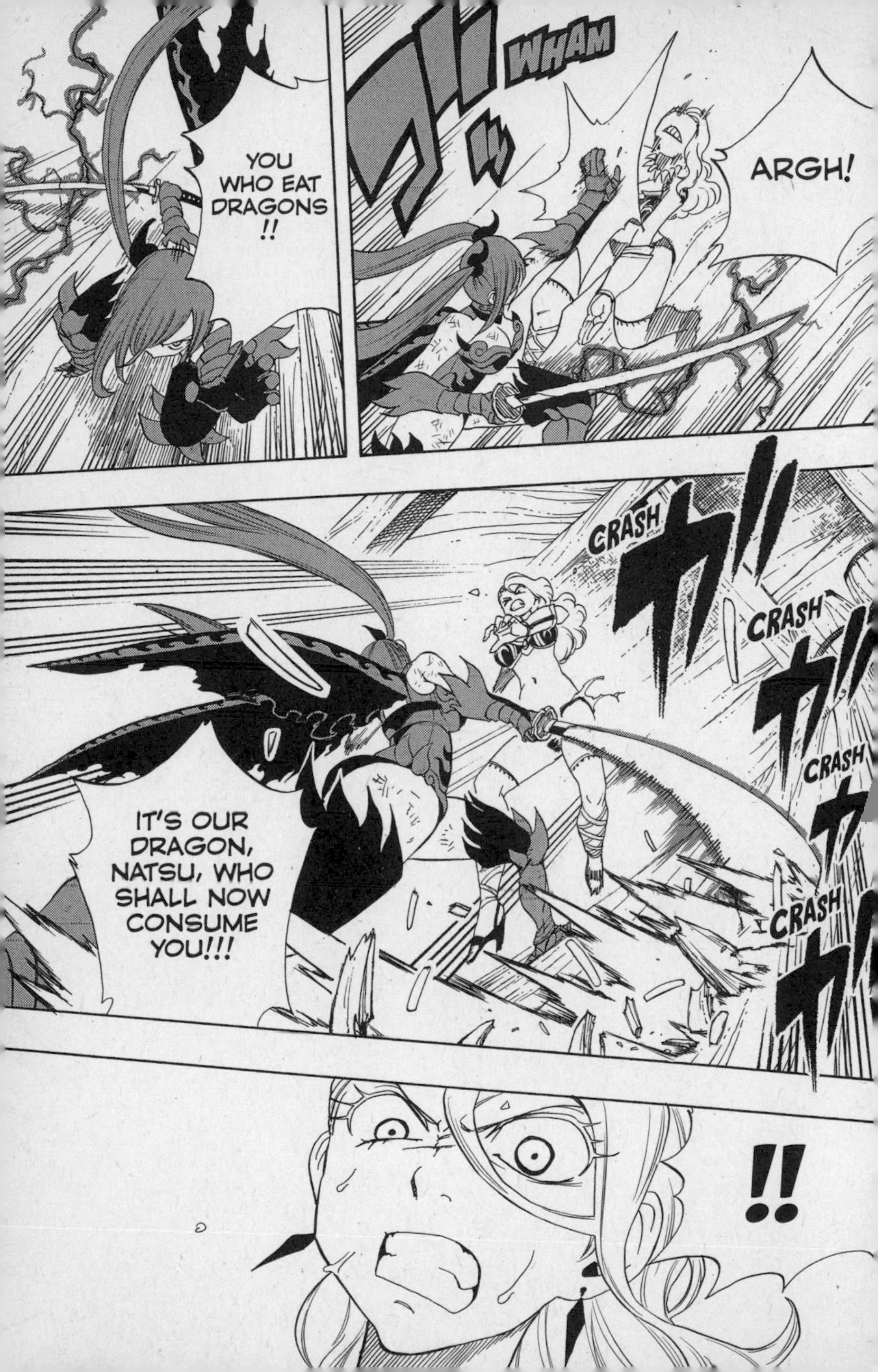
WHAM
ARGH!
YOU WHO EAT DRAGONS!!
CRASH
CRASH
CRASH
CRASH
IT'S OUR DRAGON, NATSU, WHO SHALL NOW CONSUME YOU!!!
!!

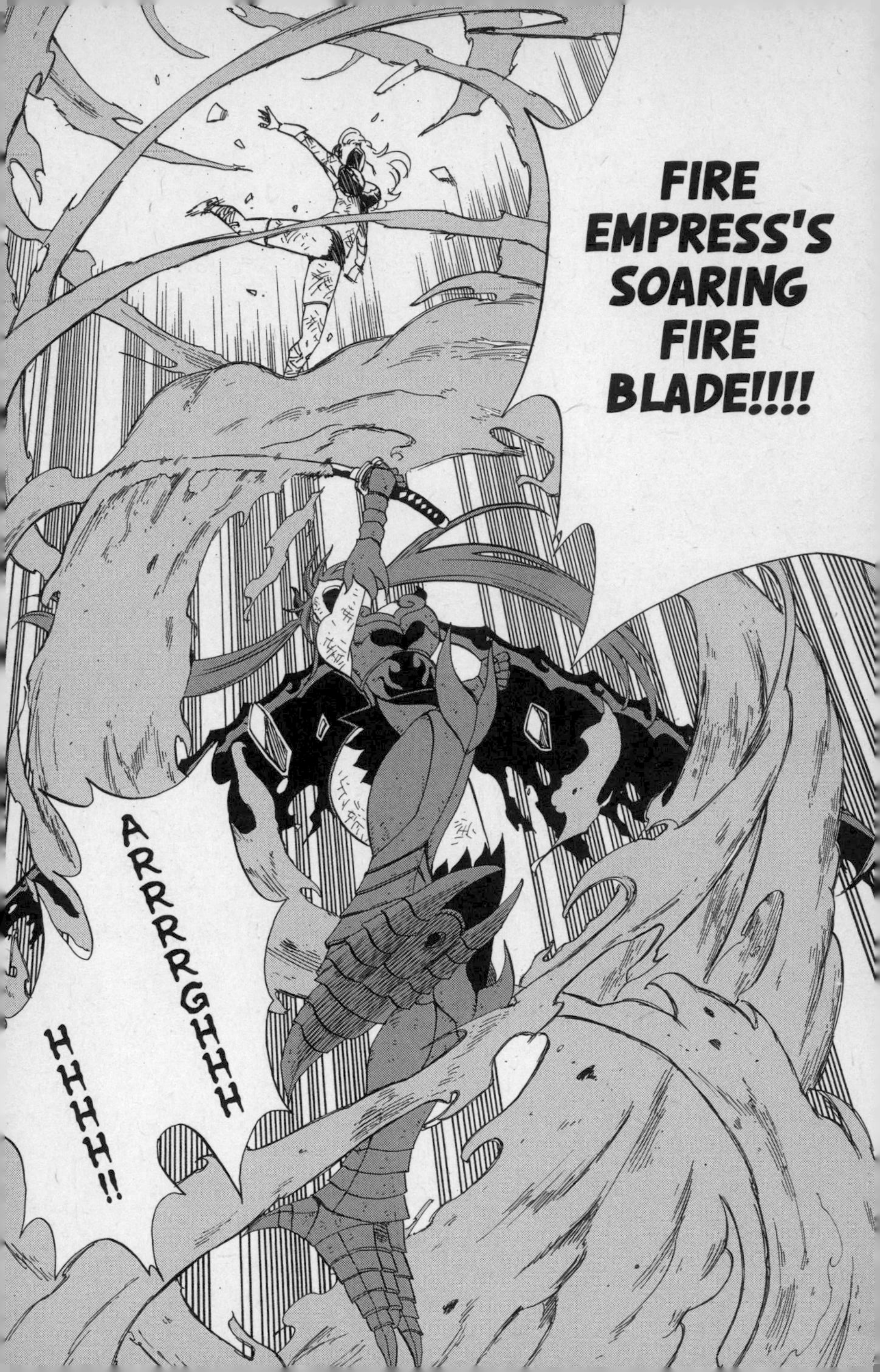
FIRE EMPRESS'S SOARING FIRE BLADE!!!!
ARRRRGHHH HHHH!!

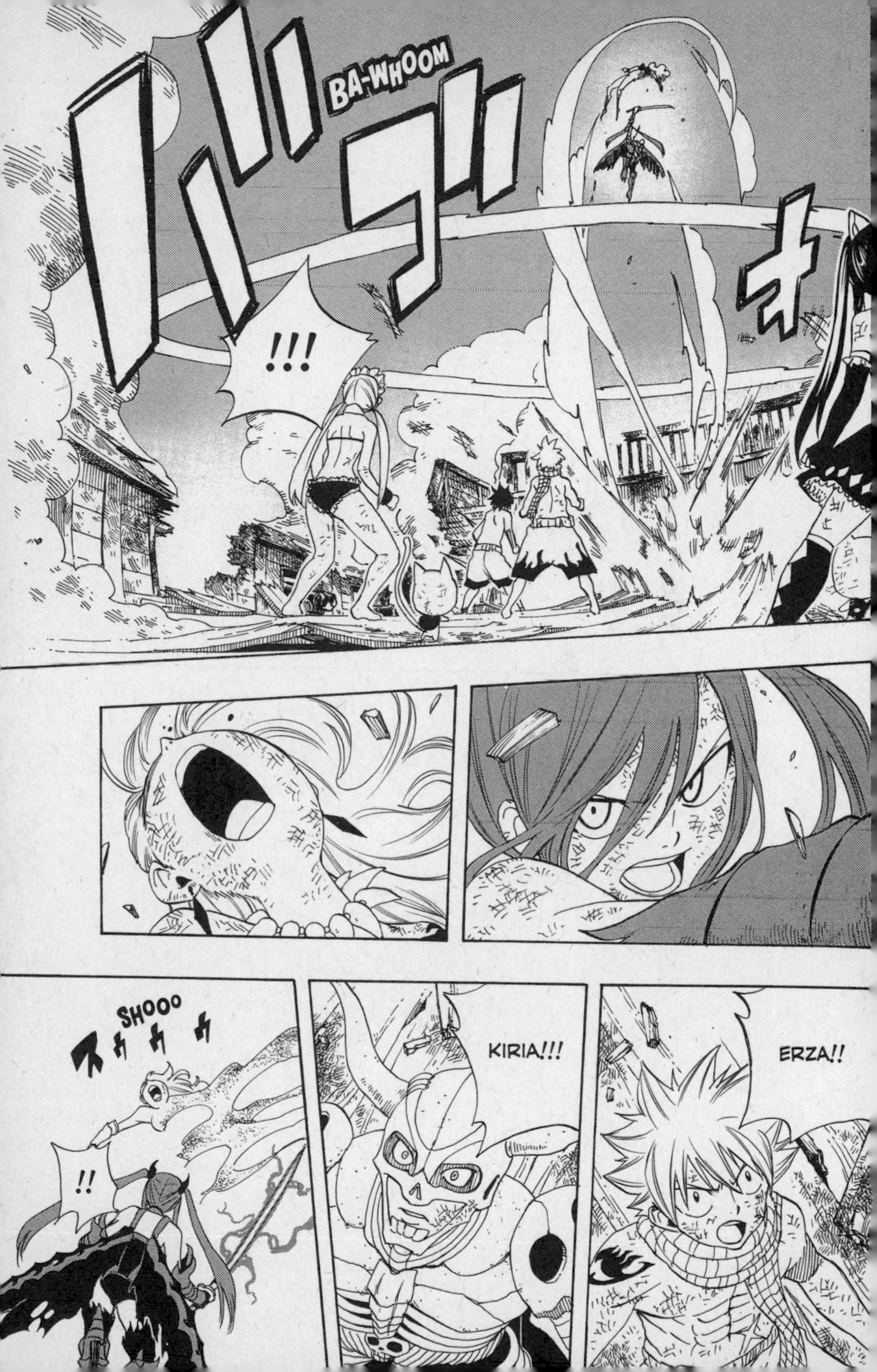
BA-WHOOM
!!!
ERZA!!
KIRIA!!!
SHOOO
!!

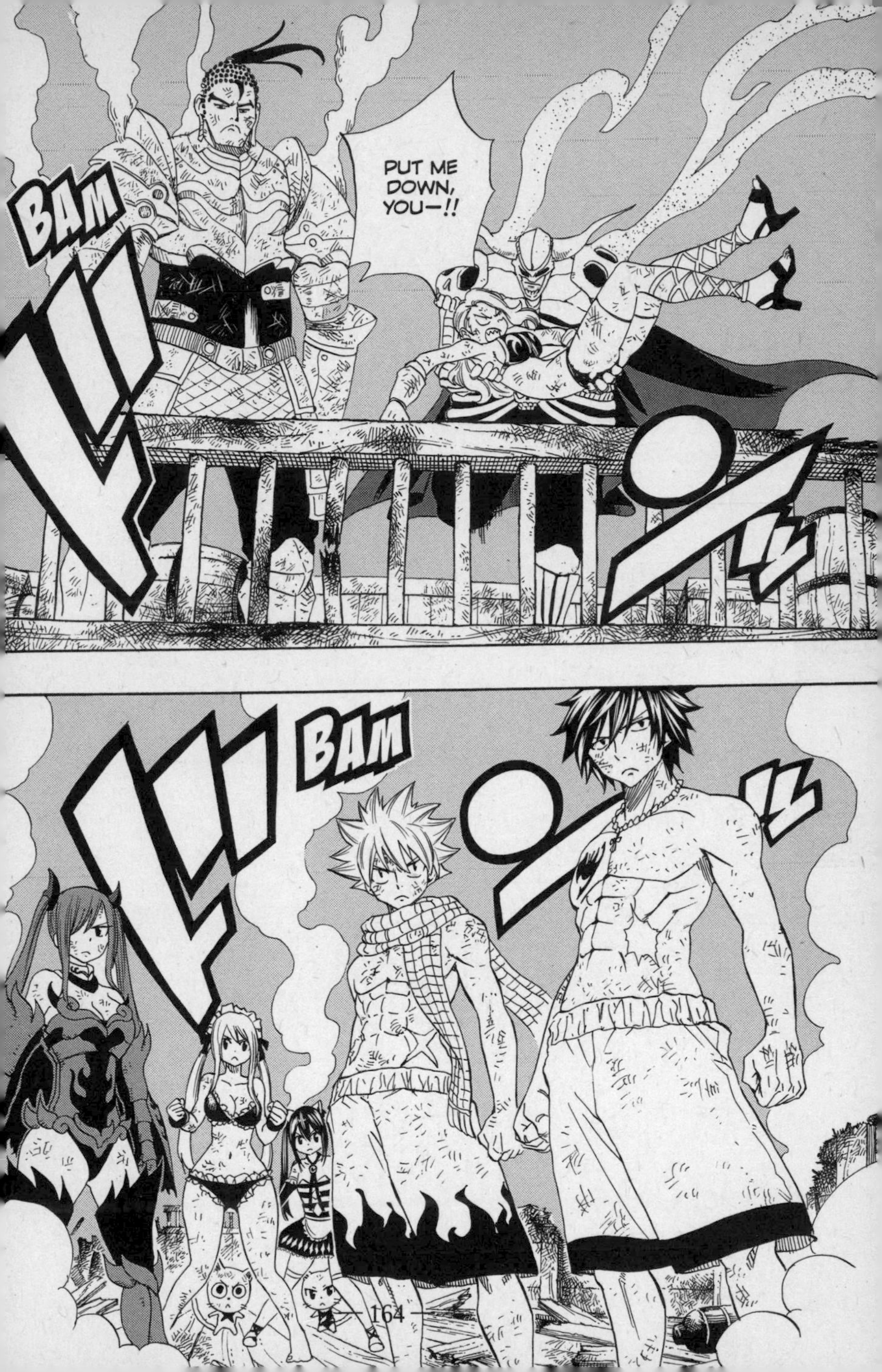
PUT ME DOWN, YOU—!!
BAM
BAM

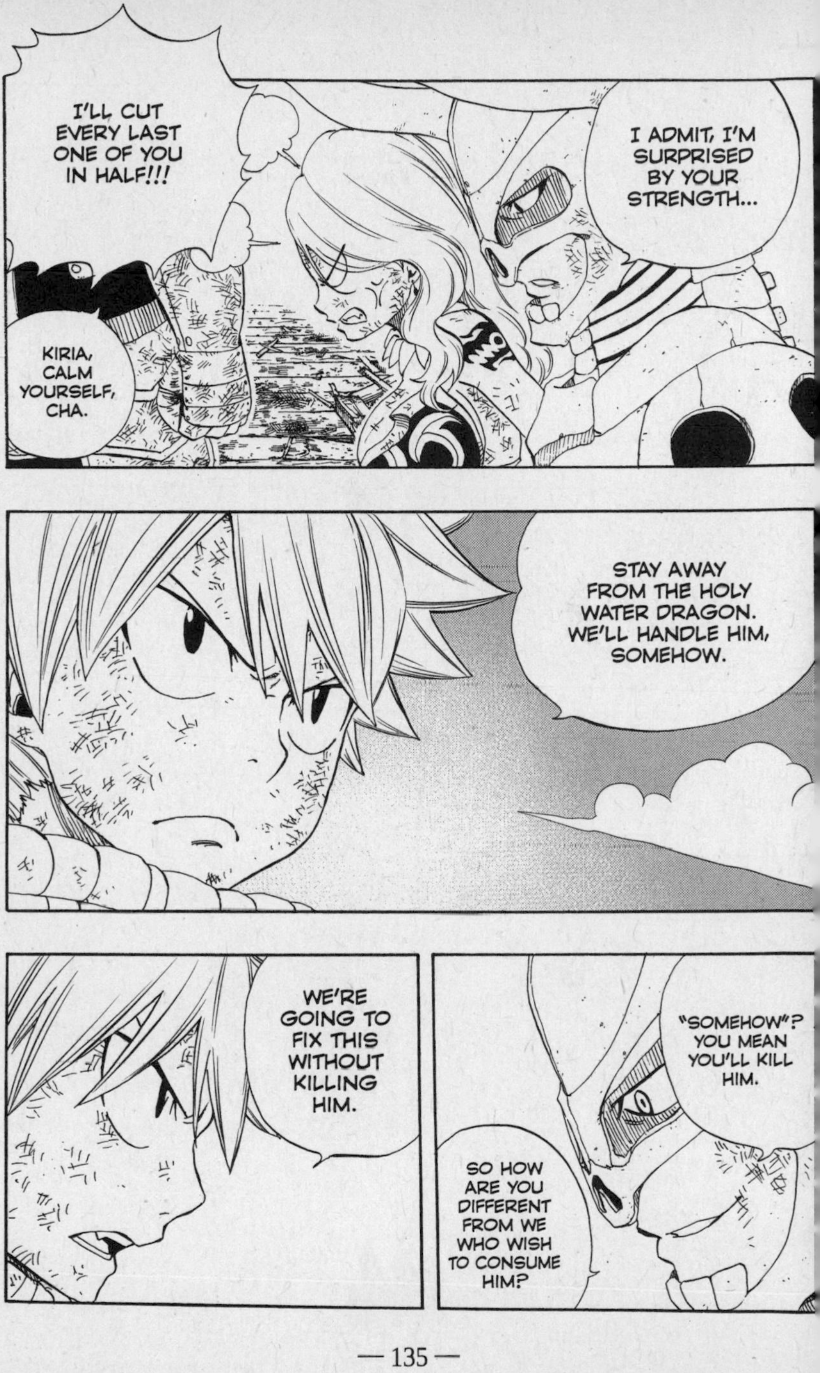
I ADMIT, I'M SURPRISED BY YOUR STRENGTH...
I'LL CUT EVERY LAST ONE OF YOU IN HALF!!!
KIRIA, CALM YOURSELF, CHA.
STAY AWAY FROM THE HOLY WATER DRAGON. WE'LL HANDLE HIM, SOMEHOW.
"SOMEHOW"? YOU MEAN YOU'LL KILL HIM.
SO HOW ARE YOU DIFFERENT FROM WE WHO WISH TO CONSUME HIM?
WE'RE GOING TO FIX THIS WITHOUT KILLING HIM.

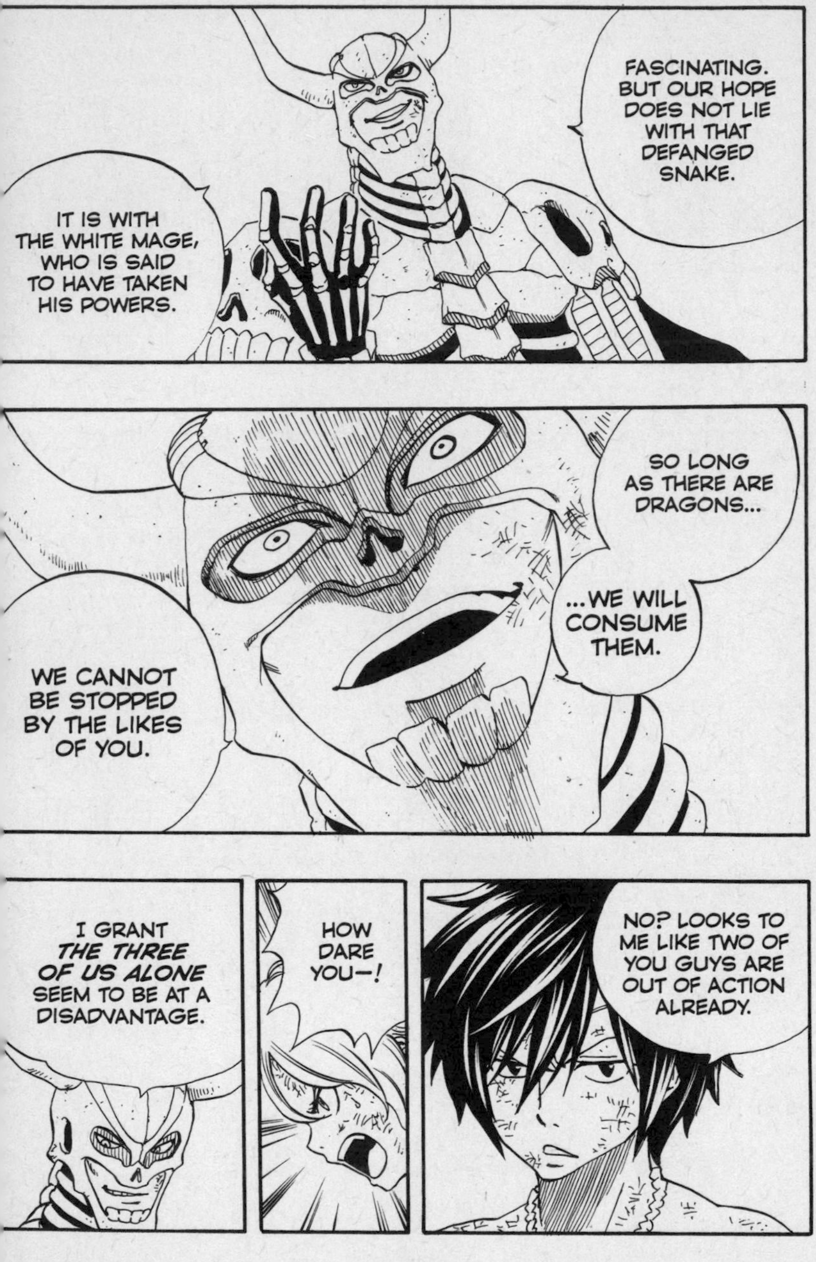
FASCINATING. BUT OUR HOPE DOES NOT LIE WITH THAT DEFANGED SNAKE.
IT IS WITH THE WHITE MAGE, WHO IS SAID TO HAVE TAKEN HIS POWERS.
SO LONG AS THERE ARE DRAGONS...
...WE WILL CONSUME THEM.
WE CANNOT BE STOPPED BY THE LIKES OF YOU.
NO? LOOKS TO ME LIKE TWO OF YOU GUYS ARE OUT OF ACTION ALREADY.
HOW DARE YOU—!
I GRANT *THE THREE OF US ALONE* SEEM TO BE AT A DISADVANTAGE.

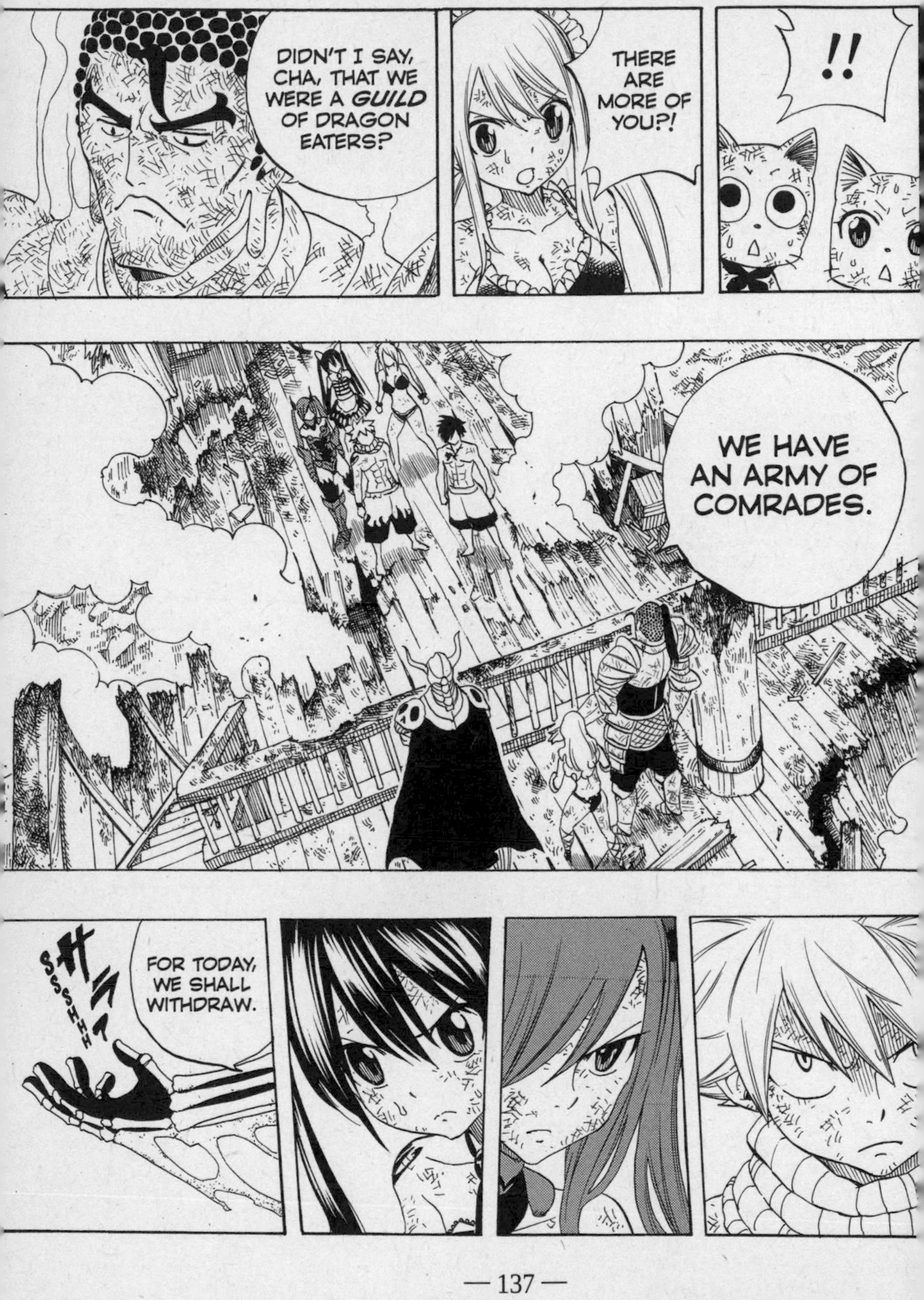
!!
THERE ARE MORE OF YOU?!
DIDN'T I SAY, CHA, THAT WE WERE A *GUILD* OF DRAGON EATERS?
WE HAVE AN ARMY OF COMRADES.
FOR TODAY, WE SHALL WITHDRAW.
SSSHHH

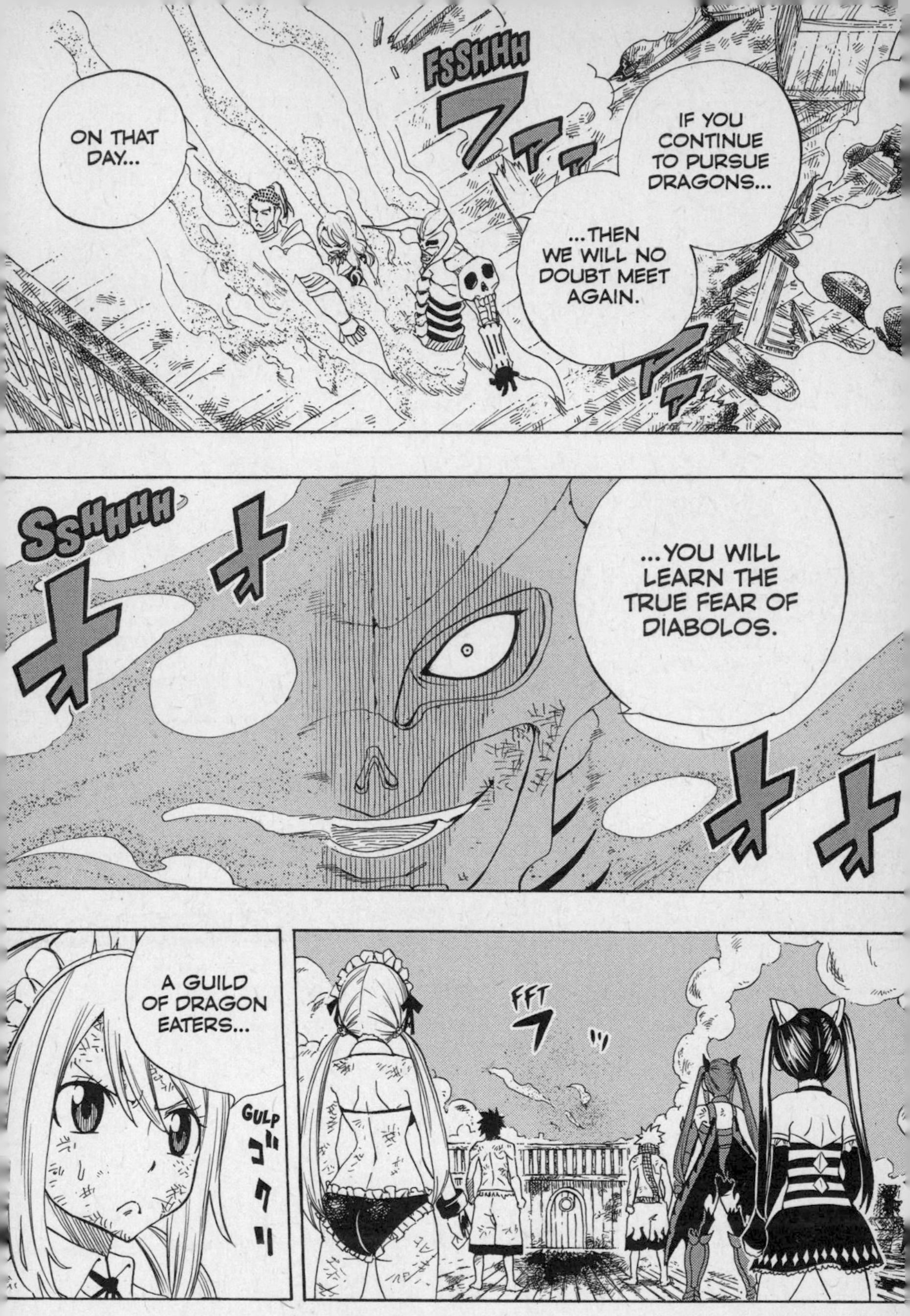
IF YOU CONTINUE TO PURSUE DRAGONS...
...THEN WE WILL NO DOUBT MEET AGAIN.
FSSHHH
ON THAT DAY...
...YOU WILL LEARN THE TRUE FEAR OF DIABOLOS.
SSHHHH
FFT
A GUILD OF DRAGON EATERS...
GULP

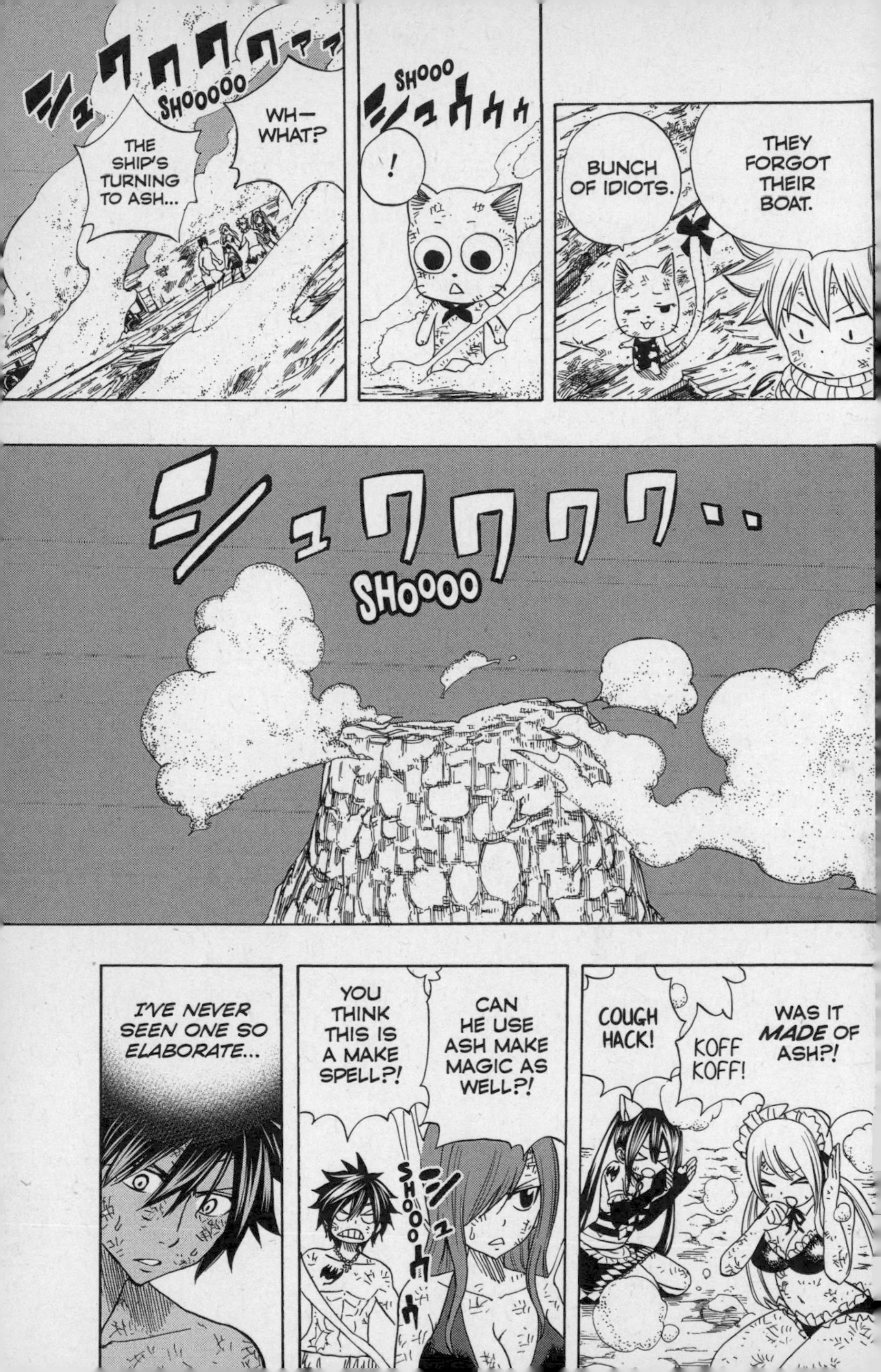
THEY FORGOT THEIR BOAT.
BUNCH OF IDIOTS.
SHOOO
!
SHOOOOO
WH— WHAT?
THE SHIP'S TURNING TO ASH...
SHOOOO
WAS IT *MADE* OF ASH?!
KOFF KOFF!
COUGH HACK!
CAN HE USE ASH MAKE MAGIC AS WELL?!
YOU THINK THIS IS A MAKE SPELL?!
SHOOO
I'VE NEVER SEEN ONE SO ELABORATE...

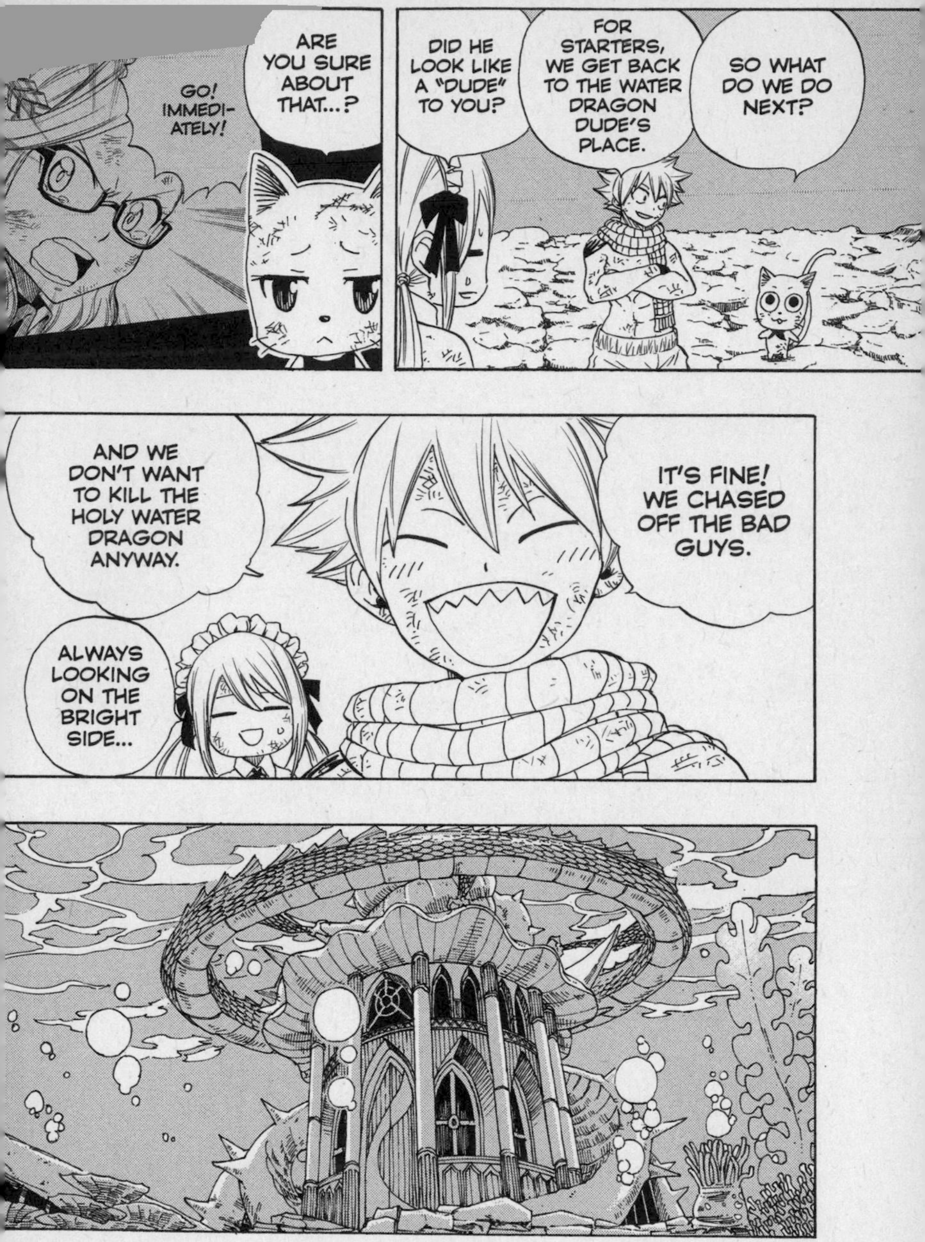
SO WHAT DO WE DO NEXT?
FOR STARTERS, WE GET BACK TO THE WATER DRAGON DUDE'S PLACE.
DID HE LOOK LIKE A "DUDE" TO YOU?
ARE YOU SURE ABOUT THAT...?
GO! IMMEDI-ATELY!
IT'S FINE! WE CHASED OFF THE BAD GUYS.
AND WE DON'T WANT TO KILL THE HOLY WATER DRAGON ANYWAY.
ALWAYS LOOKING ON THE BRIGHT SIDE...

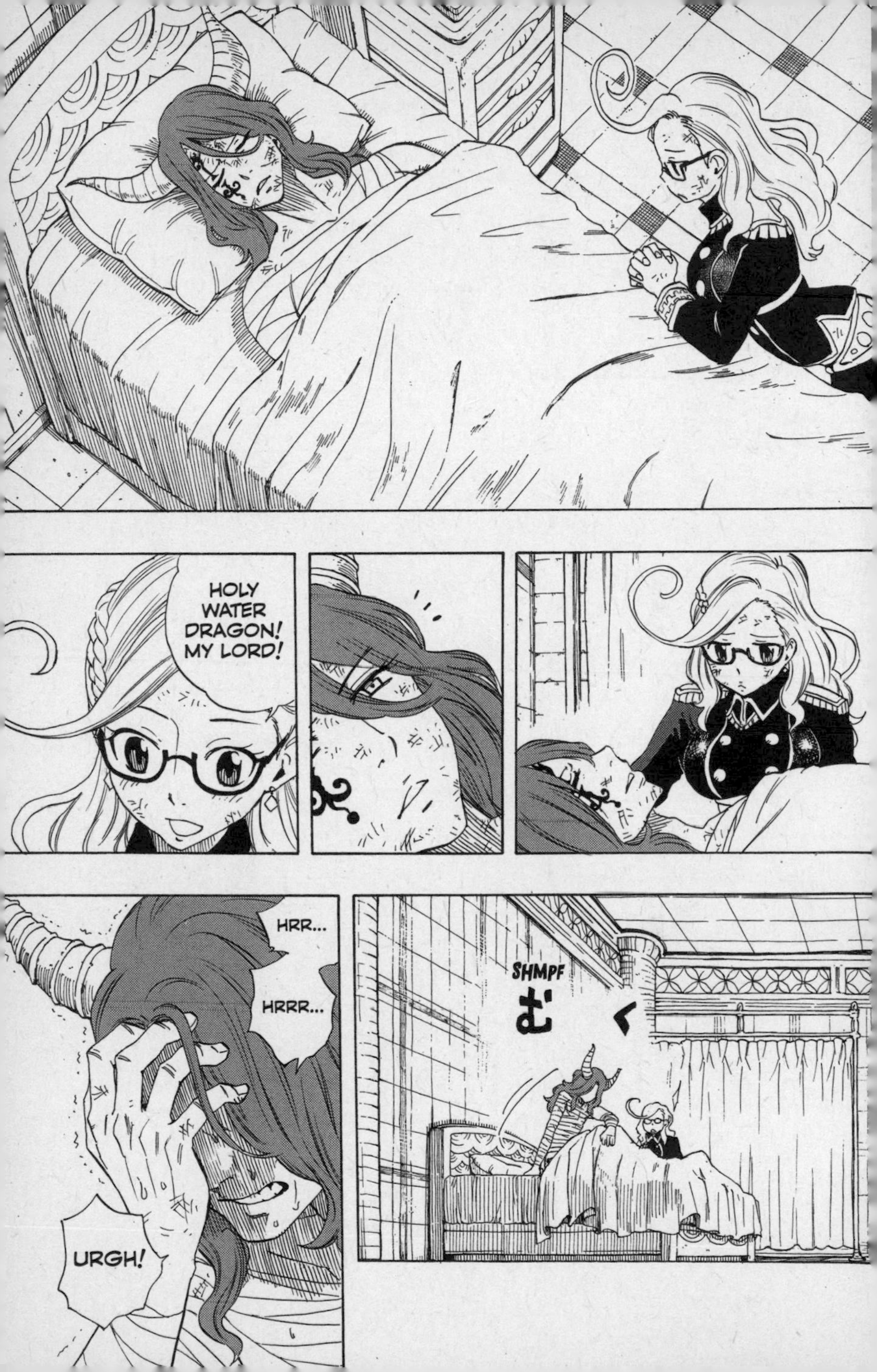
HOLY WATER DRAGON! MY LORD!
SHMPF
むく
HRR...
HRRR...
URGH!

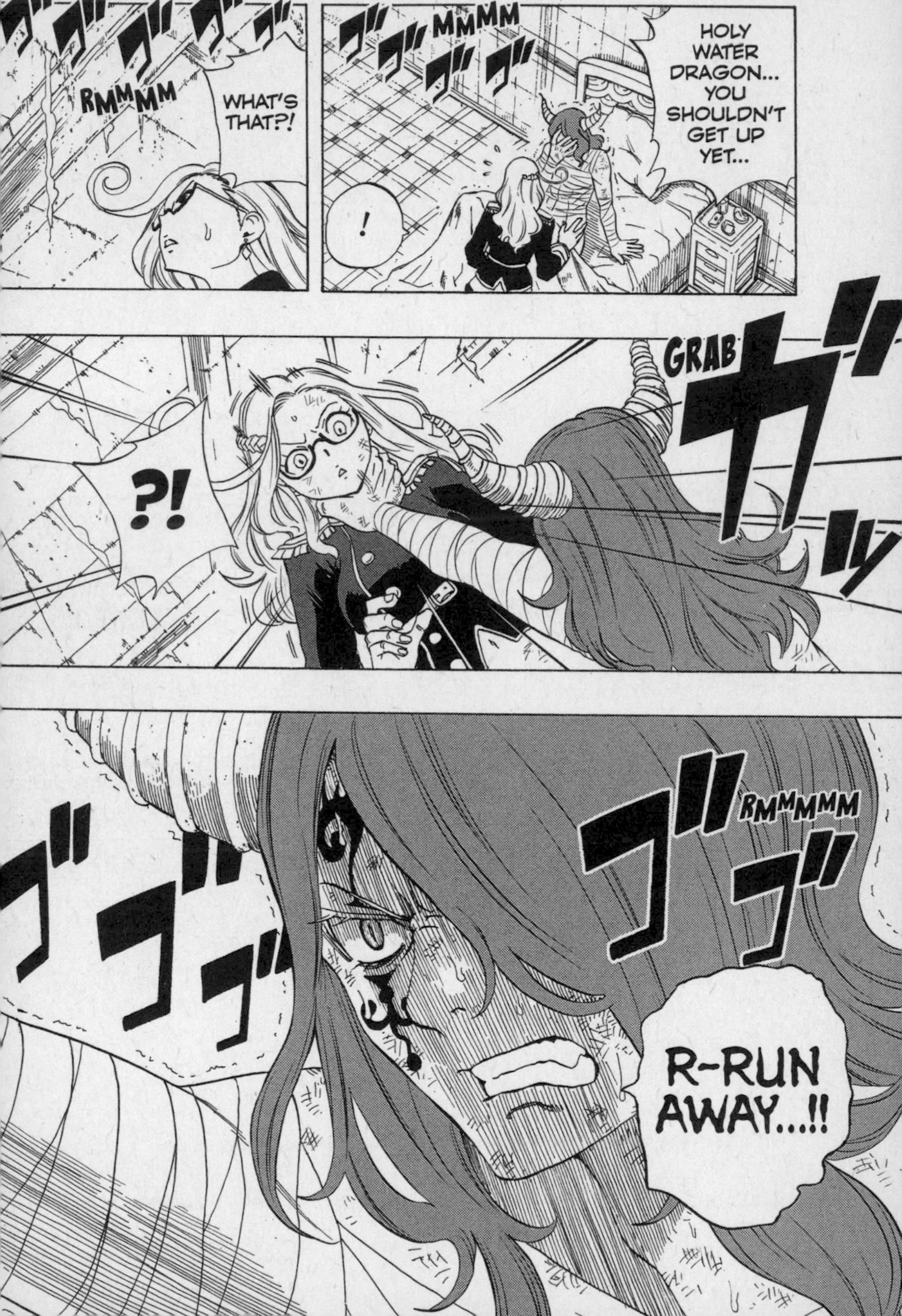
MMMM
HOLY WATER DRAGON... YOU SHOULDN'T GET UP YET...
!
RMMMM
WHAT'S THAT?!
GRAB
?!
RMMMMM
R-RUN AWAY...!!

FAIRY TAIL 100 YEARS QUEST

Chapter 17: The Holy Water Dragon

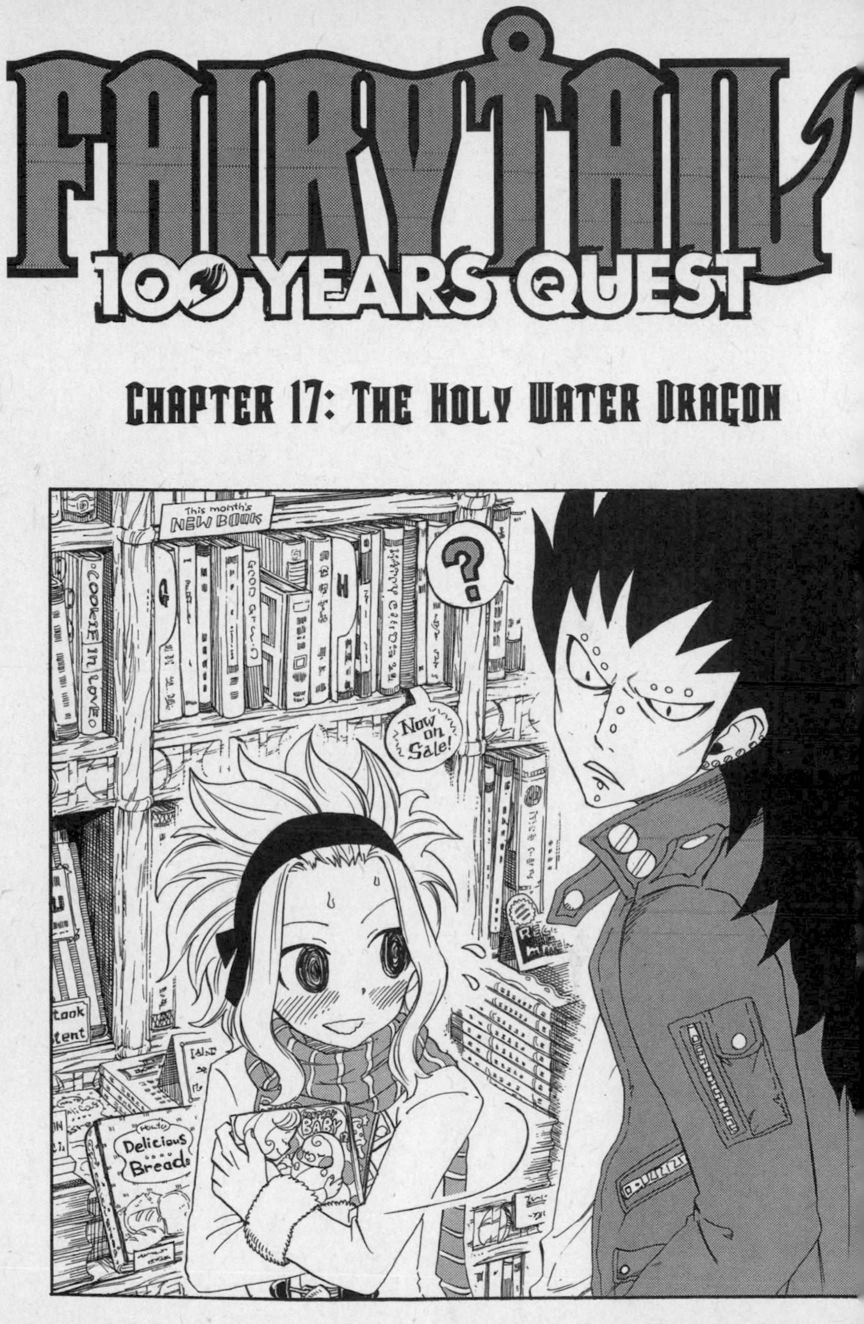
This month's NEW BOOK
?
Now on Sale!
COOKIE IN LOVE
BABY
Delicious Breads

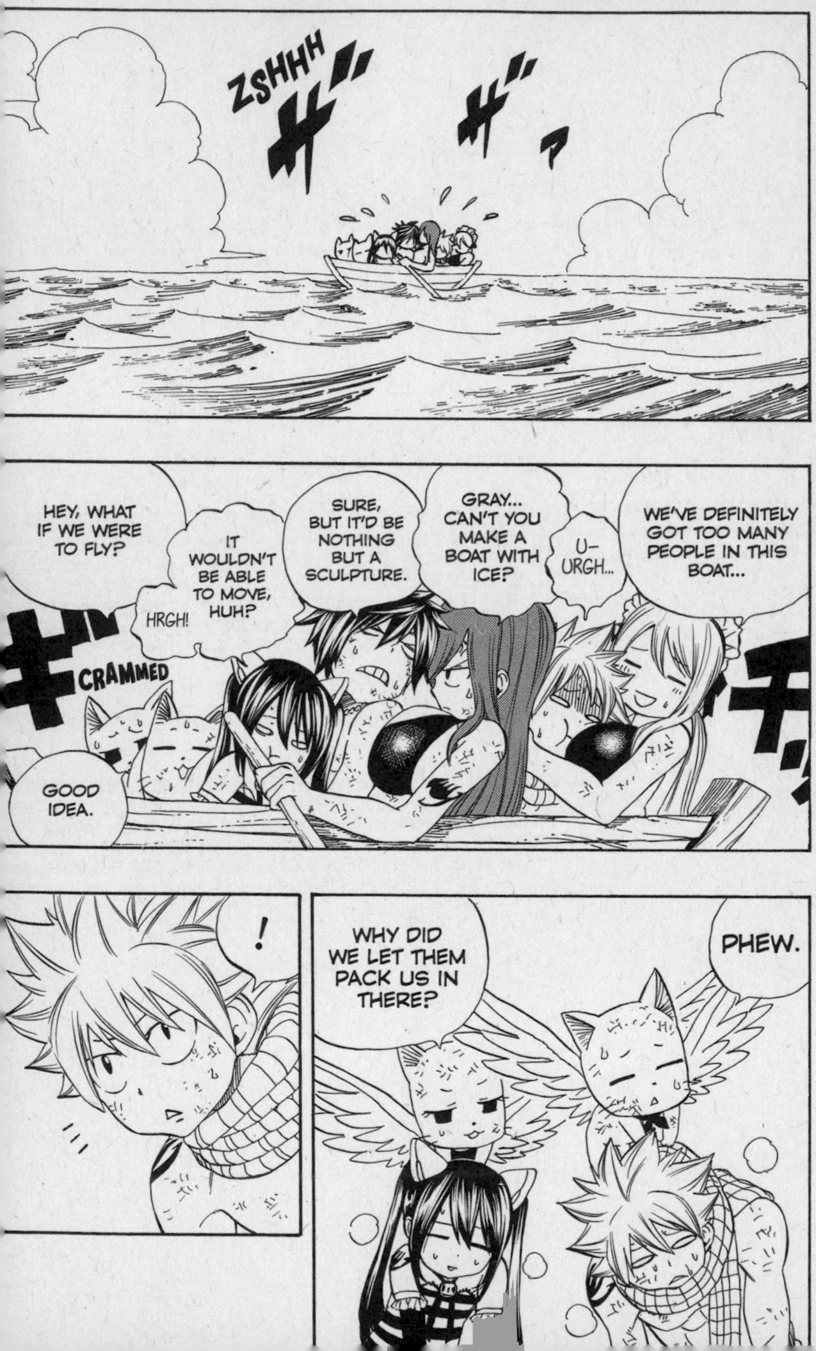
ZSHHH
WE'VE DEFINITELY GOT TOO MANY PEOPLE IN THIS BOAT...
U-URGH...
GRAY... CAN'T YOU MAKE A BOAT WITH ICE?
SURE, BUT IT'D BE NOTHING BUT A SCULPTURE.
IT WOULDN'T BE ABLE TO MOVE, HUH?
HRGH!
HEY, WHAT IF WE WERE TO FLY?
CRAMMED
GOOD IDEA.
PHEW.
WHY DID WE LET THEM PACK US IN THERE?
!

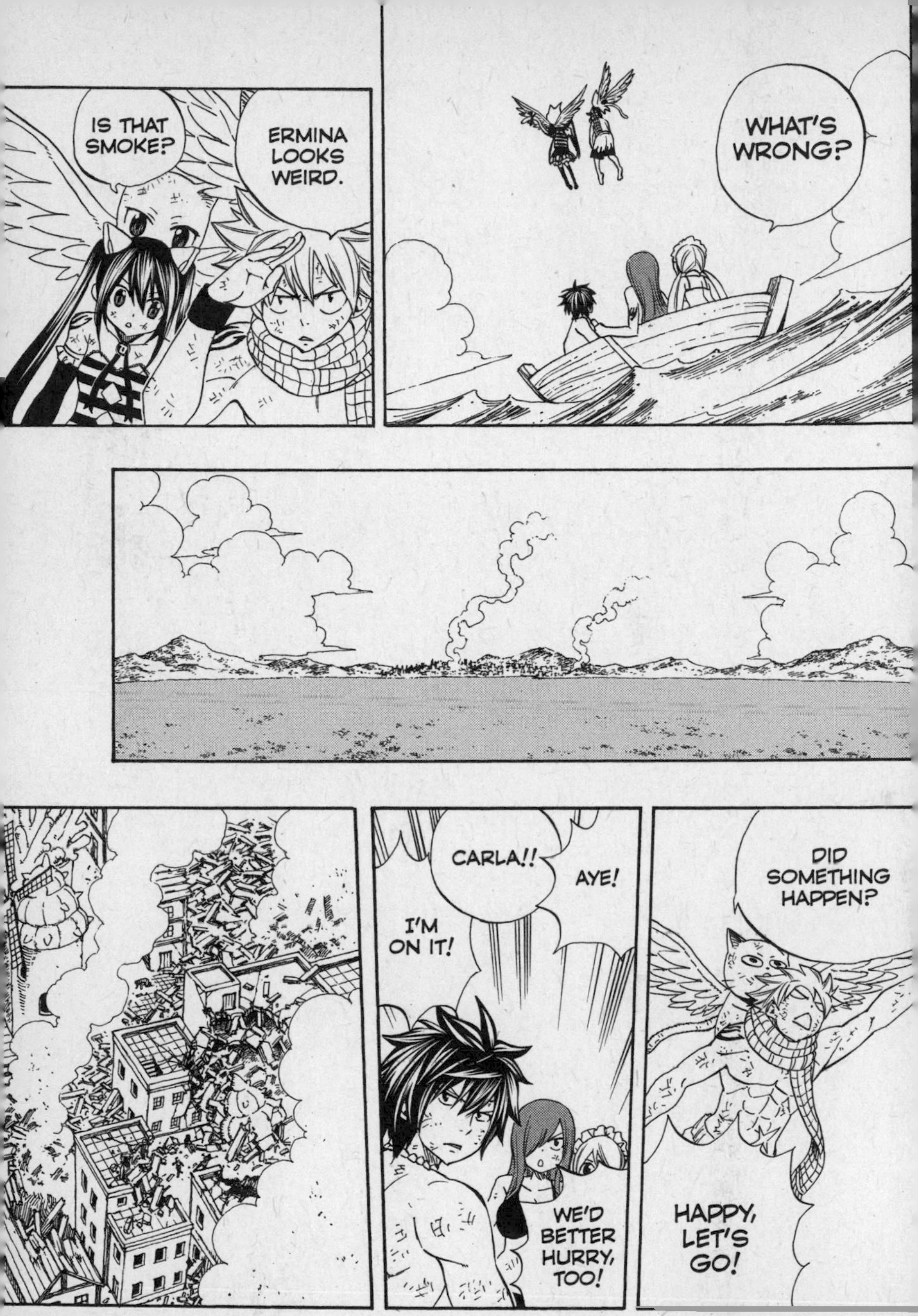
WHAT'S WRONG?
ERMINA LOOKS WEIRD.
IS THAT SMOKE?
DID SOMETHING HAPPEN?
HAPPY, LET'S GO!
AYE!
CARLA!!
I'M ON IT!
WE'D BETTER HURRY, TOO!

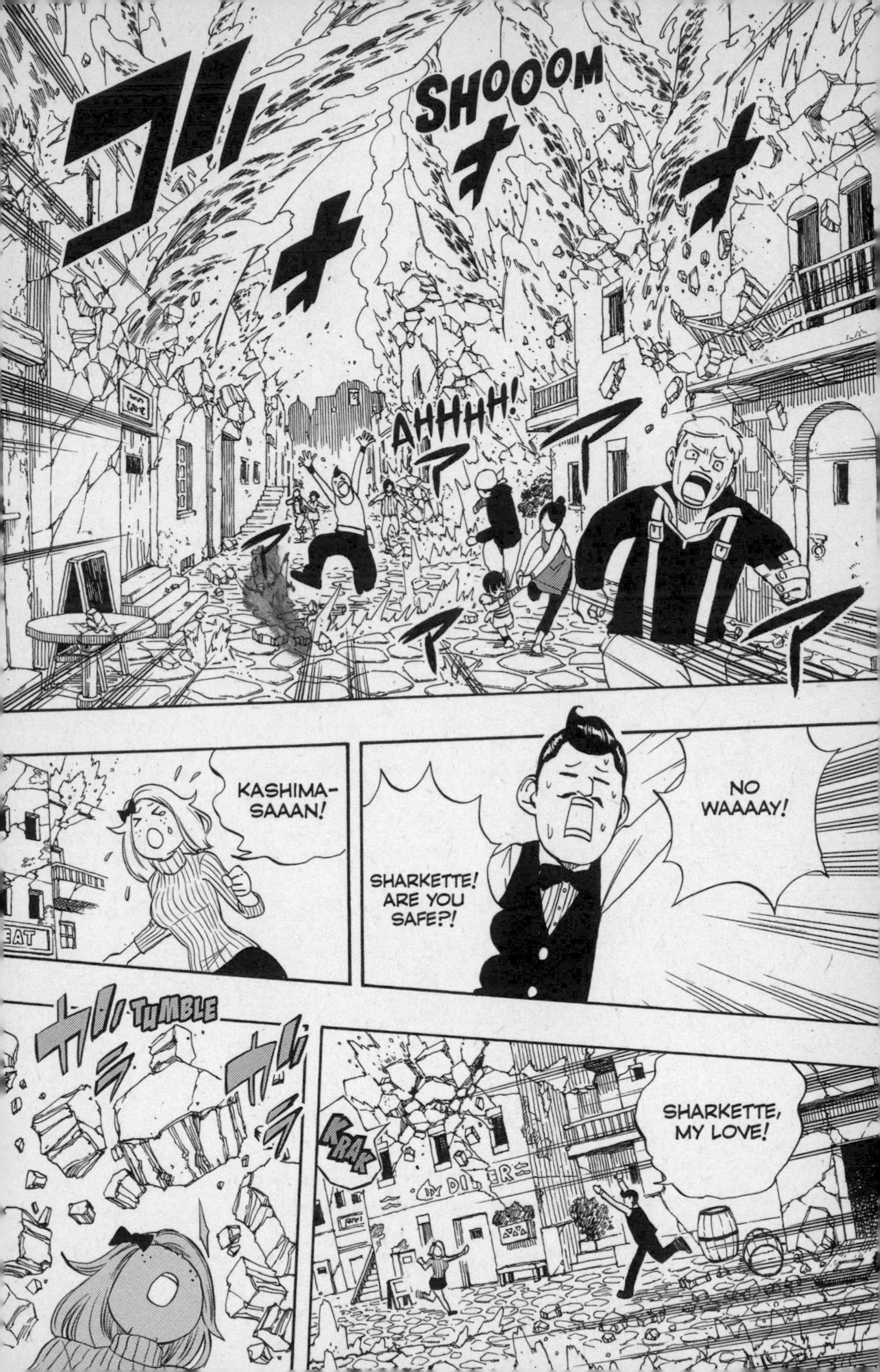
SHOOOM
AHHHH!
NO WAAAAY!
SHARKETTE! ARE YOU SAFE?!
KASHIMA-SAAAN!
SHARKETTE, MY LOVE!
KRAK
TUMBLE

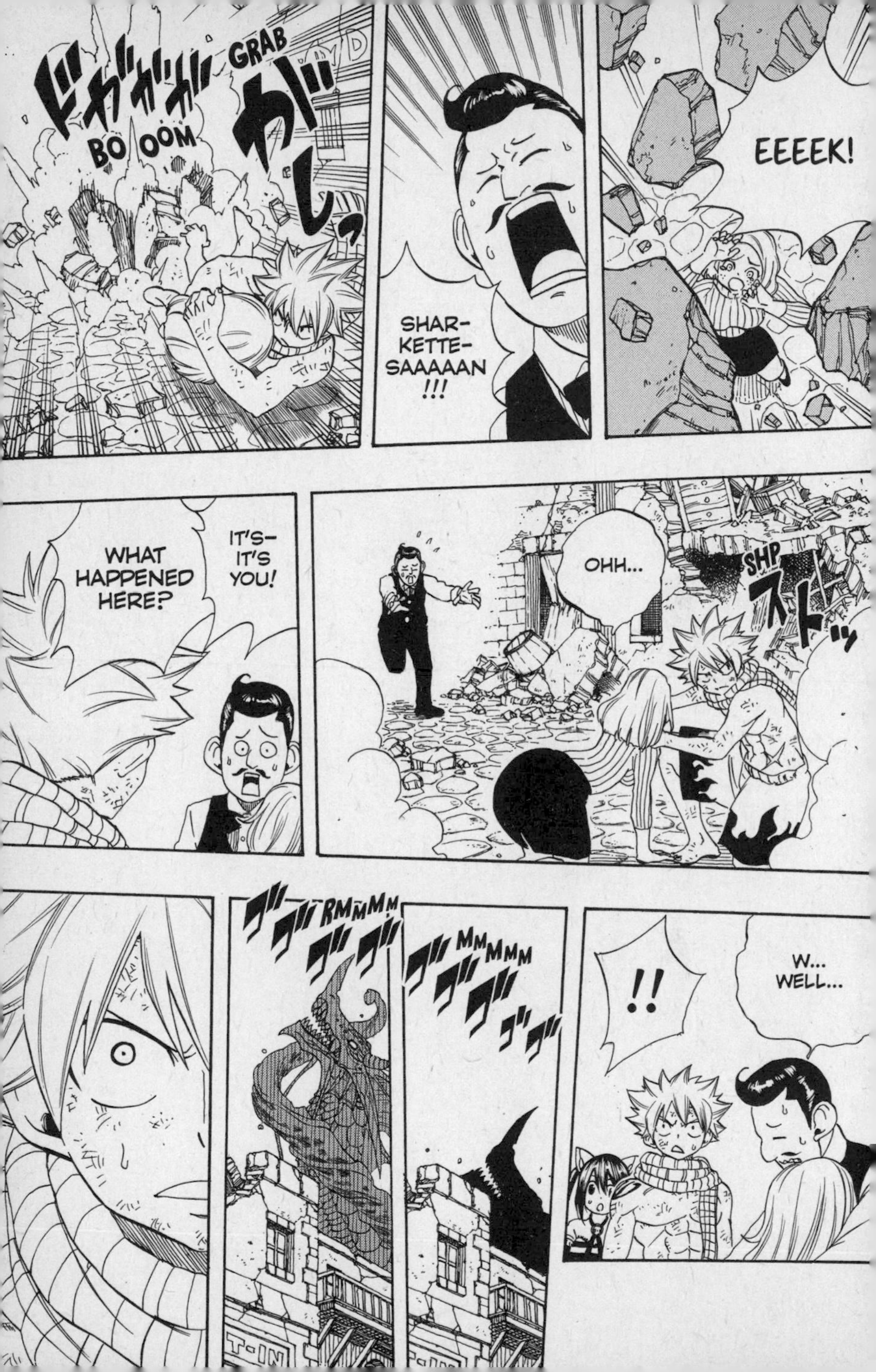
EEEEK!
SHAR-KETTE-SAAAAAN!!!
BO OOM
GRAB
OHH...
SHP
IT'S— IT'S YOU!
WHAT HAPPENED HERE?
W... WELL...
!!
MMMMM
RMMMM

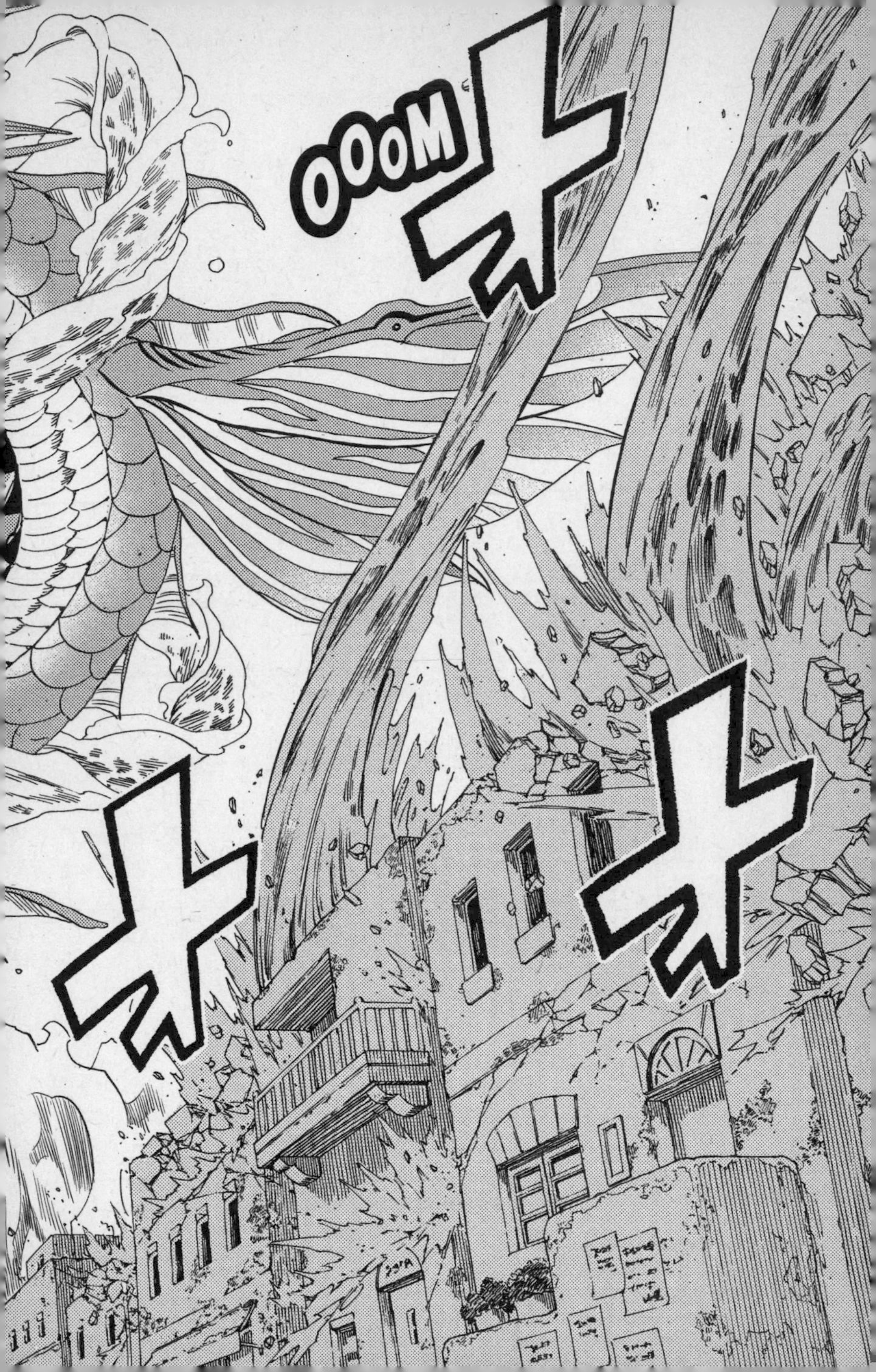
OOOM

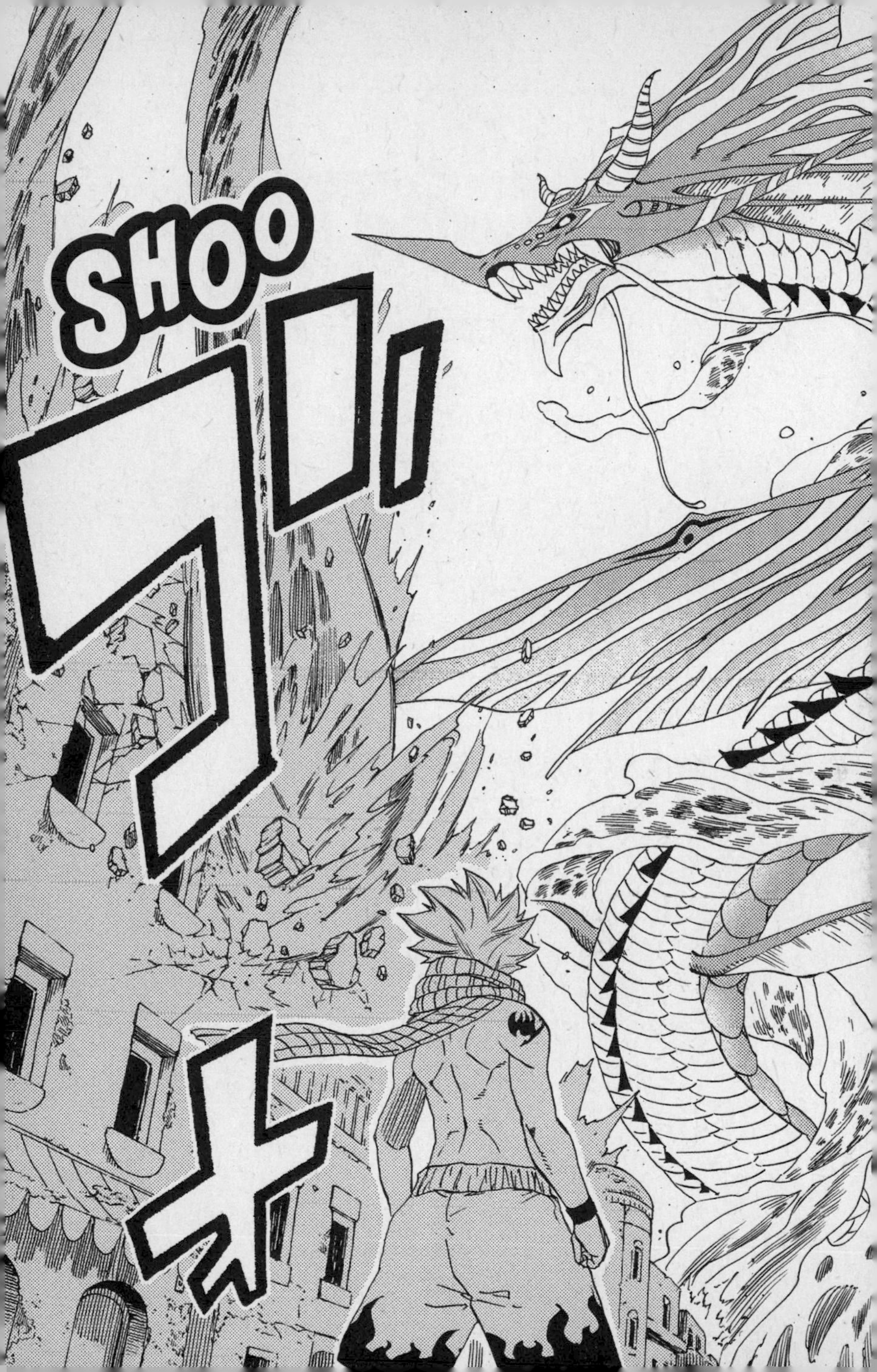
SHOO

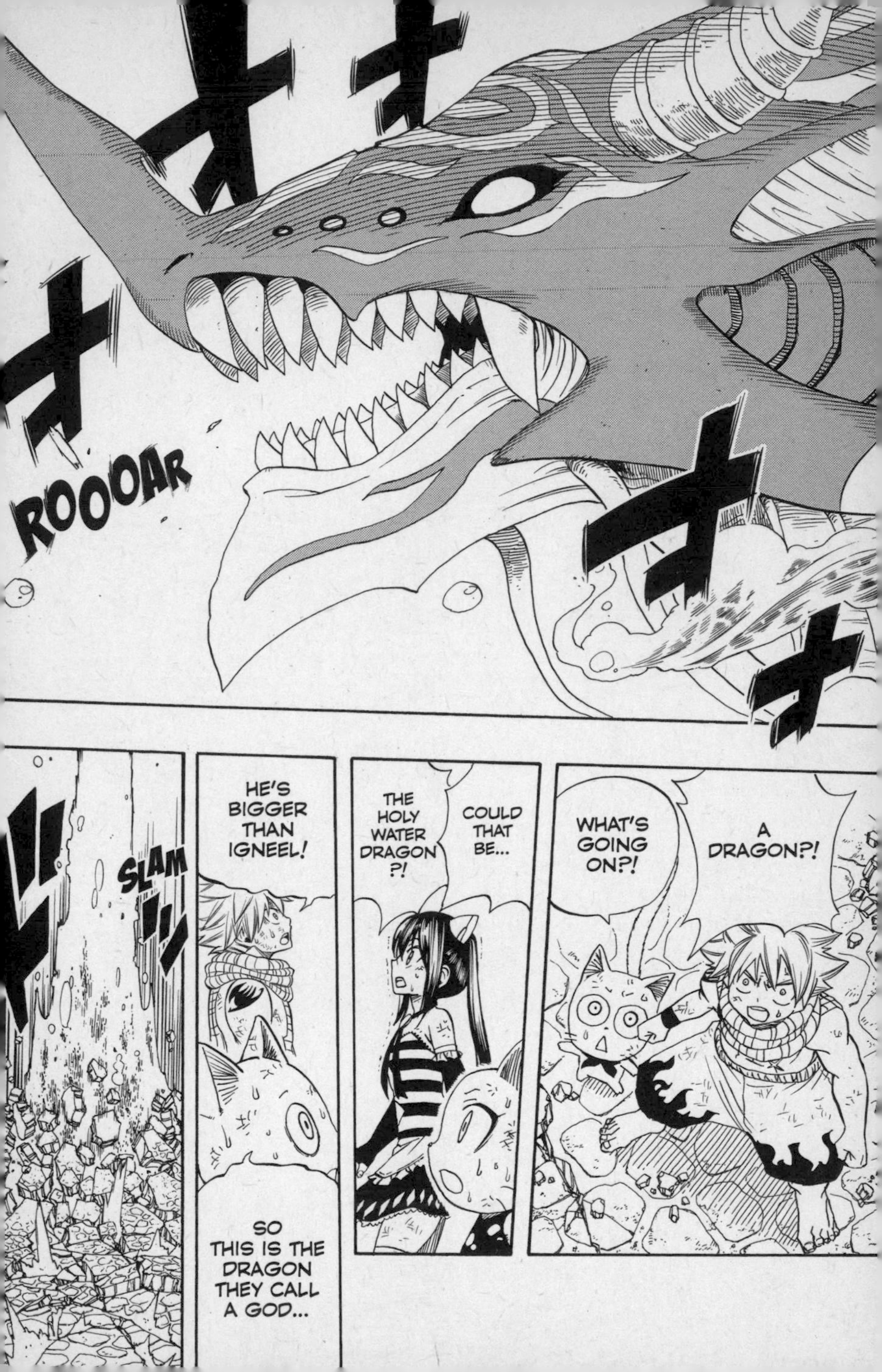
ROOOAR
A DRAGON?!
WHAT'S GOING ON?!
COULD THAT BE...
THE HOLY WATER DRAGON?!
HE'S BIGGER THAN IGNEEL!
SO THIS IS THE DRAGON THEY CALL A GOD...
SLAM

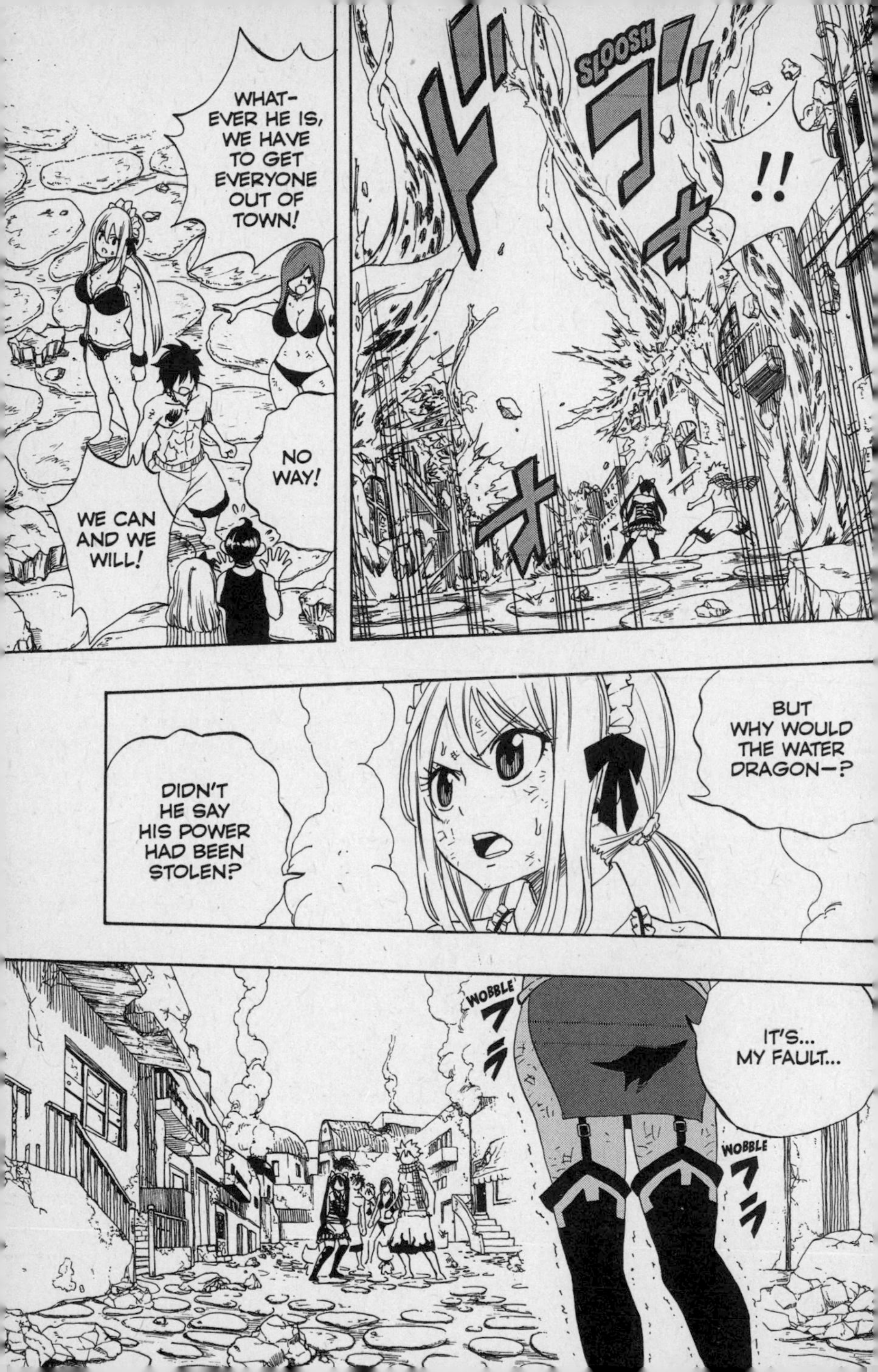
SLOOSH
!!
WHAT-EVER HE IS, WE HAVE TO GET EVERYONE OUT OF TOWN!
NO WAY!
WE CAN AND WE WILL!
BUT WHY WOULD THE WATER DRAGON—?
DIDN'T HE SAY HIS POWER HAD BEEN STOLEN?
WOBBLE
IT'S... MY FAULT...
WOBBLE

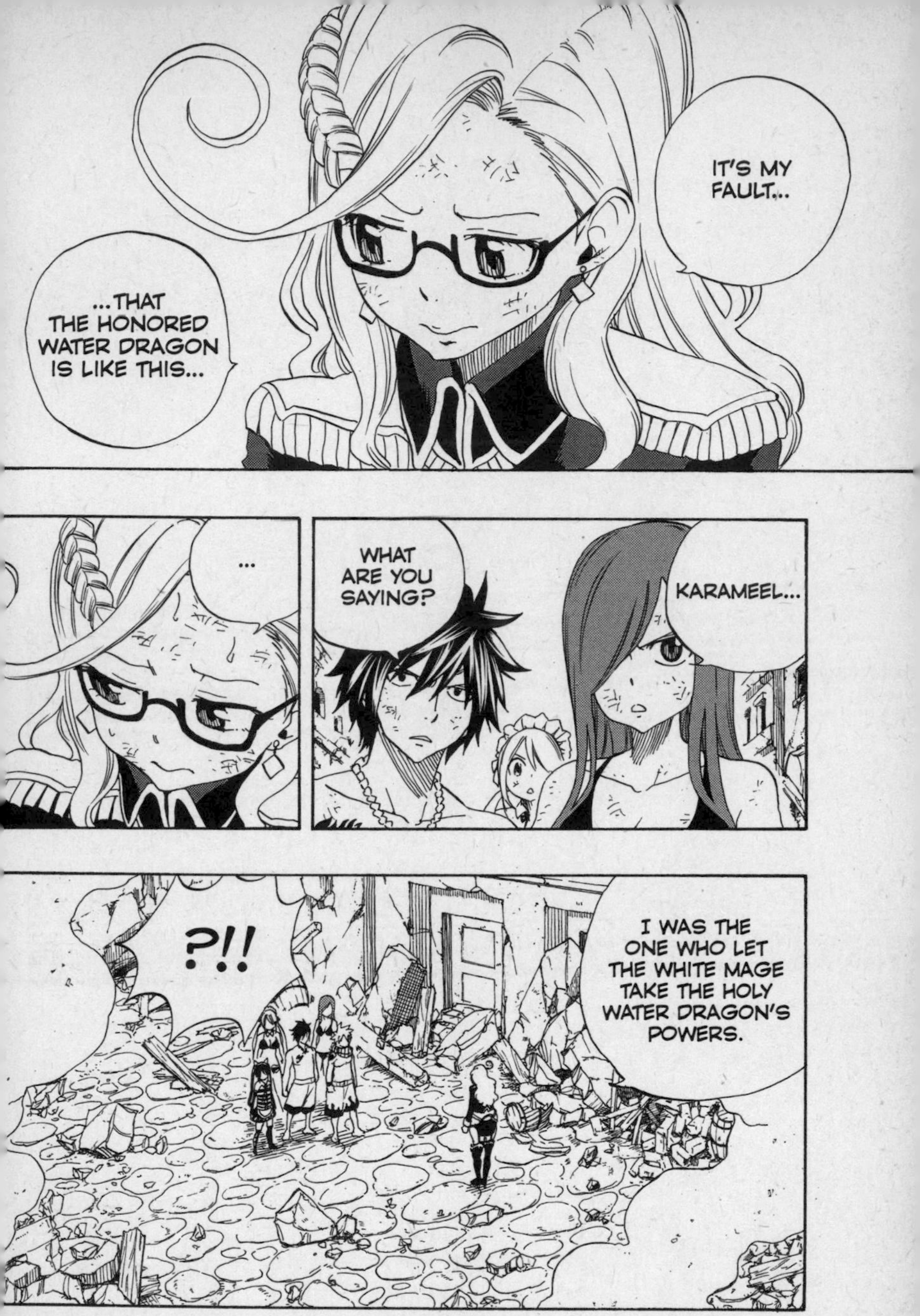
IT'S MY FAULT...
...THAT THE HONORED WATER DRAGON IS LIKE THIS...
KARAMEEL...
WHAT ARE YOU SAYING?
...
I WAS THE ONE WHO LET THE WHITE MAGE TAKE THE HOLY WATER DRAGON'S POWERS.
?!!

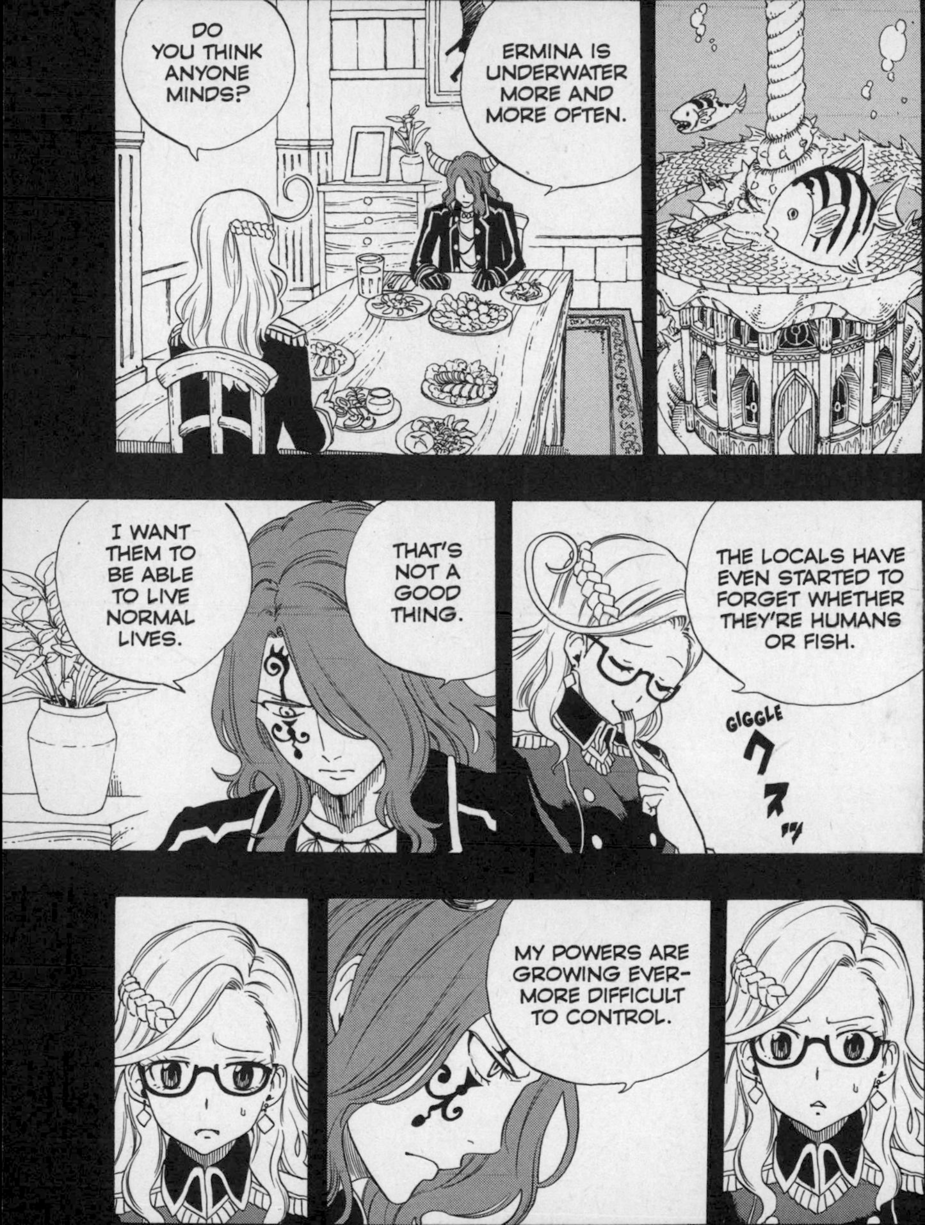
ERMINA IS UNDERWATER MORE AND MORE OFTEN.
DO YOU THINK ANYONE MINDS?
THE LOCALS HAVE EVEN STARTED TO FORGET WHETHER THEY'RE HUMANS OR FISH.
GIGGLE
THAT'S NOT A GOOD THING.
I WANT THEM TO BE ABLE TO LIVE NORMAL LIVES.
MY POWERS ARE GROWING EVER-MORE DIFFICULT TO CONTROL.

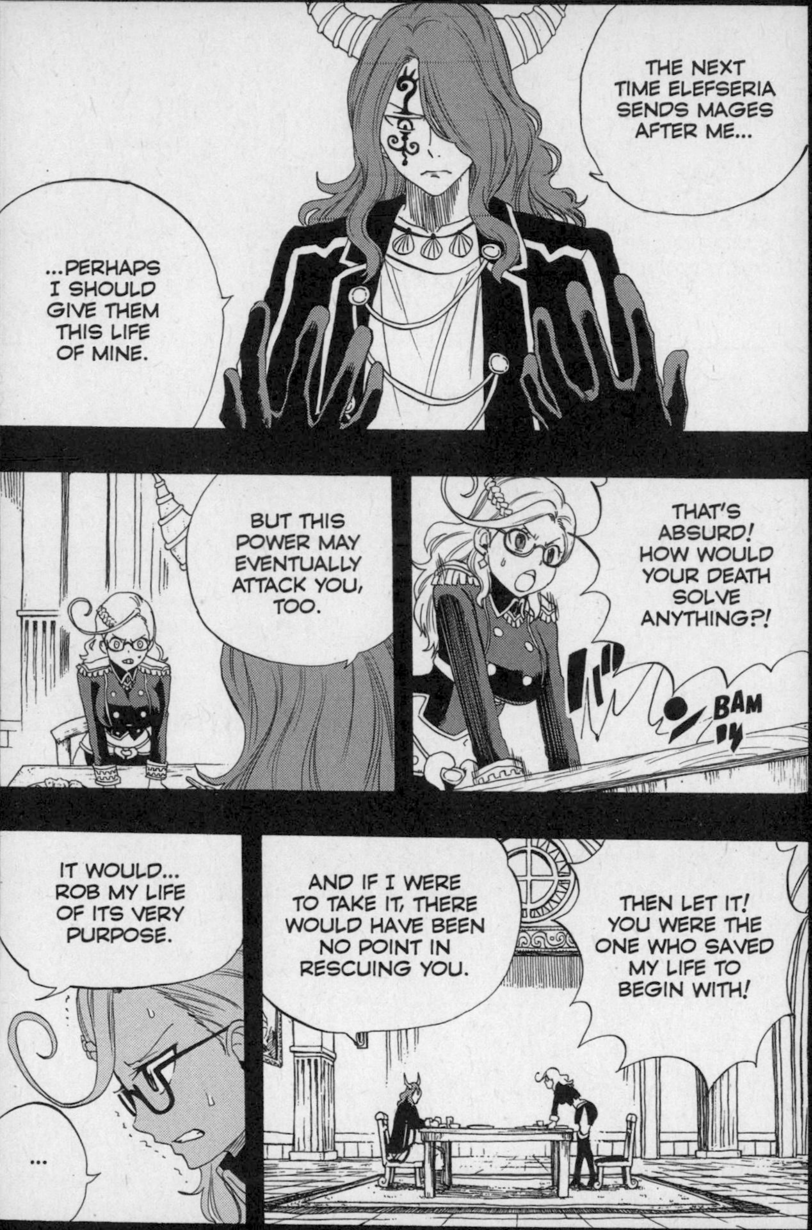
THE NEXT TIME ELEFSERIA SENDS MAGES AFTER ME...
...PERHAPS I SHOULD GIVE THEM THIS LIFE OF MINE.
THAT'S ABSURD! HOW WOULD YOUR DEATH SOLVE ANYTHING?!
BAM
BUT THIS POWER MAY EVENTUALLY ATTACK YOU, TOO.
THEN LET IT! YOU WERE THE ONE WHO SAVED MY LIFE TO BEGIN WITH!
AND IF I WERE TO TAKE IT, THERE WOULD HAVE BEEN NO POINT IN RESCUING YOU.
IT WOULD... ROB MY LIFE OF ITS VERY PURPOSE.
...

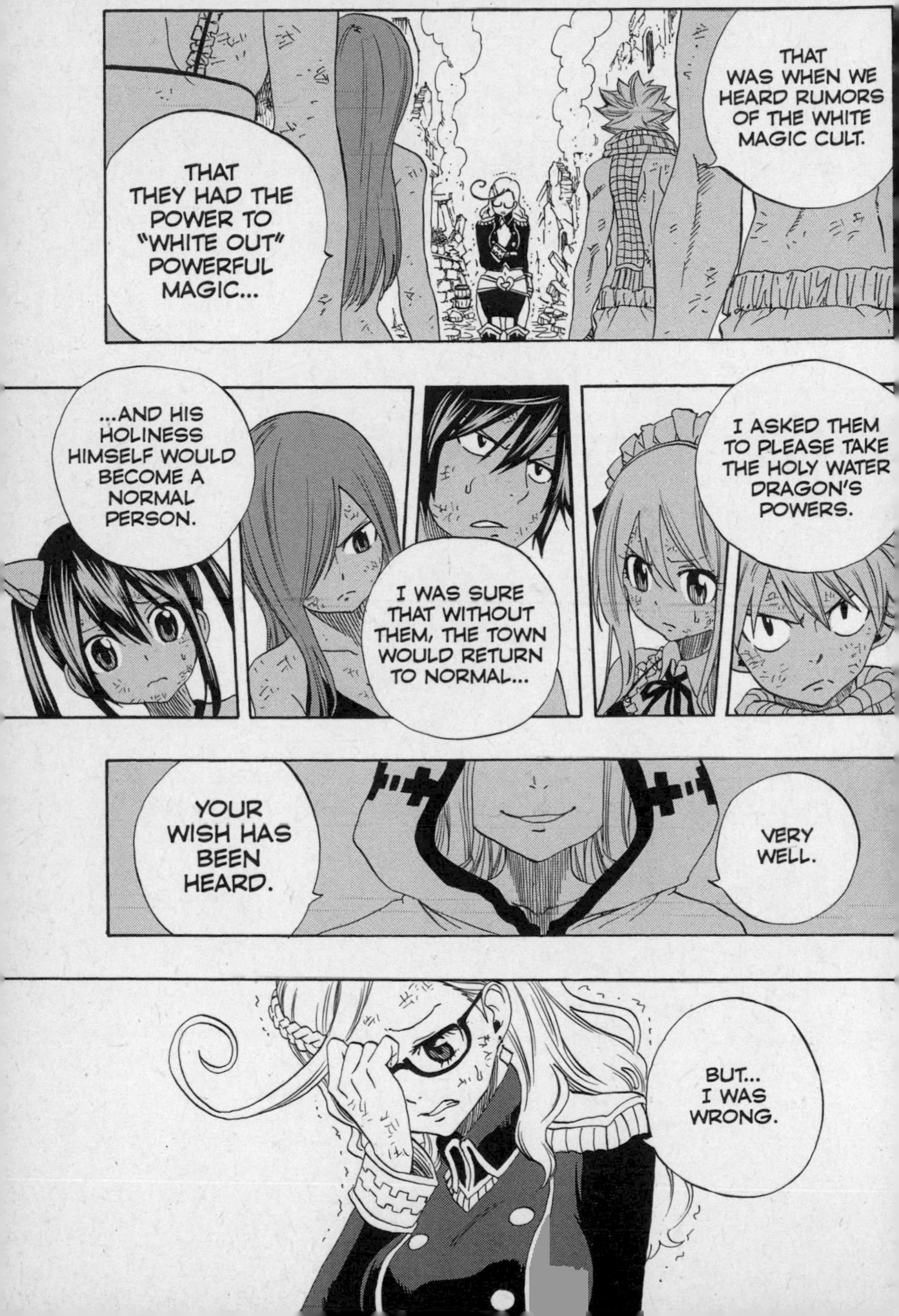
THAT WAS WHEN WE HEARD RUMORS OF THE WHITE MAGIC CULT.
THAT THEY HAD THE POWER TO "WHITE OUT" POWERFUL MAGIC...
I ASKED THEM TO PLEASE TAKE THE HOLY WATER DRAGON'S POWERS.
I WAS SURE THAT WITHOUT THEM, THE TOWN WOULD RETURN TO NORMAL...
...AND HIS HOLINESS HIMSELF WOULD BECOME A NORMAL PERSON.
VERY WELL.
YOUR WISH HAS BEEN HEARD.
BUT... I WAS WRONG.

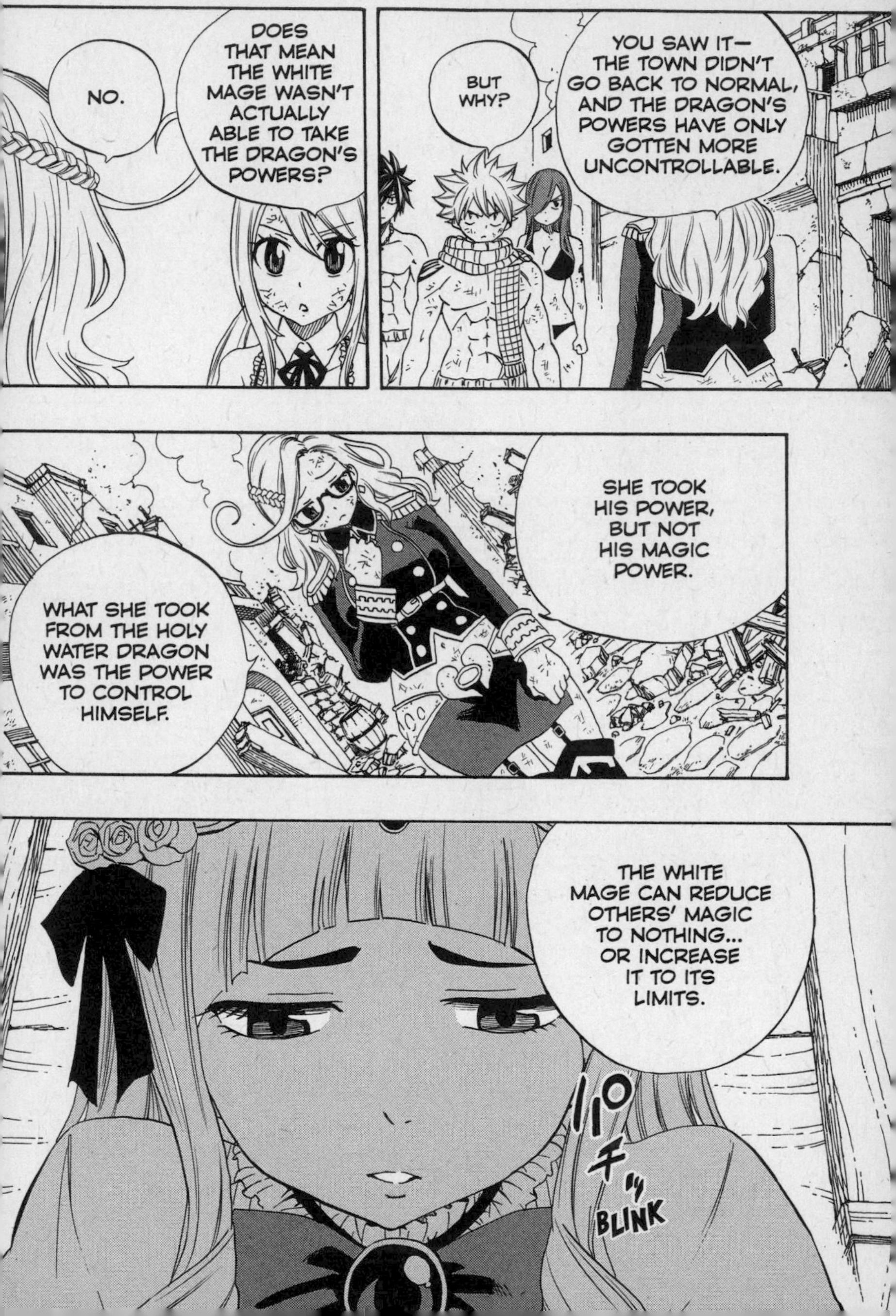
YOU SAW IT—THE TOWN DIDN'T GO BACK TO NORMAL, AND THE DRAGON'S POWERS HAVE ONLY GOTTEN MORE UNCONTROLLABLE.
BUT WHY?
DOES THAT MEAN THE WHITE MAGE WASN'T ACTUALLY ABLE TO TAKE THE DRAGON'S POWERS?
NO.
SHE TOOK HIS POWER, BUT NOT HIS MAGIC POWER.
WHAT SHE TOOK FROM THE HOLY WATER DRAGON WAS THE POWER TO CONTROL HIMSELF.
THE WHITE MAGE CAN REDUCE OTHERS' MAGIC TO NOTHING... OR INCREASE IT TO ITS LIMITS.
パチッ
BLINK

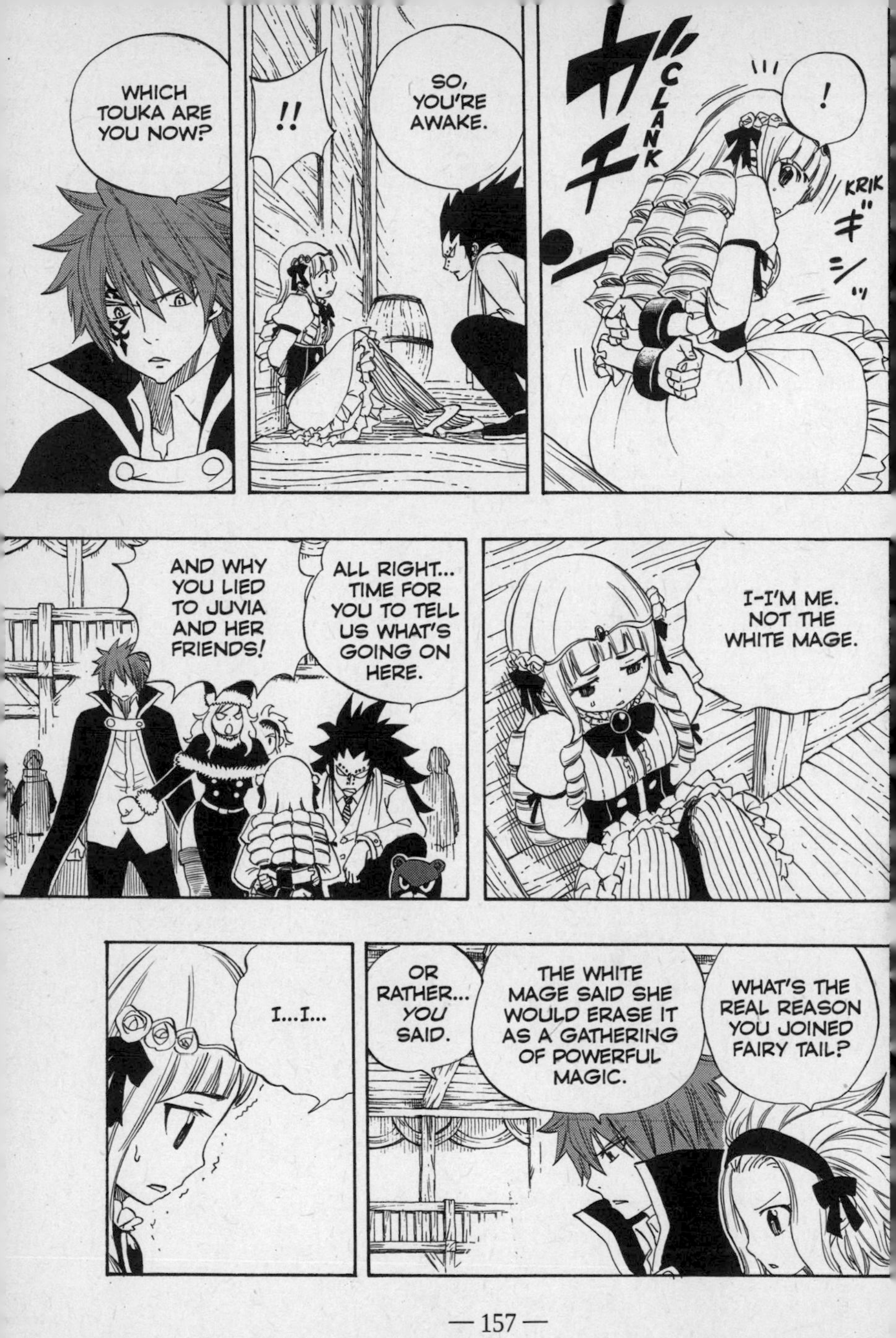
!
ガチ
CLANK
ギシッ
KRIK
SO, YOU'RE AWAKE.
!!
WHICH TOUKA ARE YOU NOW?
I-I'M ME. NOT THE WHITE MAGE.
ALL RIGHT... TIME FOR YOU TO TELL US WHAT'S GOING ON HERE.
AND WHY YOU LIED TO JUVIA AND HER FRIENDS!
WHAT'S THE REAL REASON YOU JOINED FAIRY TAIL?
THE WHITE MAGE SAID SHE WOULD ERASE IT AS A GATHERING OF POWERFUL MAGIC.
OR RATHER... *YOU* SAID.
I...I...

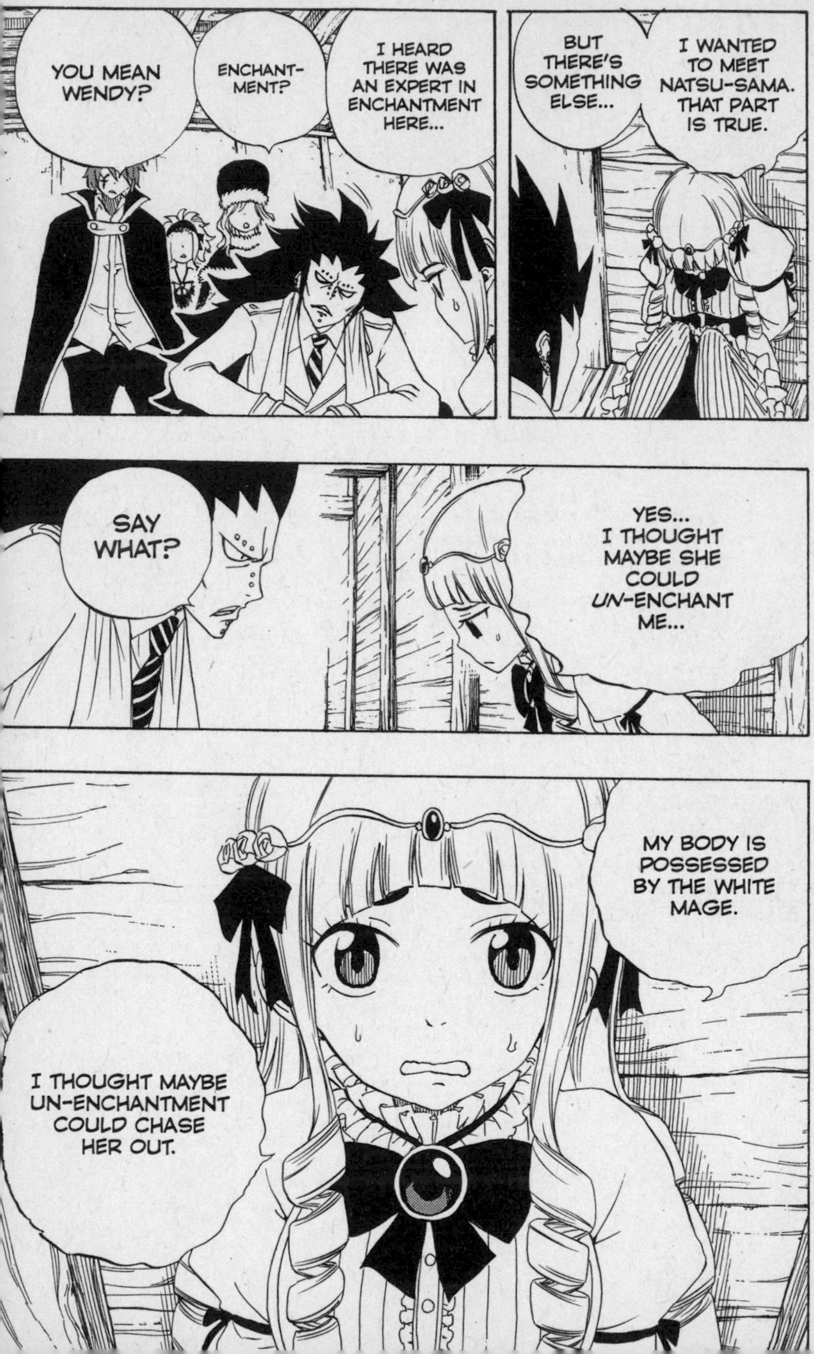
I WANTED TO MEET NATSU-SAMA. THAT PART IS TRUE.
BUT THERE'S SOMETHING ELSE...
I HEARD THERE WAS AN EXPERT IN ENCHANTMENT HERE...
ENCHANT-MENT?
YOU MEAN WENDY?
YES... I THOUGHT MAYBE SHE COULD *UN*-ENCHANT ME...
SAY WHAT?
MY BODY IS POSSESSED BY THE WHITE MAGE.
I THOUGHT MAYBE UN-ENCHANTMENT COULD CHASE HER OUT.

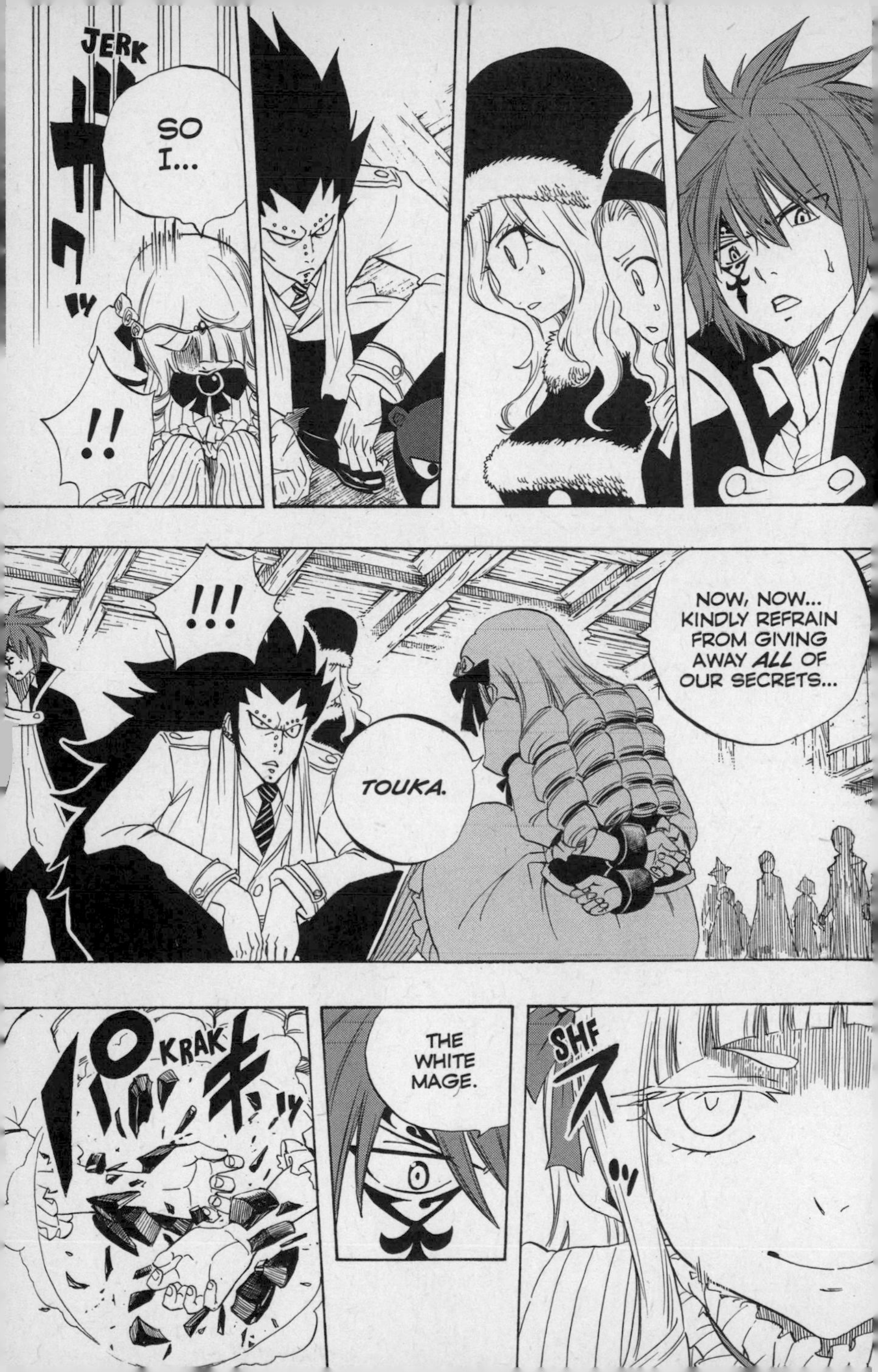
JERK
SO I...
!!
NOW, NOW... KINDLY REFRAIN FROM GIVING AWAY ALL OF OUR SECRETS...
!!!
TOUKA.
SHF
THE WHITE MAGE.
KRAK

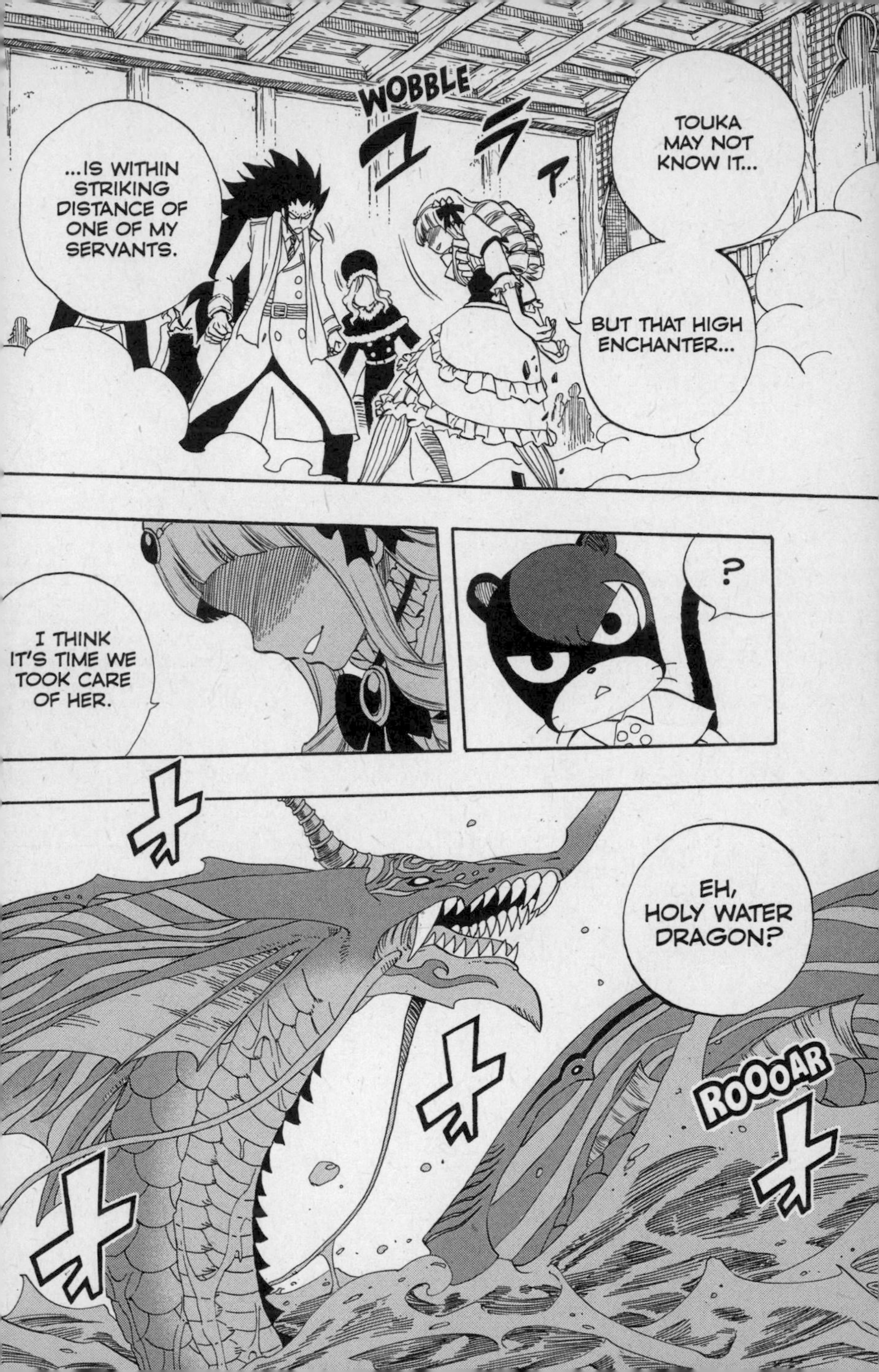
TOUKA MAY NOT KNOW IT...
BUT THAT HIGH ENCHANTER...
WOBBLE
ユラァ
...IS WITHIN STRIKING DISTANCE OF ONE OF MY SERVANTS.
?
I THINK IT'S TIME WE TOOK CARE OF HER.
EH, HOLY WATER DRAGON?
ROOOAR

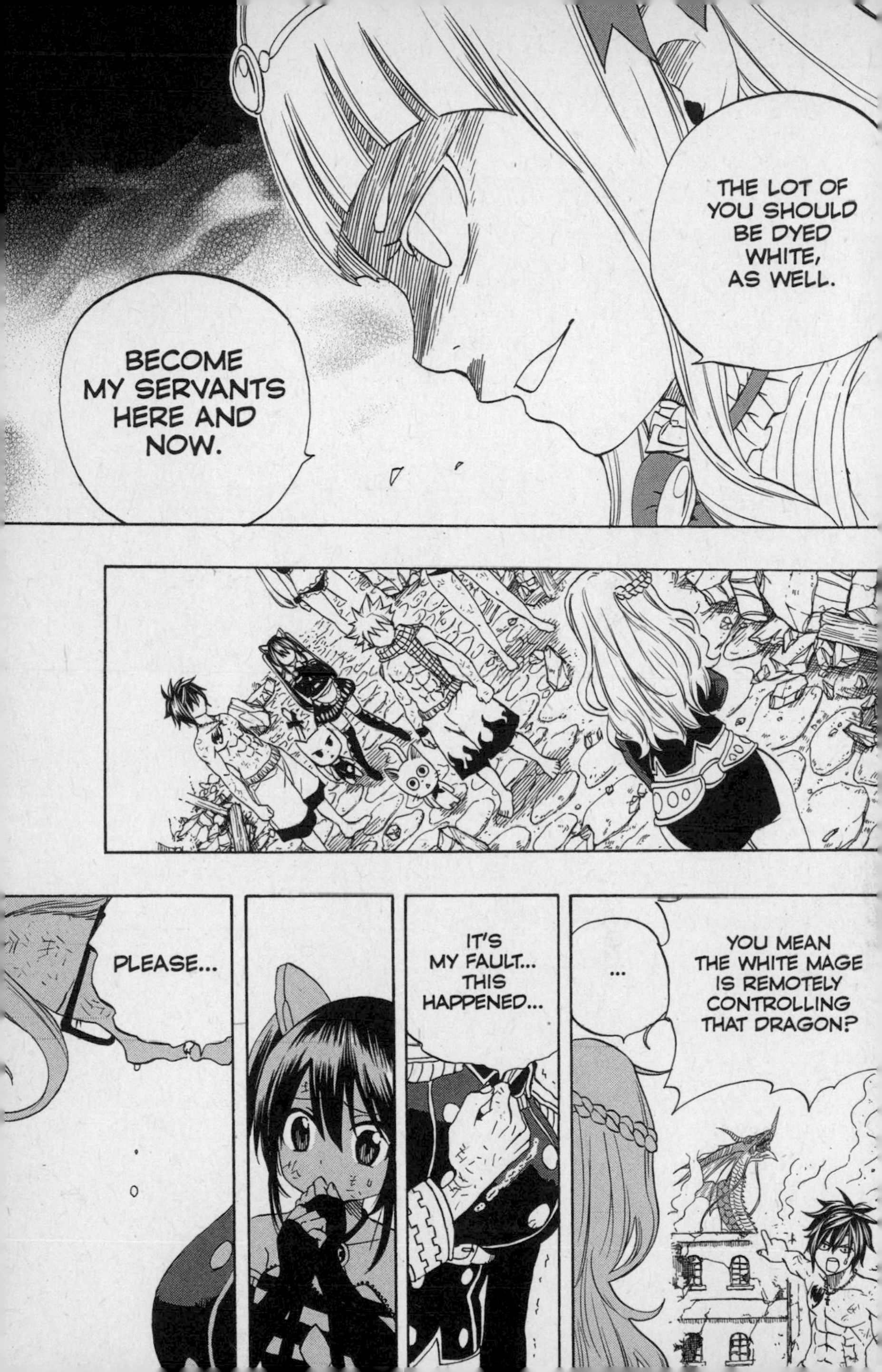
THE LOT OF YOU SHOULD BE DYED WHITE, AS WELL.
BECOME MY SERVANTS HERE AND NOW.
YOU MEAN THE WHITE MAGE IS REMOTELY CONTROLLING THAT DRAGON?
...
IT'S MY FAULT... THIS HAPPENED...
PLEASE...

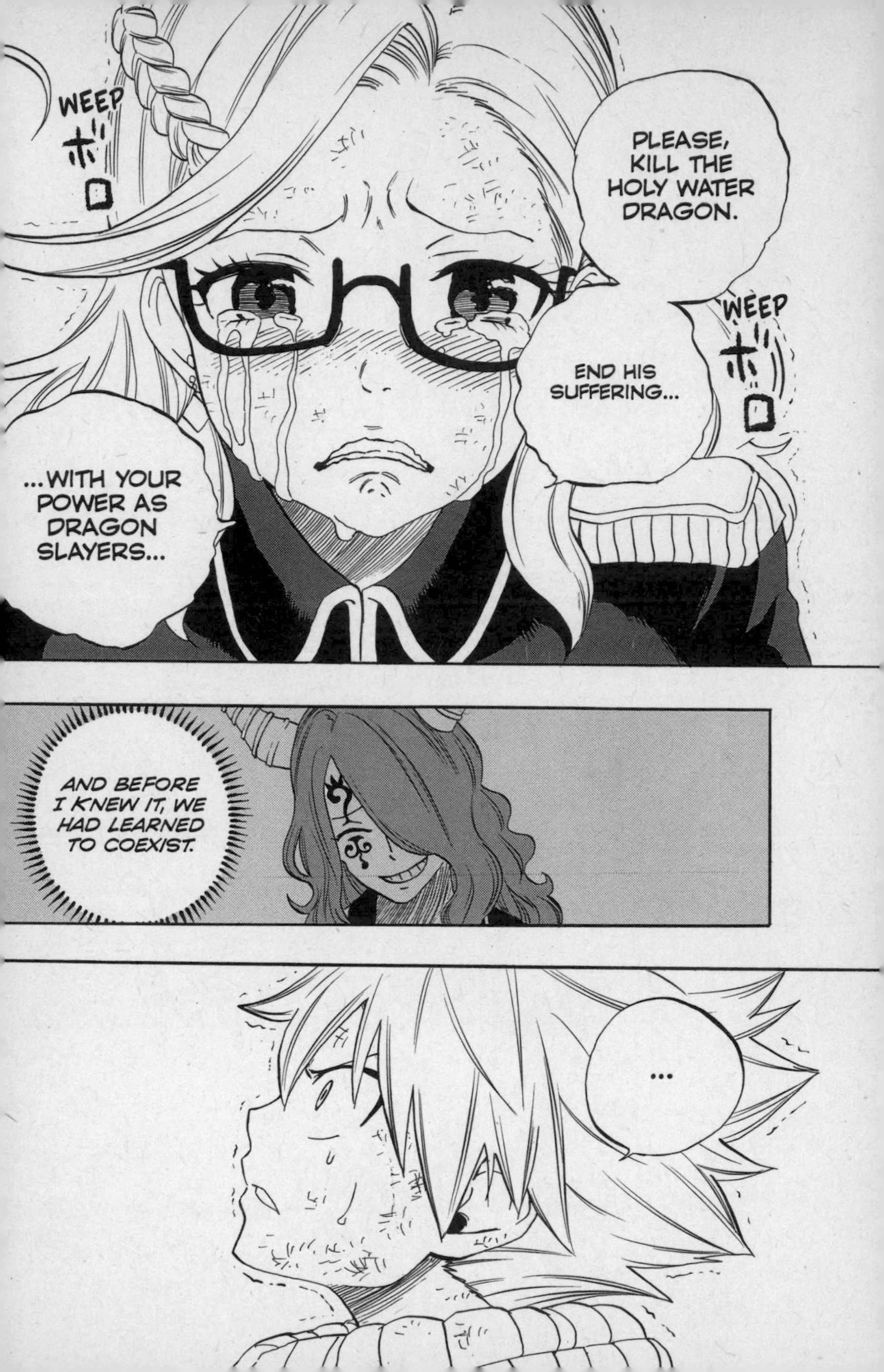
PLEASE, KILL THE HOLY WATER DRAGON.
WEEP
ボロ
END HIS SUFFERING...
WEEP
ボロ
...WITH YOUR POWER AS DRAGON SLAYERS...
AND BEFORE I KNEW IT, WE HAD LEARNED TO COEXIST.
...

FAIRY TAIL 100 YEARS QUEST

Chapter 18: A Bitter Choice

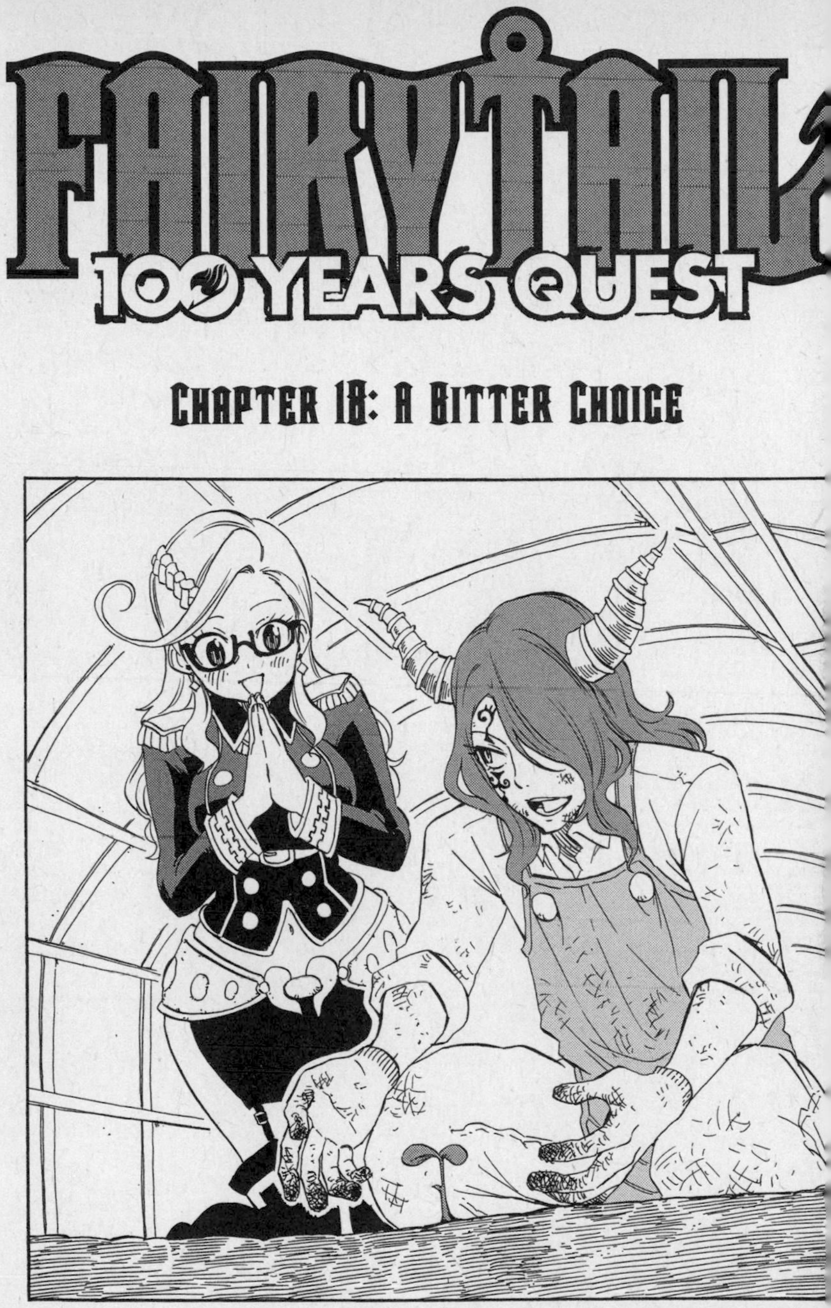

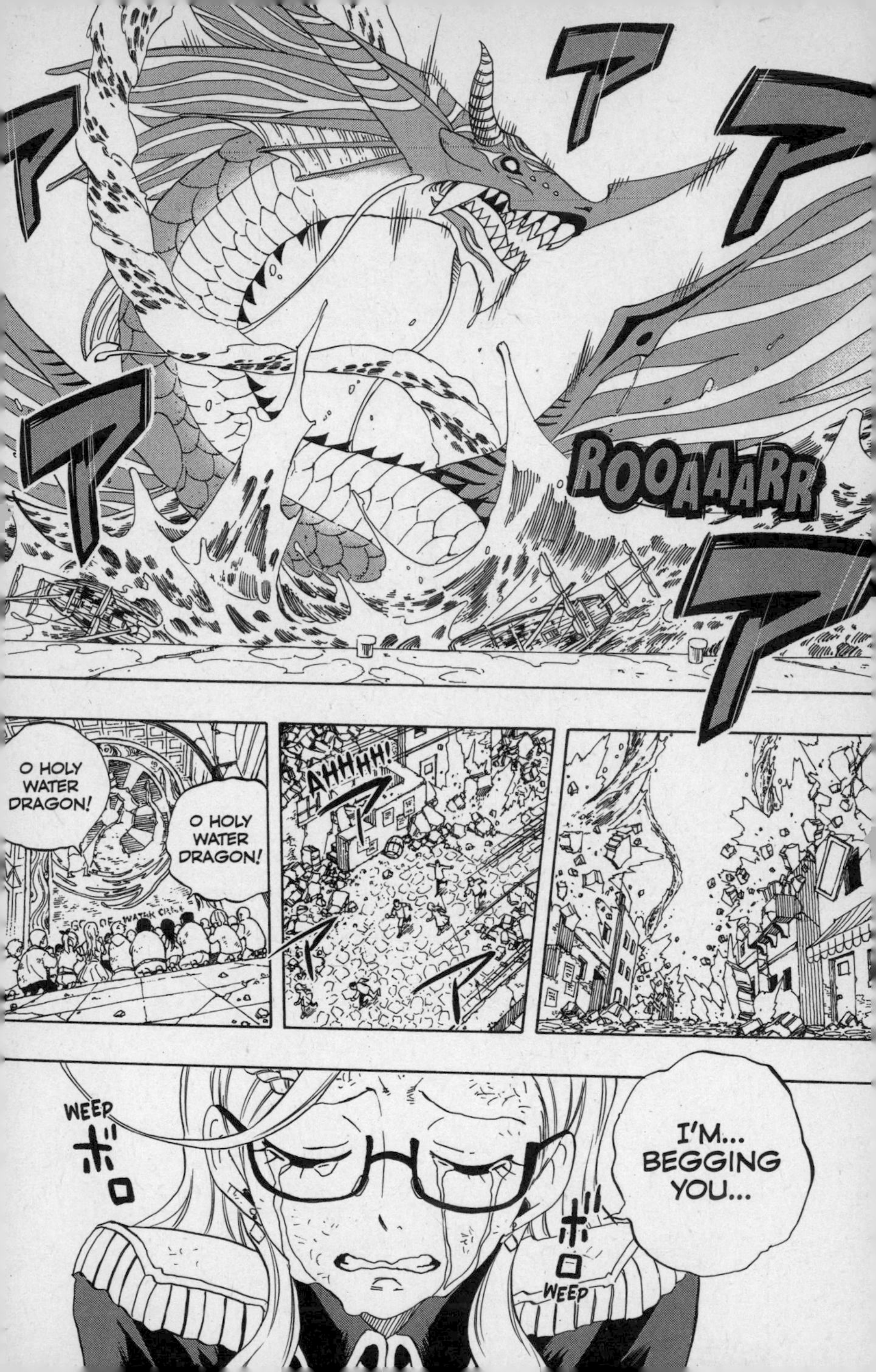

ROOAAARR
AHHHH!
O HOLY WATER DRAGON!
O HOLY WATER DRAGON!
I'M... BEGGING YOU...
WEEP
ボロ
ボロ
WEEP

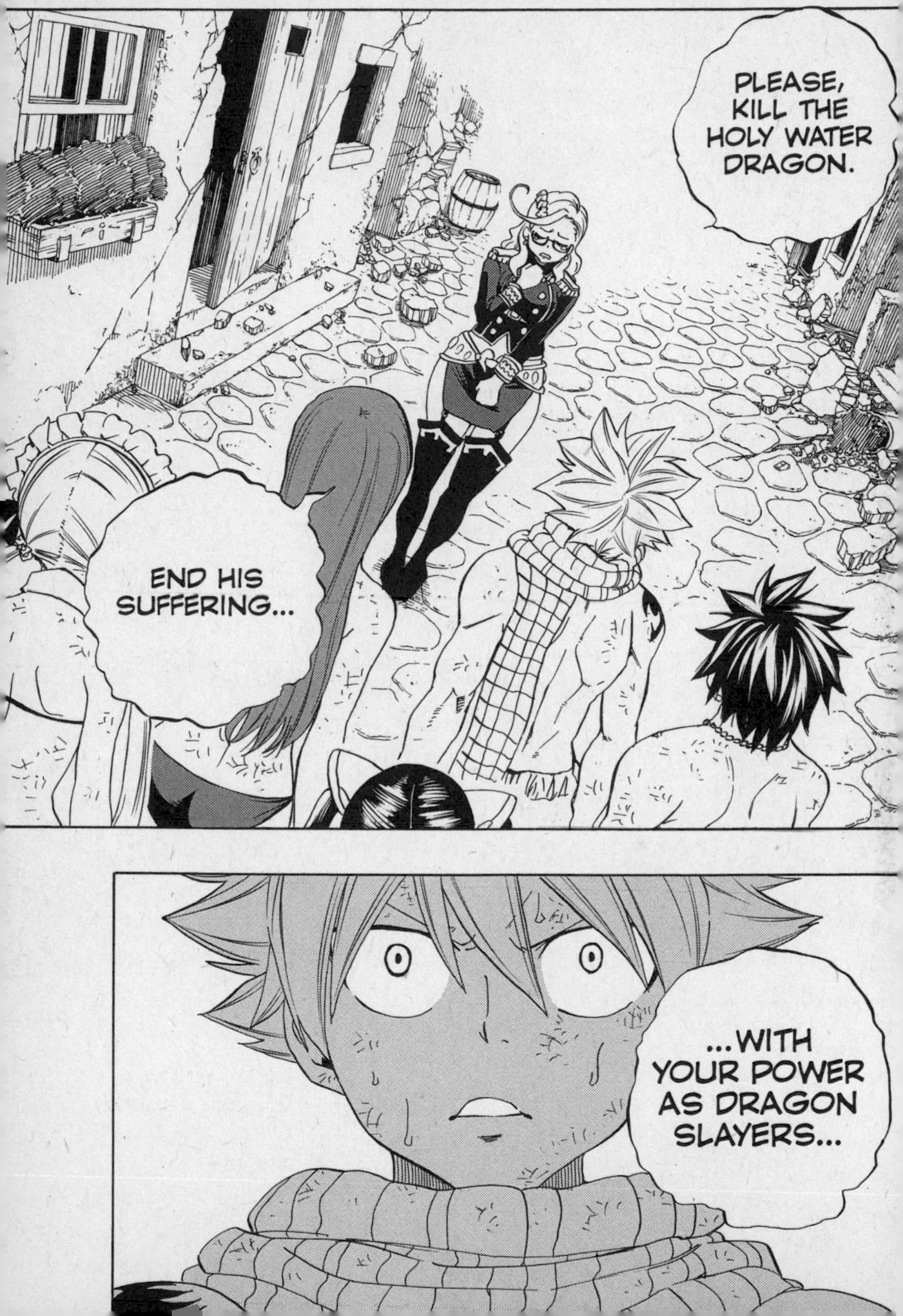
PLEASE, KILL THE HOLY WATER DRAGON.
END HIS SUFFERING...
...WITH YOUR POWER AS DRAGON SLAYERS...

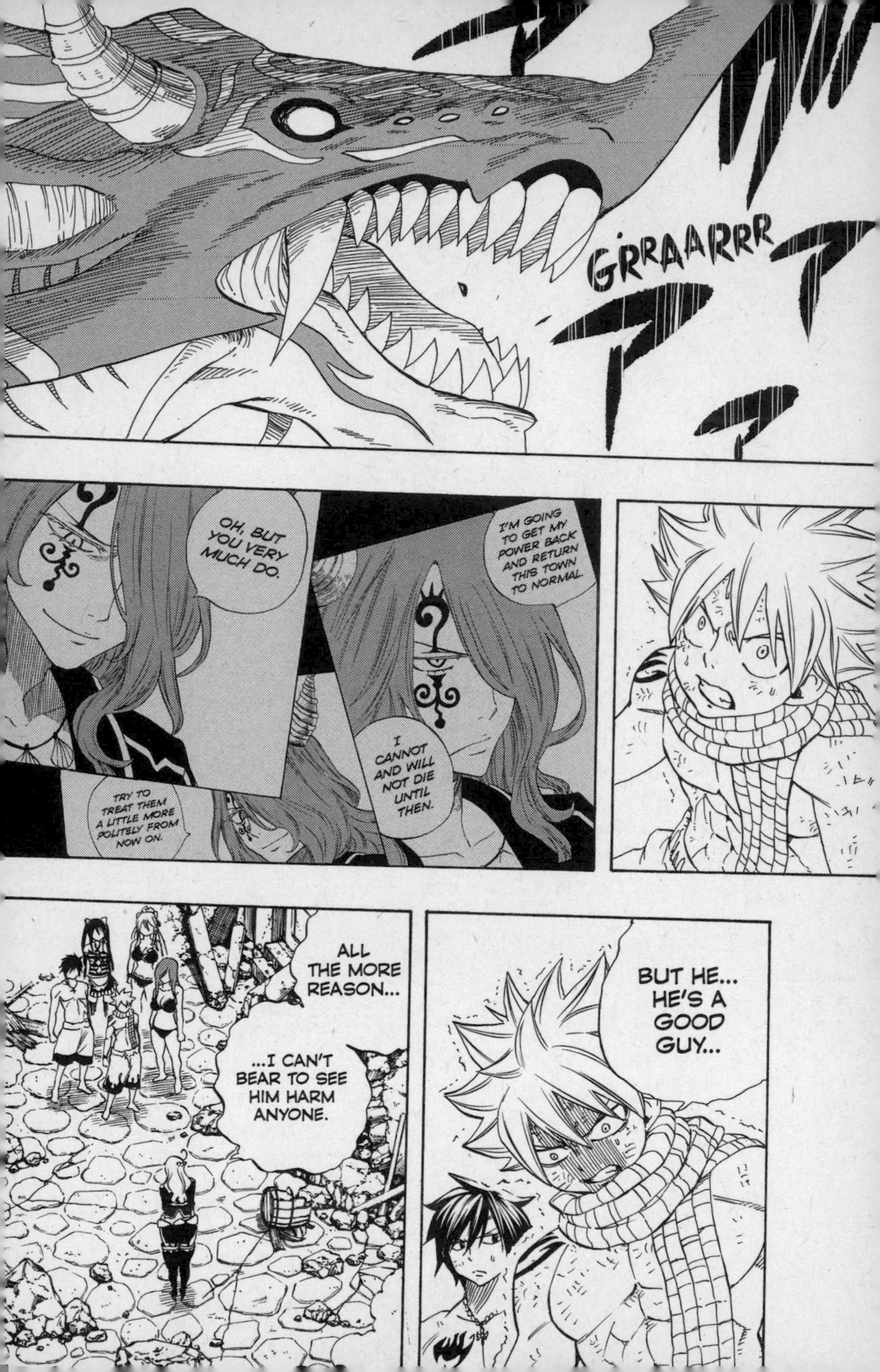
GRRAARRR
I'M GOING TO GET MY POWER BACK AND RETURN THIS TOWN TO NORMAL.
I CANNOT AND WILL NOT DIE UNTIL THEN.
OH, BUT YOU VERY MUCH DO.
TRY TO TREAT THEM A LITTLE MORE POLITELY FROM NOW ON.
BUT HE... HE'S A GOOD GUY...
ALL THE MORE REASON...
...I CAN'T BEAR TO SEE HIM HARM ANYONE.

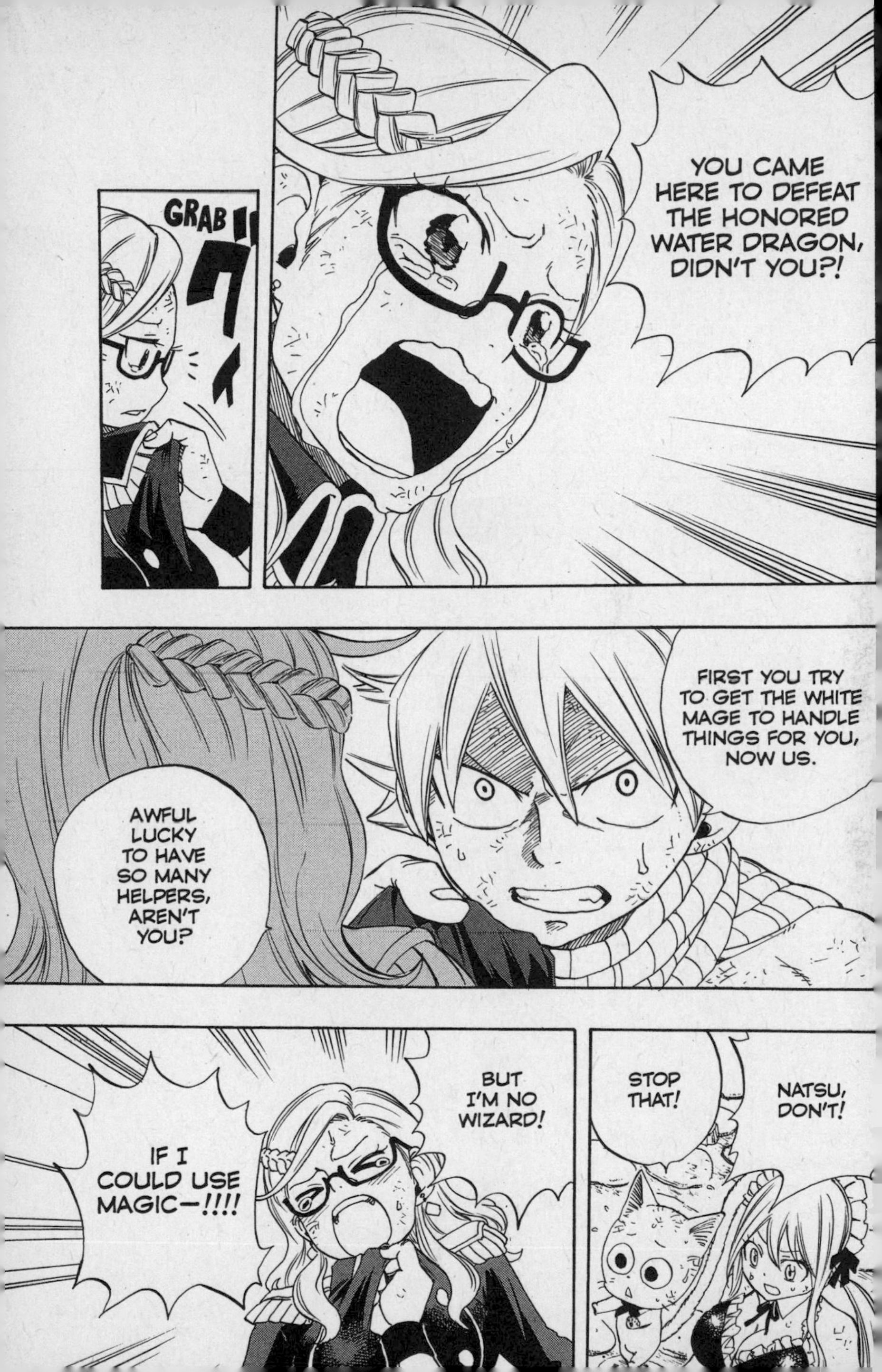
YOU CAME HERE TO DEFEAT THE HONORED WATER DRAGON, DIDN'T YOU?!
GRAB
FIRST YOU TRY TO GET THE WHITE MAGE TO HANDLE THINGS FOR YOU, NOW US.
AWFUL LUCKY TO HAVE SO MANY HELPERS, AREN'T YOU?
NATSU, DON'T!
STOP THAT!
BUT I'M NO WIZARD!
IF I COULD USE MAGIC—!!!!

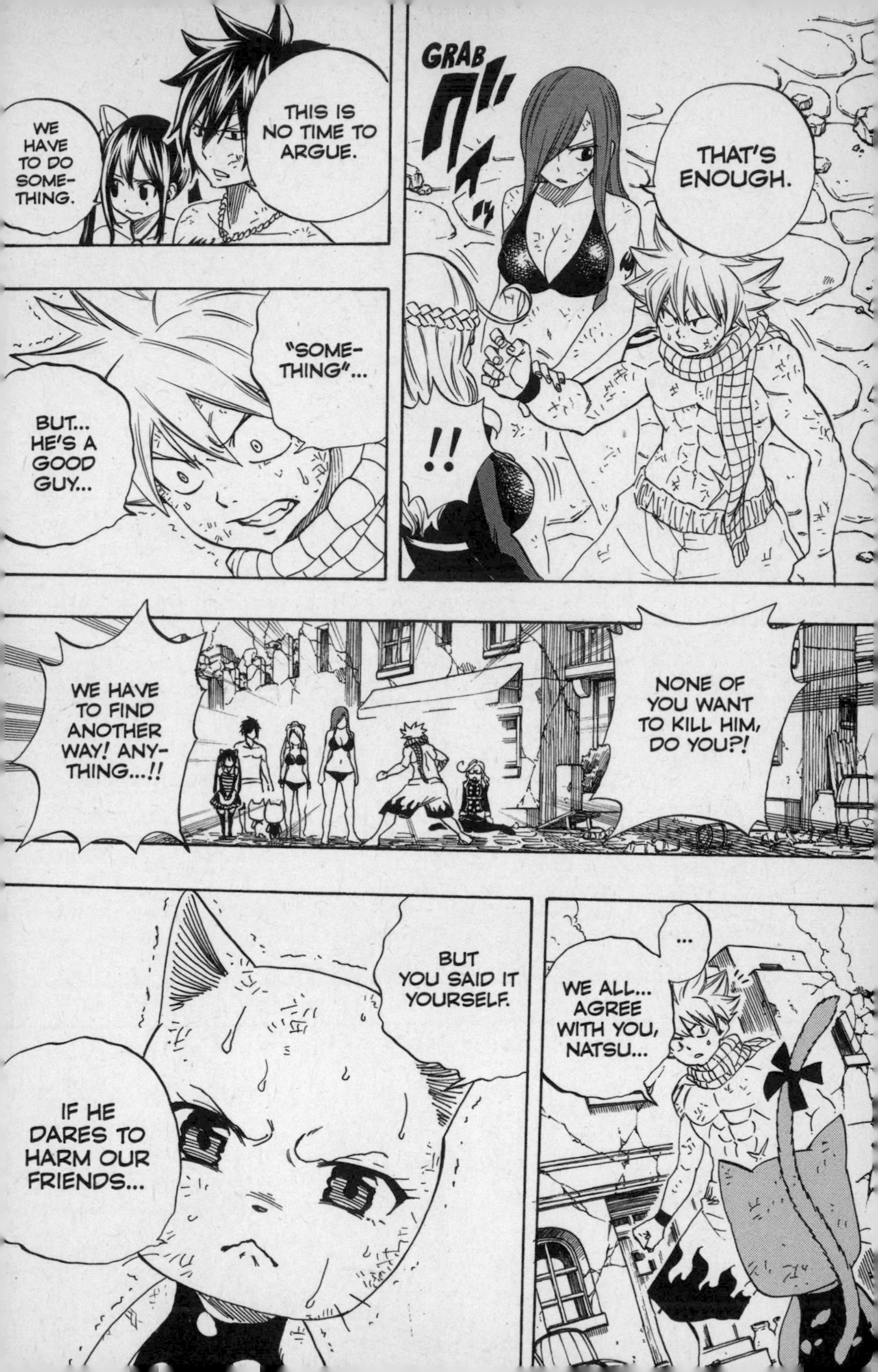
GRAB
THAT'S ENOUGH.
!!
THIS IS NO TIME TO ARGUE.
WE HAVE TO DO SOME-THING.
"SOME-THING"...
BUT... HE'S A GOOD GUY...
NONE OF YOU WANT TO KILL HIM, DO YOU?!
WE HAVE TO FIND ANOTHER WAY! ANY-THING...!!
...
WE ALL... AGREE WITH YOU, NATSU...
BUT YOU SAID IT YOURSELF.
IF HE DARES TO HARM OUR FRIENDS...

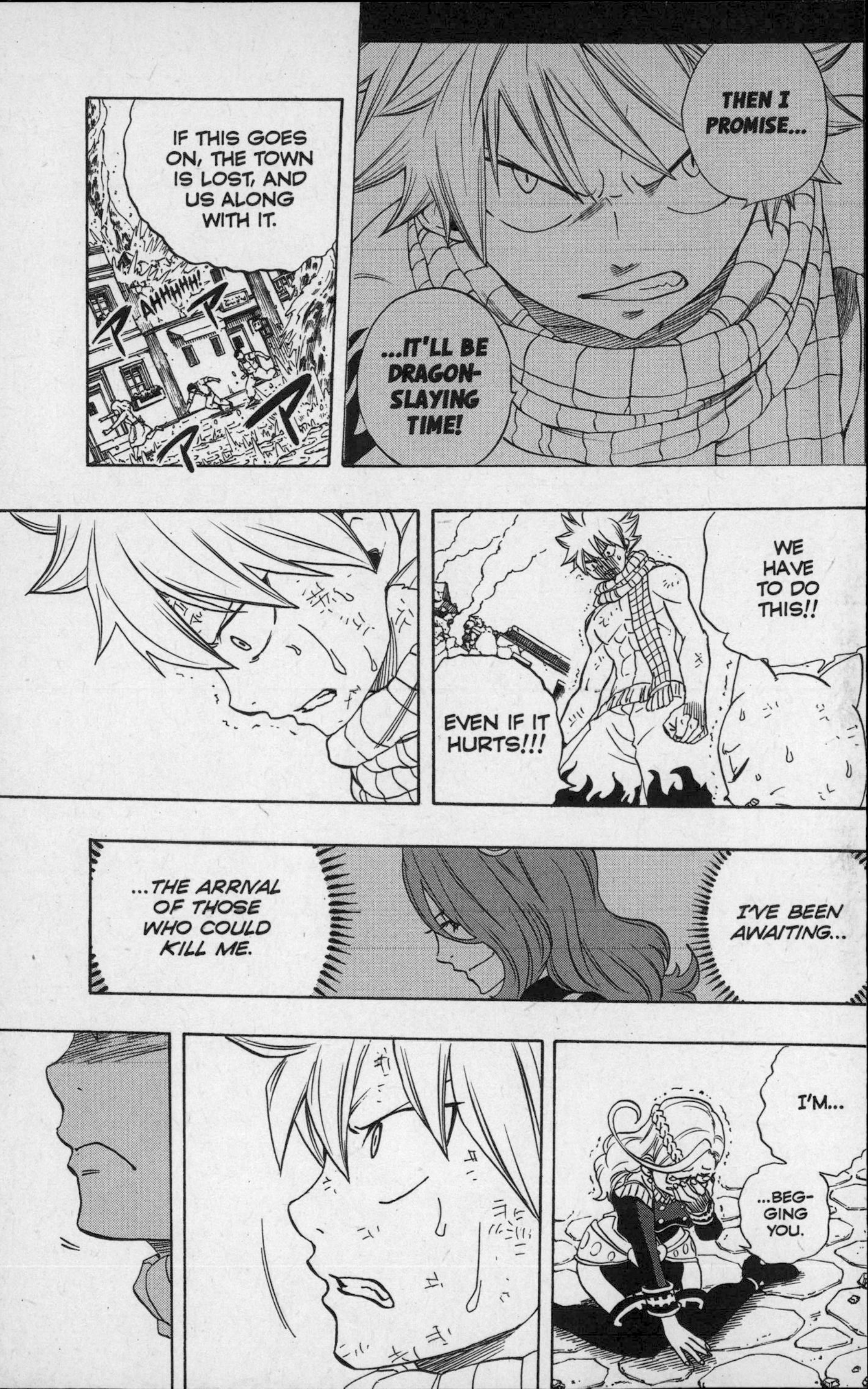
THEN I PROMISE...
...IT'LL BE DRAGON-SLAYING TIME!
IF THIS GOES ON, THE TOWN IS LOST, AND US ALONG WITH IT.
AHHHHHH!
WE HAVE TO DO THIS!!
EVEN IF IT HURTS!!!
I'VE BEEN AWAITING...
...THE ARRIVAL OF THOSE WHO COULD KILL ME.
I'M...
...BEG-GING YOU.

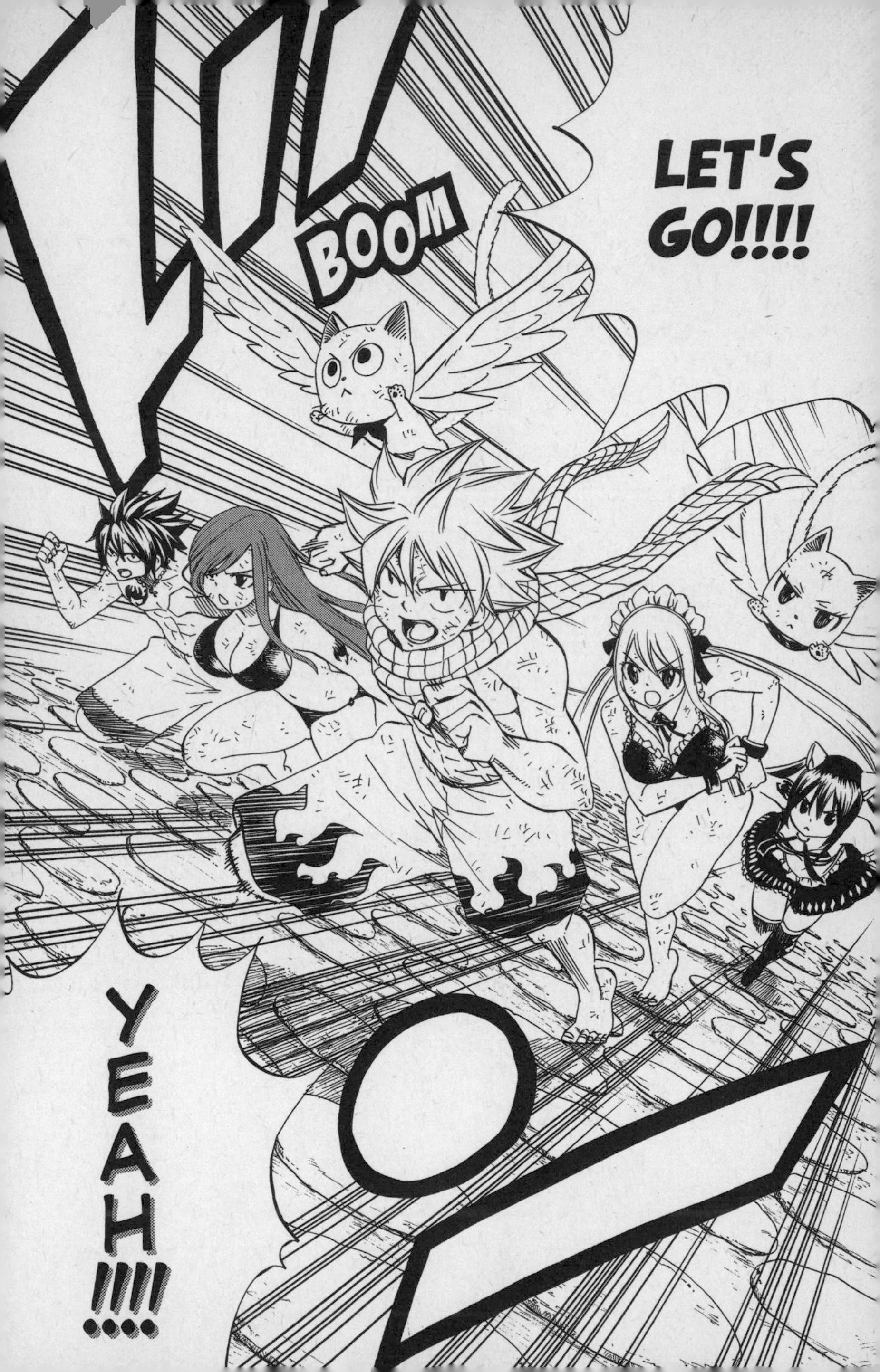
LET'S GO!!!!
BOOM
YEAH!!!!

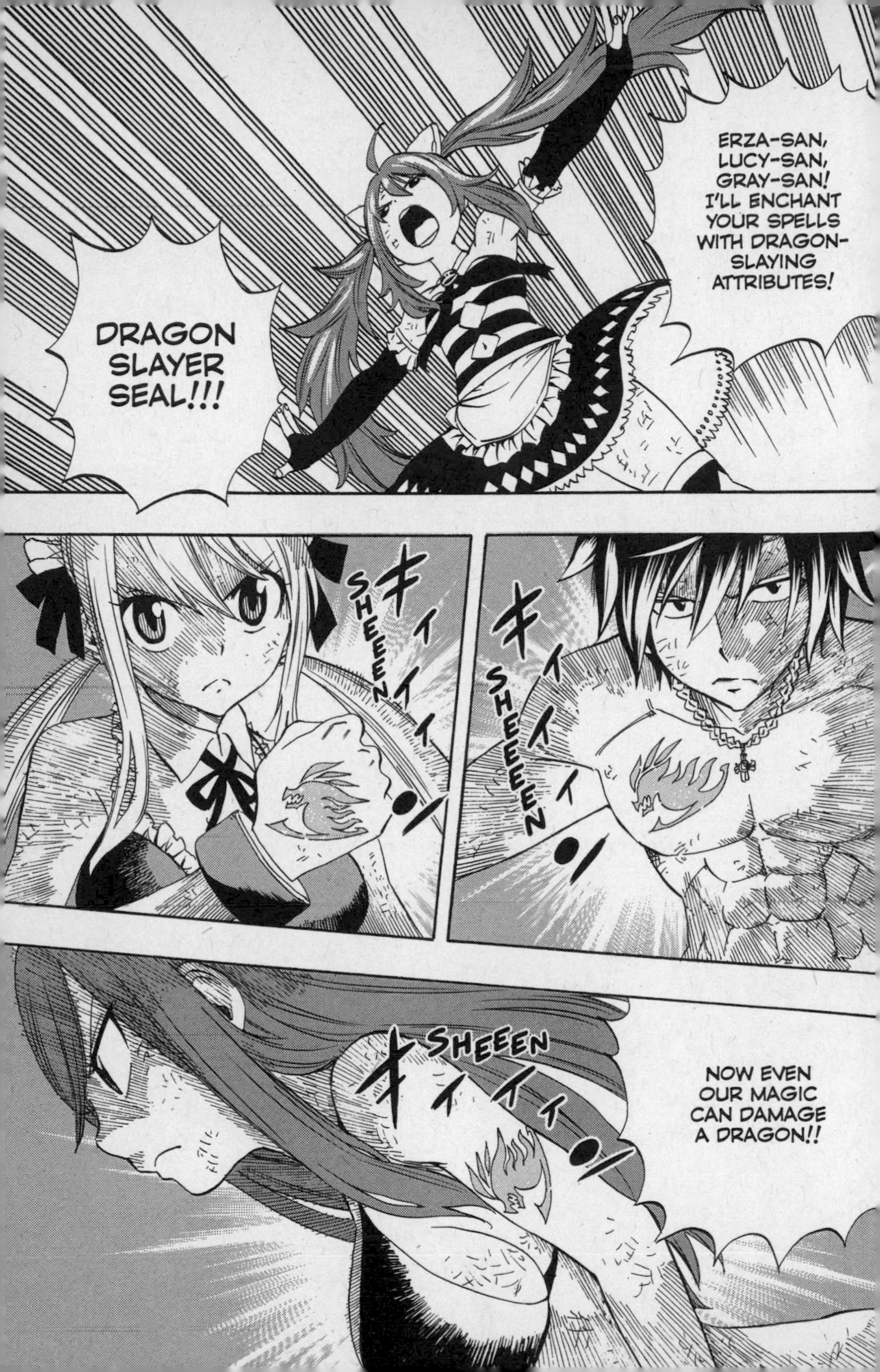
ERZA-SAN, LUCY-SAN, GRAY-SAN! I'LL ENCHANT YOUR SPELLS WITH DRAGON-SLAYING ATTRIBUTES!
DRAGON SLAYER SEAL!!!
SHEEEEEN
SHEEEN
NOW EVEN OUR MAGIC CAN DAMAGE A DRAGON!!
SHEEEN

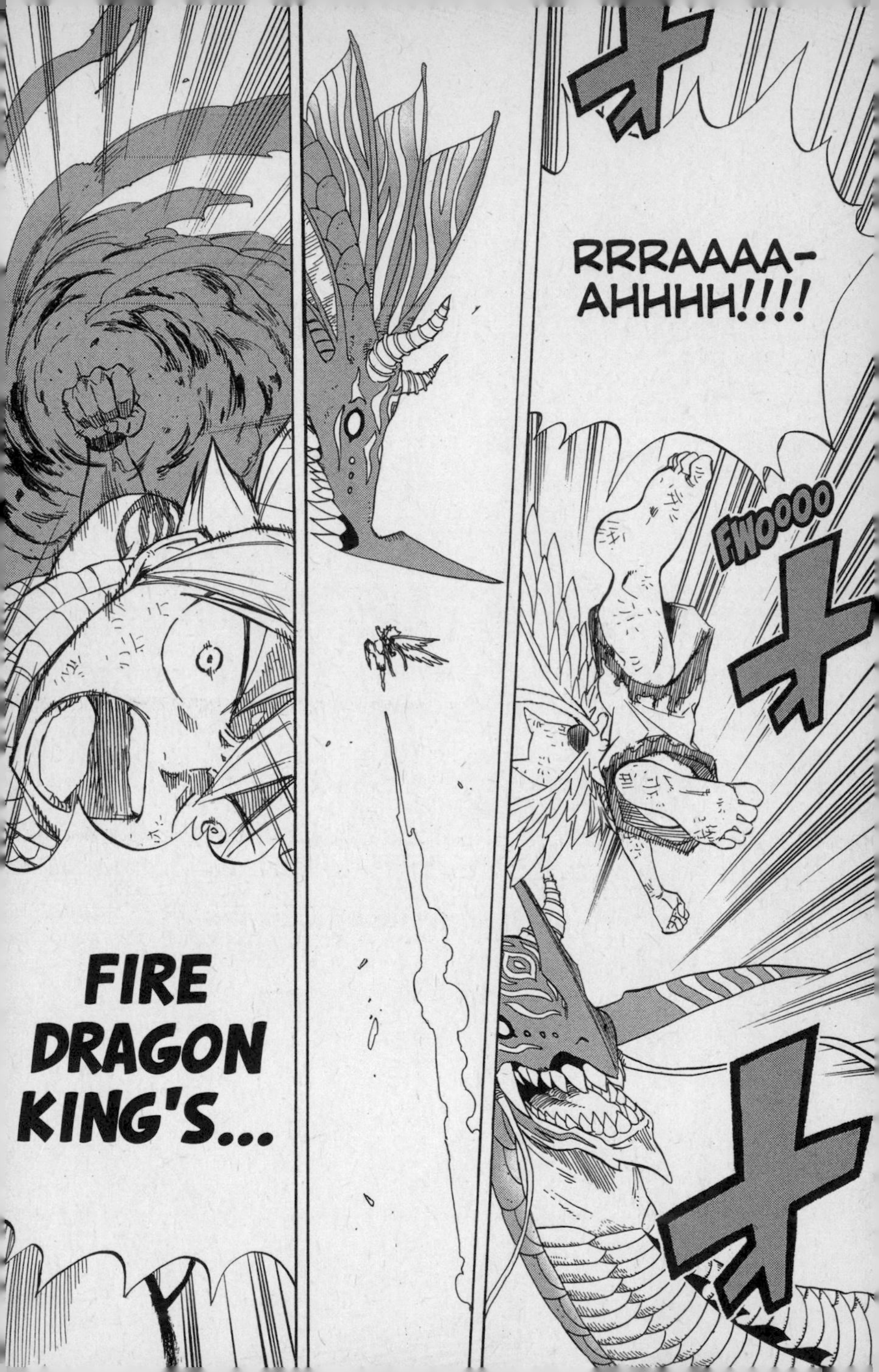
RRRAAAA-AHHHH!!!!
FWOOOO
FIRE DRAGON KING'S...

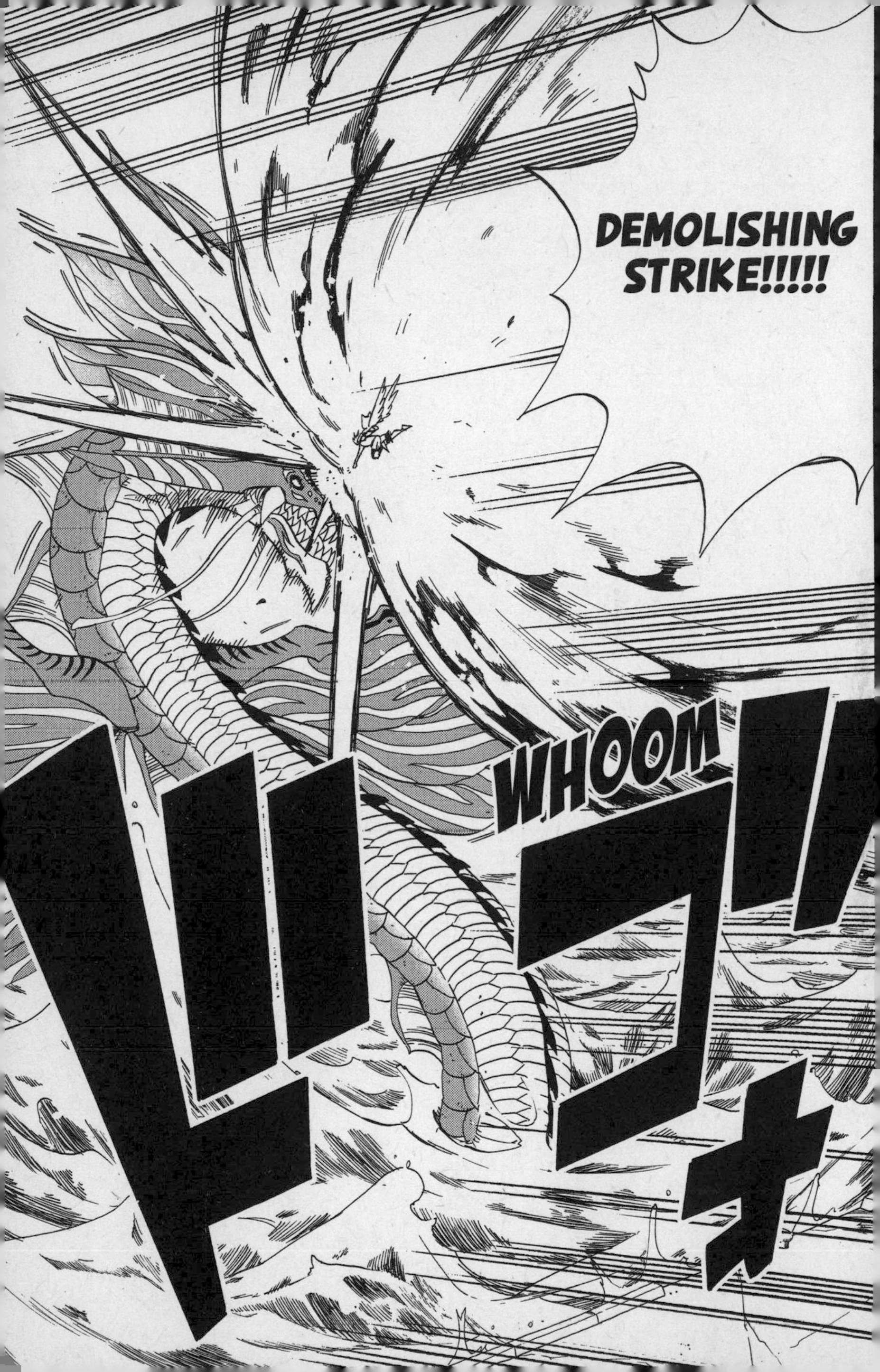
DEMOLISHING STRIKE!!!!!
WHOOM

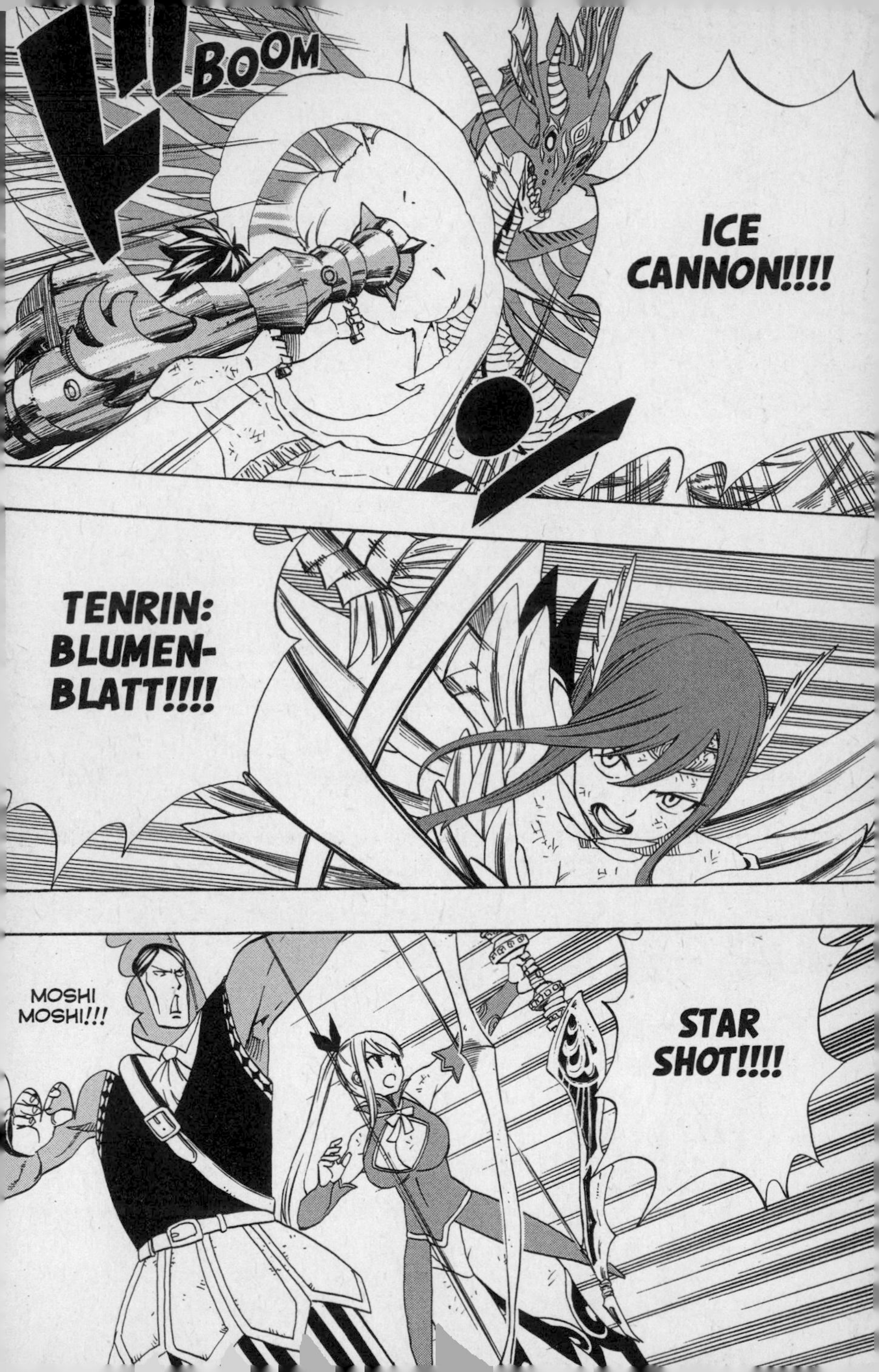
ICE CANNON!!!!
BOOM
TENRIN: BLUMEN-BLATT!!!!
STAR SHOT!!!!
MOSHI MOSHI!!!

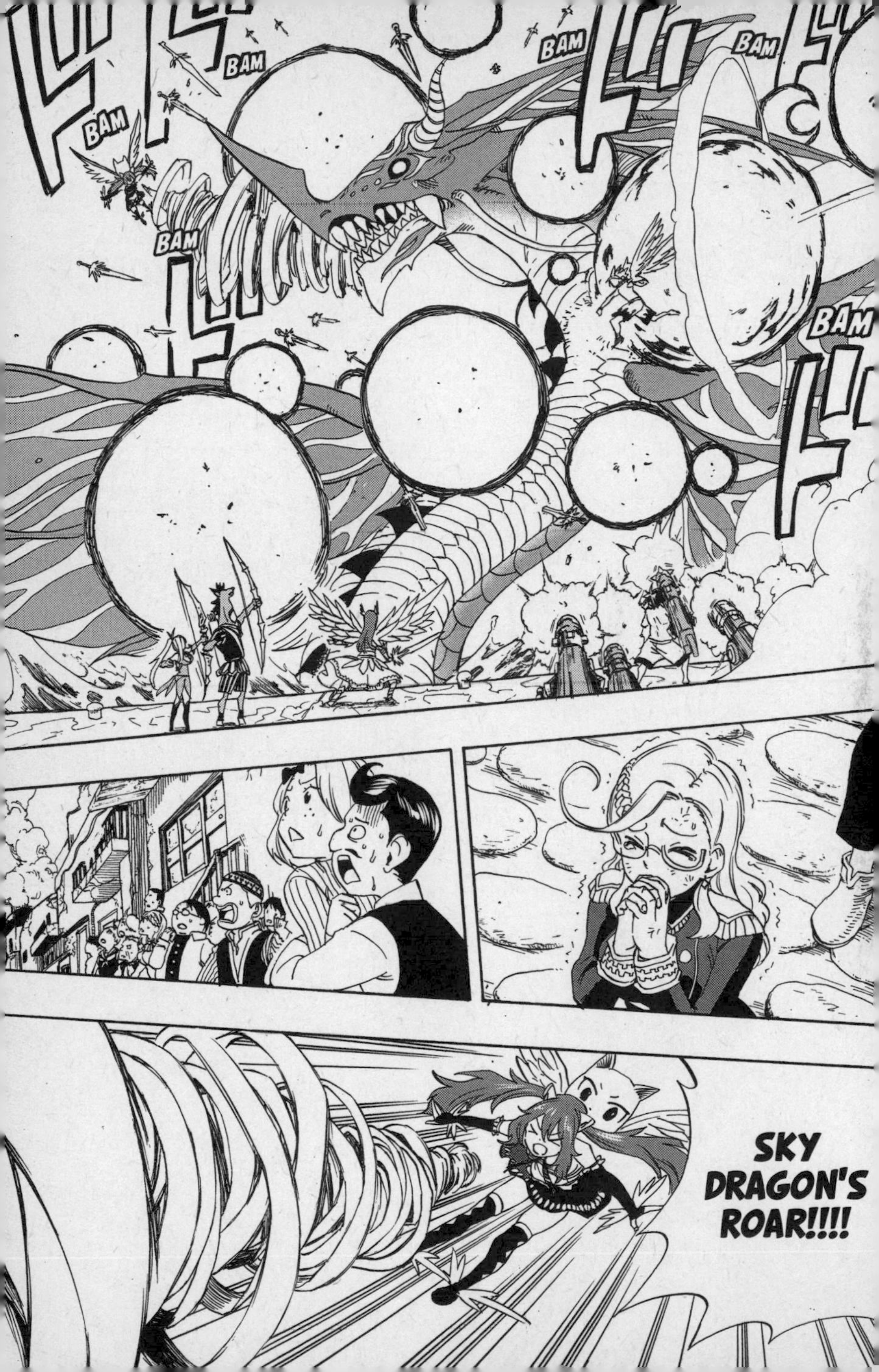
BAM
BAM
BAM
BAM
BAM
BAM
SKY DRAGON'S ROAR!!!!

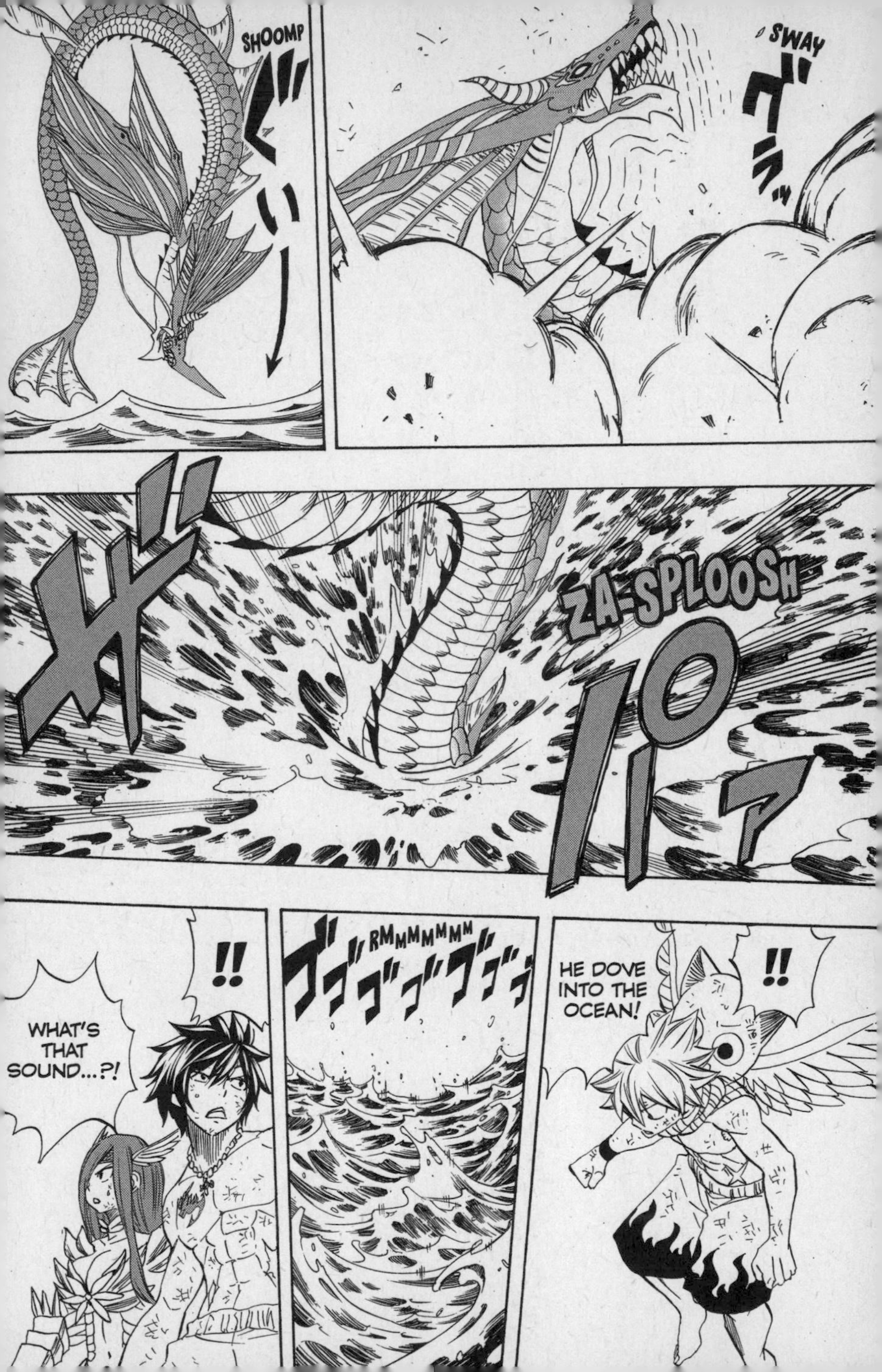
SWAY
SHOOMP
ZA-SPLOOSH
!!
HE DOVE INTO THE OCEAN!
RMMMMMMM
!!
WHAT'S THAT SOUND...?!

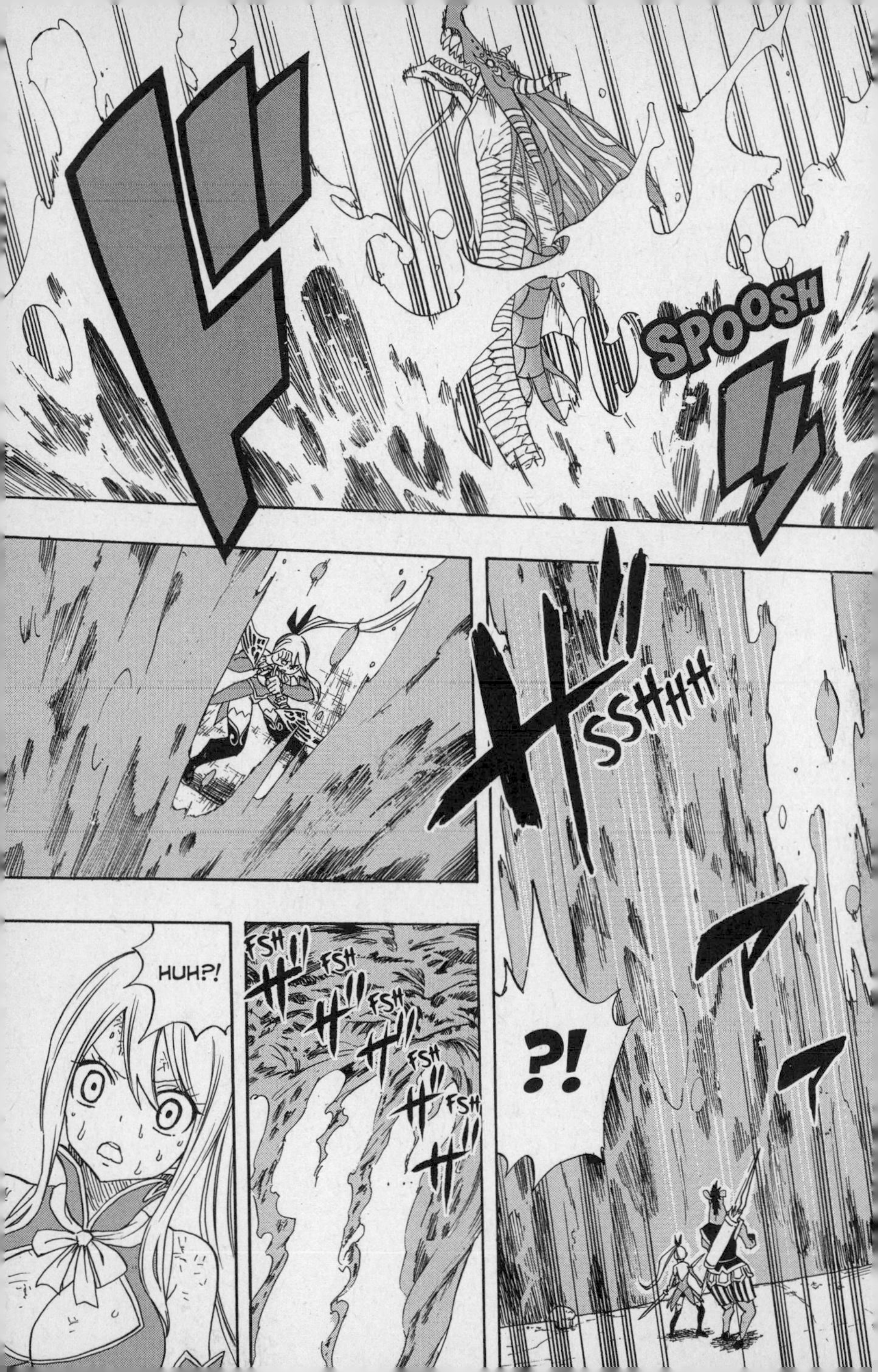
SPOOSH
SSHHH
?!
FSH
FSH
FSH
FSH
FSH
HUH?!

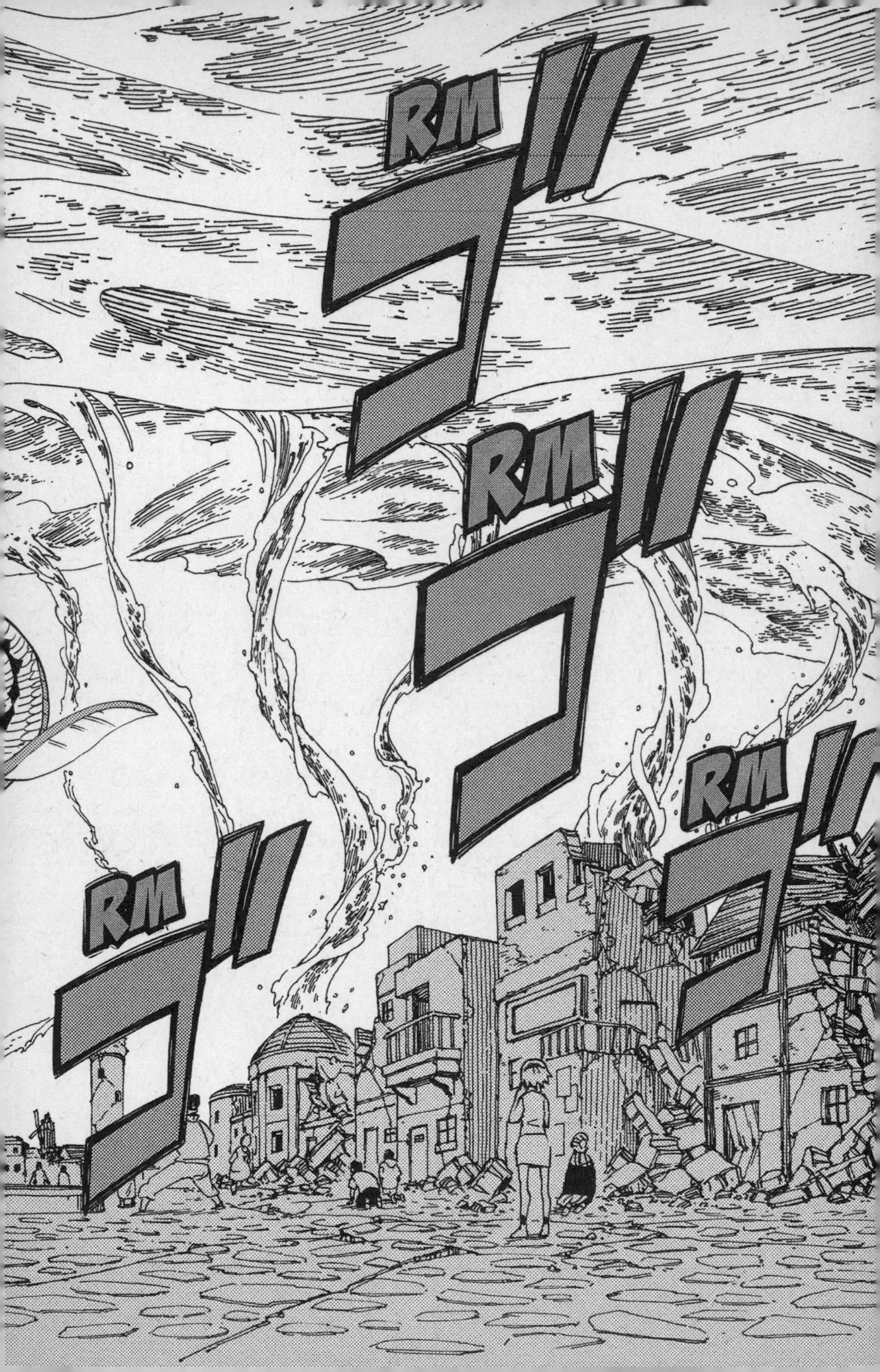
RM
RM
RM
RM

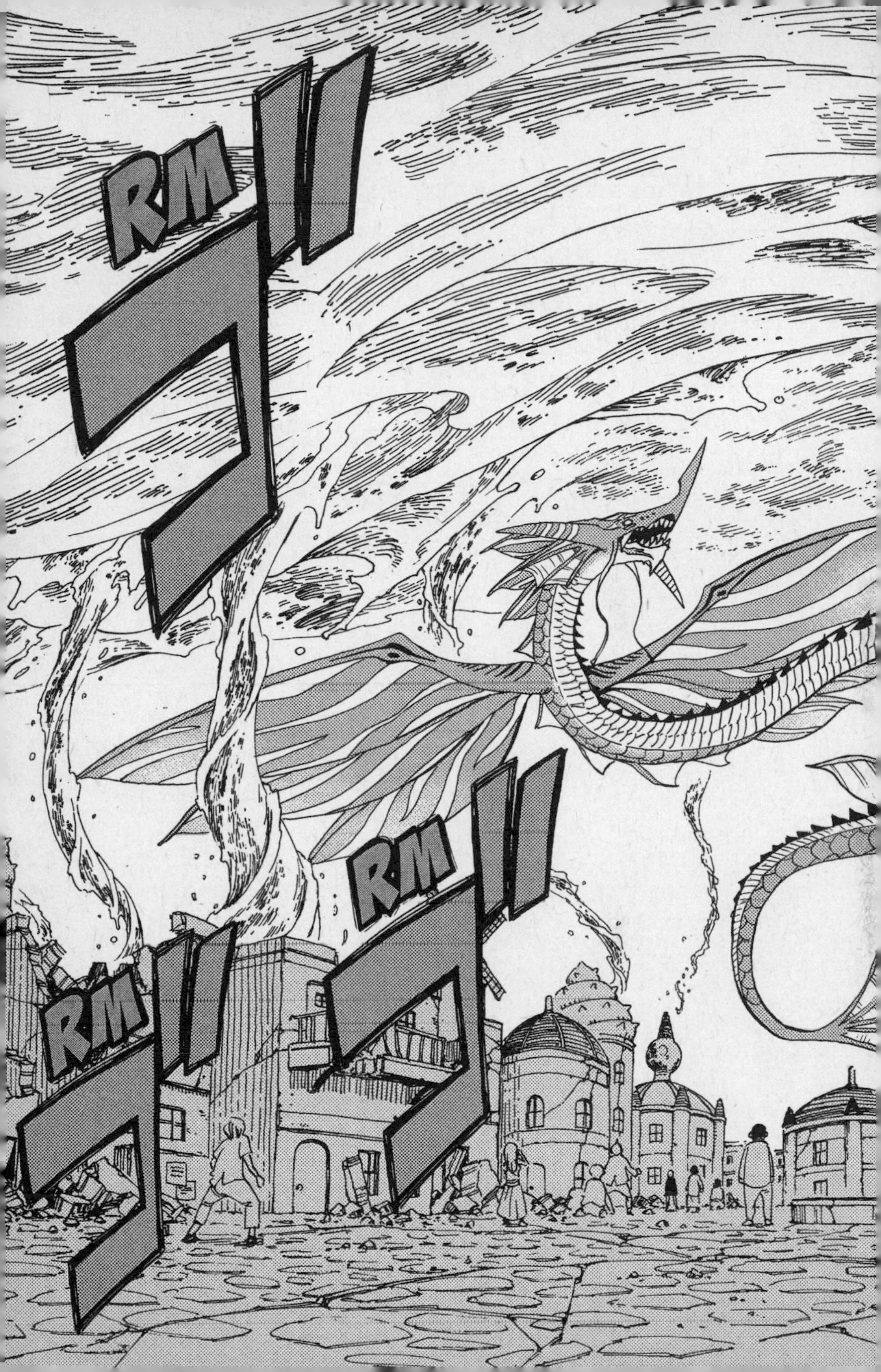
RM
RM
RM

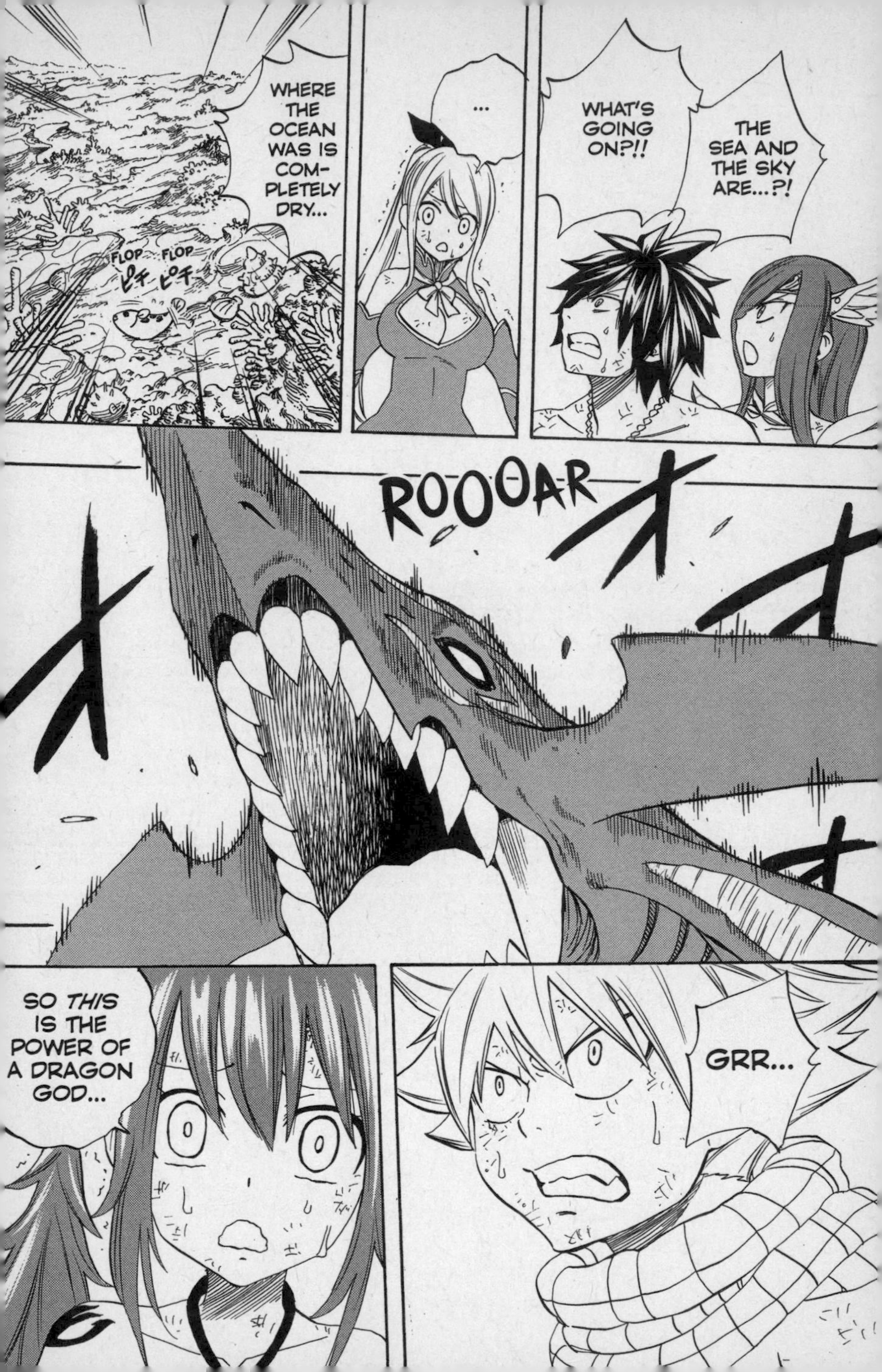
THE SEA AND THE SKY ARE...?!
WHAT'S GOING ON?!!
...
WHERE THE OCEAN WAS IS COM-PLETELY DRY...
FLOP FLOP
ピチ ピチ
ROOOAR
GRR...
SO *THIS* IS THE POWER OF A DRAGON GOD...

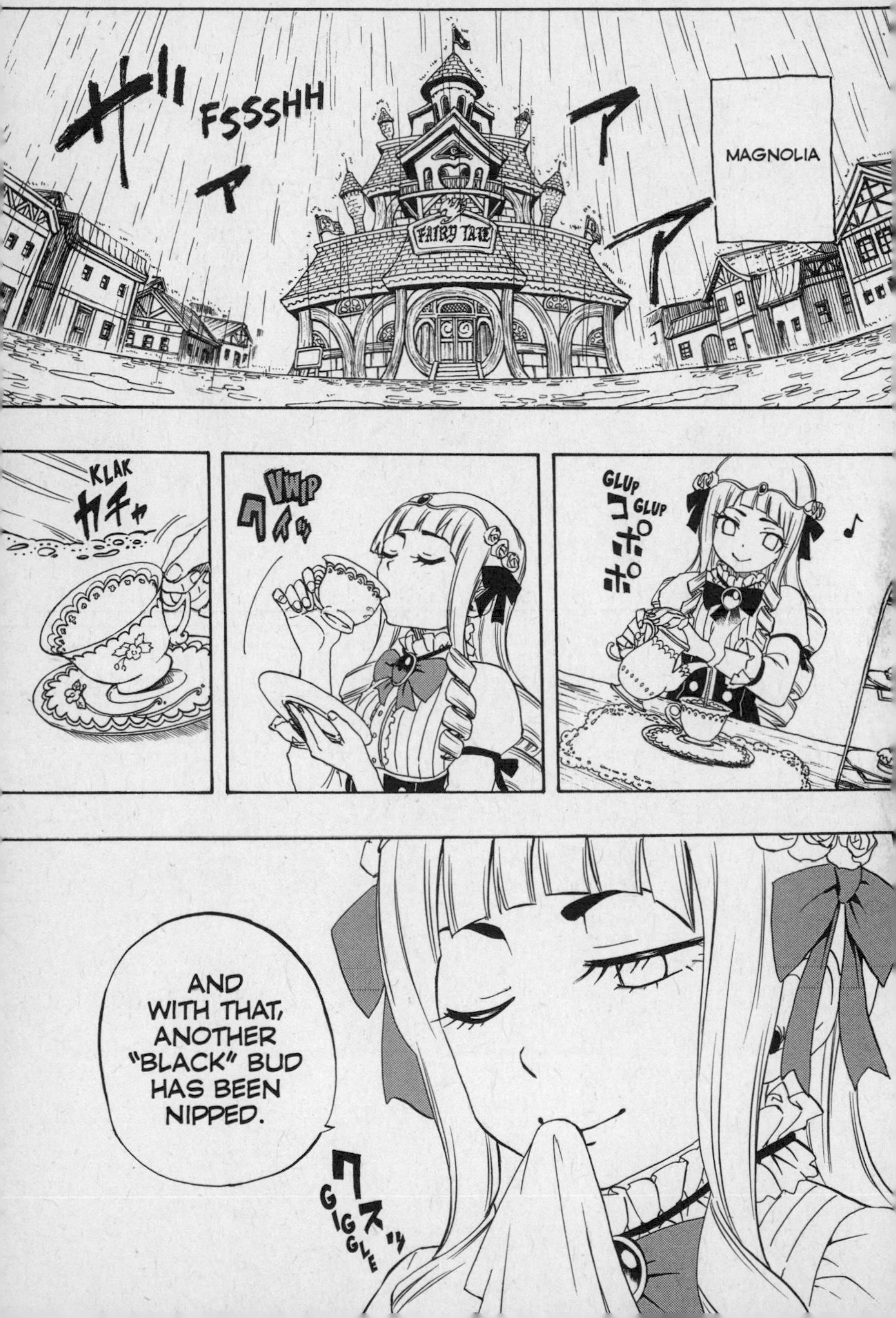
MAGNOLIA
FSSSHH
FAIRY TAIL
GLUP GLUP
コポポポ
VWIP
クイッ
KLAK
カチャ
AND WITH THAT, ANOTHER "BLACK" BUD HAS BEEN NIPPED.
GIGGLE
クスッ

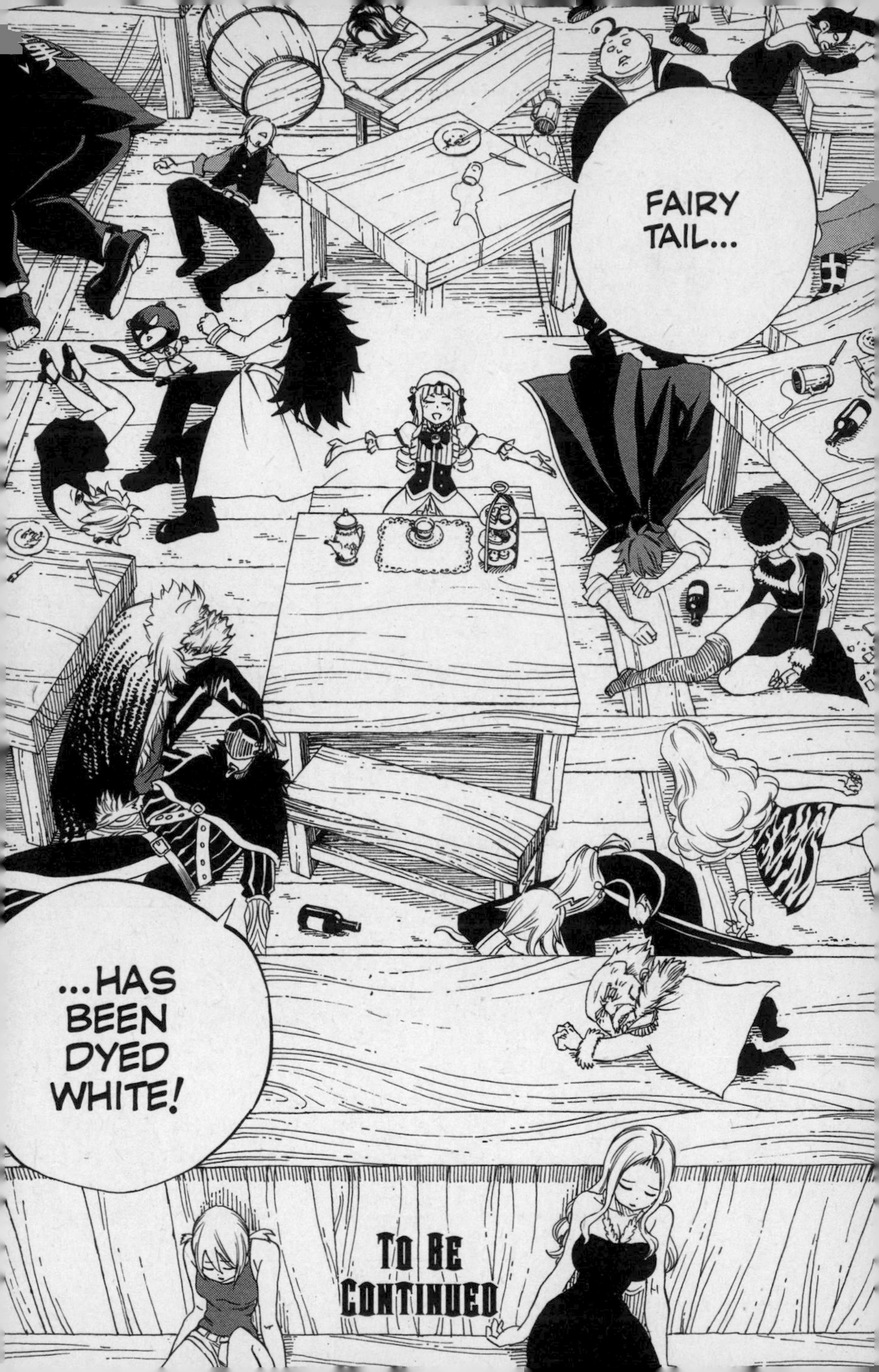
FAIRY TAIL...
...HAS BEEN DYED WHITE!
TO BE CONTINUED

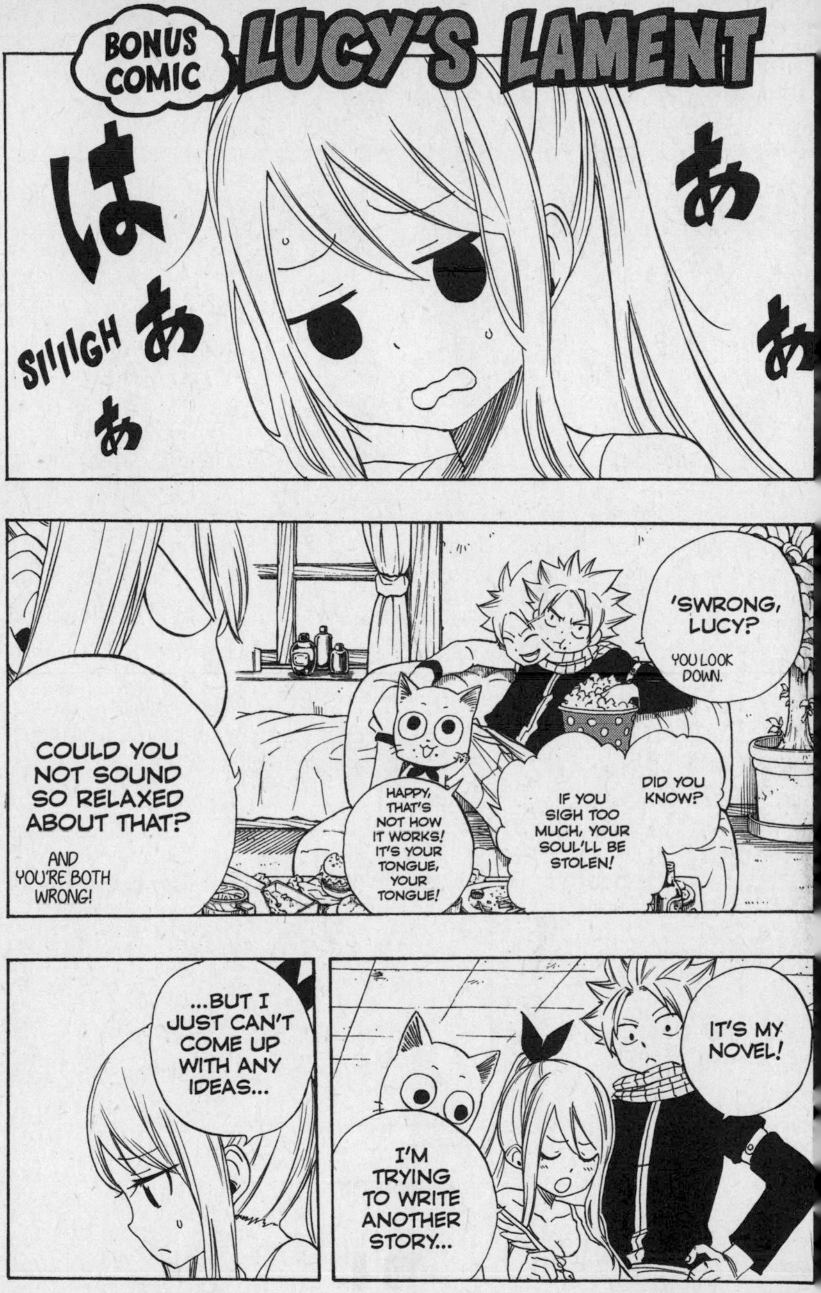
BONUS COMIC
LUCY'S LAMENT
ああ
はあ
SIIIGH
ああ
'SWRONG, LUCY?
YOU LOOK DOWN.
DID YOU KNOW?
IF YOU SIGH TOO MUCH, YOUR SOUL'LL BE STOLEN!
HAPPY, THAT'S NOT HOW IT WORKS! IT'S YOUR TONGUE, YOUR TONGUE!
COULD YOU NOT SOUND SO RELAXED ABOUT THAT?
AND YOU'RE BOTH WRONG!
IT'S MY NOVEL!
I'M TRYING TO WRITE ANOTHER STORY...
...BUT I JUST CAN'T COME UP WITH ANY IDEAS...

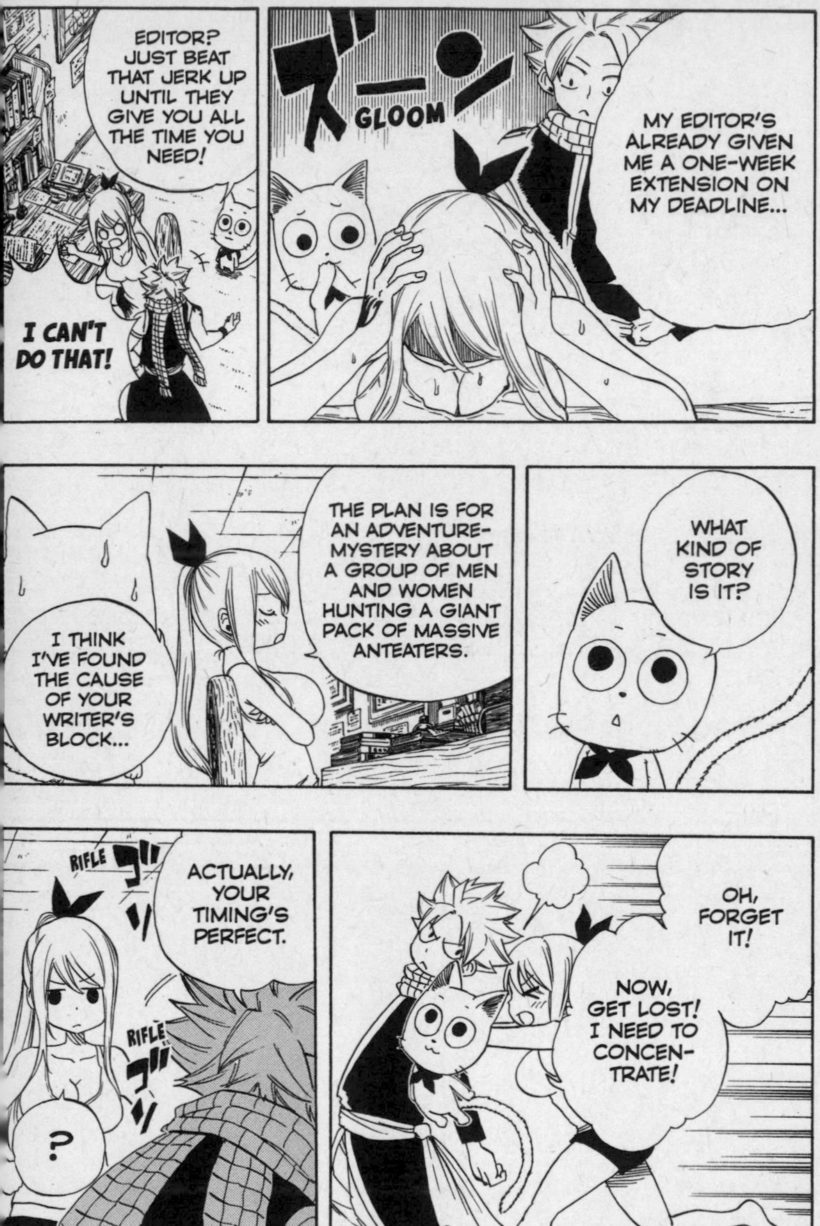
GLOOM
MY EDITOR'S ALREADY GIVEN ME A ONE-WEEK EXTENSION ON MY DEADLINE...
EDITOR? JUST BEAT THAT JERK UP UNTIL THEY GIVE YOU ALL THE TIME YOU NEED!
I CAN'T DO THAT!
WHAT KIND OF STORY IS IT?
THE PLAN IS FOR AN ADVENTURE-MYSTERY ABOUT A GROUP OF MEN AND WOMEN HUNTING A GIANT PACK OF MASSIVE ANTEATERS.
I THINK I'VE FOUND THE CAUSE OF YOUR WRITER'S BLOCK...
OH, FORGET IT!
NOW, GET LOST! I NEED TO CONCEN-TRATE!
ACTUALLY, YOUR TIMING'S PERFECT.
RIFLE
RIFLE
?

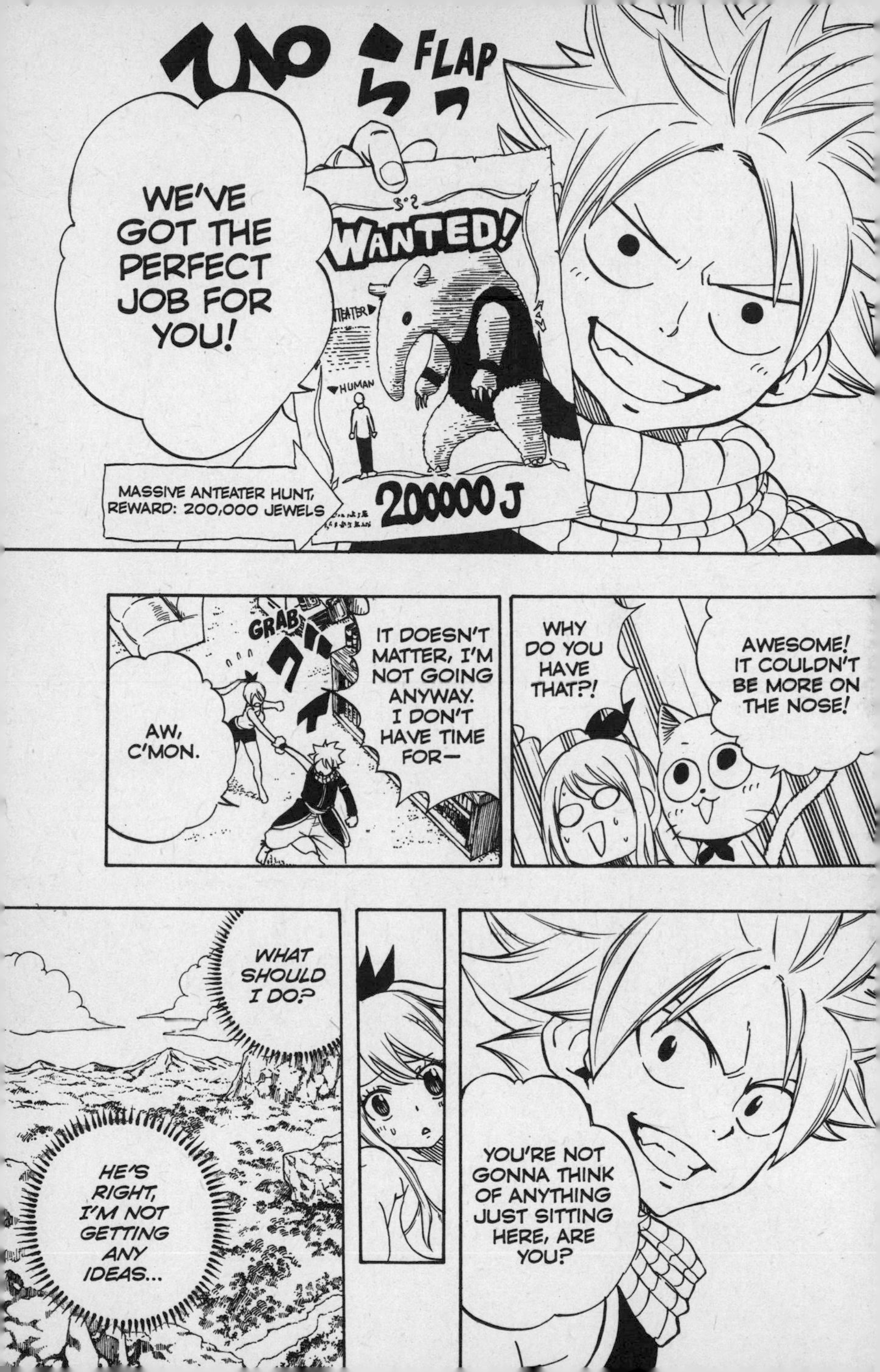
FLAP
WE'VE GOT THE PERFECT JOB FOR YOU!
WANTED!
HUMAN
200000 J
MASSIVE ANTEATER HUNT, REWARD: 200,000 JEWELS
AWESOME! IT COULDN'T BE MORE ON THE NOSE!
WHY DO YOU HAVE THAT?!
IT DOESN'T MATTER, I'M NOT GOING ANYWAY. I DON'T HAVE TIME FOR—
GRAB
AW, C'MON.
YOU'RE NOT GONNA THINK OF ANYTHING JUST SITTING HERE, ARE YOU?
WHAT SHOULD I DO?
HE'S RIGHT, I'M NOT GETTING ANY IDEAS...

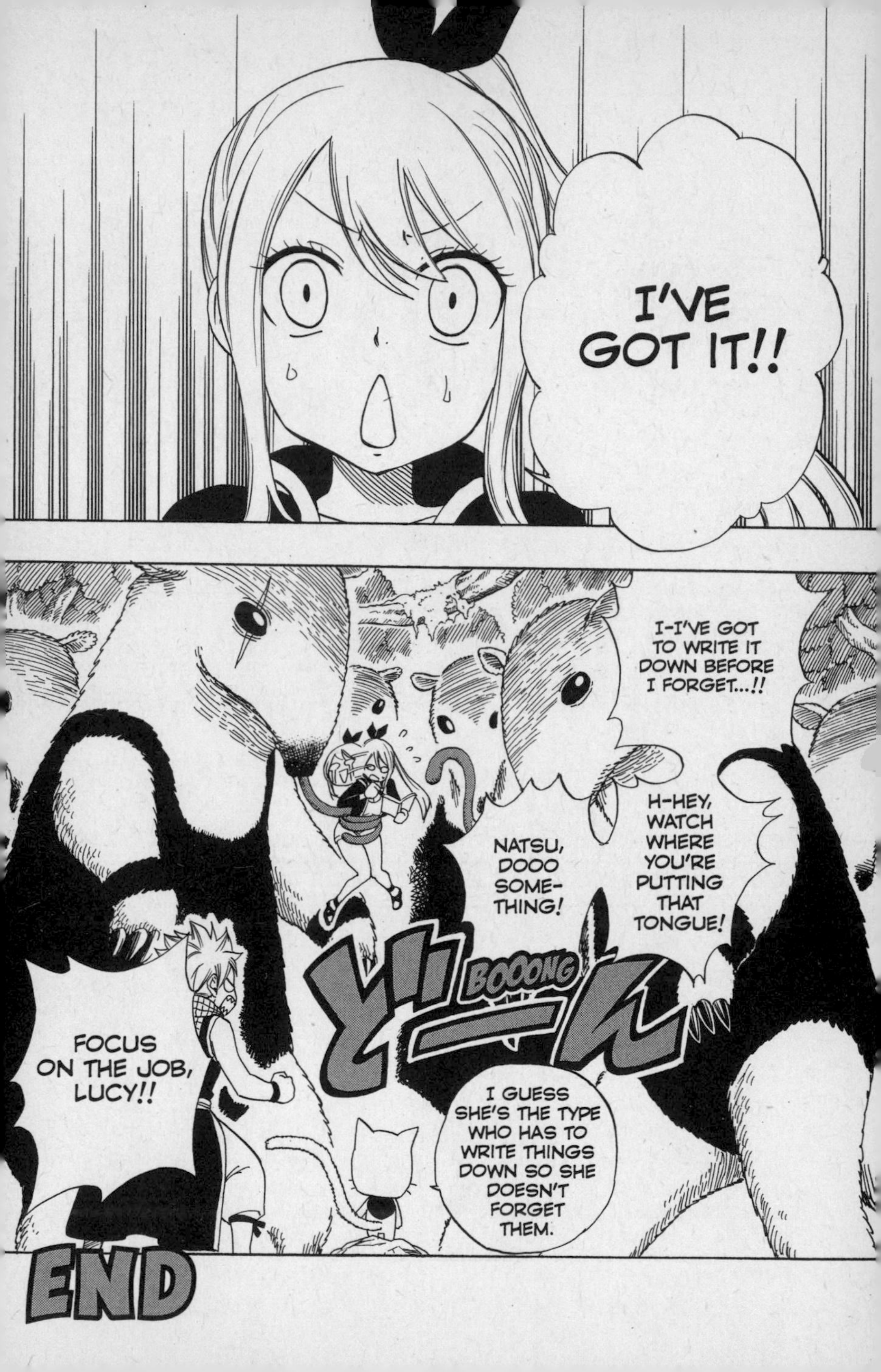
I'VE GOT IT!!
I-I'VE GOT TO WRITE IT DOWN BEFORE I FORGET...!!
H-HEY, WATCH WHERE YOU'RE PUTTING THAT TONGUE!
NATSU, DOOO SOME-THING!
どーん
BOOONG
I GUESS SHE'S THE TYPE WHO HAS TO WRITE THINGS DOWN SO SHE DOESN'T FORGET THEM.
FOCUS ON THE JOB, LUCY!!
END

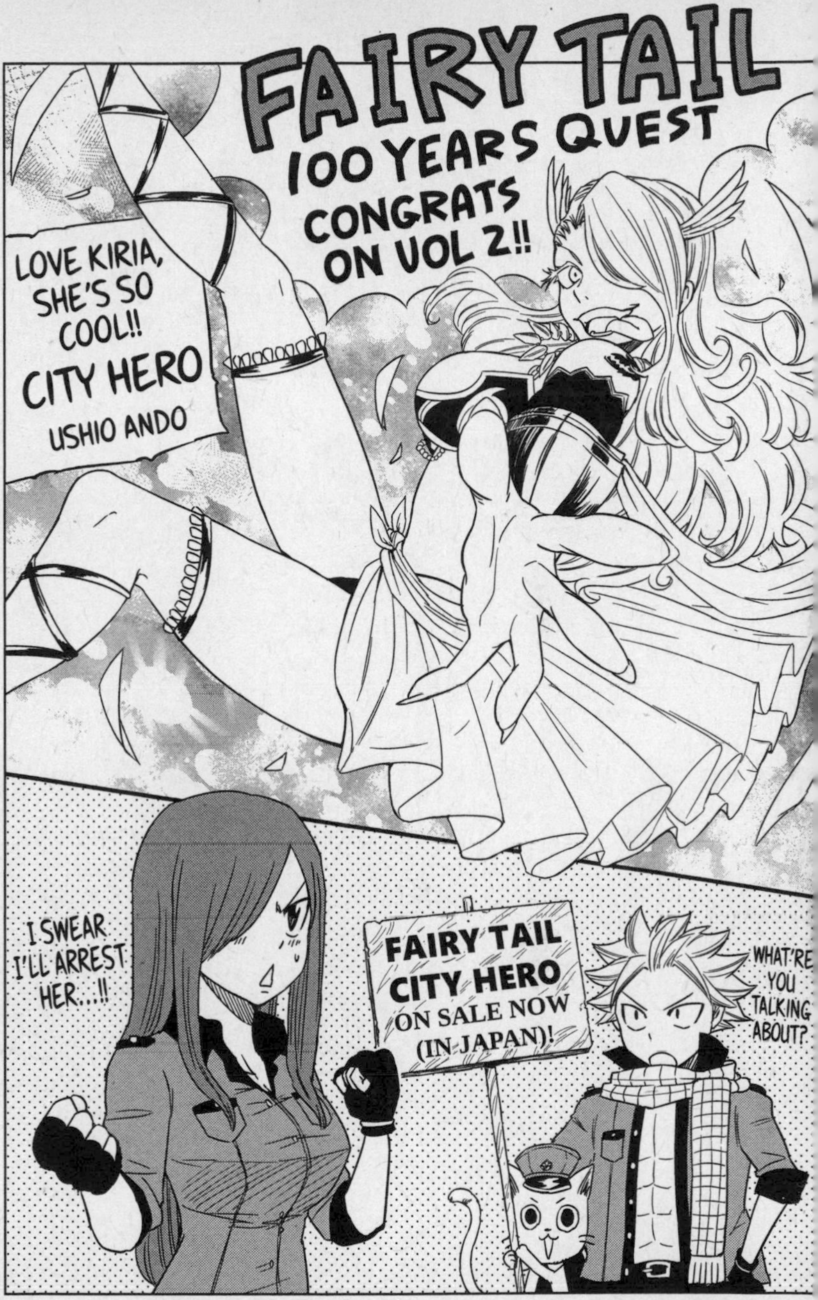
FAIRY TAIL
100 YEARS QUEST
CONGRATS ON VOL 2!!
LOVE KIRIA, SHE'S SO COOL!!
CITY HERO
USHIO ANDO
WHAT'RE YOU TALKING ABOUT?
FAIRY TAIL CITY HERO ON SALE NOW (IN JAPAN)!
I SWEAR I'LL ARREST HER...!!

DE ART RETURNS

(FUKUOKA PREFECTURE   POTTA)

UEDA-SENSEI, MASHIMA-SENSEI--

I'M ROOTING FOR YOU!

▲ THIS IS SUPER CUTE, AND REALLY SHOWS THE FRIENDSHIP BETWEEN WENDY AND CARLA!

(TOKUSHIMA PREFECTURE   TOSHIHIRO MIKI)

MADMOLE HAS FAIRY TAIL PAJAMAS CHA!

▲ I LIKE WHAT THEY'VE DONE WITH THIS VERY SMALL SPACE.

(IBARAKI PREFECTURE   KAE SHIBATA)

▲ LUCY PRAYING FOR A REUNION... EXCELLENT!

(AICHI PREFECTURE   NANASE-KUN)

I'M ROOTING FOR YOU!

CAN'T WAIT FOR MORE FAIRY TAIL!

▲ GRAY, SO SEXY... AND JUVIA, CUTE!!

(OKAYAMA PREFECTURE   NINJIN)

TOUKA

▼ FOCUS ON TOUKA!! AMAZED SHE'D TURN OUT LIKE THIS...

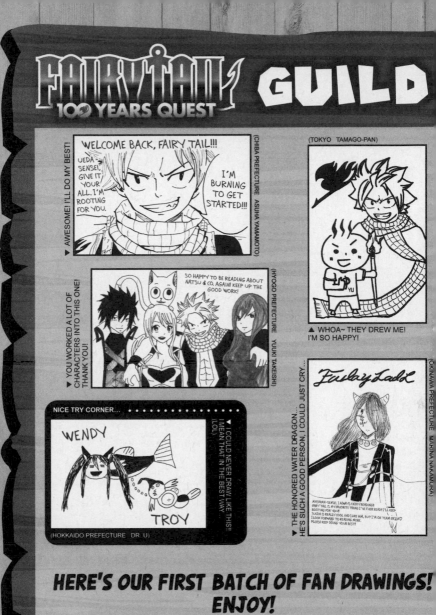

FAIRY TAIL 100 YEARS QUEST GUILD

(TOKYO TAMAGO-PAN)

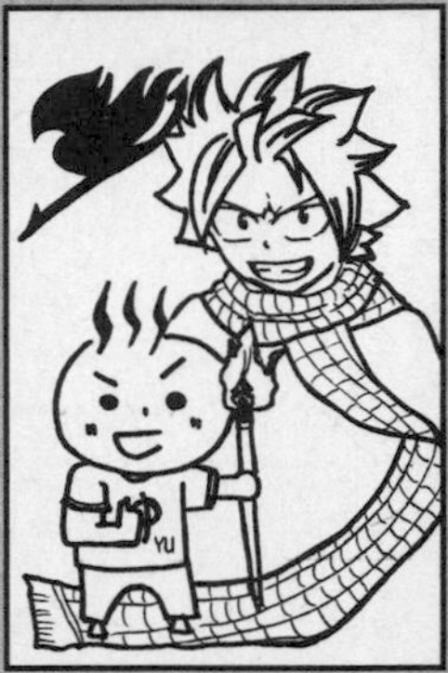
YU

▲ WHOA~ THEY DREW ME! I'M SO HAPPY!

(OKINAWA PREFECTURE MAKINA NAKAMURA)

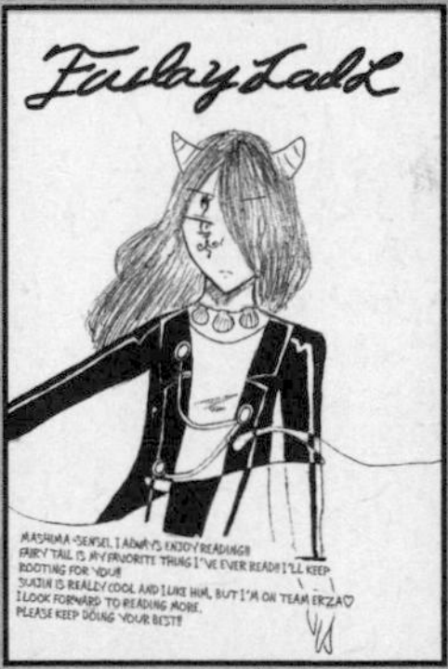
MASHIMA-SENSEI, I ALWAYS ENJOY READING!!
FAIRY TAIL IS MY FAVORITE THING I'VE EVER READ!! I'LL KEEP
ROOTING FOR YOU!!
SUIJIN IS REALLY COOL AND I LIKE HIM, BUT I'M ON TEAM ERZA♡
I LOOK FORWARD TO READING MORE.
PLEASE KEEP DOING YOUR BEST!!

▼ THE HONORED WATER DRAGON... HE'S SUCH A GOOD PERSON, I COULD JUST CRY...

(CHIBA PREFECTURE ASUHA YAMAMOTO)

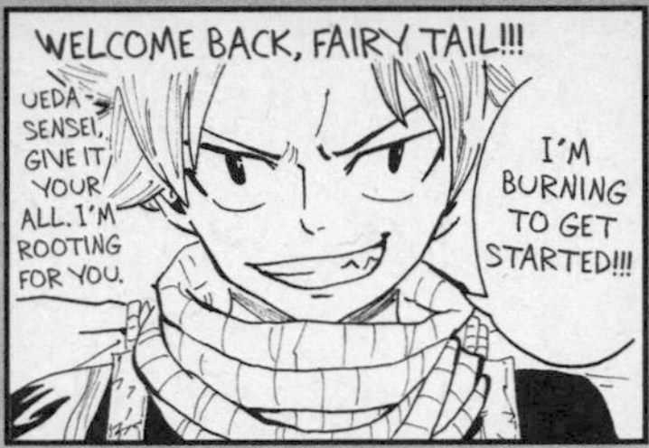
WELCOME BACK, FAIRY TAIL!!!
UEDA-SENSEI, GIVE IT YOUR ALL. I'M ROOTING FOR YOU.
I'M BURNING TO GET STARTED!!!

▼ AWESOME! I'LL DO MY BEST!

(HYOGO PREFECTURE YUUKI TAKEISHI)

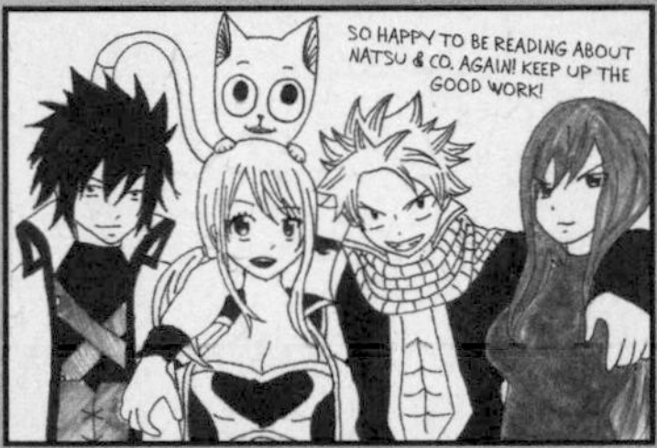
SO HAPPY TO BE READING ABOUT NATSU & CO. AGAIN! KEEP UP THE GOOD WORK!

▼ YOU WORKED A LOT OF CHARACTERS INTO THIS ONE! THANK YOU!

NICE TRY CORNER...

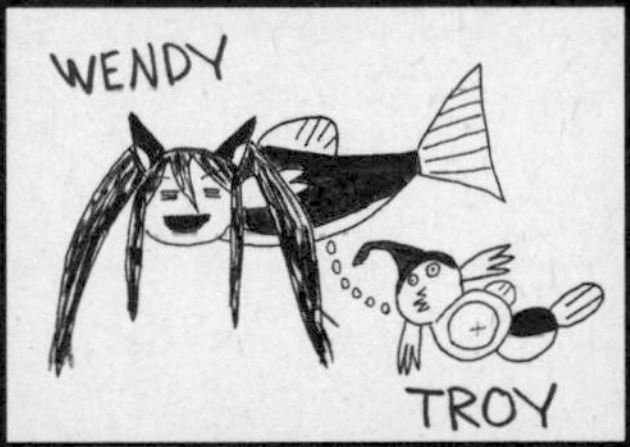
WENDY
TROY

▼ I CCULD NEVER DRAW LIKE THIS!! I MEAN THAT IN THE BEST WAY... (LOL)

(HOKKAIDO PREFECTURE DR U)

HERE'S OUR FIRST BATCH OF FAN DRAWINGS! ENJOY!

EDITOR'S NOTE: DRAWING SUBMISSIONS LIMITED TO JAPAN.

TRANSLATION NOTES

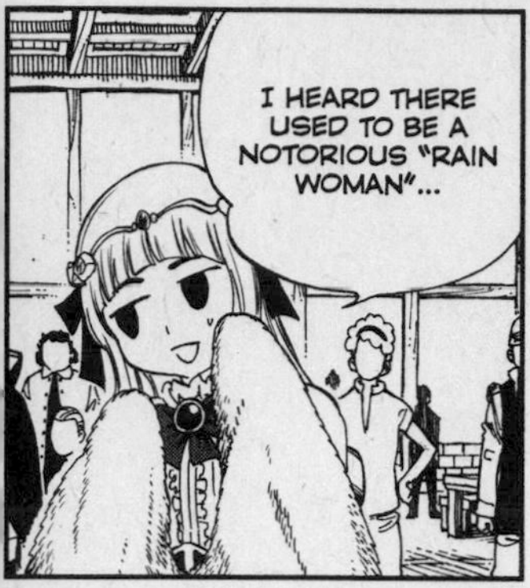
I HEARD THERE USED TO BE A NOTORIOUS "RAIN WOMAN"...

Rain Woman, page 95

Ame onna, or rain woman, can either refer to a spirit of folklore said to cause rain, or it can literally mean a woman whose presence or actions are believed to cause precipitation.

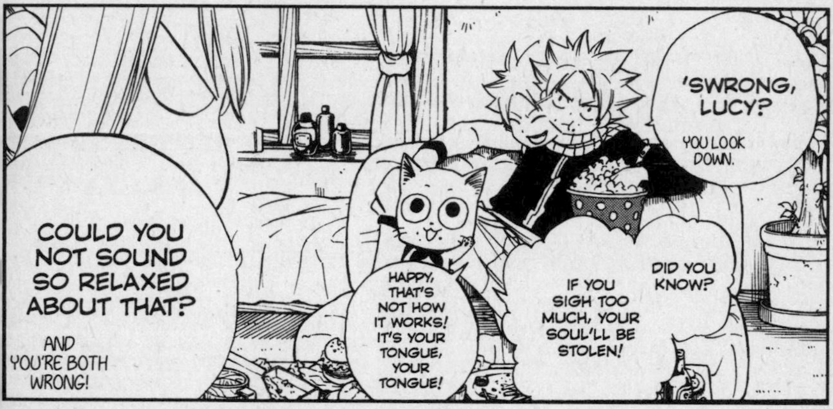
'SWRONG, LUCY?
YOU LOOK DOWN.
DID YOU KNOW?
IF YOU SIGH TOO MUCH, YOUR SOUL'LL BE STOLEN!
HAPPY, THAT'S NOT HOW IT WORKS! IT'S YOUR TONGUE, YOUR TONGUE!
COULD YOU NOT SOUND SO RELAXED ABOUT THAT?
AND YOU'RE BOTH WRONG!

If You Sigh…, page 183

Both Natsu and Happy seem to be a little confused about this tradition. It's common to say in Japanese that "too much sighing chases happiness away," but also that "if you lie, Enma (the King of the underworld) will steal your tongue." The guys seem to have mixed these two ideas together.

FAIRY TAIL
100 YEARS QUEST

A Kodansha Comics Trade Paperback Original
FAIRY TAIL: 100 Years Quest 2 copyright © 2019 Hiro Mashima/Atsuo Ueda
English translation copyright © 2019 Hiro Mashima/Atsuo Ueda

Published in the United States by Kodansha Comics, an imprint of
Kodansha USA Publishing, LLC, New York.

Publication rights for this English edition arranged through
Kodansha Ltd., Tokyo.

First published in Japan in 2019 by Kodansha Ltd., Tokyo.

ISBN 978-1-63236-893-5

Printed in the United States of America.

www.kodanshacomics.com

9 8 7 6 5 4 3 2 1
Translation: Kevin Steinbach
Lettering: Phil Christie

Kodansha Comics edition cover design by Phil Balsman

Publisher: Kiichiro Sugawara
Managing editor: Maya Rosewood
Vice president of marketing & publicity: Naho Yamada

Director of publishing services: Ben Applegate
Associate director of operations: Stephen Pakula
Publishing services managing editor: Noelle Webster
Assistant production manager: Emi Lotto